COLORS OF

Australia

AA Publishing

Author: Terry Marsh

Produced by AA Publishing

Published by AA Publishing (a trading name of Automobile Association Developments Limited, whose registered office is Fanum House, Basing View, Basingstoke, Hampshire RG21 4EA; registered number 1878835)

ISBN-10: 0-7495-4669-7
ISBN-13: 978-0-7495-4669-4

A02530

A CIP catalogue record for this book is available from the British Library.

Layouts by Andrew Milne Design
Printed and bound in China

COLORS OF

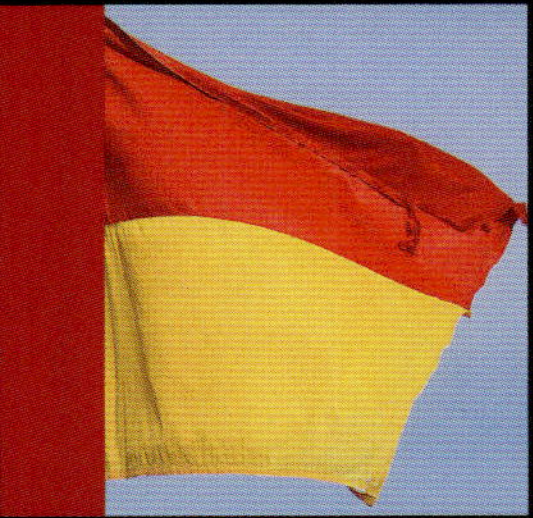
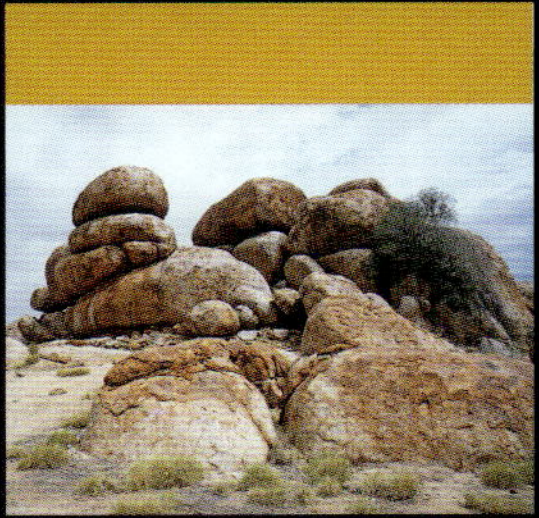
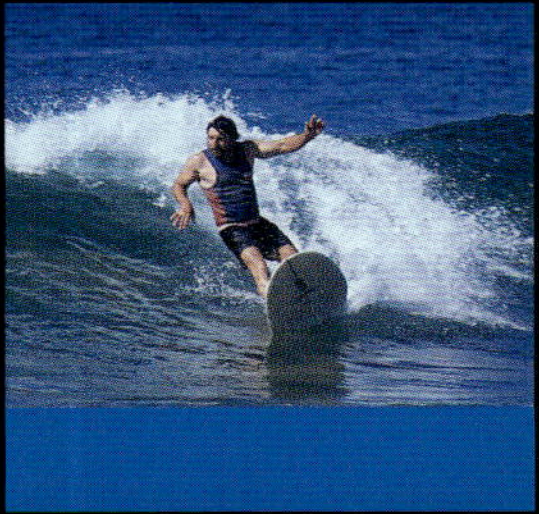
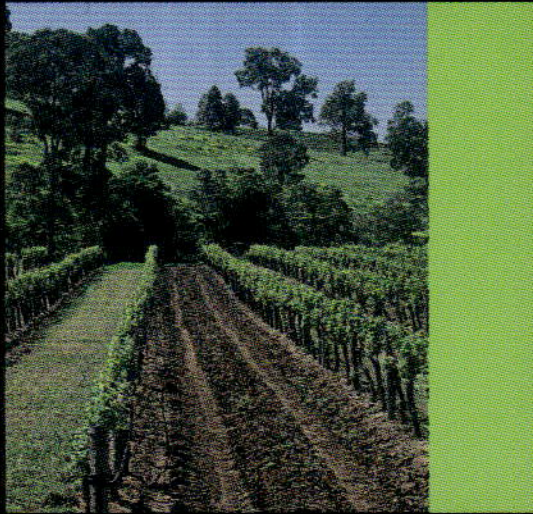

Australia

CONT

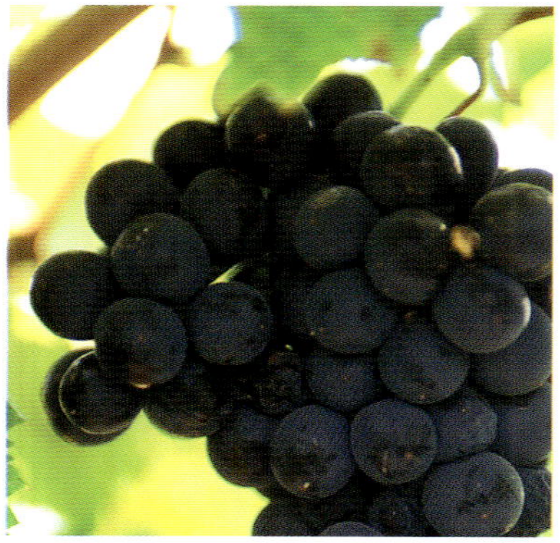

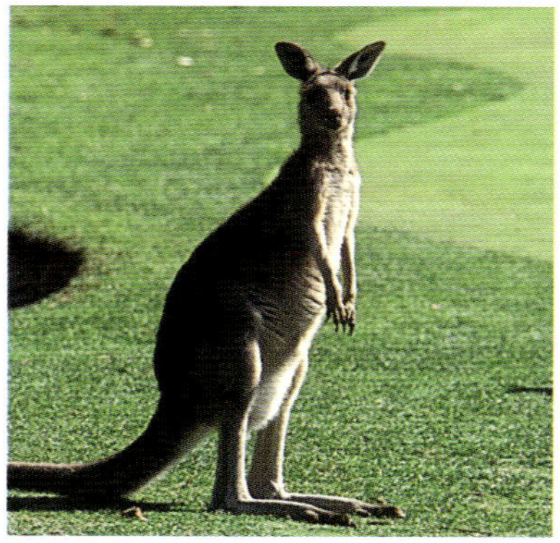

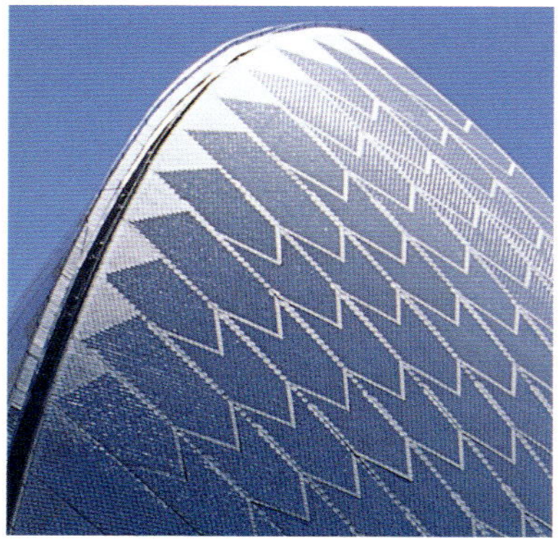

ENTS

COLORS OF **AUSTRALIA**

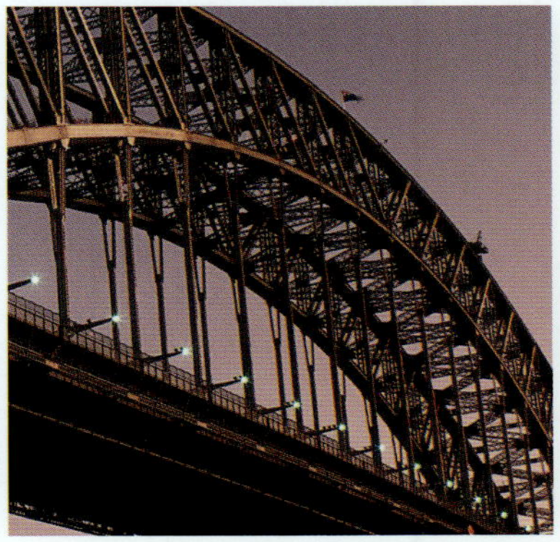

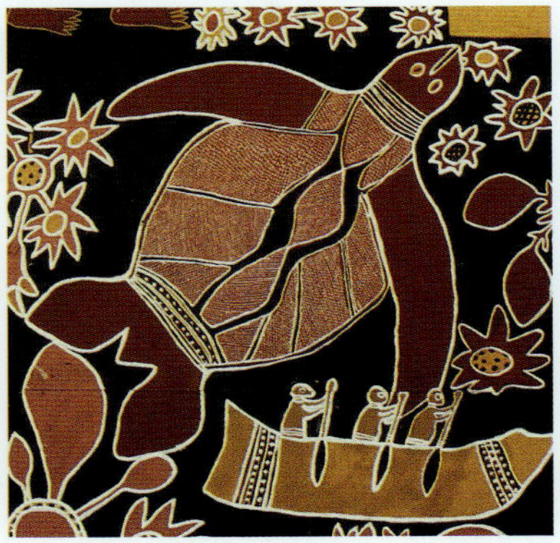

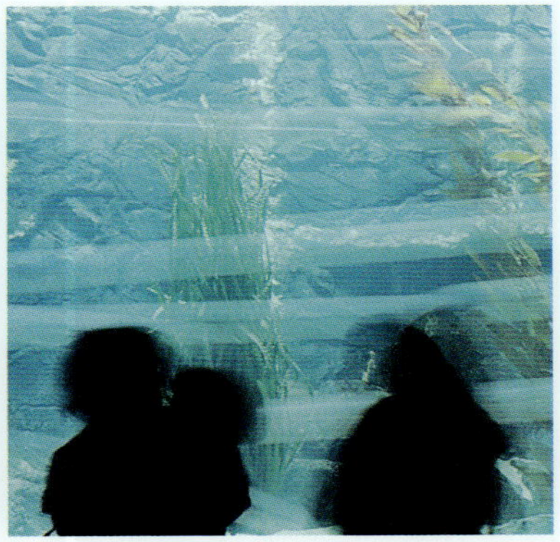

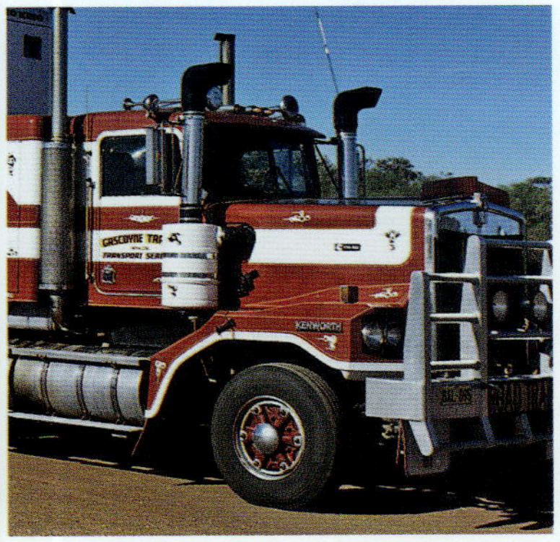

NTRO

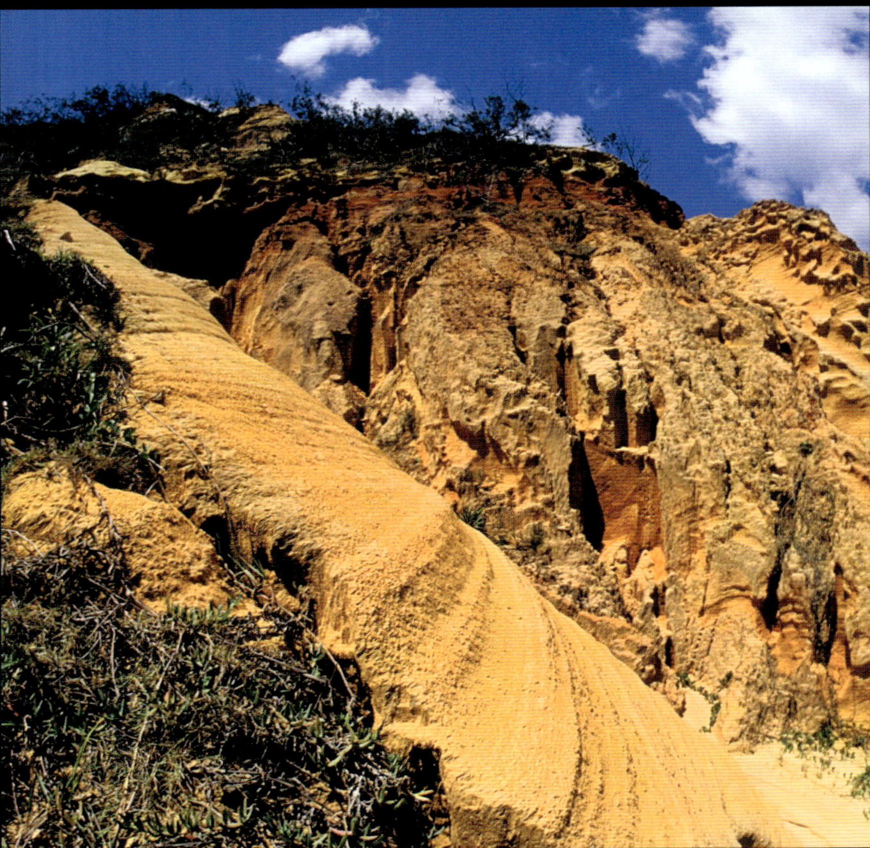

JCTION

COLORS OF AUSTRALIA: **INTRODUCTION**

ustralia is a paradox: it is the world's oldest continent—and, for that matter, its largest island—yet it is the world's youngest eveloped country, its early history barely beyond living memory. Youthfulness and vibrancy are hallmarks of modern Australia.The nd has been inhabited by indigenous ("Aboriginal") people for more than fifty thousand years (some think it is closer to one undred and fifty thousand years), but was only settled (by the British) little more than two hundred years ago. Since then Australia as metamorphosed from a penal colony into a colorful and youthful nation with a population of around twenty million, almost all them living in eight major cities.

he landscape

part from a few iconic symbols, like Uluru (Ayers Rock), Sydney Opera House, and the Harbour Bridge, the enduring image of ustralia is one of the "Outback," dust plains dotted with salt bush and spinifex, cinnamon-red deserts stretching as far as the eye an see, deep river gorges, outlandish rock formations, intense colors, and vivid blue skies. Other than for a few small towns that prang up to meet a particular purpose, this imagery remains valid, and even today most of the Outback, the real Outback hundreds f miles from anywhere, is rough, pioneering country where only the foolhardy venture unprepared. The Outback is at the heart of ustralia, one of the most ancient landforms in the world. Here rain may not fall for years, clouds seldom appear, and temperatures equently rise to more than a human can safely withstand for any length of time.

Covering an area almost as large as the United States, or the entire European continent, Australia's landscape is diverse, mbracing lush forests in Tasmania, tropical rain forests and reefs in the "Top End", high plateaux across the Great Dividing Range nd almost 29,000 miles of coastline. Yet 70 percent of the country is arid, its people and communities clinging to the coastal fringes; ery little development exists more than 30 miles inland. The vastness is inescapable in what is one of the world's emptiest countries.

Veird, wonderful, and only here

ew countries boast a more weird and distinctive native array of flora and fauna than Australia. Millions of years of isolation from ther land masses have produced species that are wonderful, unique, sometimes seriously odd, and often dangerous. Australia has ore venomous snakes than any other country, both of the world's most venomous spiders, and the world's most deadly octopuses. ortunately, none of these is especially interested in humans, and usually avoids contact, leaving visitors free to marvel at the more readily evident, often wacky, species that live here, like the kangaroo and wallaby, the koala bear, the emu, and the crocodiles, or the less obvious marsupial mole that "swims" through the sand leaving no burrow behind it, and the frog that lays eggs. Throw in trees that shed their bark rather than their leaves, rivers without water, lakes of pink salt, trees that sting, and plants that have evolved to conserve water, and you begin to get the idea that there is something unusual about this country. Some mammals are so unique that they have their own scientific classification—monotremes. One, the enigmatic platypus, lives in an aquatic environment, suckles its young like a mammal, yet lays eggs, and has a beak like a duck's. The other monotreme, the spiny echidna, is something of an irascible pin cushion in design.

The indigenous people

Aboriginal means indigenous, and from a time when their numbers of around three hundred thousand represented the total population of Australia, today Aboriginal people constitute just 1.5 percent. For thousands of years, the Aboriginal people led a nomadic existence, a race of hunter-gatherers traveling light and living in temporary dwellings. Most moved around in small groups and, as a result, evolved into numerous clans, divided by traditions, and with as many as five hundred different languages. For the Aboriginal people, the world and its people were created by the Creation ancestors during a period known as the Dreamtime, in essence, a type of religious ideology that even today forms the basis of Aboriginal life.

The arrival of Europeans proved disastrous for the Aboriginal people. Although the immediate four years following the arrival of the First Fleet in 1788 saw no Aboriginal fatalities, thousands were later killed in hostilities—the whole Aboriginal population of Tasmania, for example, was completely annihilated—or by unfamiliar diseases, often intentionally introduced by white settlers, against which they had no resistance. In some parts of the country, there was a time when Aboriginal people were treated as vermin and shot on sight. In the last thirty years, efforts have been made to address this lack of understanding and to promote Australia's native heritage.

In 1992, the doctrine of *terra nullius*—the notion that at the time of the British settlement, Australia belonged to no one and was therefore legally unoccupied—was famously overturned in the High Court. The Native Title Act followed and paved the way for the Aboriginal people to claim

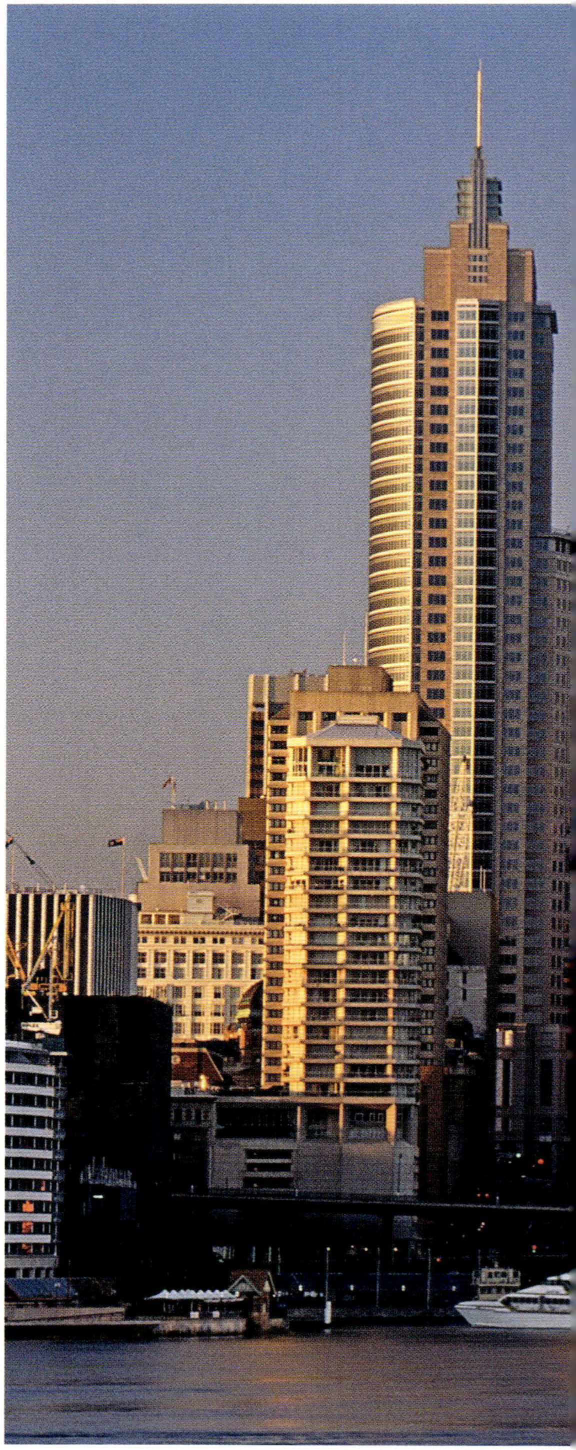

Previous page: Red Canyon, Fraser Island, the world's largest sand island. This World Heritage Listed site became an eco-tourism venue after its timber and sand mining industries ceased.

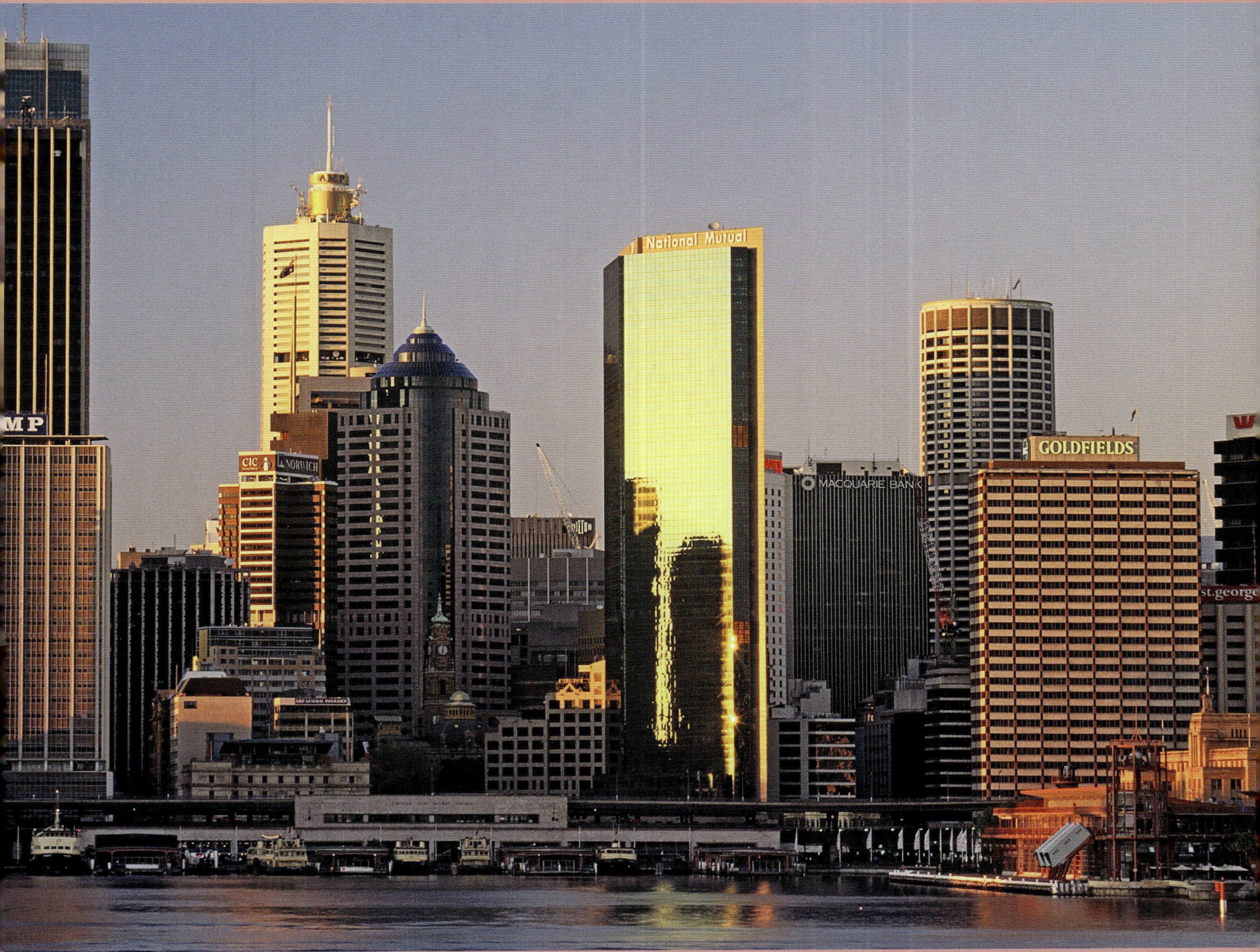

The soaring city skyline of high-rise office buildings that make up Sydney's CBD (Central Business District) is a stunning sight at any time, but especially at dawn, from Milson's Point.

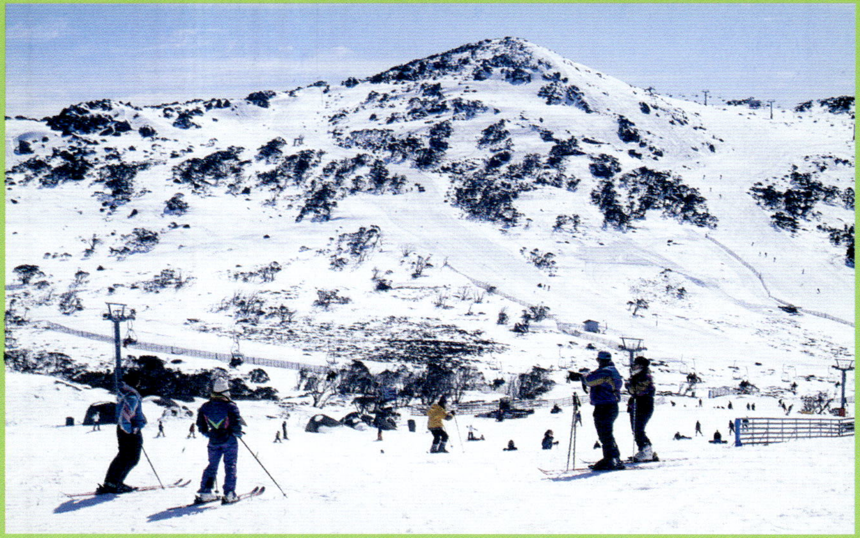

their land back if they could establish unbroken occupancy. Ironically, this apparent milestone decision is founded on the requirement that indigenous people with no adequate means of communication with the early Europeans, no fundamental concept of land ownership, and no material documentation, have to prove their occupancy of the land.

After years of neglect, the situation of the Aboriginal people is now high on the political agenda. Most Australians support the efforts of reconciliation and are increasingly aware of the continent's rich Aboriginal heritage.

The true Aussie

The myth that portrays the true Aussie as a dusty, sun-wizened jackaroo (or jillaroo), riding the Outback ranges herding sheep and cattle, or some sun-dried fossicker panning for gold, is about as valid as portraying every American as a gun-toting, tobacco-chewing cowboy or every Brit as a bowler-wearing, umbrella-carrying, pinstripe-suited snob. Portraying Aussies as youthful, happy, hedonistic, open-minded, easy-going, self-improving, enthusiastic, tanned, and often attractive or handsome, is much closer to the mark.

Leisure and sport are crucial to the Aussie way of life: work is the tedious bit in between the footie, or the fishing, beach picnics, and barbies. Taking life and authority seriously is not the Aussie way; having fun and enjoying a healthy lifestyle is. On car bumpers you'll find a sticker that sums it all up: "Everyone needs something to believe in. I believe I'll have another beer." That's not to portray the nation as one of alcoholics, but with almost a thousand wineries spread across every state, it's a wonder it's not. What makes the difference is that your man-in-the-street Aussie covets a healthy lifestyle where most things are done in moderation, and few to excess. Sport, excitement, enthusiasm, and getting involved are part of everyday life. But if you want to get into a conversation with the locals, you need to know how the local team is faring. Among men especially, sport seems to be the major topic of conversation, and while you may be tempted to think of this as something of a fixation, the reality is that it's based on real national success in athletics, swimming, cricket, rugby, cycling, boxing, and tennis.

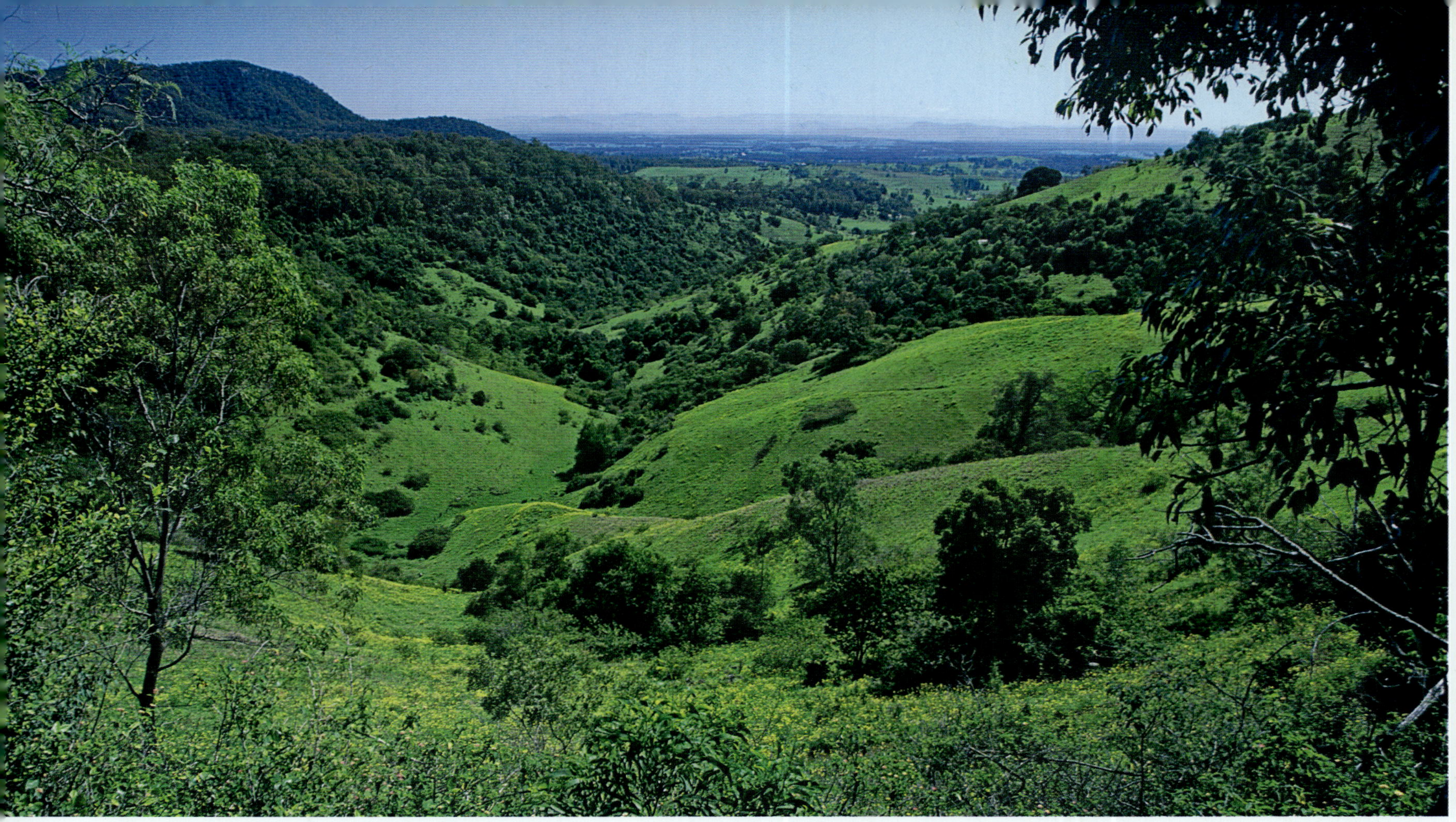

With virtually all Australians living within a few hours' drive of a beach, it's not surprising that the country is the home of beach culture, in spite of a host of deadly perils that inhabit the coastal waters, like box jellyfish, blue-ringed octopus, saltwater crocodiles, and sharks. On sunny summer days—which is most of them—you might be forgiven for thinking that the entire population has gone surfing. And the popular beaches, whether huge sweeping crescents or sheltered coves, are stacked with tanned, beautiful bodies basking on the sands or making the most of the deep blue waves. How could it be otherwise? The coast is where 80 percent of the population lives, pursuing The Great Australian Dream of living on their own plot of land, in a brick house with red-tiled roof, plenty of room for the kids to play and a barbecue ("barbie") in the back yard.

Life in the cities

Life in Australia's cities is surprisingly cosmopolitan. A multi-cultural society now exists, fuelled by post-War immigration policies, which brought in people from Europe and, more recently, southeast Asia, and has done much to reduce Australia's Anglocentrism. Each of the cities is remarkably different. Sydney is bustling and the de facto capital of the country, though the

The fertile Hunter Valley (top), is just a two-hour drive north of Sydney. Perisher Blue Ski Resort in the Snowy Mountains (above) offers alpine ski runs, cross-country skiing, and snow boarding. Next page: The Great Barrier Reef.

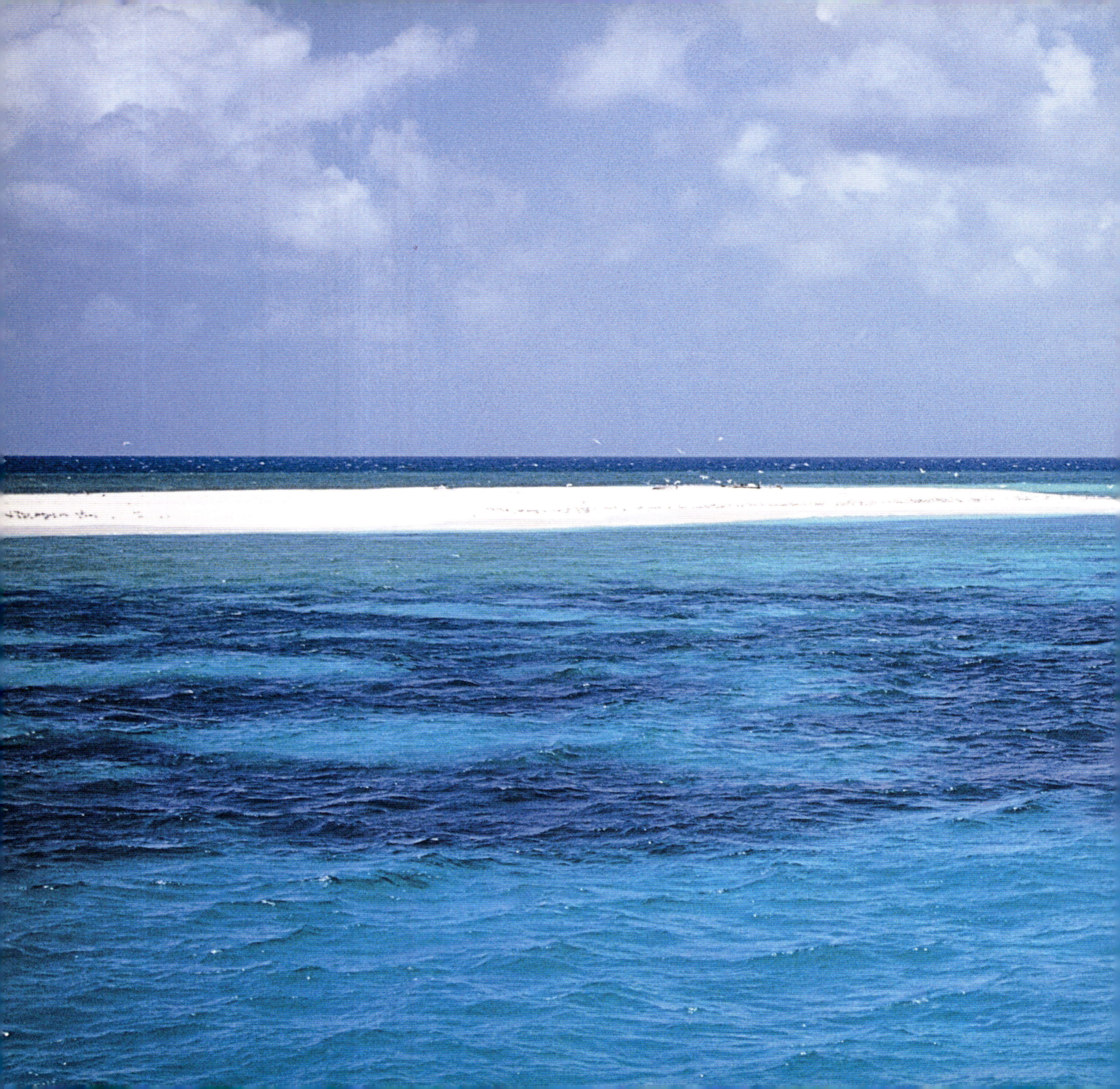

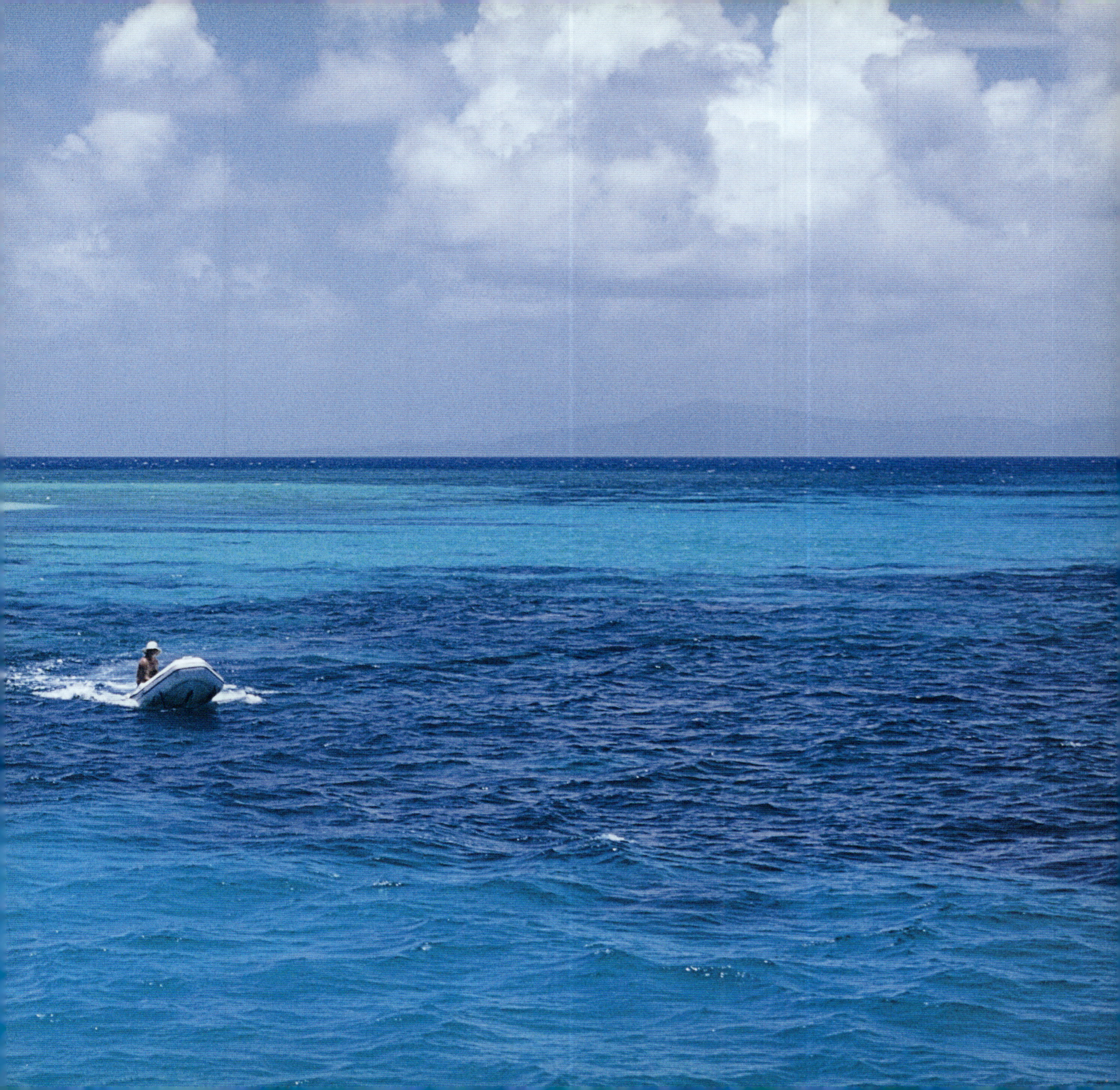

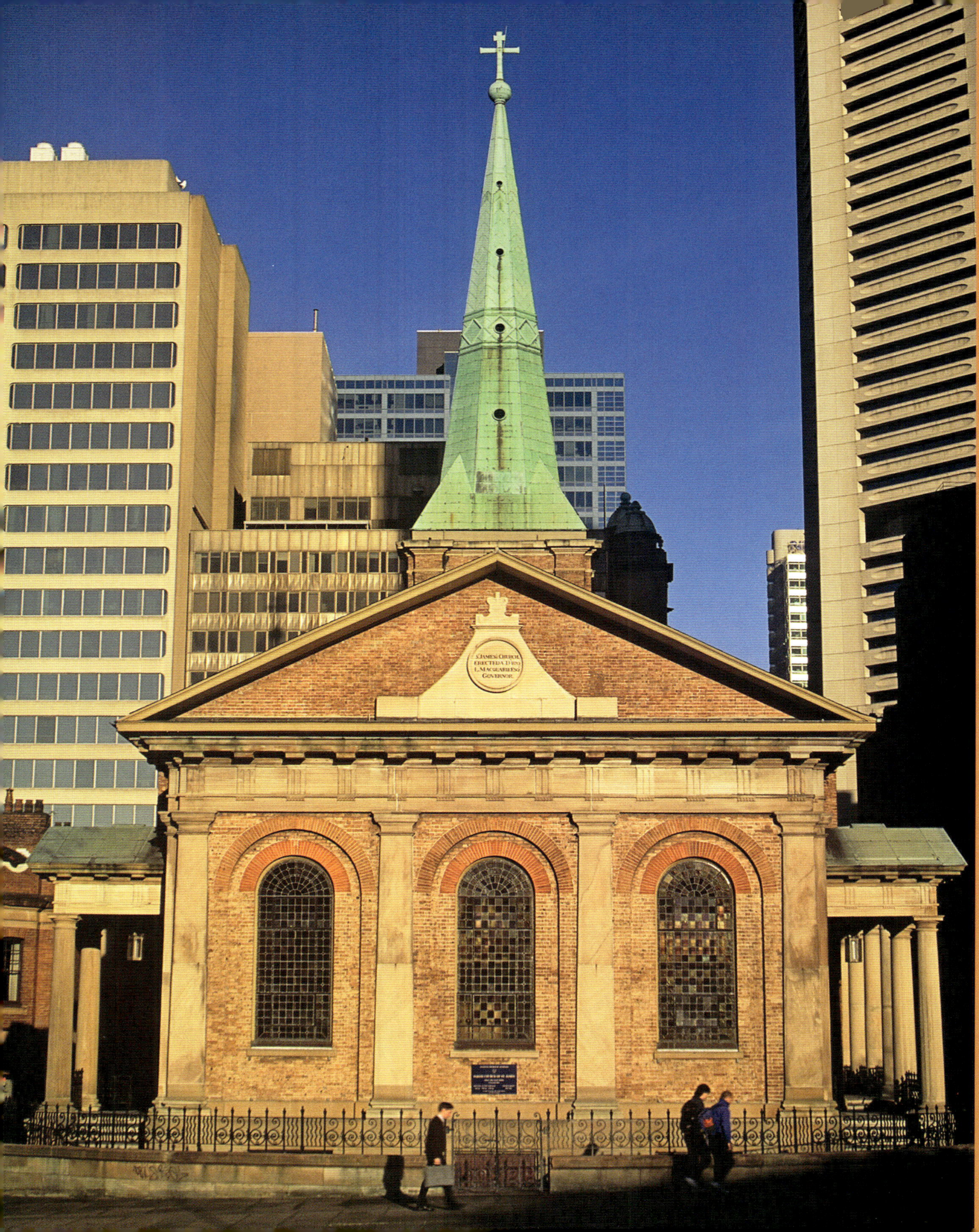

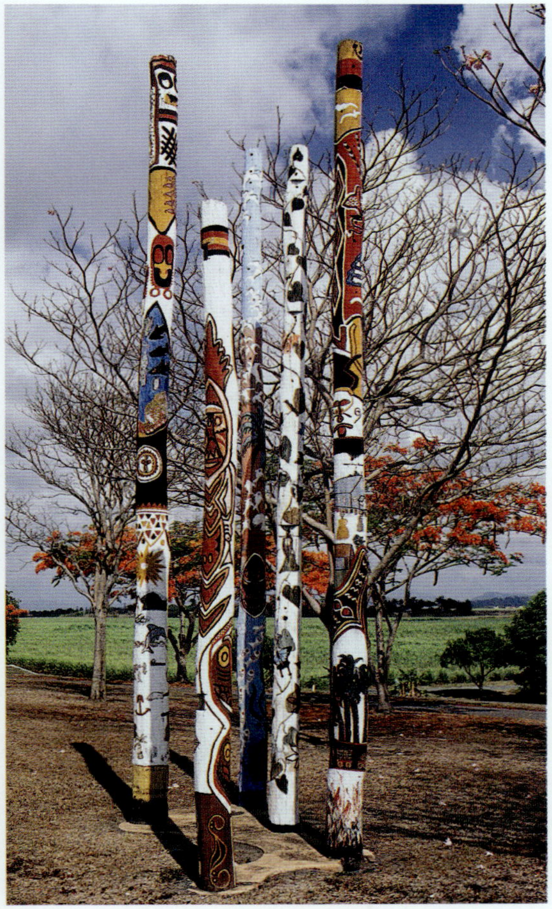

political capital is Canberra, a set of artificial communities in search of a city. Melbourne has a relaxing and delightful café culture that is a marked contrast to the energetic lifestyle of Brisbane. Adelaide, a city of rectangular blocks, has a peculiar charm and a splendid Chinatown, while Hobart, birthplace of Errol Flynn and capital of Tasmania has a distinct maritime feel and some fine streets lined with heritage buildings. Perth and Darwin are both such remote cities that they evolve largely without the influence of mainstream Australia. Perth is modern, bright, and bustling, but earnestly relaxed; Darwin, tropical, humid, and not given to anything suddenly energetic.

Arts and culture

For many years Australia was looked on as a cultural wasteland, not only by the world in general, but by many Australian people, too. Often, talented Australians had to go overseas to make a name. But, as with World War I, World War II fueled a resurgent nationalism, one, however, that this time sought a radical independence from Britain. The development of new iconographies of identity in the previous two decades, and especially in the 1930s, provided much of the basis for the nationalisms of the 1940s and 1950s.

Suddenly, Australian poets and short-story writers started to make progress, helped by the inspired by the works of the legendary "Banjo" Paterson (who wrote *The Man from Snowy River* and the words for the Australian cult anthem *Waltzing Matilda*). Many of the new wave of writers celebrated the bush, its male traditions of "mateship," and Aussie nationalism. What arose in consequence was a great and distinctive Australian literary voice which ran throughout the twentieth century and continues into the twenty-first.

The nationalistic enthusiasm also spread to the other arts as writers produced plays very much in the Australian idiom, and a recognisable school of landscape painting evolved. By the mid-1970s, painting and sculpture were in such vogue that there was much talk of an 'art boom', when artworks commanded very high prices.

Opposite: Old and new—the church of St James juxtaposed against modern offices in Sydney.
Above: Aboriginal totem poles in Lagoons Recreation Reserve, Mackay, in Central Queensland.

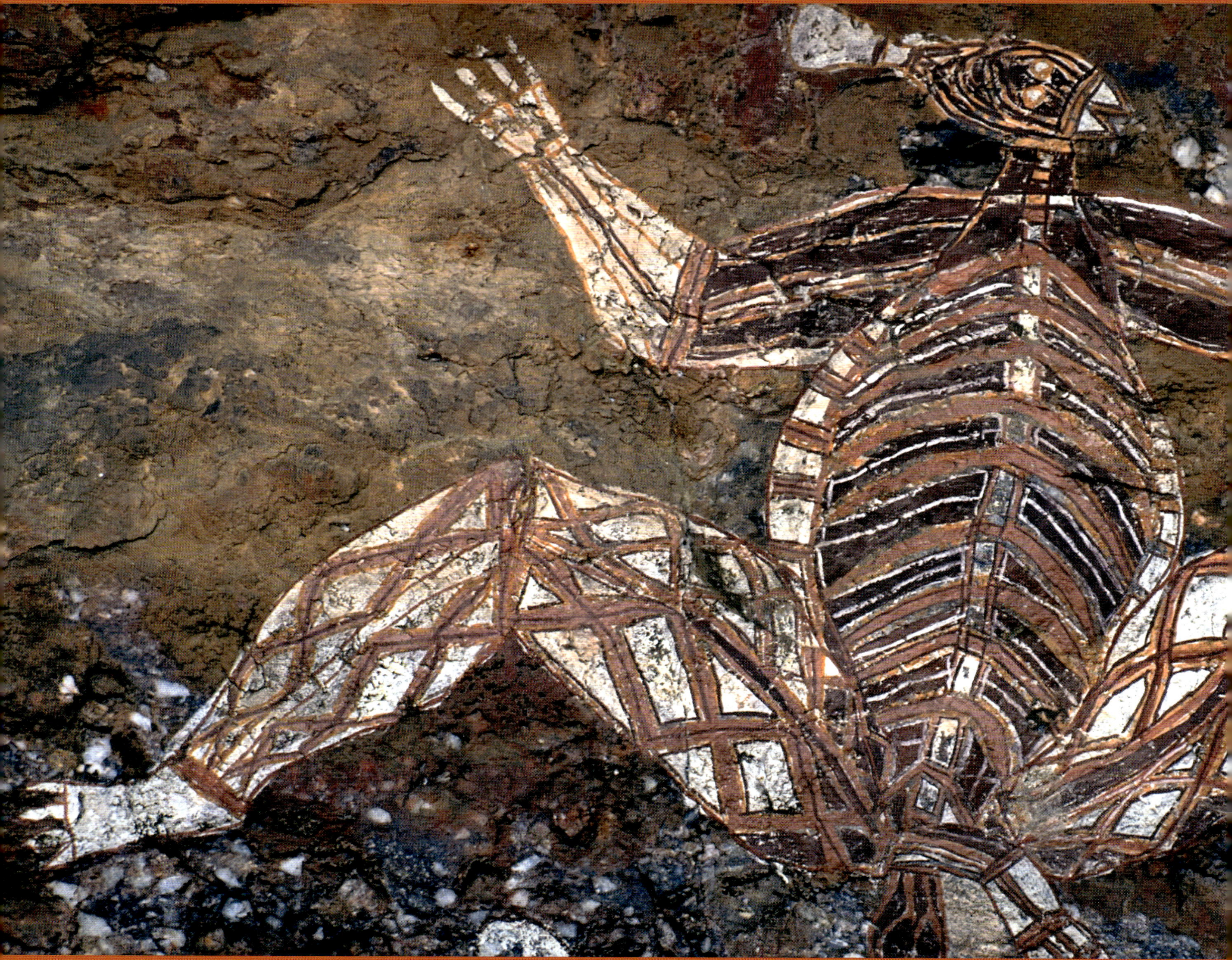

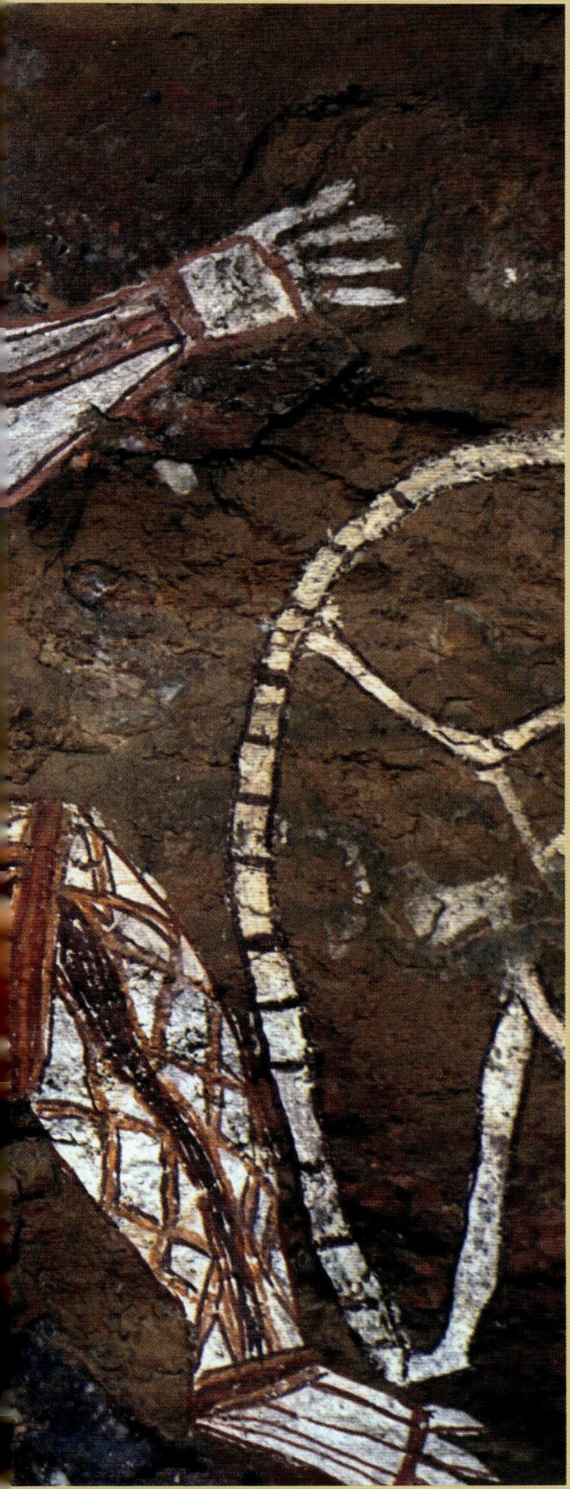

Aboriginal art

Aboriginal rock art is the longest-surviving living tradition of art in the world. Arnhem Land and the adjacent Kakadu National Park contain some of the finest rock paintings, many thought to have been made before the last Ice Age. Early forms of artistic Aboriginal expression, dating back more than thirty thousand years, were rock carvings and body painting. Like Christian stained-glass windows in cathedrals, Aboriginal art essentially involves story telling; here using keynote myths, rituals, sorcery, and magic, to describe their Dreaming, the stories of creation, their beliefs, and their spirituality. The strong relationship between the ancestral beings of the "time before time", the Dreamtime, with the landscape and every living creature they created, is the foundation of this art.

As in conventional art forms, the modern form of Aboriginal art began to develop in the 1970s, mainly in Arnhem Land and Papunya, a region to the west of Alice Springs. Here, Aboriginal artists were encouraged to paint their tribal designs onto bark sheets stripped from stringybark trees. Later, modern paints, mostly polymers, were used, and this inspired a new genre, the strongly symbolic dot style associated with the central deserts. Modern Aboriginal art commands good prices, but don't be surprised while walking through Alice Springs or settling down for an evening meal to be offered artwork at an affordable price. It will be genuine. It will be original. But will it be art?

The memories linger

Back home, the memories linger. But those of time spent in cities rarely transcend experiences in the Outback. Nor is there artwork more splendid than that of the starlit heavens seen from the darkness of the Centre, with the scent of eucalyptus and only the sound of crickets for company. And the images of Uluṟu, Kata Tjuṯa, Wattarka (Kings Canyon) and the Outback towns will prevail long after all others have faded. The true colors of Australia are those closest to its heart. And from its heart Australia offers a rare beauty, serenity, and a oneness with nature that is never forgotten.

Aboriginal rock art at Nourlangie Rock in Kakadu National Park, Northern Territory.

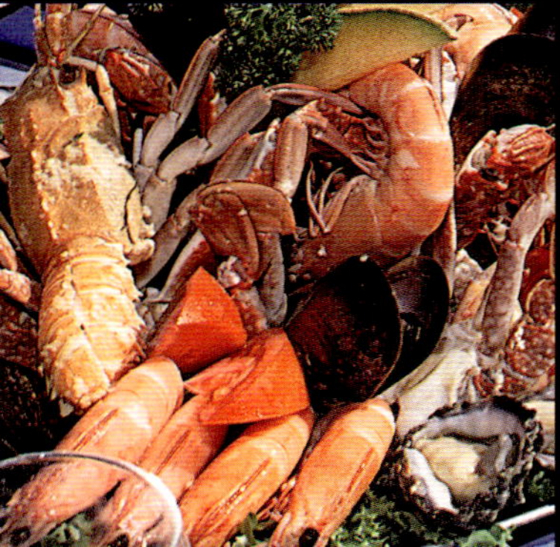

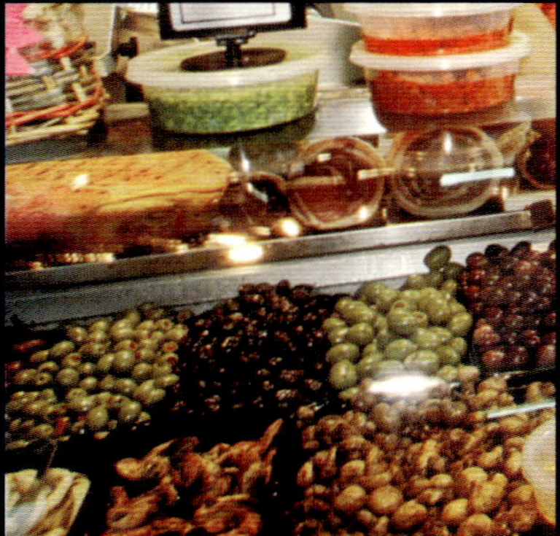

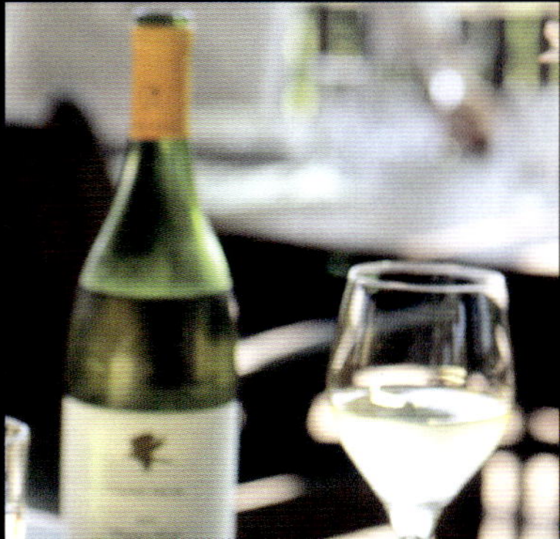

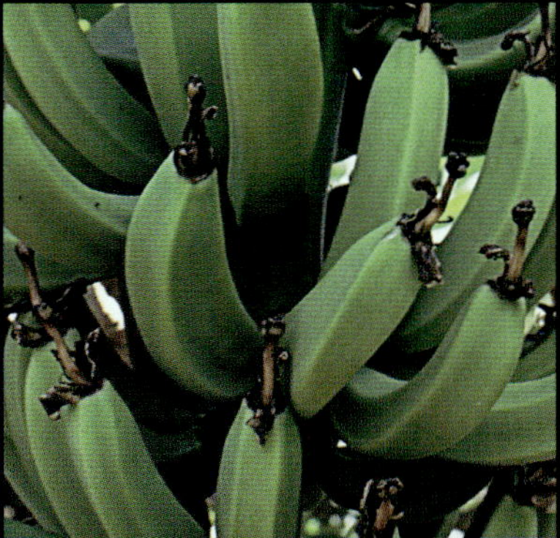

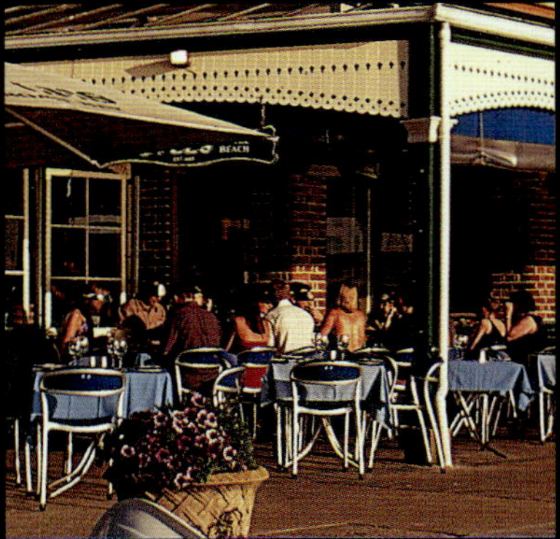

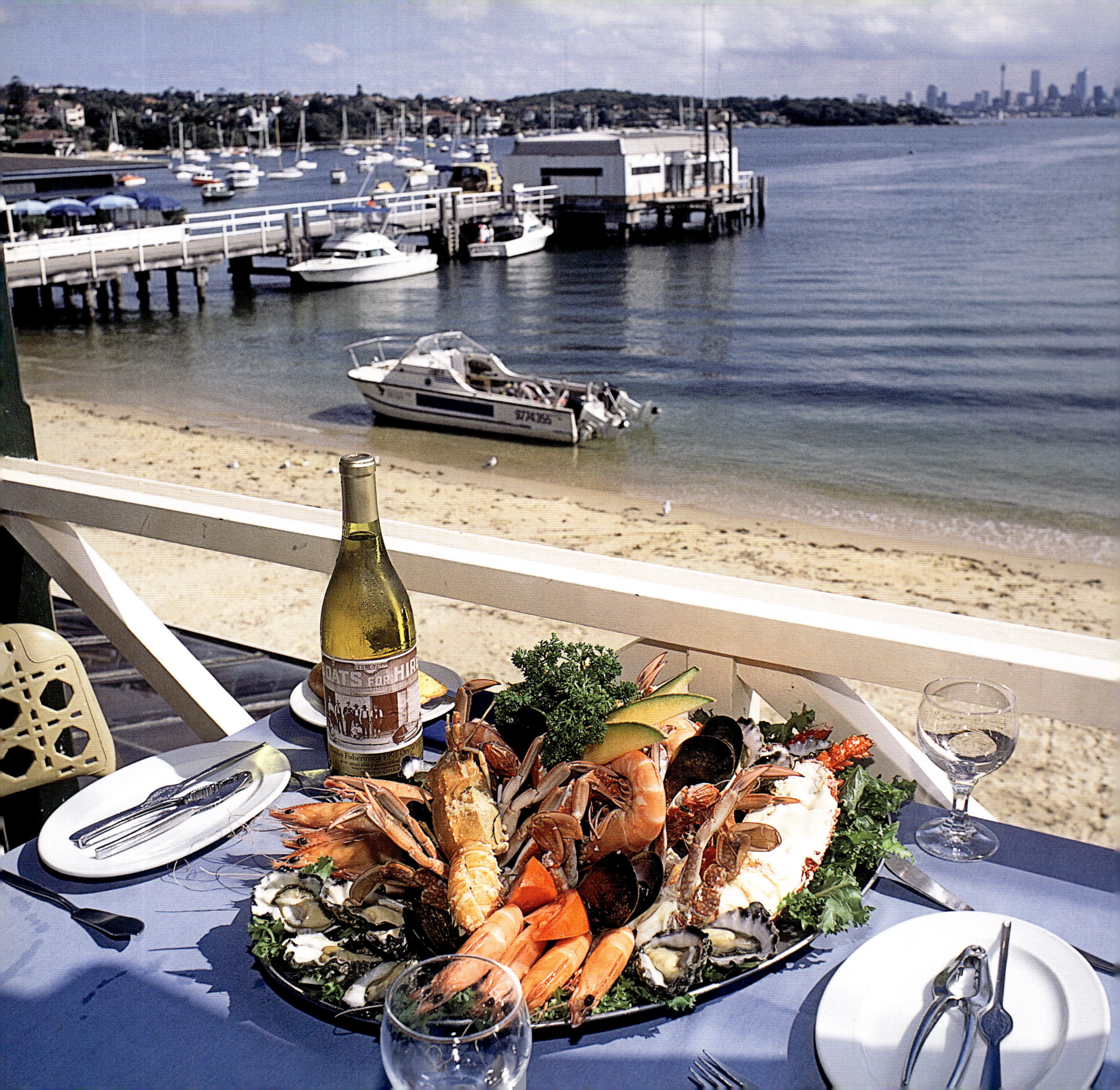

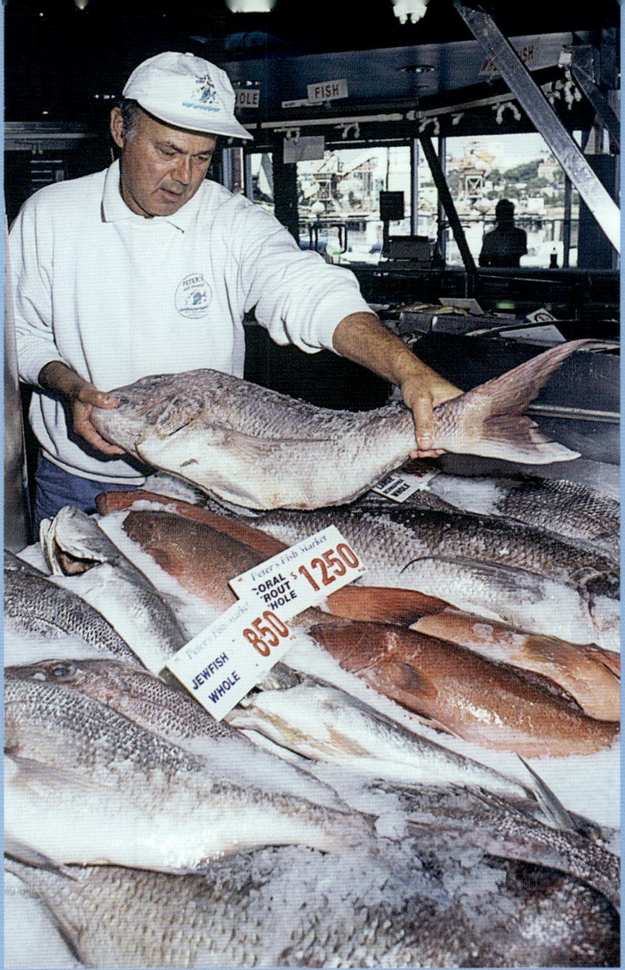

SEAFOOD AL FRESCO

Australian cuisine is a talented blend of culinary influences from many parts of the world, notably Asia. The seafood, lamb, emu steaks, kangaroo, and crocodile meat offered by restaurants in major cities is complemented by cosmopolitan dishes of lasagne, kebabs, moussaka, dim sums, curries, bouillabaisse, venison, Creole carri poule, goulash, lahksa, and frankfurters. In Alice Springs, at the very heart of Australia, one restaurant even serves "Swiss-Indian-Australian" cuisine.

The Aboriginal people have been using natural food resources for thousands of years, so it should be no surprise to find bushfoods in modern cooking: deliciously tangy fruits from the rain forests, aromatic herbs from the woodlands, zingy pepperleaf and delicate snowberries from the southern highlands, and spicy bush tomatoes from the desert.

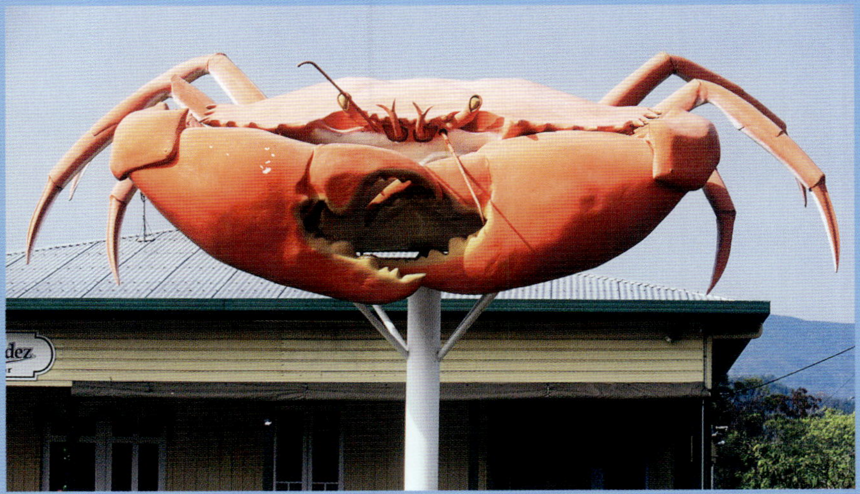

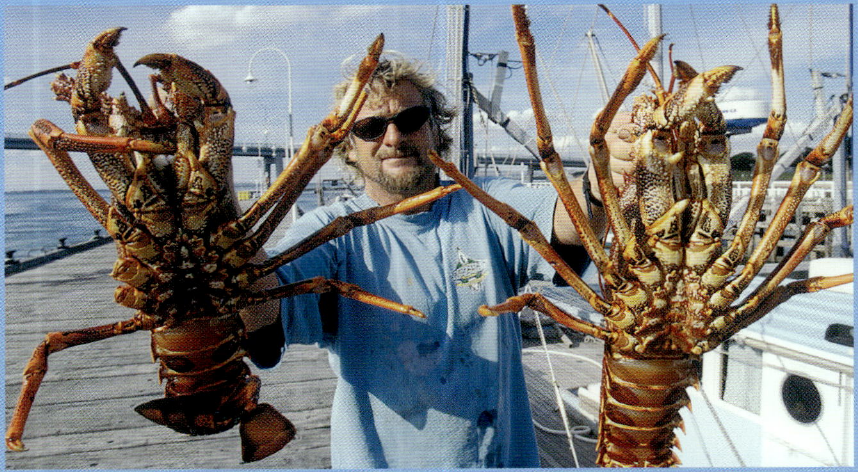

With most Australians living by the sea, it's not surprising that seafood of all shapes and sizes is a major ingredient in Aussie cuisine, like giant crab, rock lobster, and barramundi.

Straight from the sea, fresh and still kicking. While "If it swims, you can eat it" isn't a wholly reliable rule-of-thumb, the list of edible species is long, and they are invariably delicious.

FOOD GALORE

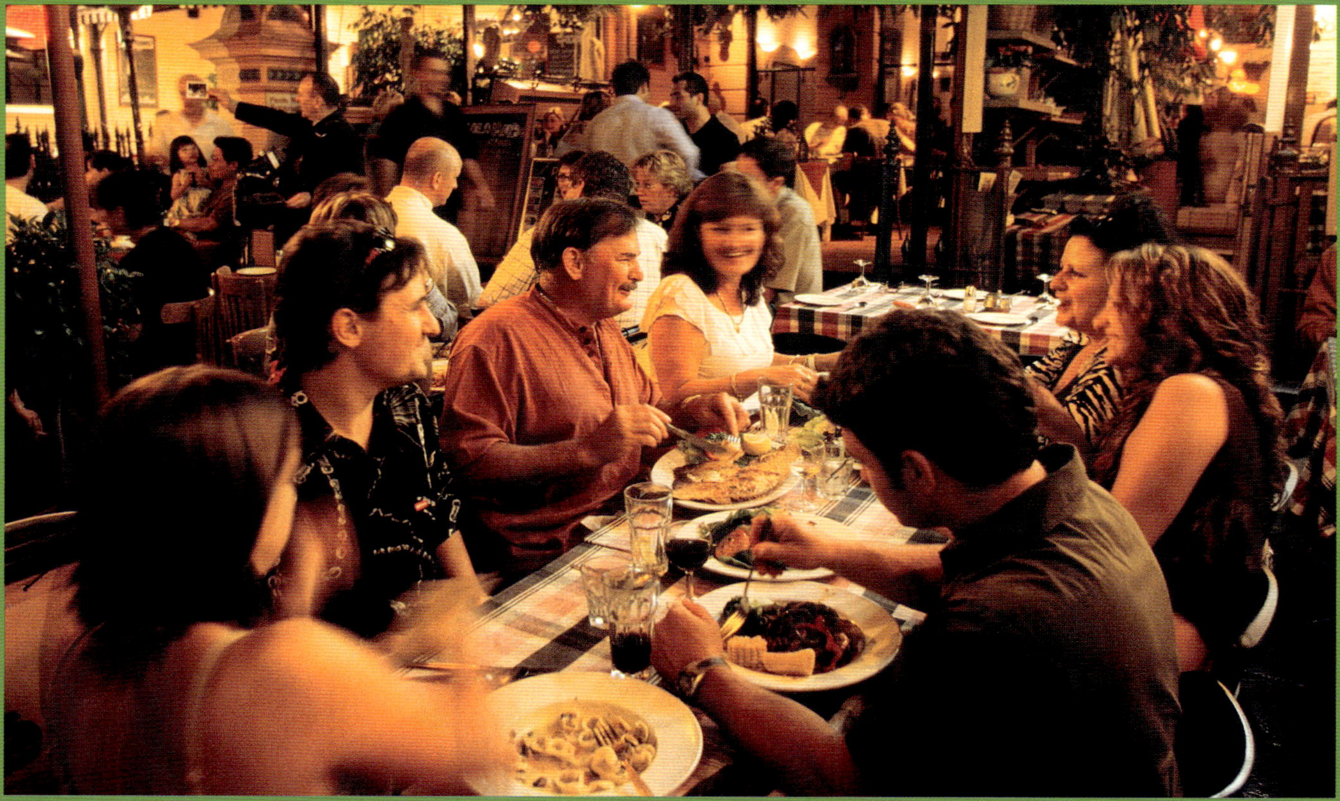

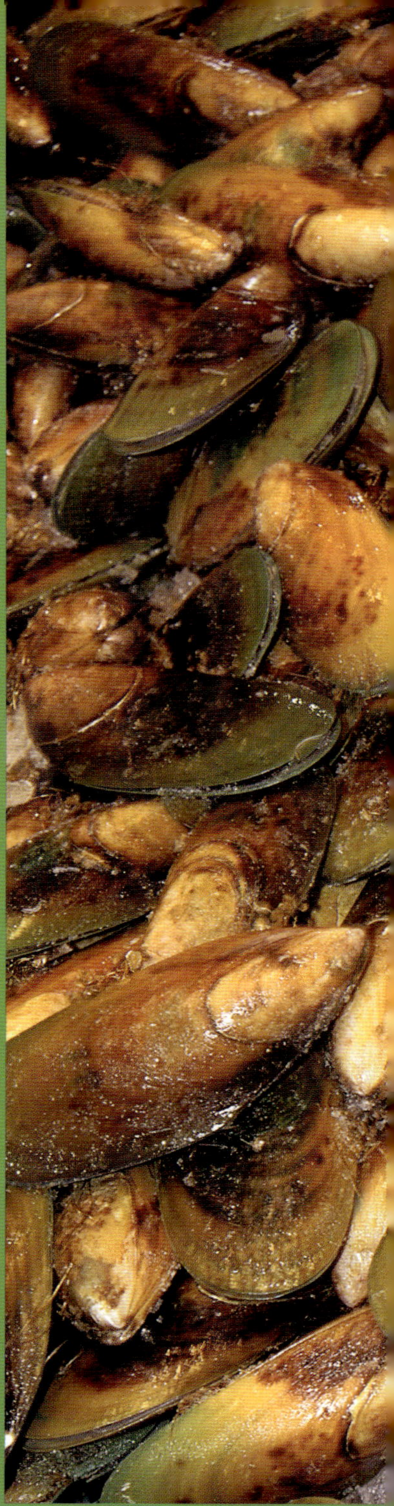

Although seafood dominates, the Australians are not slow to consume indigenous food supplies like venison, quail, crocodile, emu, kangaroo, and, if you can believe it, road kill. The bustling Lygon Street cafés in Melbourne are as much a social venue as a place to eat.

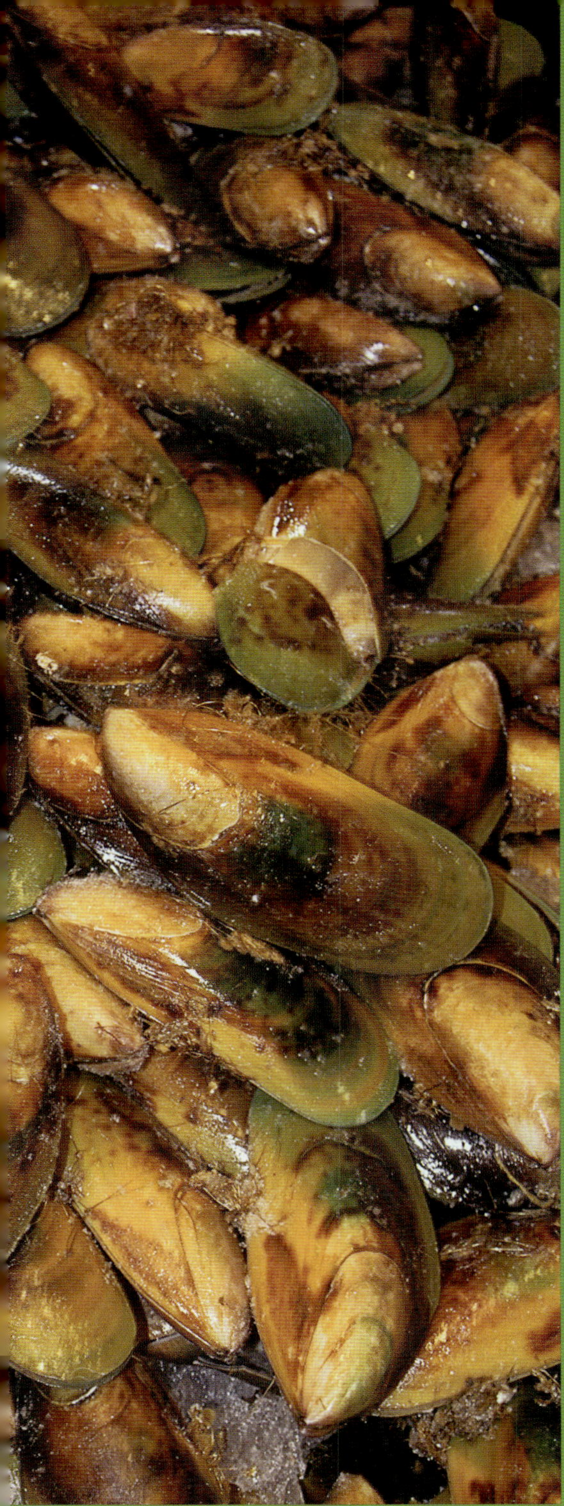

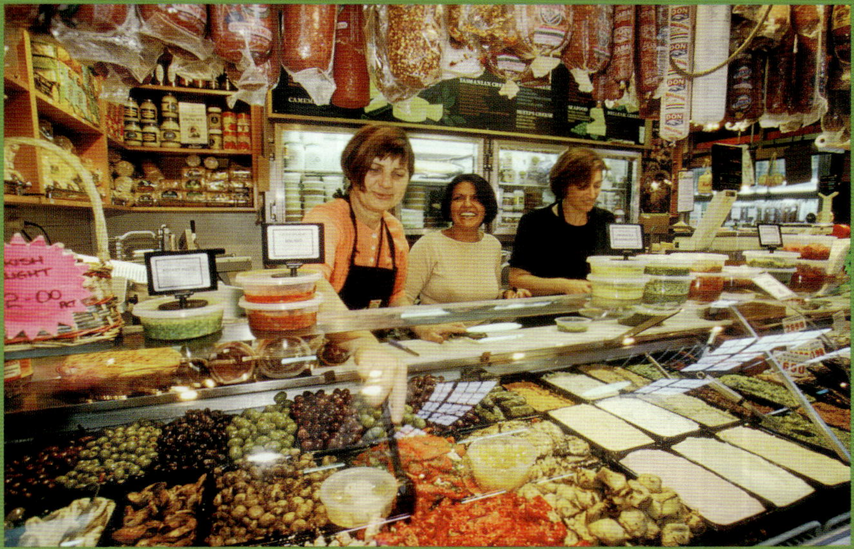

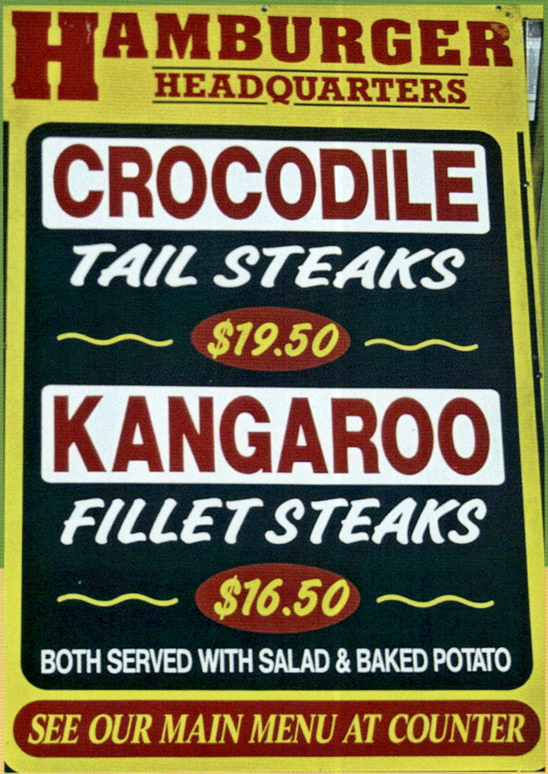

Tina's Deli in Queen Victoria Market, Melbourne (top right), reflects the wide range of food available in Australia. The market was established in 1878, and is the largest open-air market in the Southern Hemisphere.

FINE & FRUITY

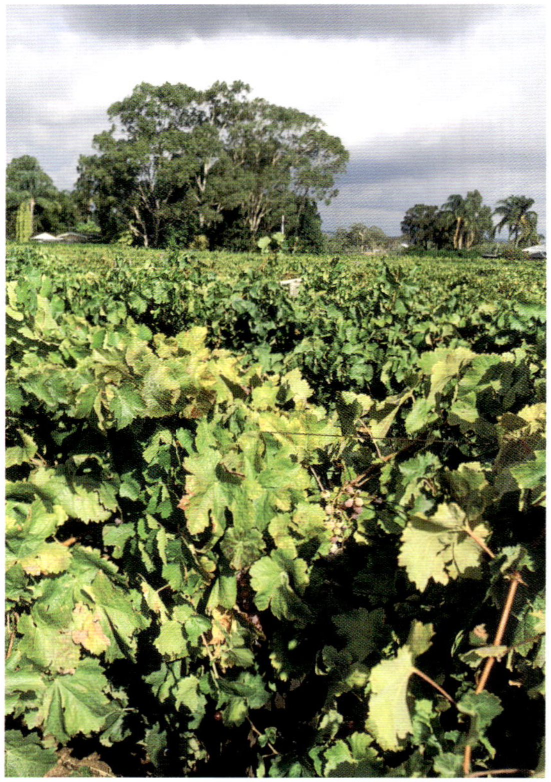

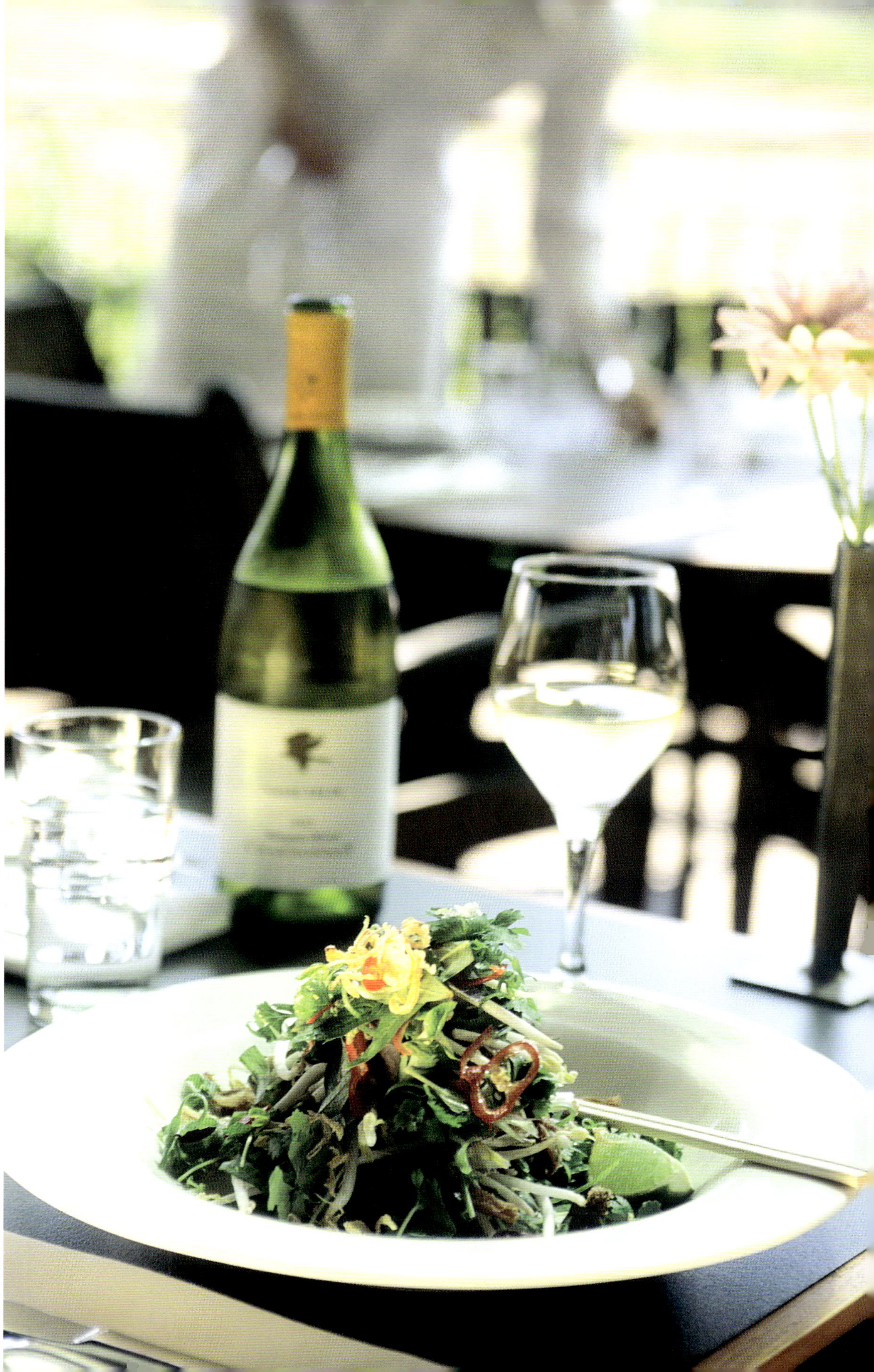

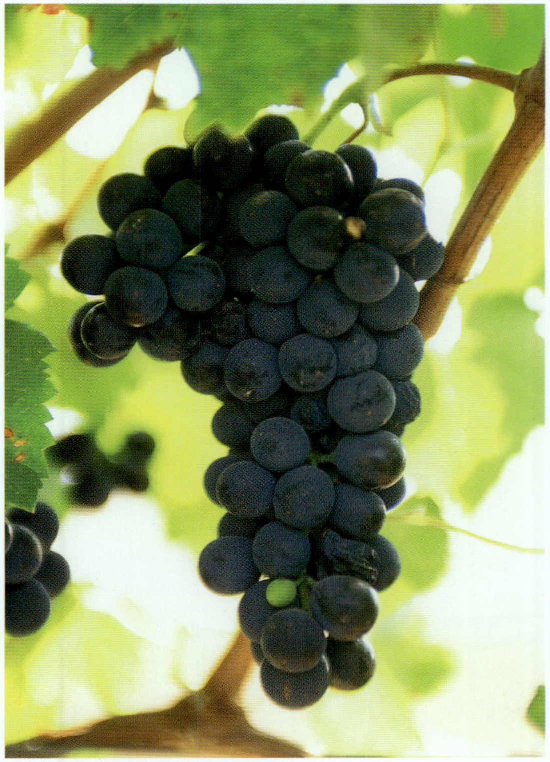

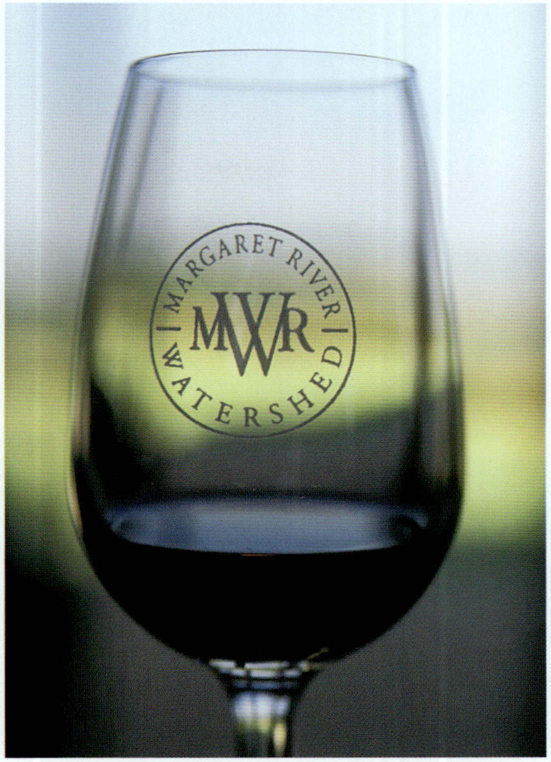

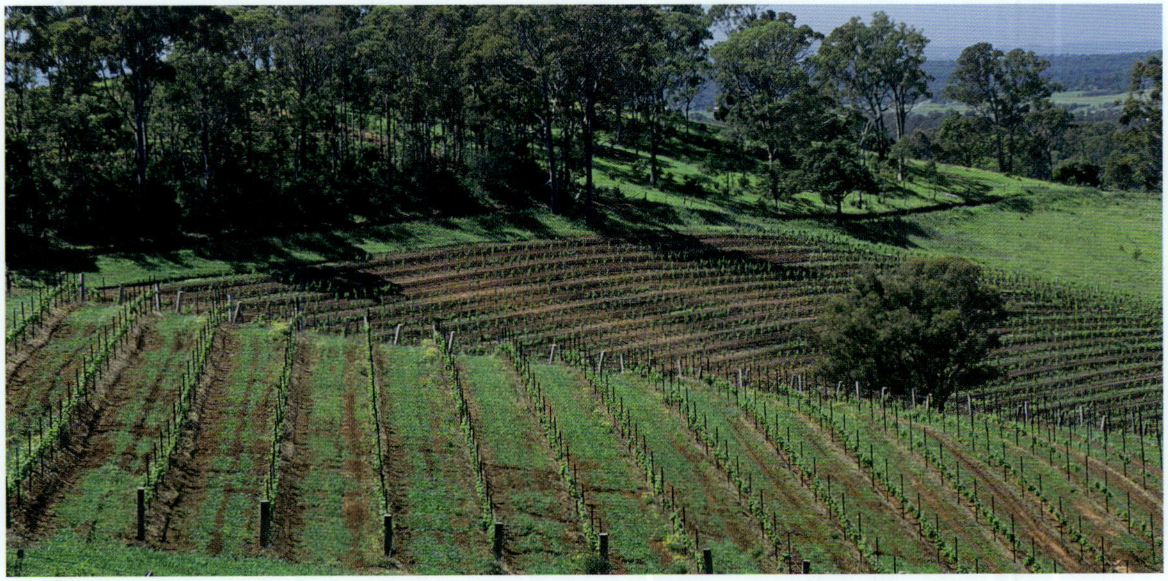

Across Australia, soil types vary from deep black volcanic loams to sandy soils over gravel, and rich red clays over limestone, providing the foundation for wines of stunning diversity. The geographic richness of Australia blended with the winemakers' quest for innovation has developed a diversity of winemaking techniques and styles, and wines to suit every palate, every dish.

Next page: Vasse Felix winery and restaurant at Margaret River, Western Australia.

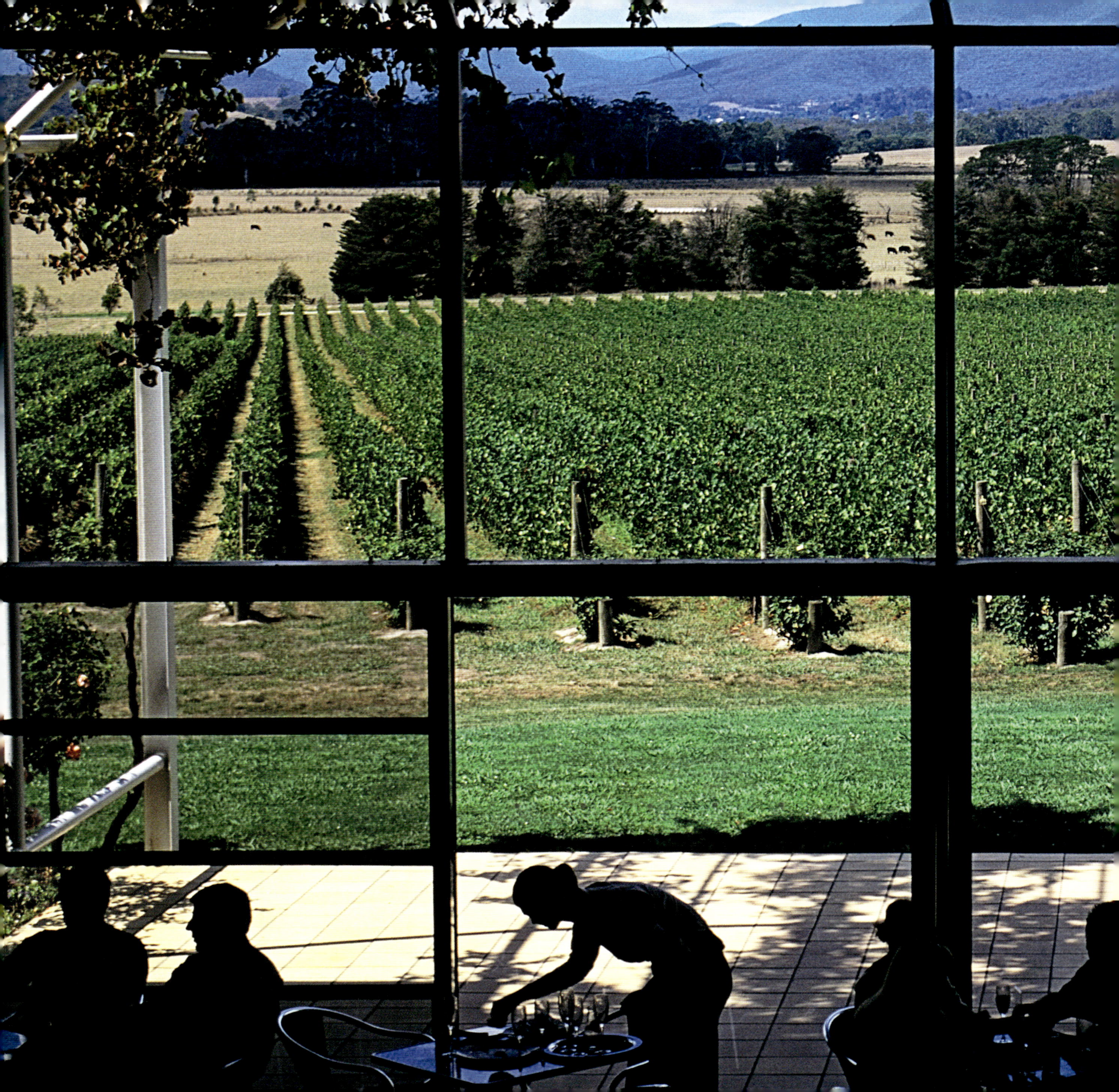

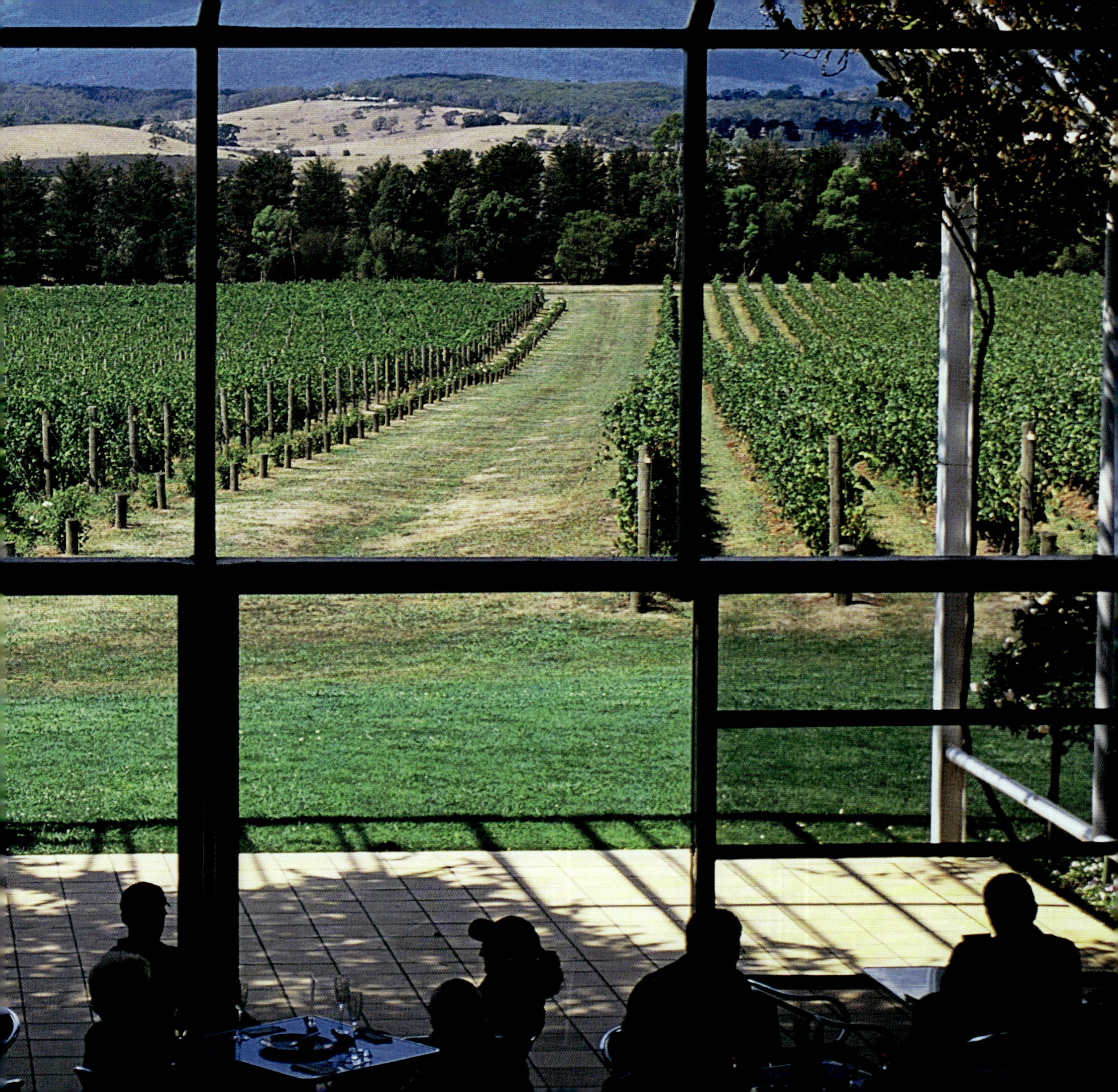

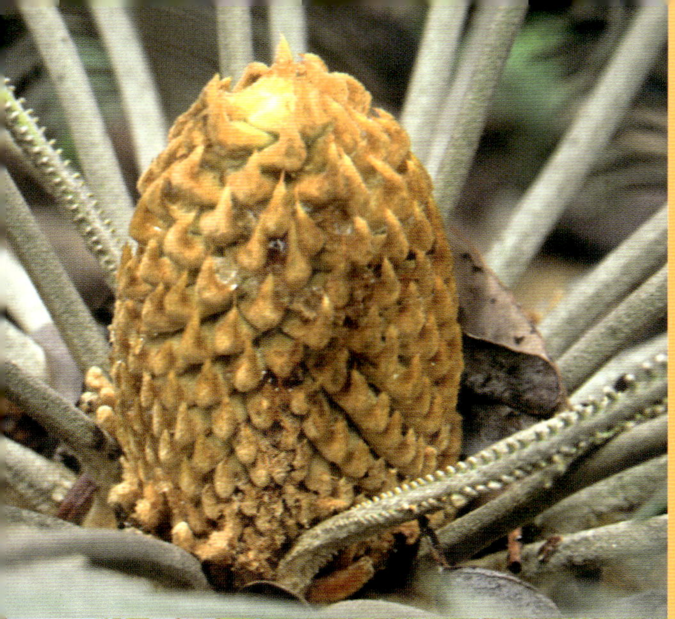
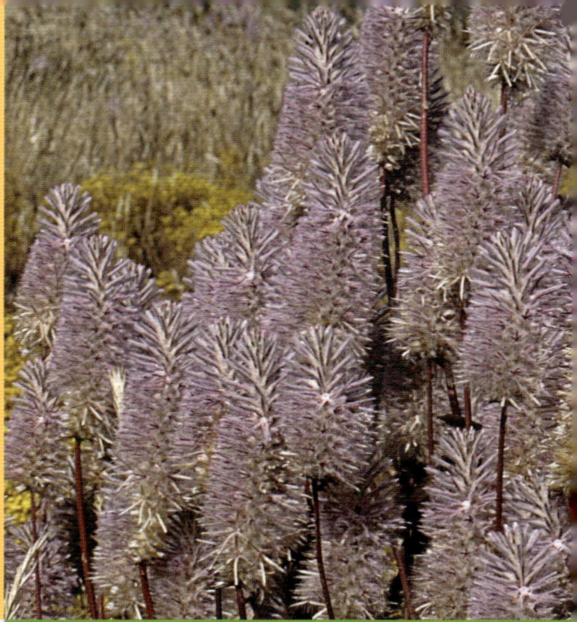
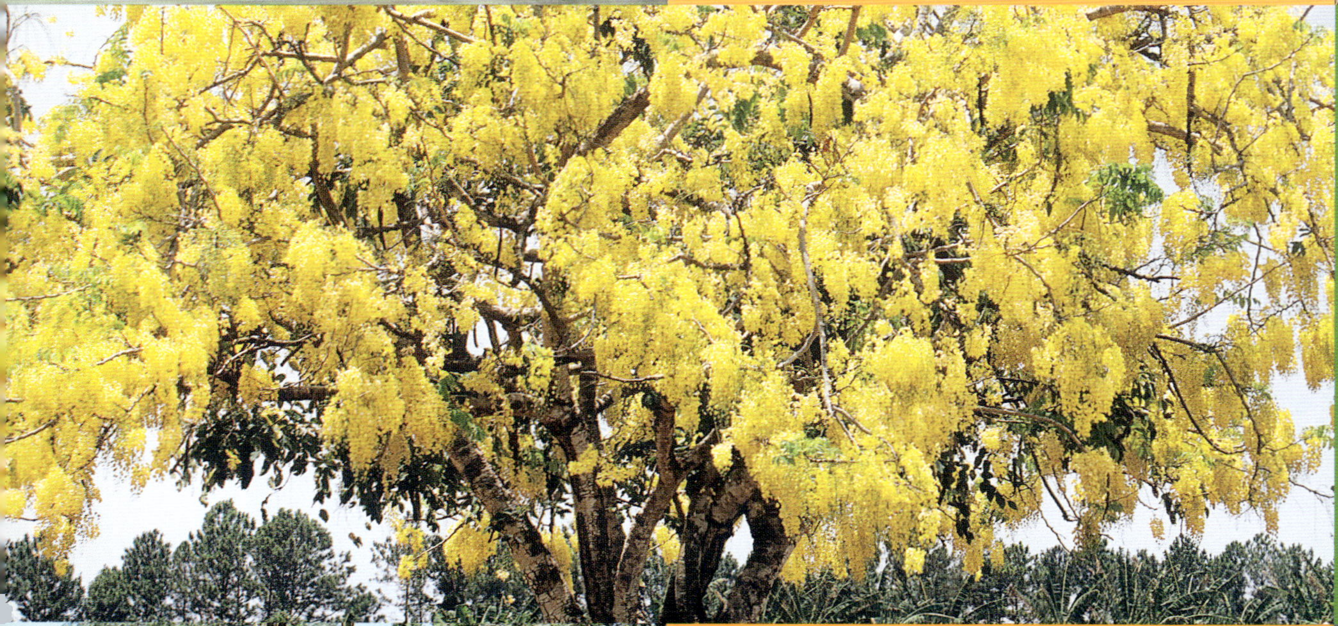
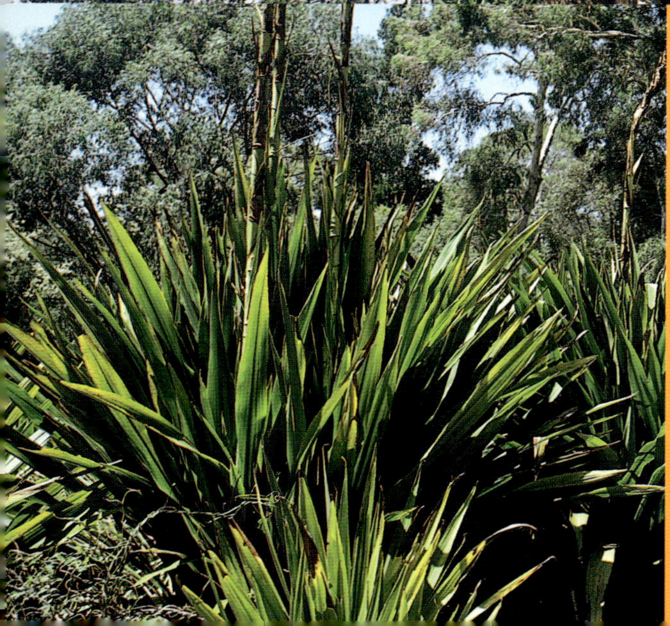
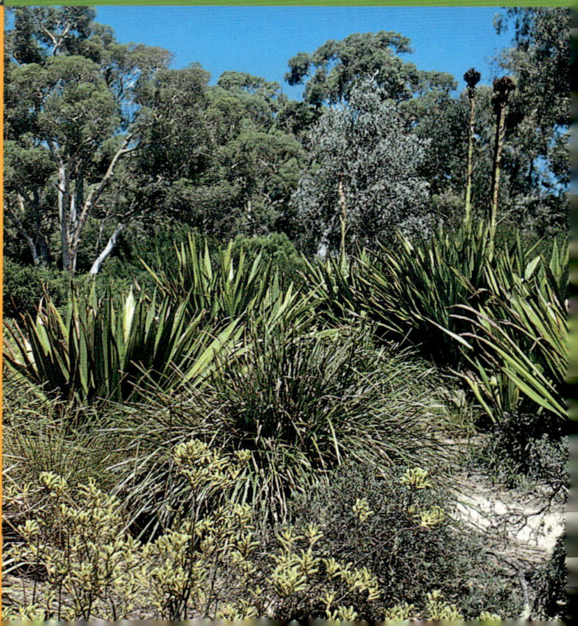

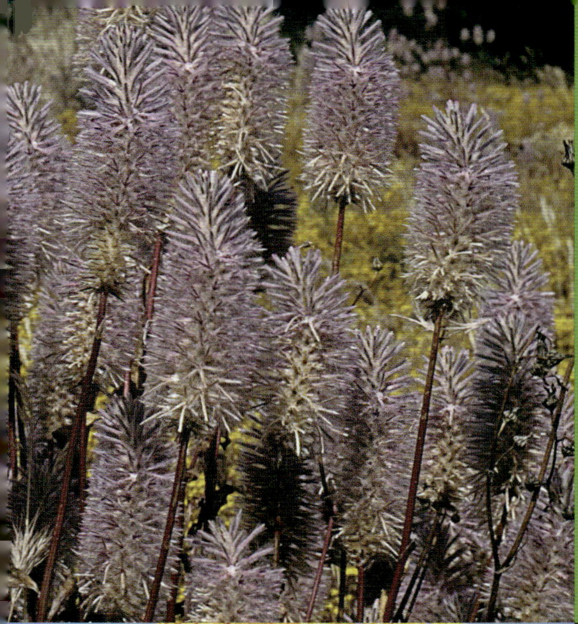
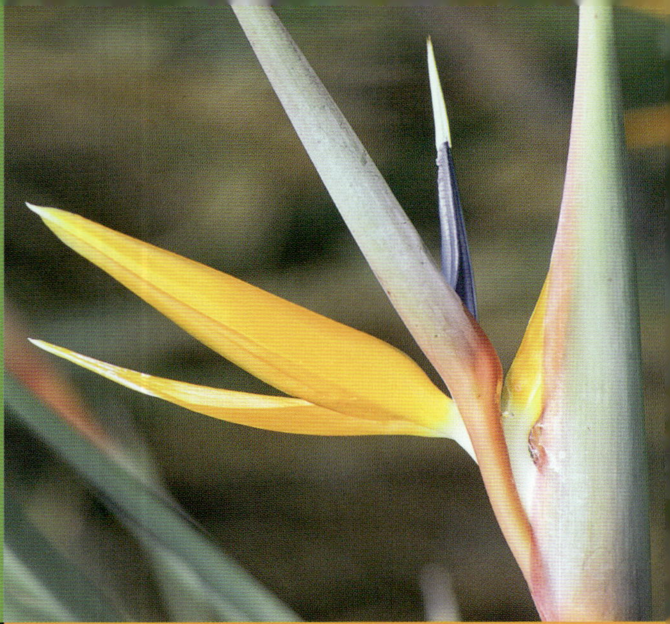
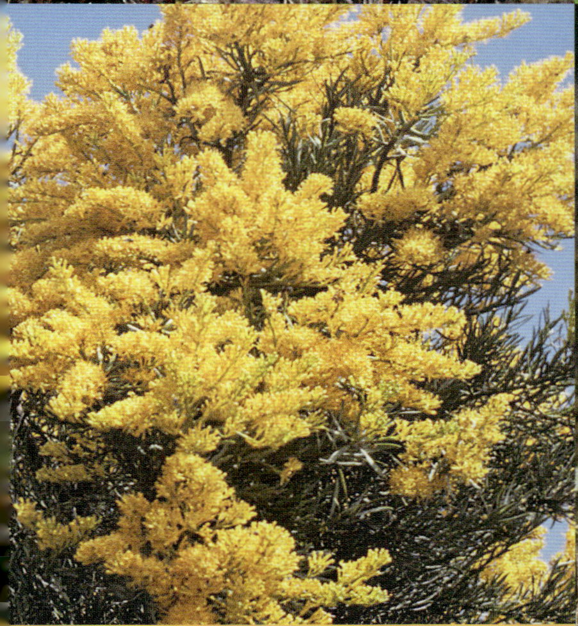
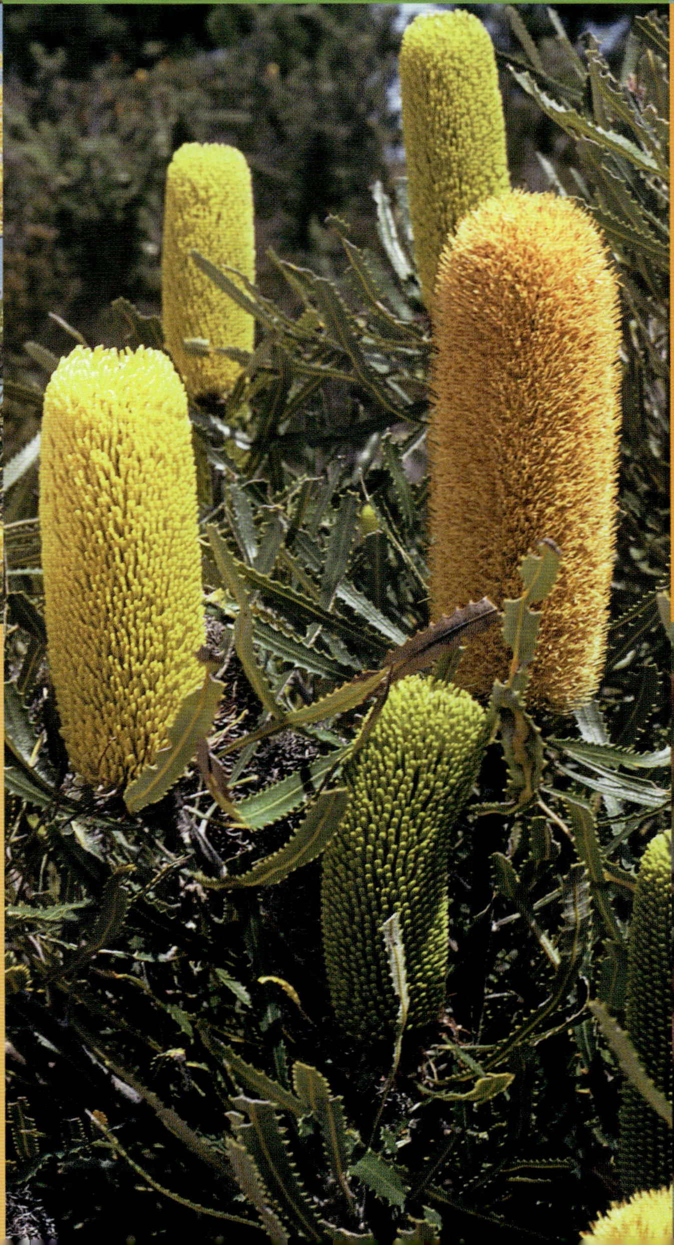
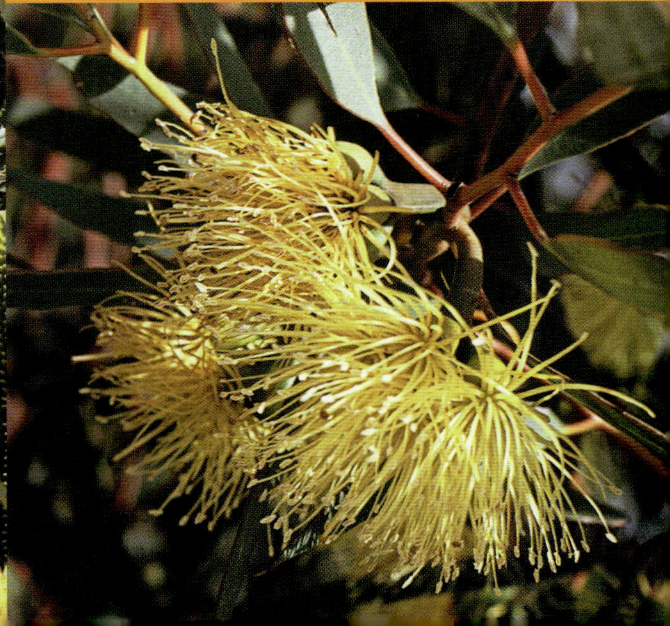

NATURAL PRODUCE

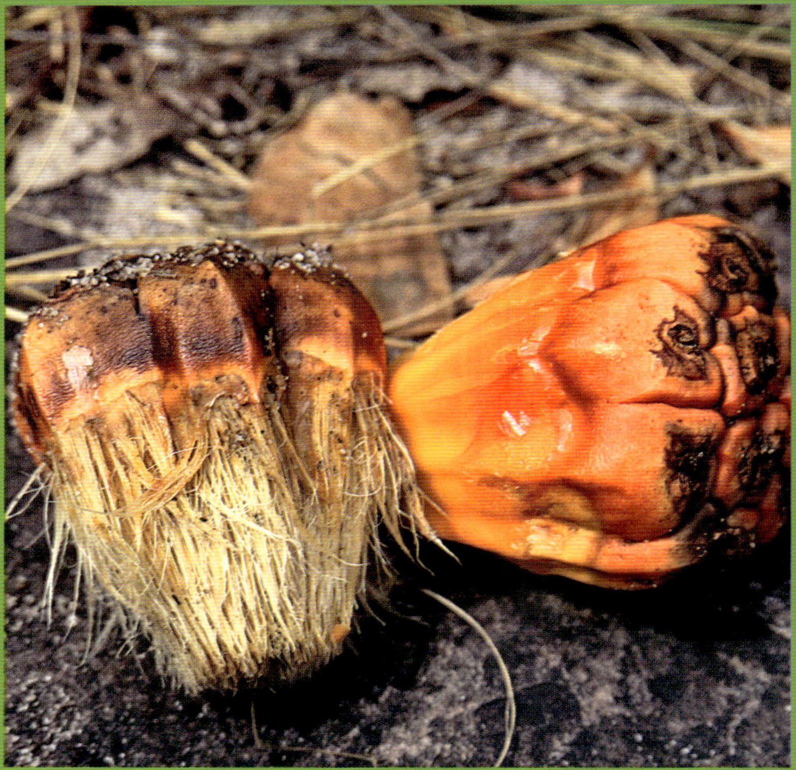

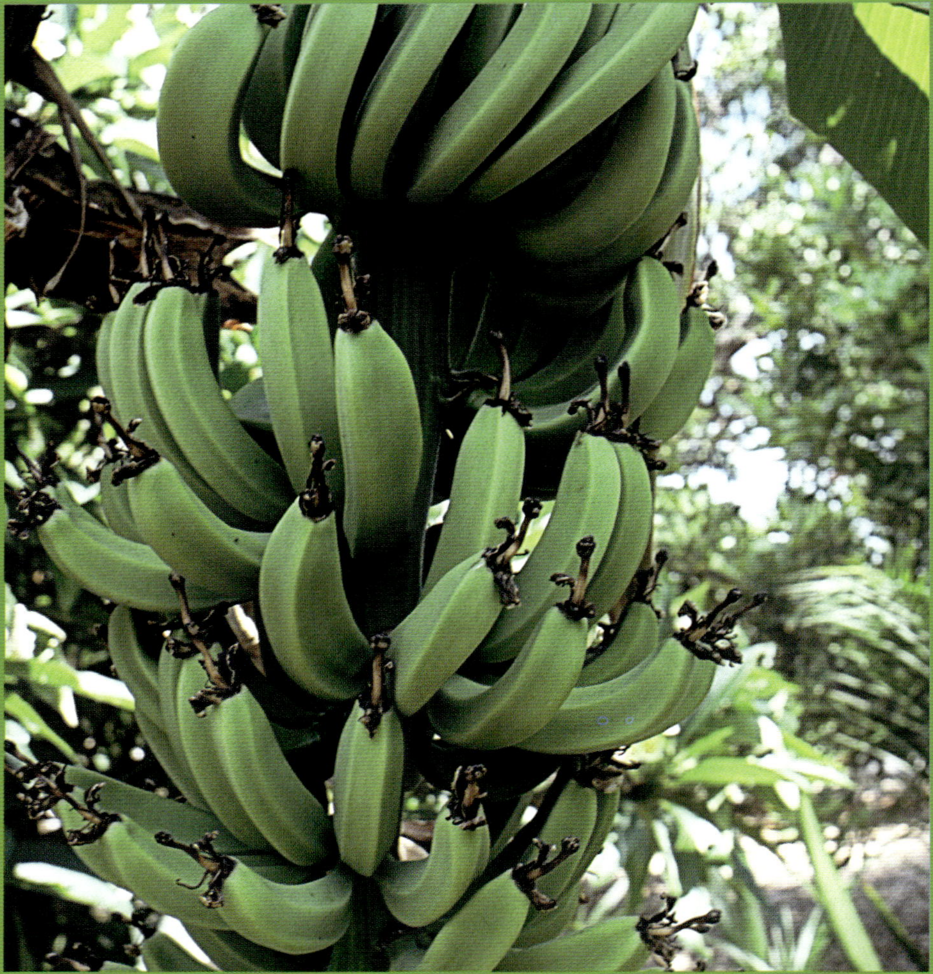

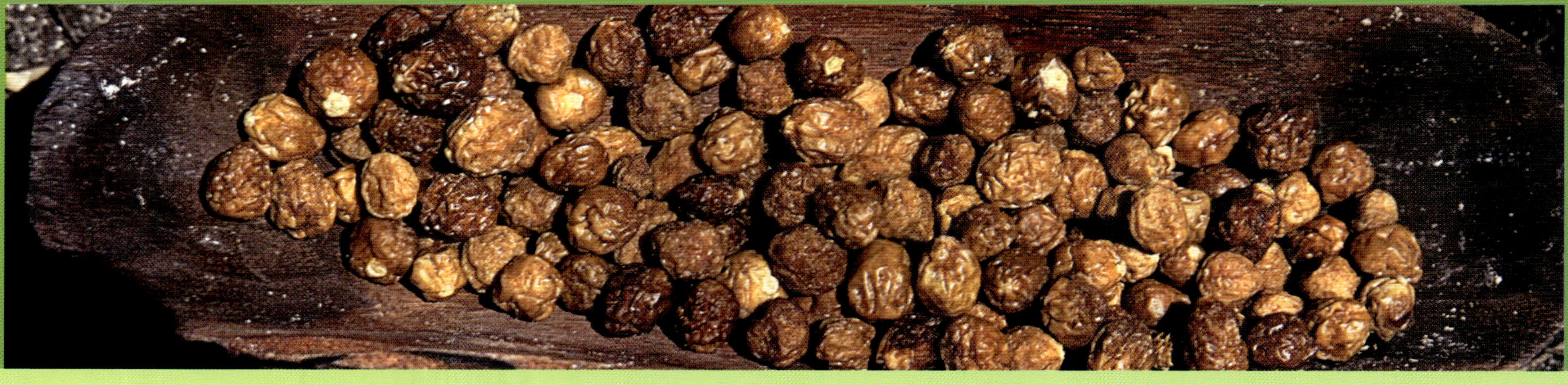

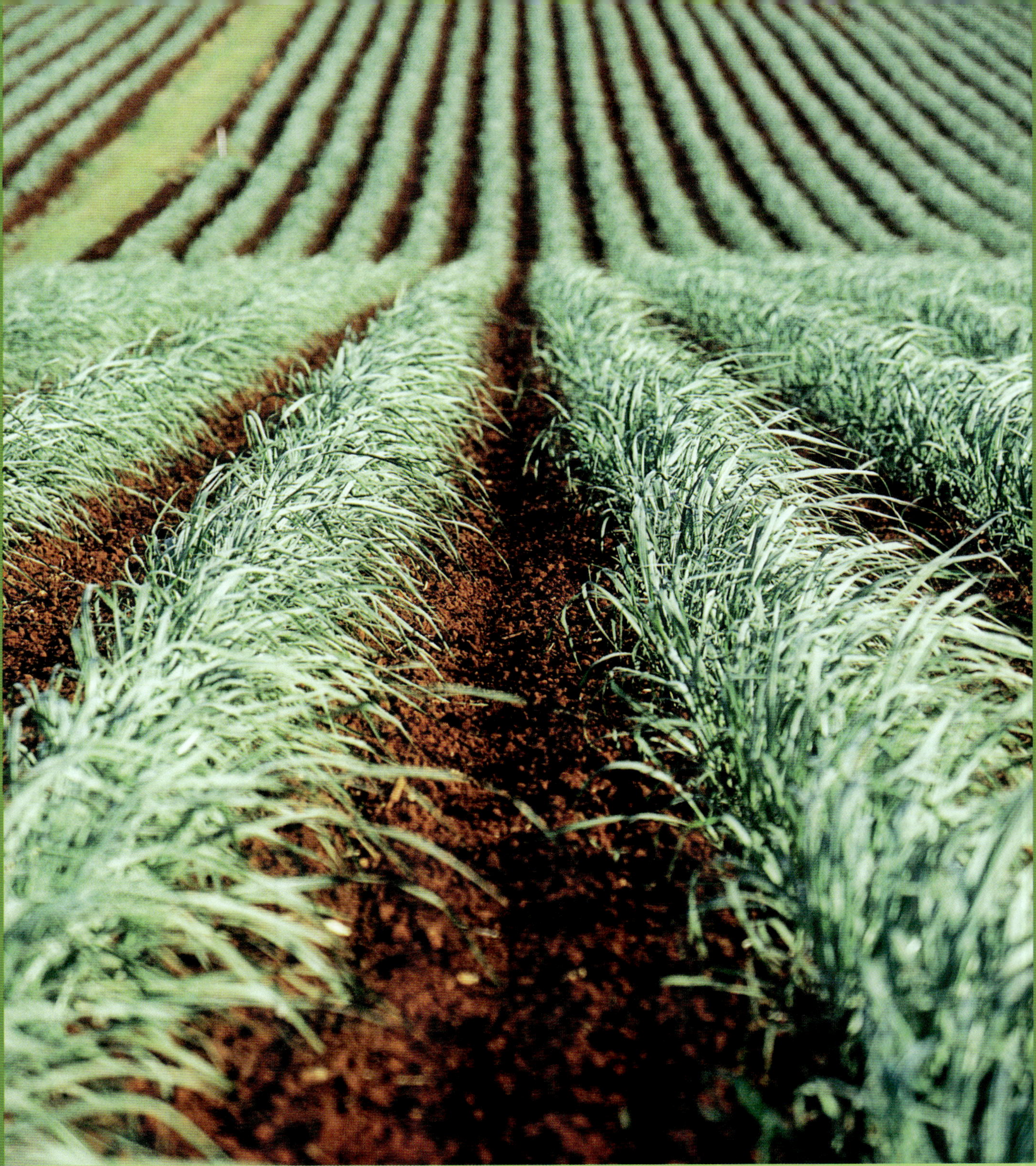

Australia's environment, one of the least polluted in the world, produces the freshest fruit and vegetables both familiar (like bananas) and not-so-well-known, like custard apple, lychee, persimmon, asparagus, avocado, eggplant, Chinese cabbage, sugar crop (above), and zucchini. Bushtucker food, like bush raisins (left, in a wooden bowl) and pandanus fruits (far left), are also in plentiful supply. The diversity of climates also generates a range of harvesting times, enabling crops to be grown in the north in winter months to supplement those grown in the south during the summer.

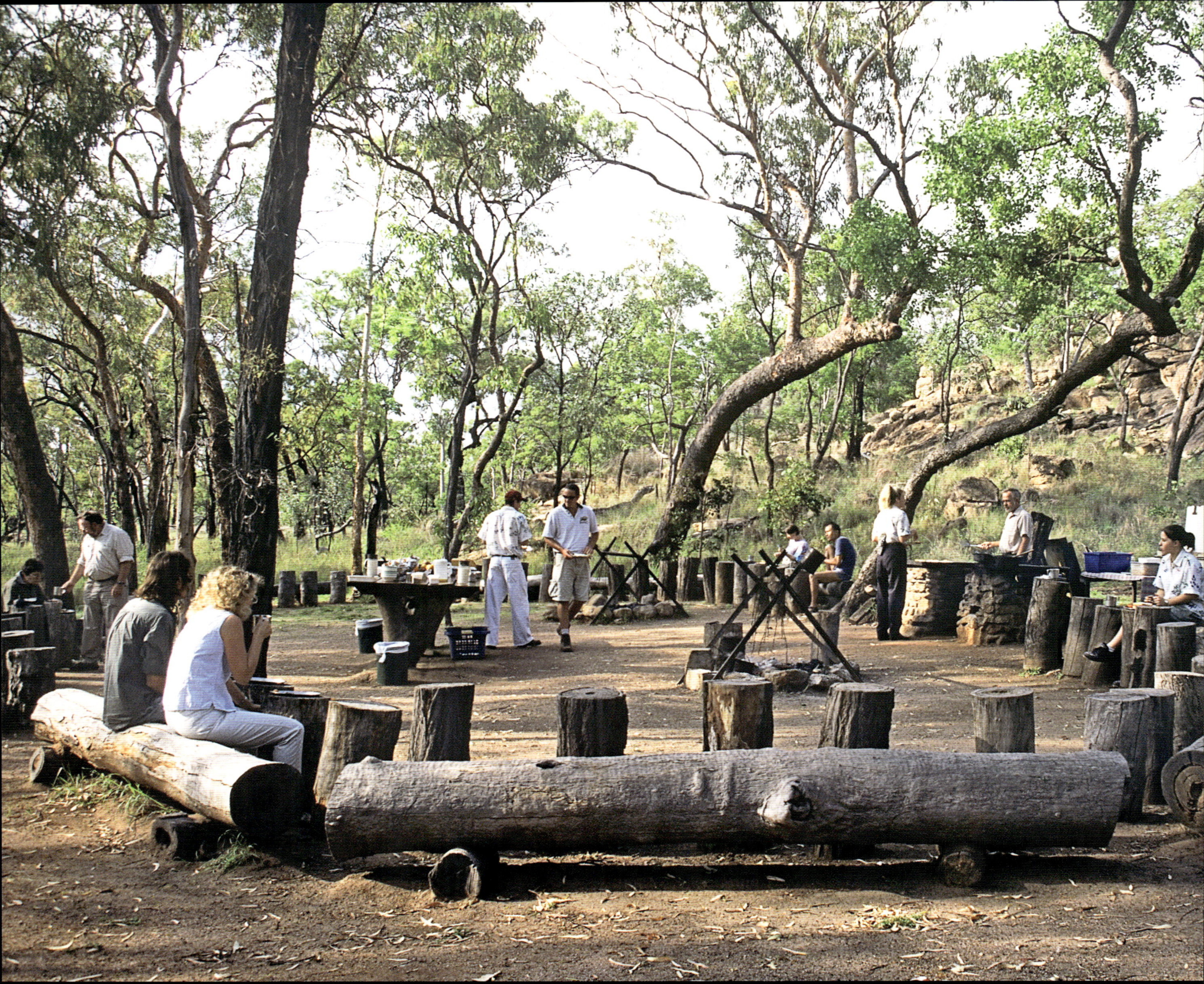

These outback travelers are settling down for a traditional “bush breakfast” at a campsite in Undara, Queensland. Eating out, literally, like this, has its limitations, but the experience is still not one to be missed. The opposite experience is a meal at a sophisticated waterfront city restaurant.

EATING OUT

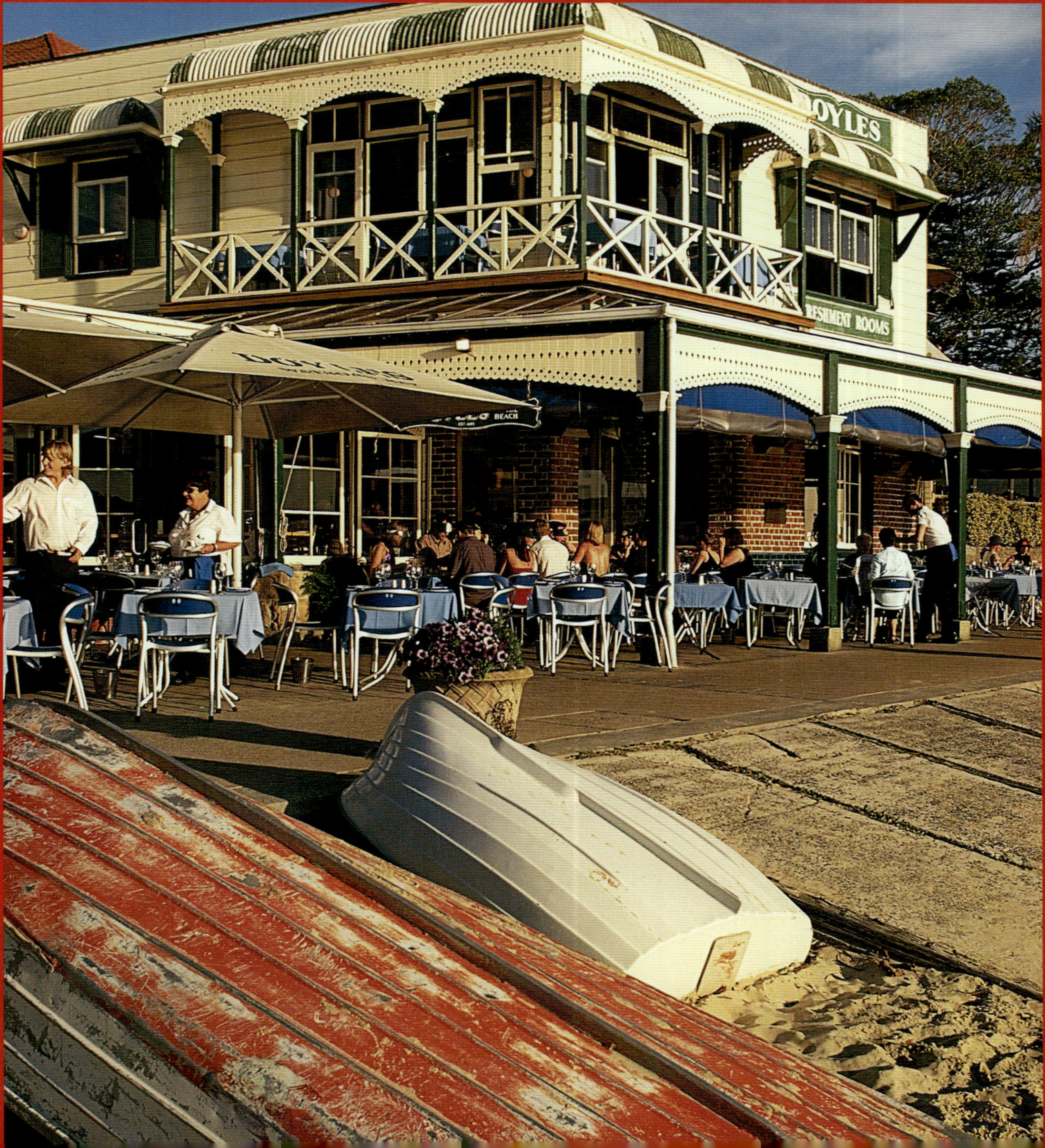

LIFE & PEOPLE

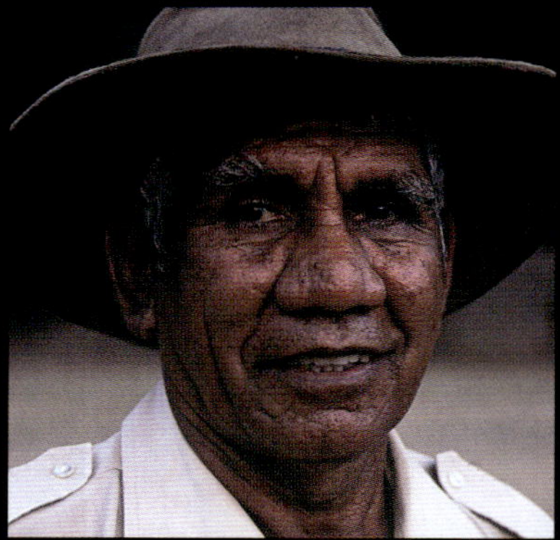

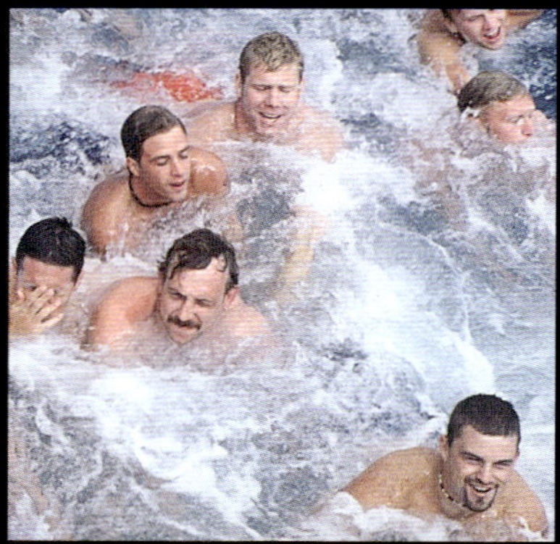

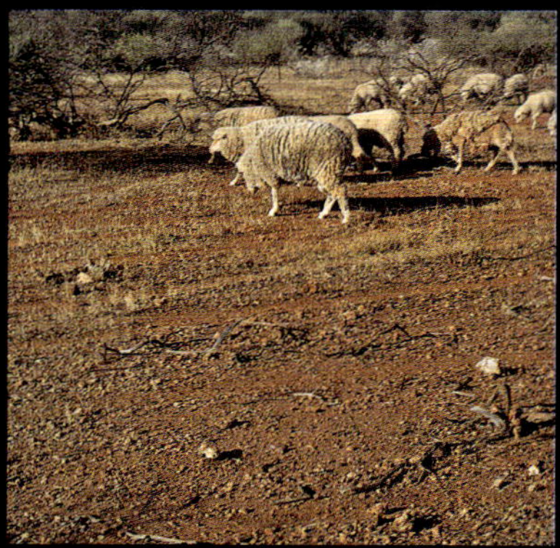

2

COLORS OF AUSTRALIA: LIFE & PEOPLE

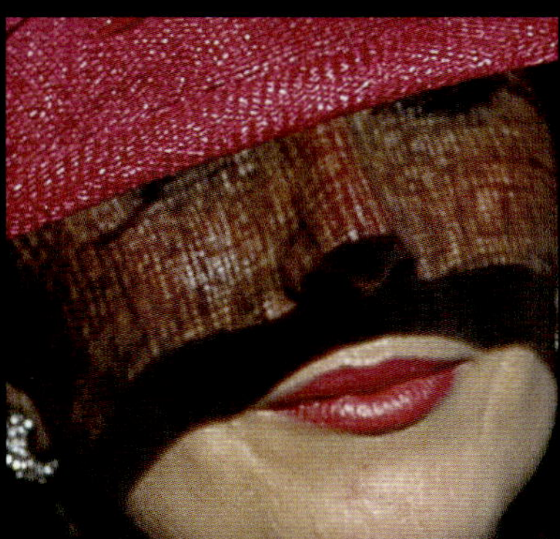

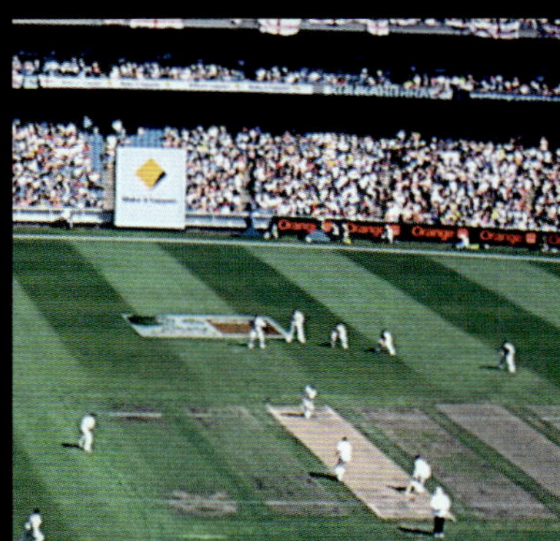

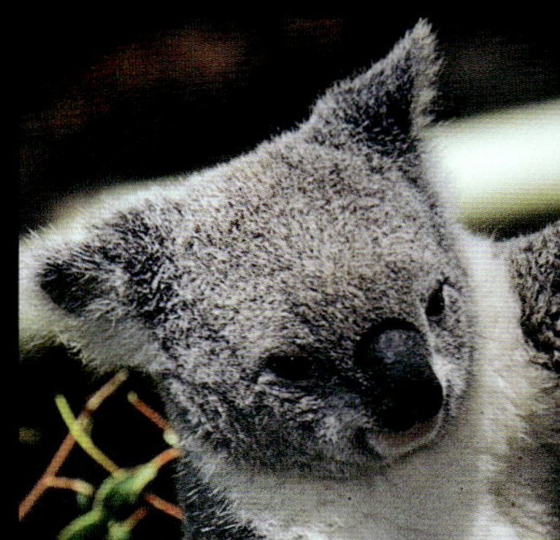

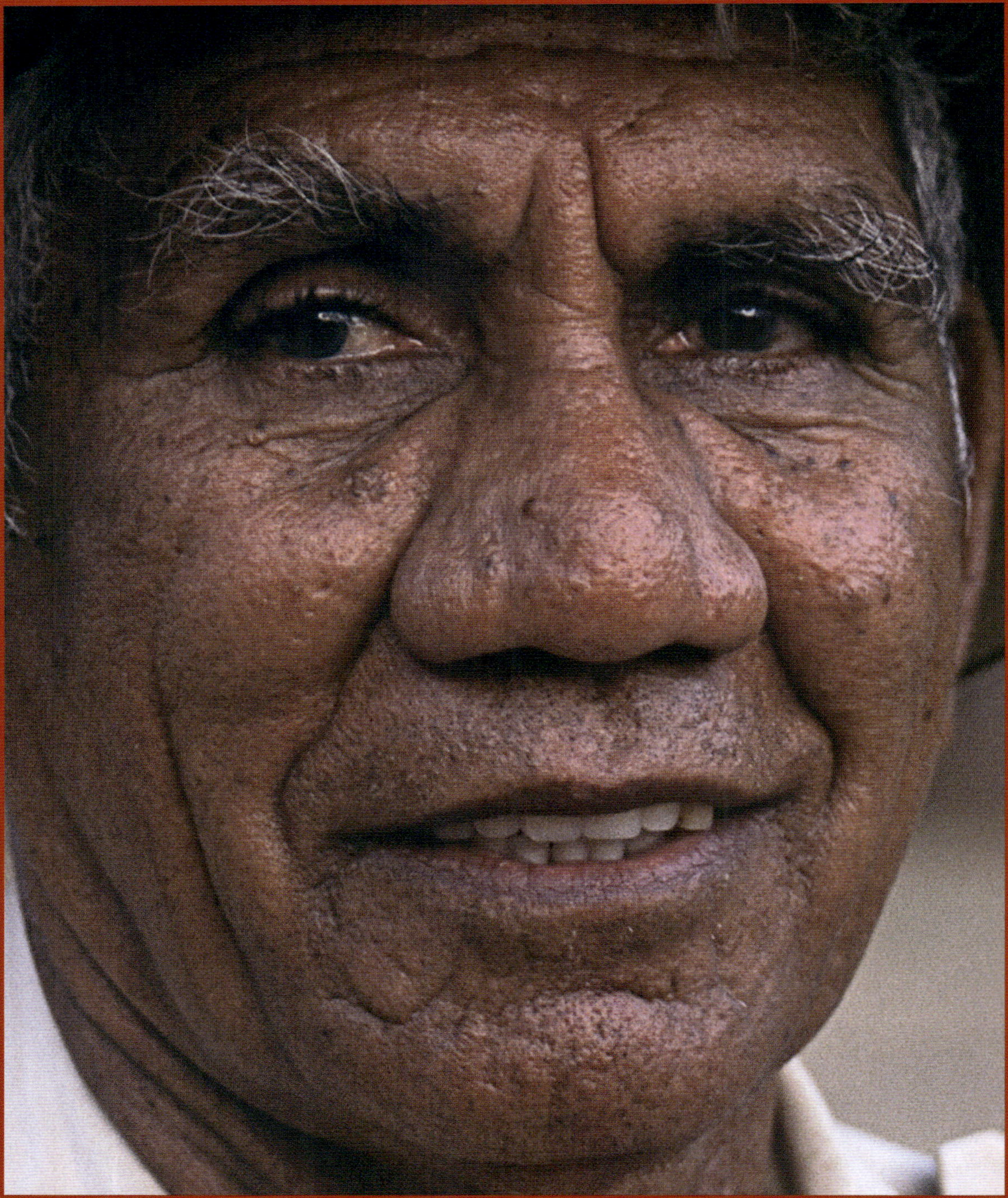

THE REAL THING

Today Aboriginal people constitute just 1.5 percent of the population but their traditional lifestyles have not declined. Traditions are very much alive and include skills such as pandanus leaf weaving (opposite right) in Manyallaluk, and face painting ready for a welcoming dance on the Tiwi Islands.

Frenzy, fun, and frivolity are key ingredients of a fast and energetic, often determined, lifestyle characterized by a love of sports, healthy competition, good food, good wine—and poking fun at officialdom. Happily, the dry and usually harmless Aussie sense of humor is never far from the surface of everyday life, and its people inordinately friendly and welcoming. Life in Australia is unquestionably for living.

There is a keenness and enthusiasm for everything that is at once both invigorating and almost tangible, be it politics, surfing, Australian Rules Football, music and opera, exploring the Outback, reveling in glorious sunsets, or simply relaxing on a beach. Yet, for a nation with so much energy, so much commitment, so much going on, it is paradoxical that the underlying rule of thumb is not to take anything too seriously. Life, it seems, is far too short for that.

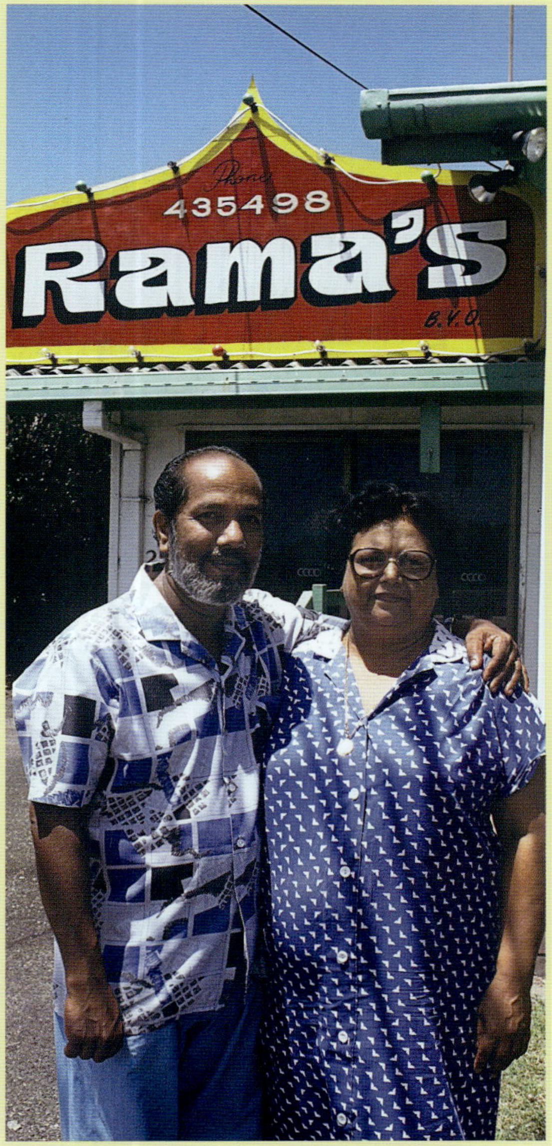

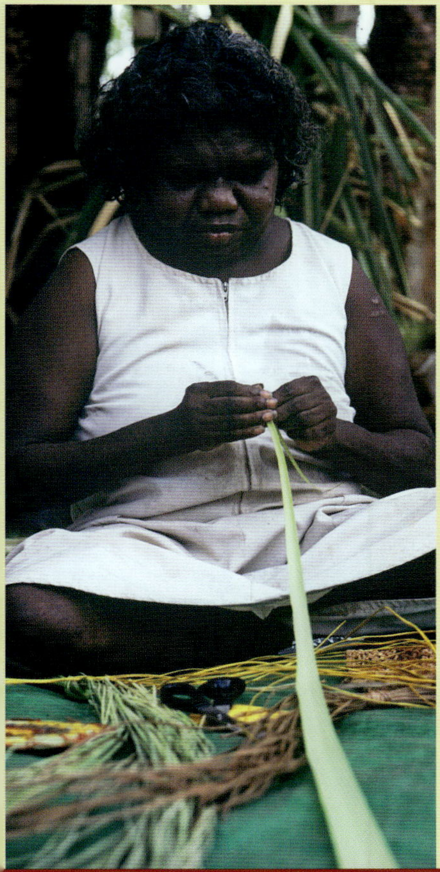

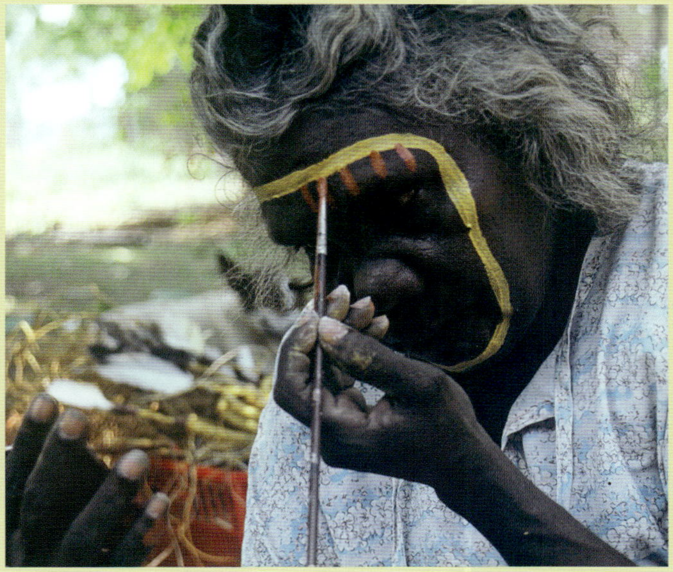

ENJOY LIFE

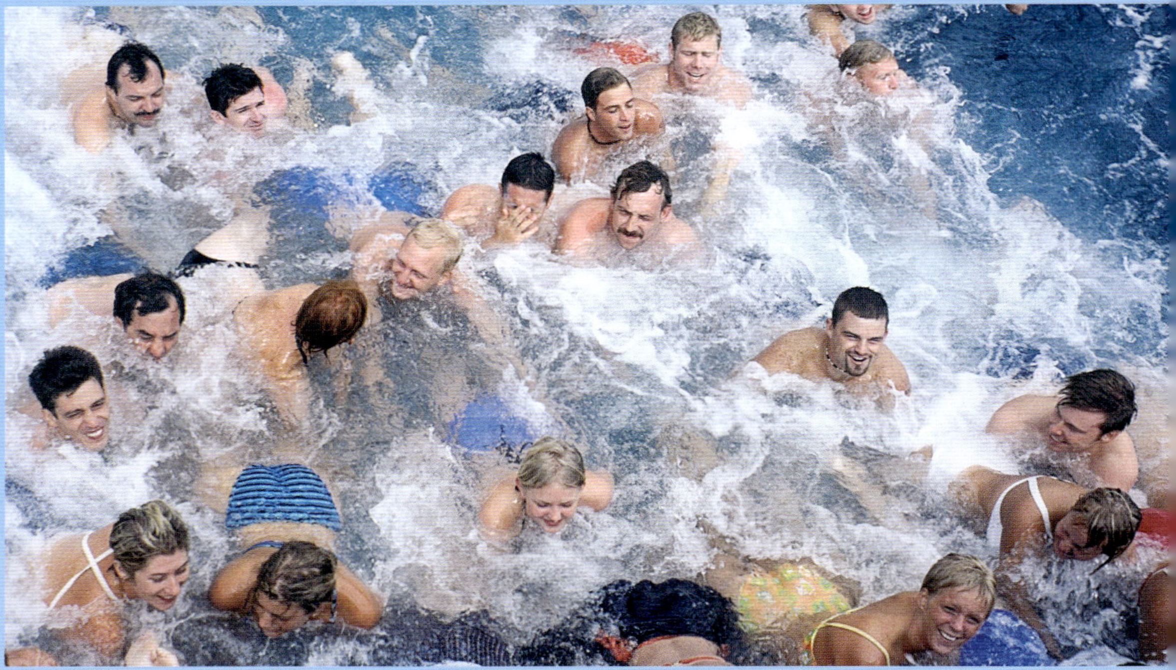

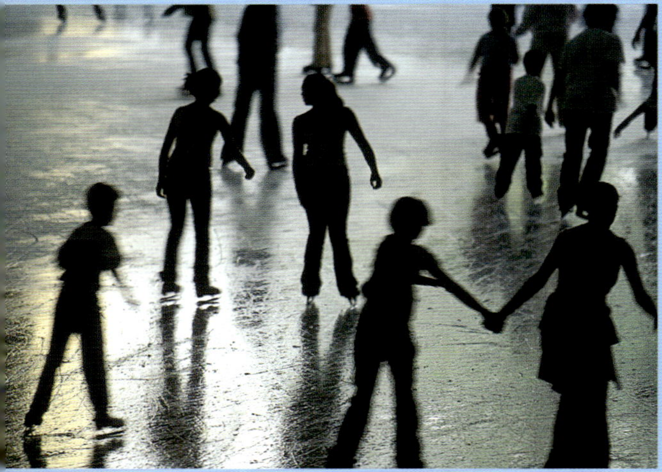

Having fun is high on everyone's agenda in this hedonistic but light-hearted society, whether simply ice-skating in the Macquarie Centre, Sydney, or boom netting (being towed alongside a boat on a big net) off the Whitsunday Islands, Queensland.

Right: Singing their hearts out—the Australian Girls' Choir perform at the Darling Harbour Carnivale, Sydney.
Next page: Celebrating Chinese New Year in Melbourne's Chinatown.

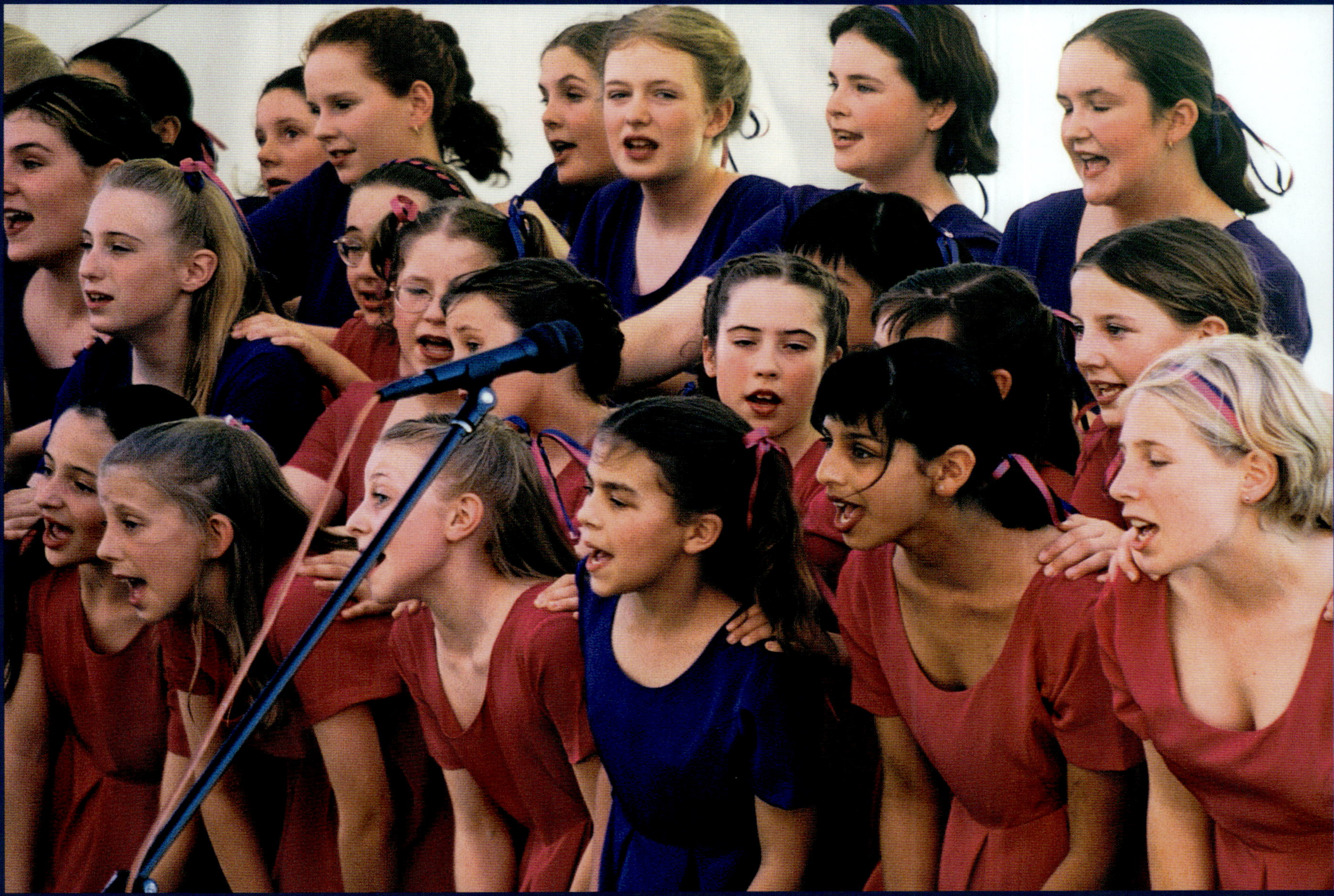

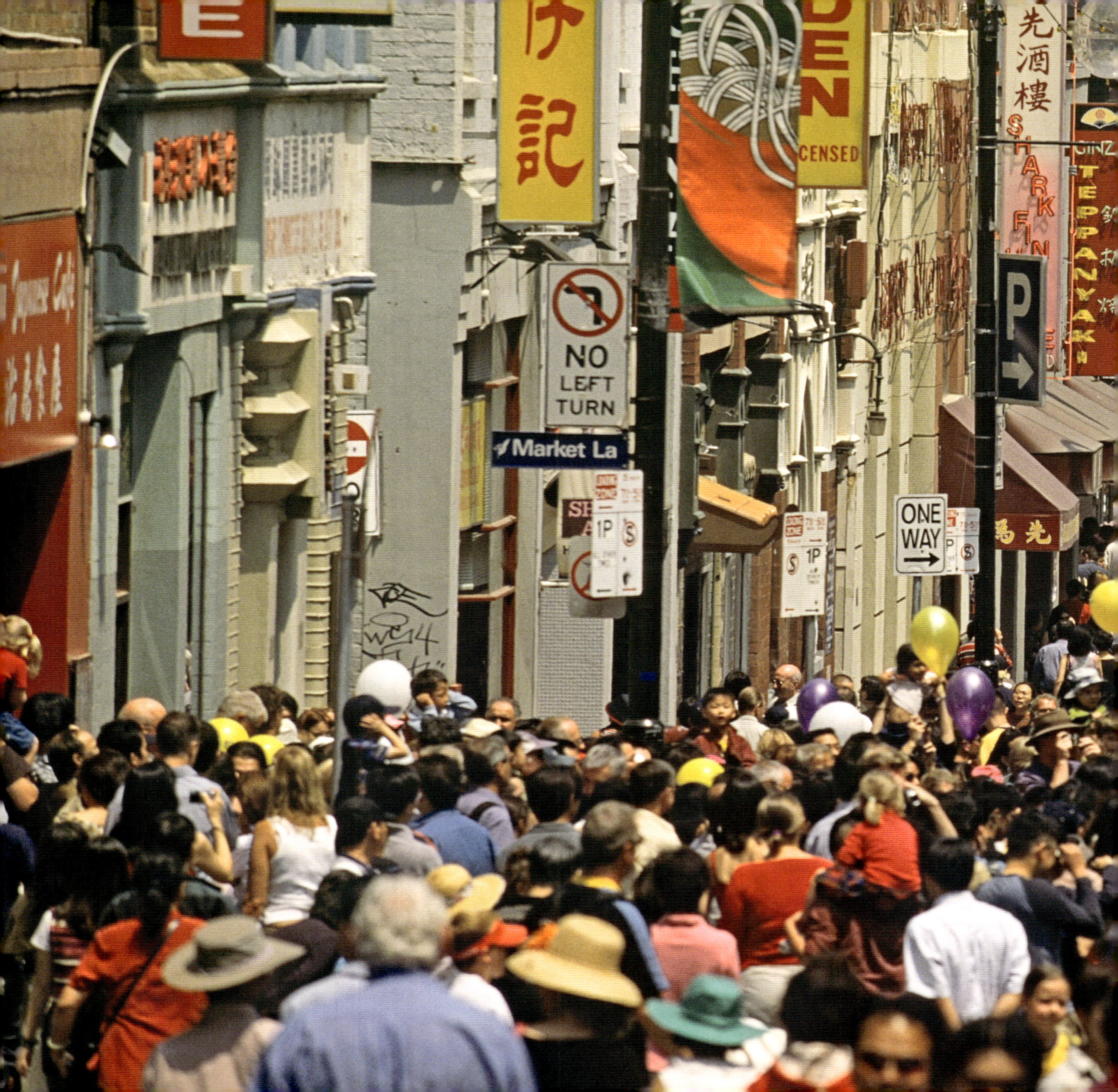

記
DEN
CENSED
先酒樓
SHARK FIN
TEPPANYAKI
P
NO LEFT TURN
Market La
ONE WAY
1P

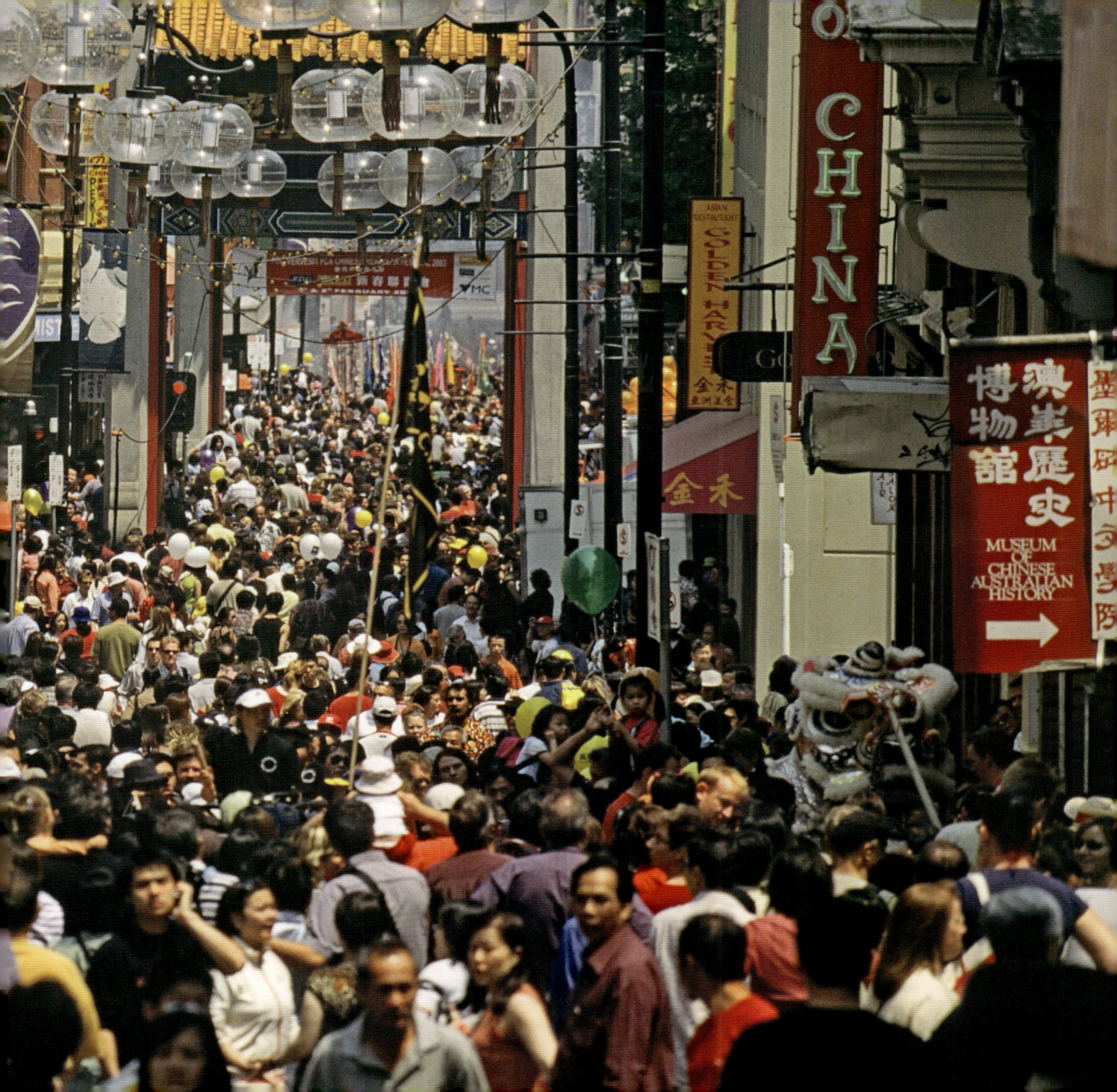
CHINA
澳華歷史博物館
MUSEUM OF CHINESE AUSTRALIAN HISTORY
金禾

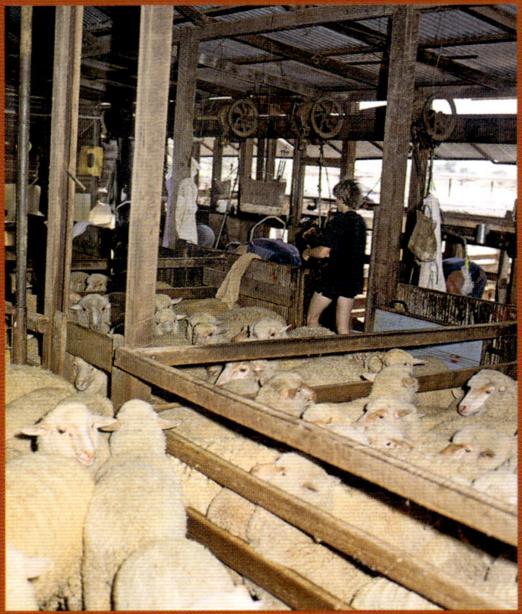

OUTBACK LIFE

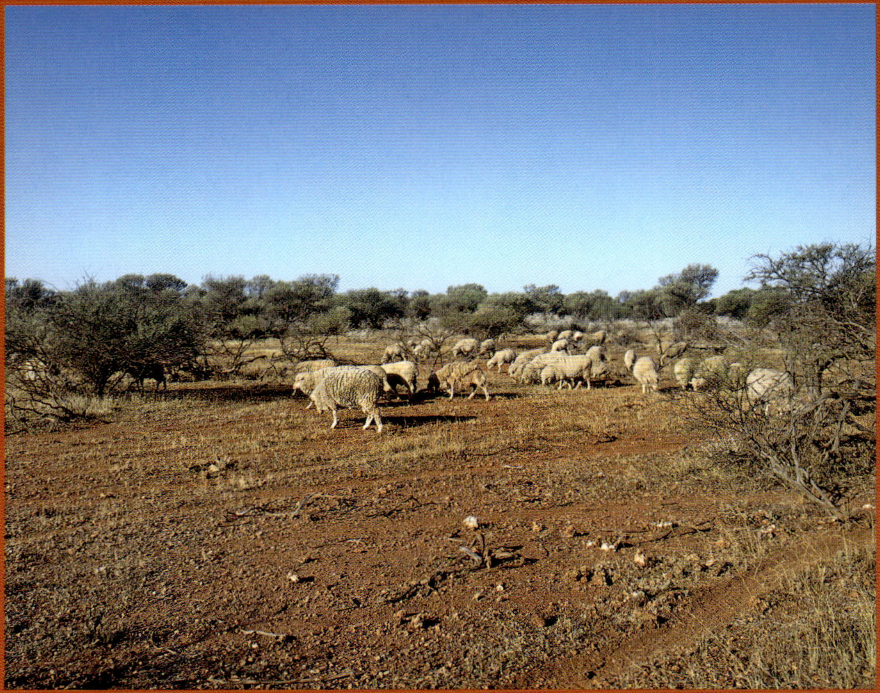

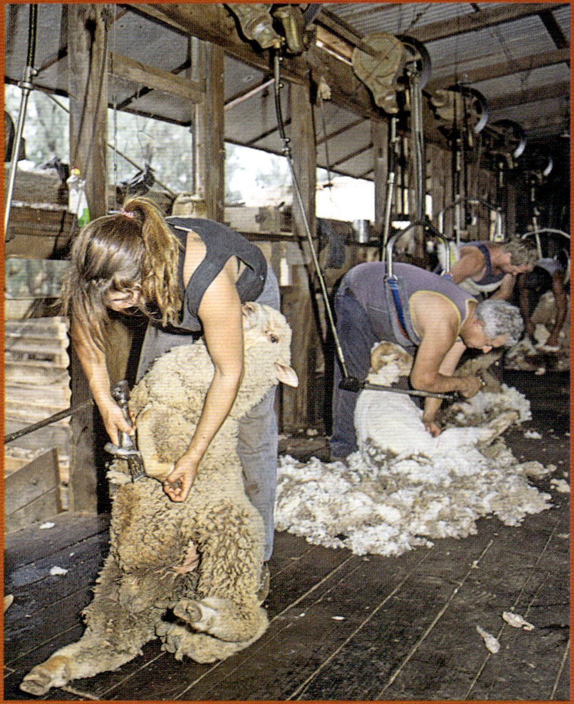

It takes a special kind of person to live in the Outback. Sheep and cattle are the reasons for being here, though the backbreaking job of sheep shearing is not exclusively a male preserve. It's lonely, quiet, and miles from anywhere: self reliance and mutual dependence are essential.

Pubs are the focus of Outback life after a hard day's work, like the William Creek Pub (opposite), on the Oodnadatta Track. The track began as an Aboriginal trade route, but was later used by the Overland Telegraph Line and the railway to Alice Springs. These pubs are, well, rather idiosyncratic.

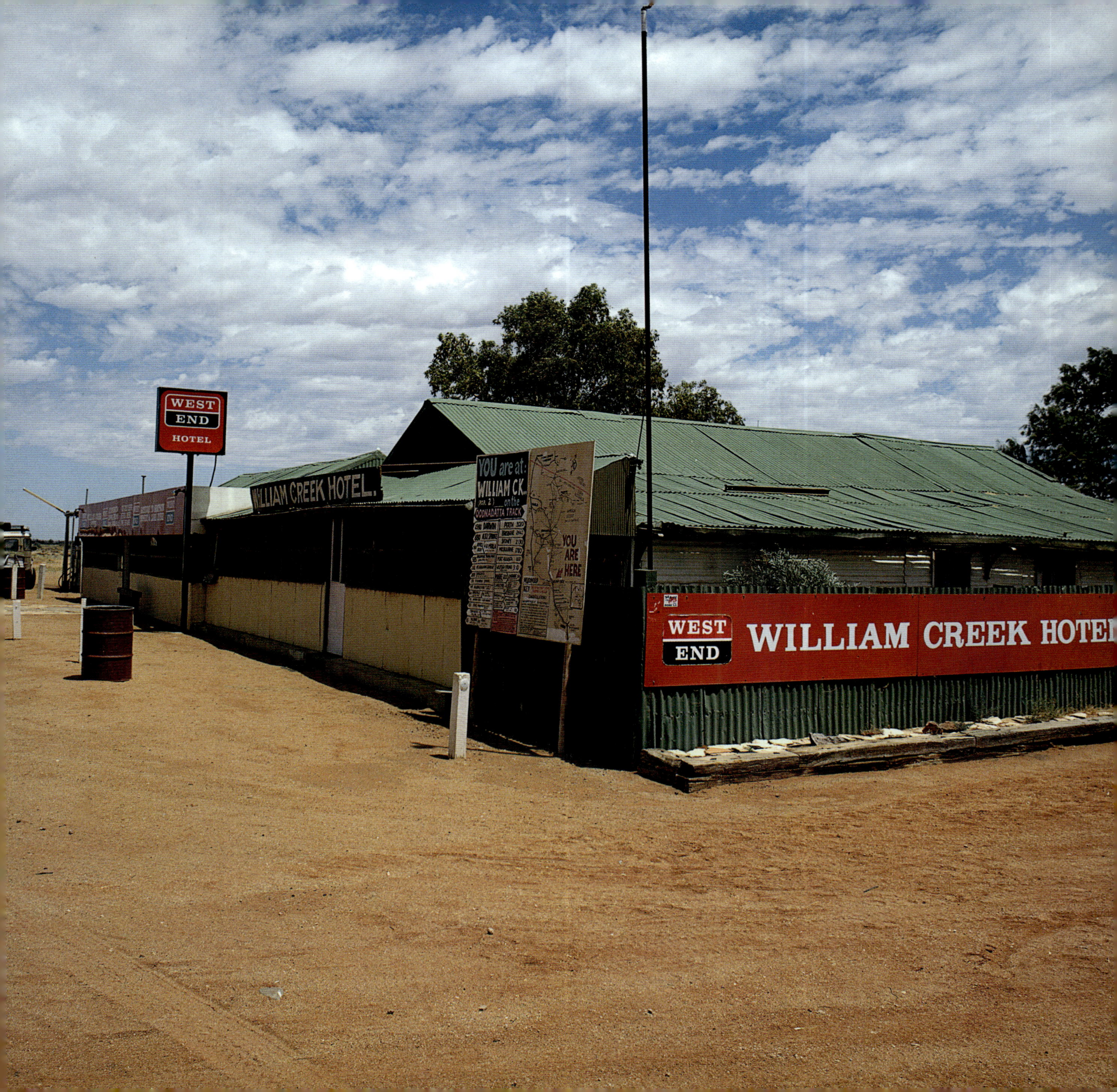
WEST END HOTEL
WILLIAM CREEK HOTEL.
YOU are at: WILLIAM CK.
OODNADATTA TRACK
YOU ARE HERE
WEST END
WILLIAM CREEK HOTE

SEX IN THE CITY

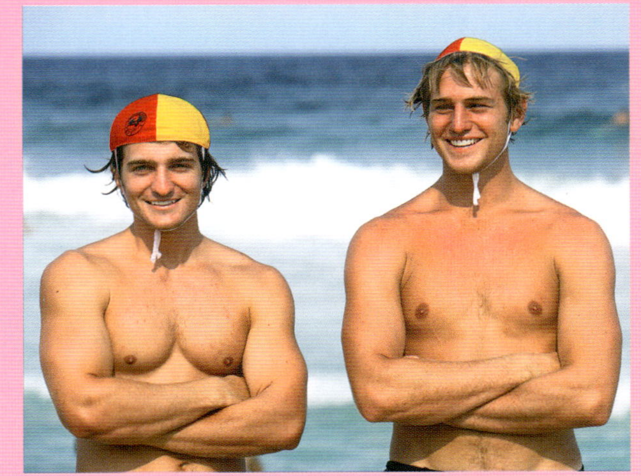

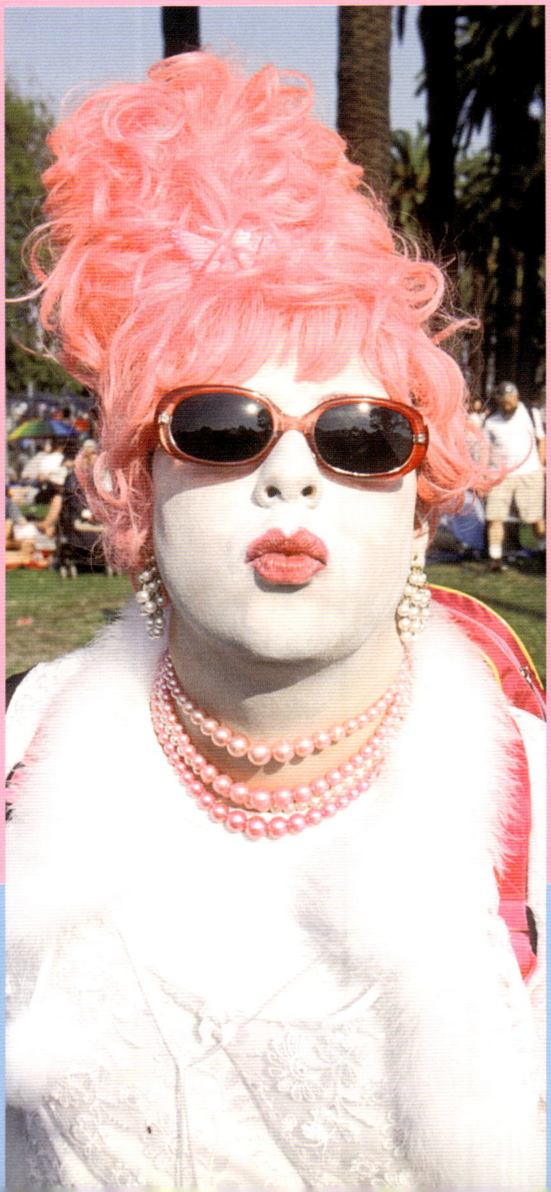

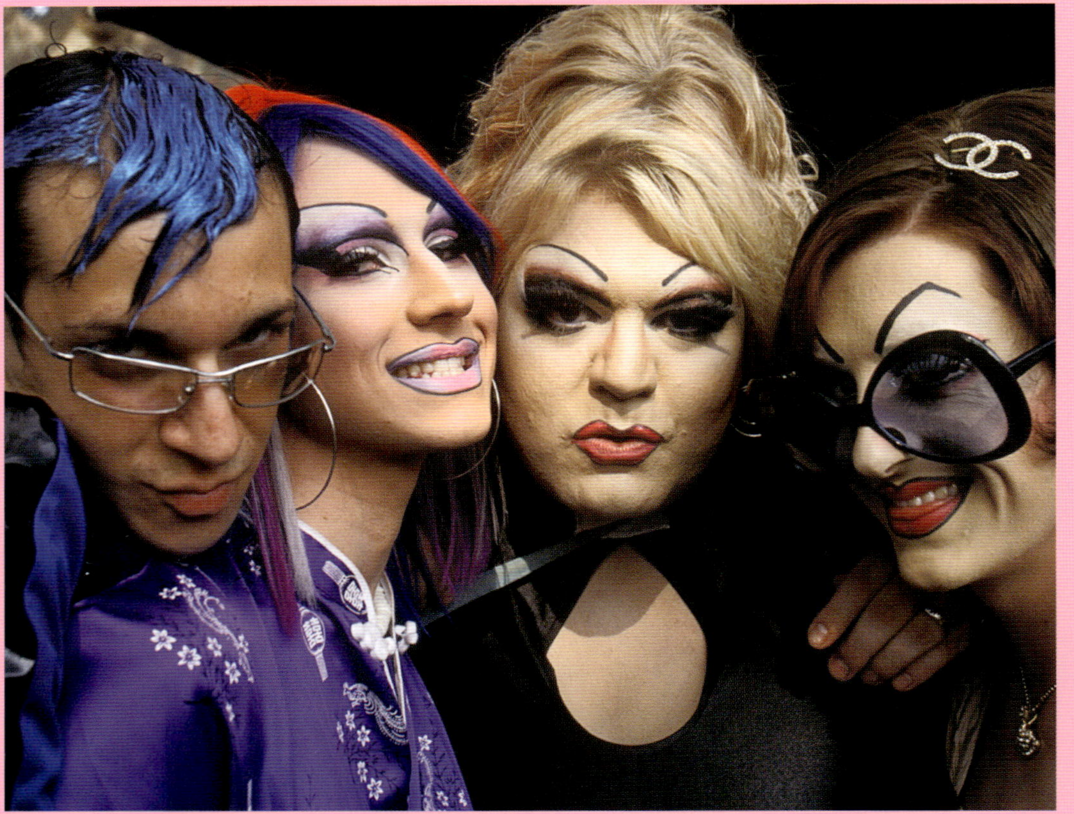

From a lively gay scene, with regular festivals where anything can happen and usually does, to the simple attractions of beautiful women and bronzed lifeguards, Australia takes it all in its stride. It's about looking good and feeling good.

Major gay festivals, such as Mardi Gras, and dance parties like the Sleaze Ball, Pride, and Mid-Summa, tend to be concentrated in Sydney and Melbourne. But the smaller cities and even some country centers have well-established gay scenes too.

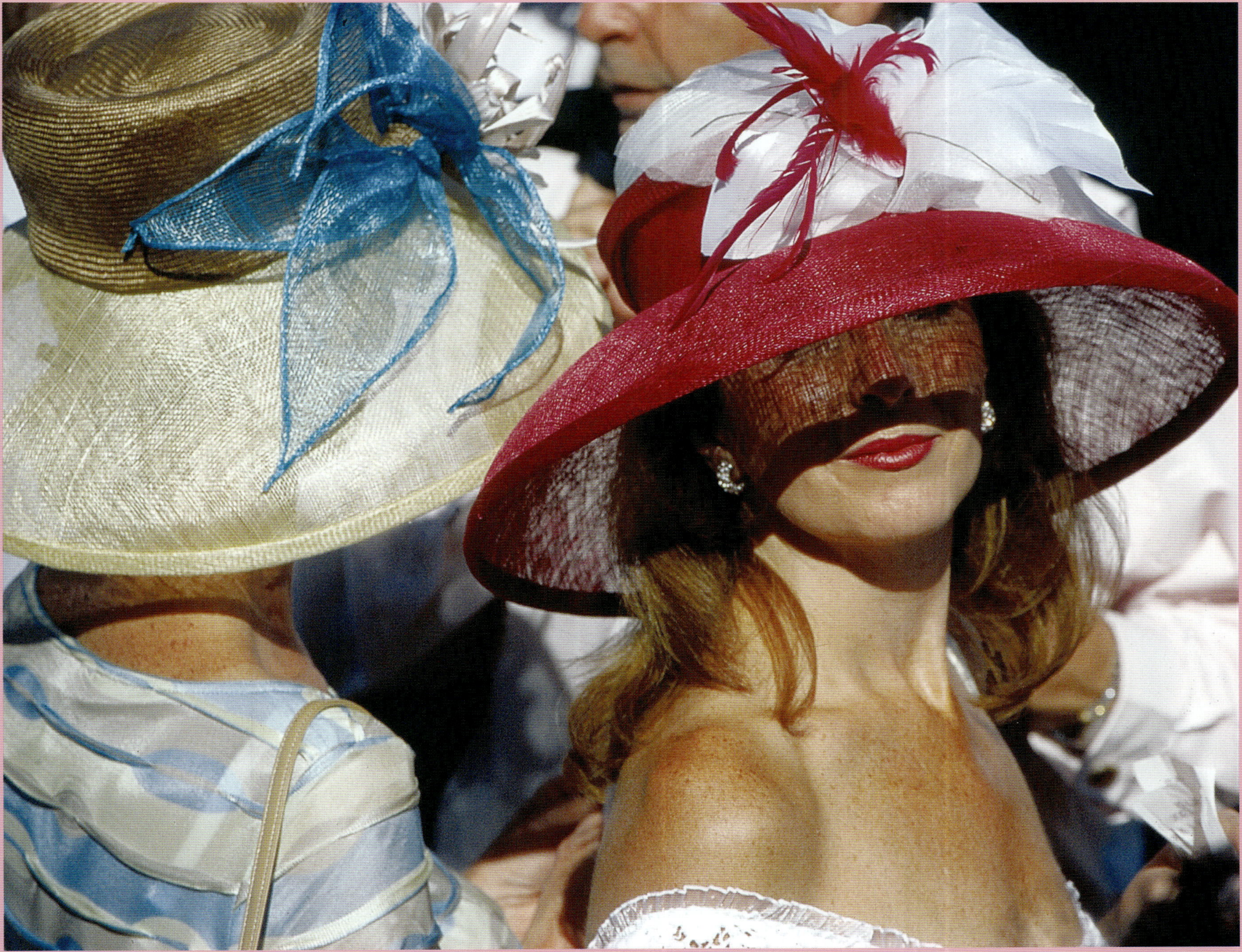

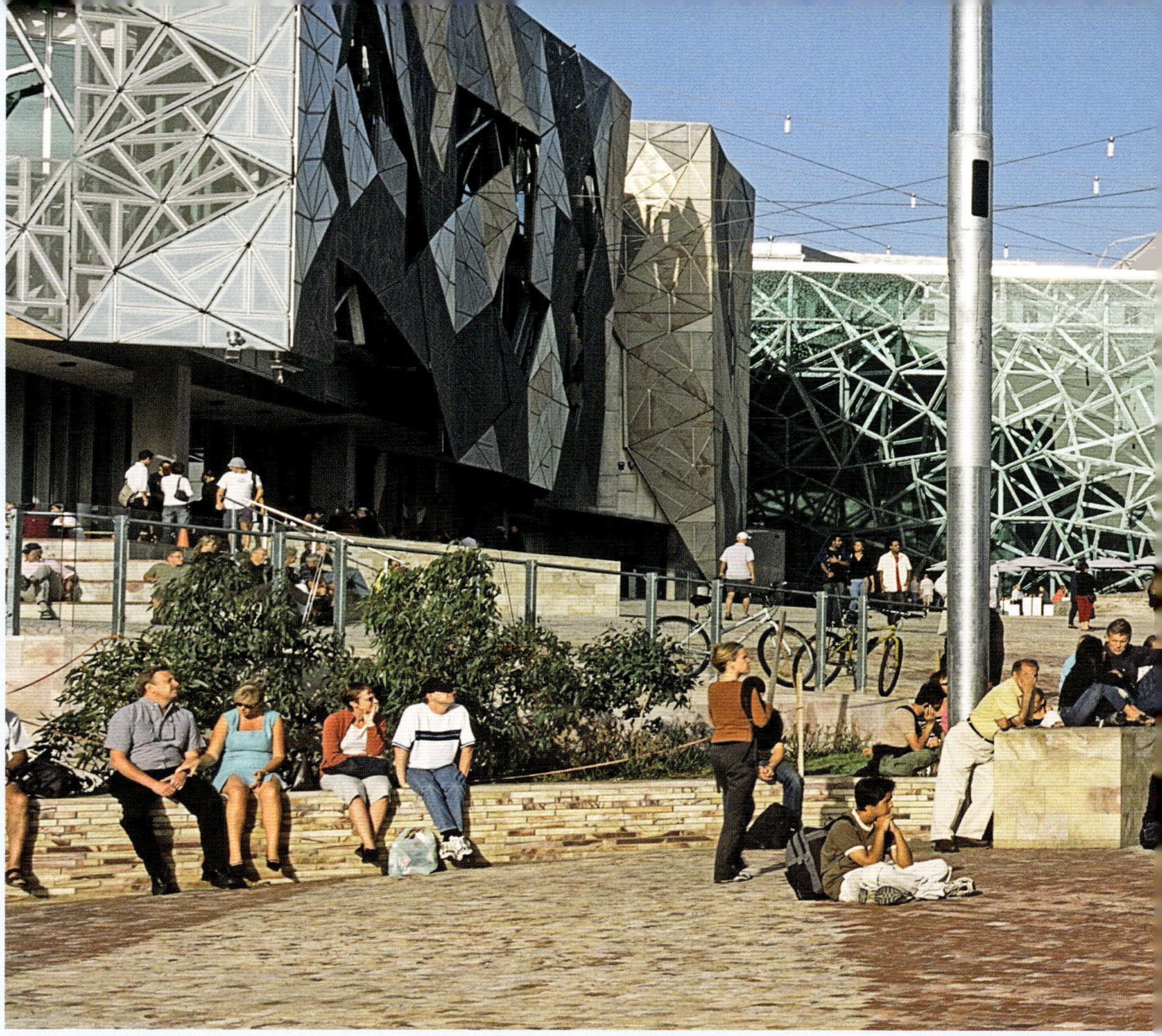

URBAN CHIC

The size of a city block, Federation Square, Melbourne, at the very center of the city, is a living, breathing focus for the city's community life, bringing together a creative mix of galleries, cinemas, restaurants, cafés, bars, festivals, events, and public open spaces.

You seldom need to look far to find something happening, whether a blues and jazz festival, street theater, art exhibitions, dance, or simply university students having a good time.

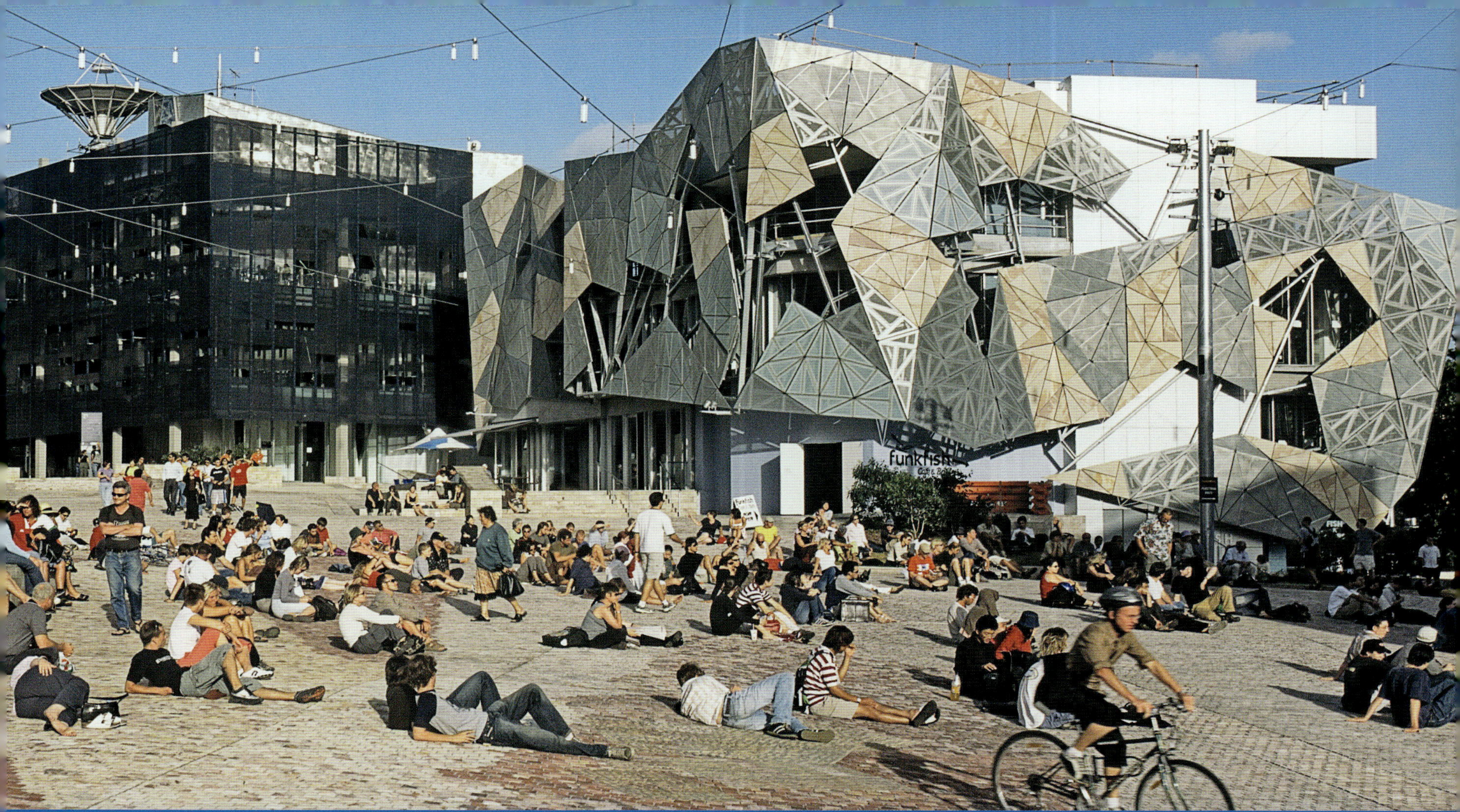

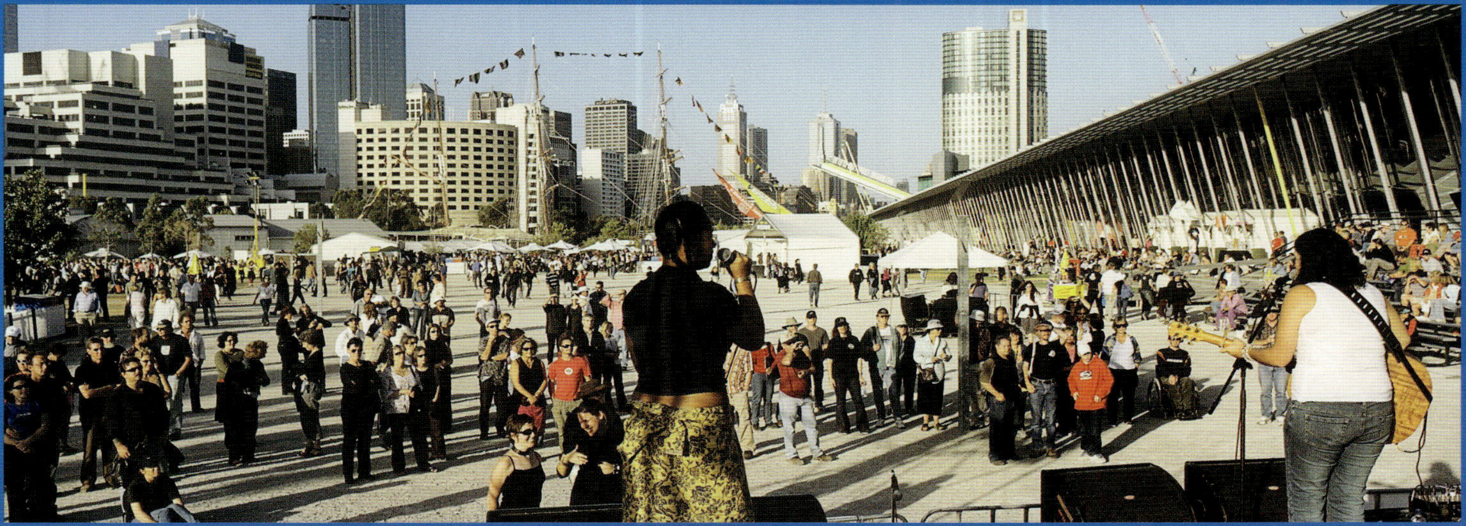

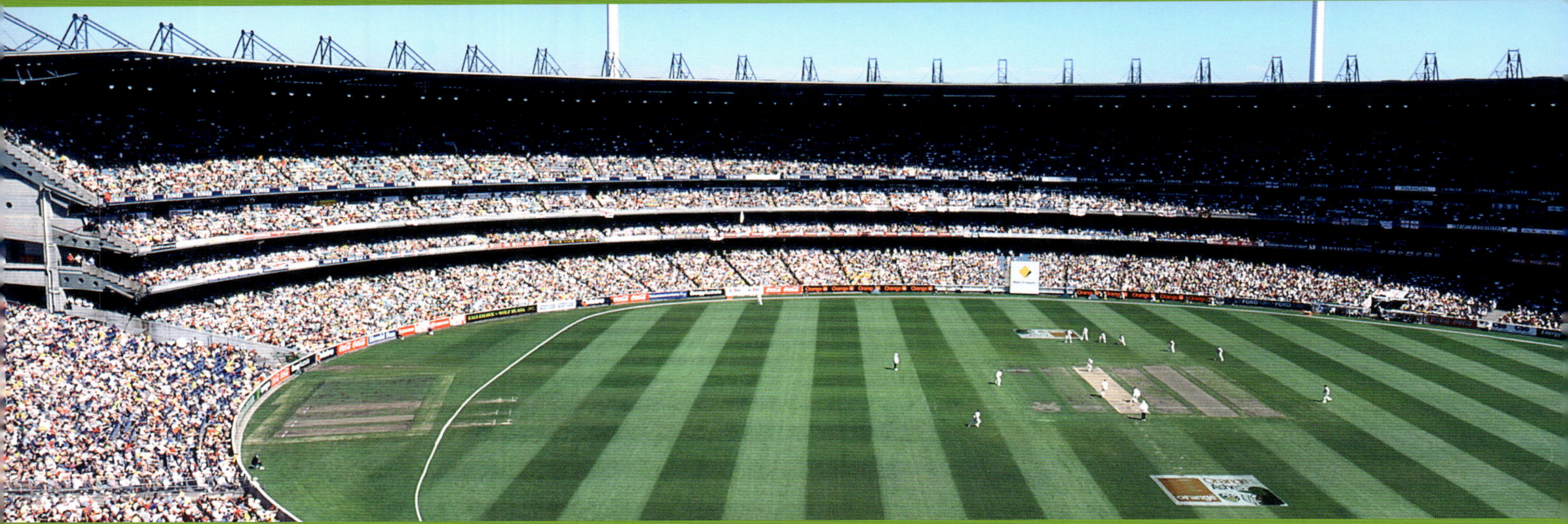

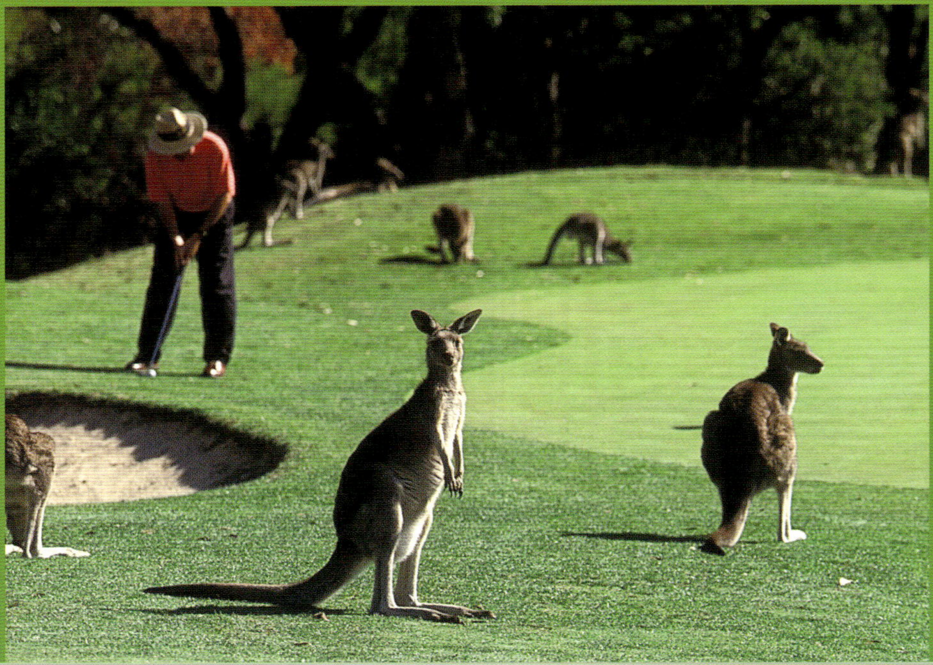

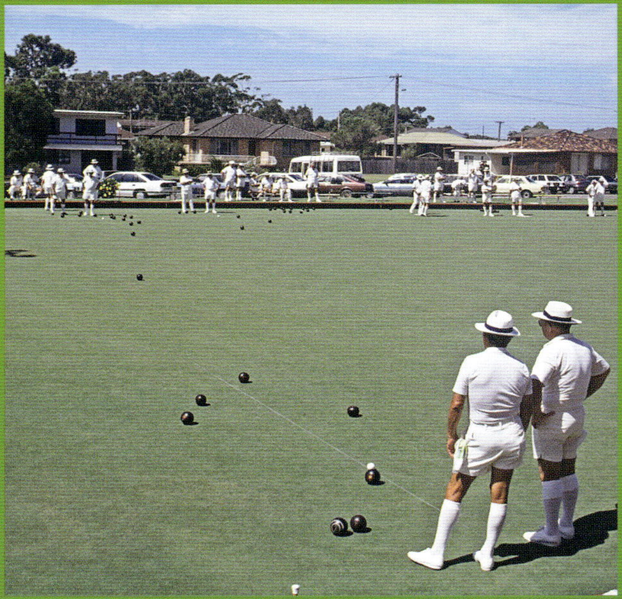

Leisure and sport are crucial to the Aussie way of life. The competitive urge of modern Australians is best illustrated in their approach to sport. Winning is vital, yet on the odd occasion Australia loses, they are first to acknowledge the better team.

Sport is as much for watching as taking part, whether it is cricket, tennis, golf, bowls, racing, soccer, or the curious hybrid of Australian Rules Football, about which Aussies are passionate, and visitors mystified.

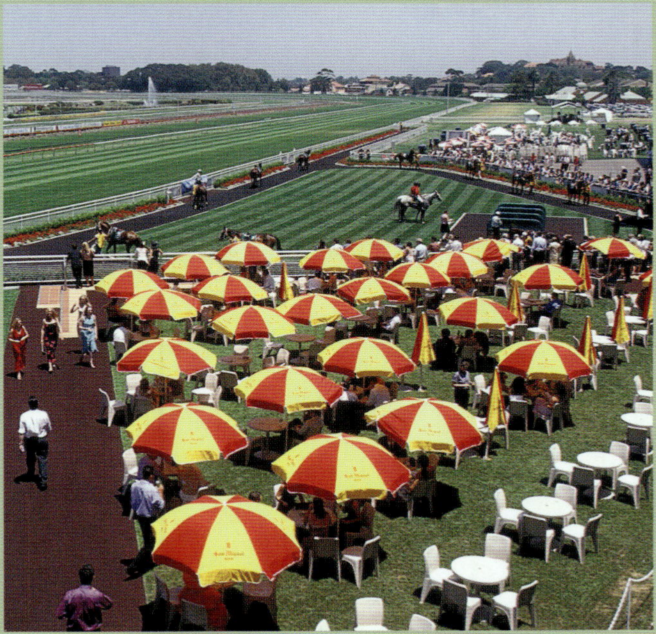

THIS SPORTING LIFE

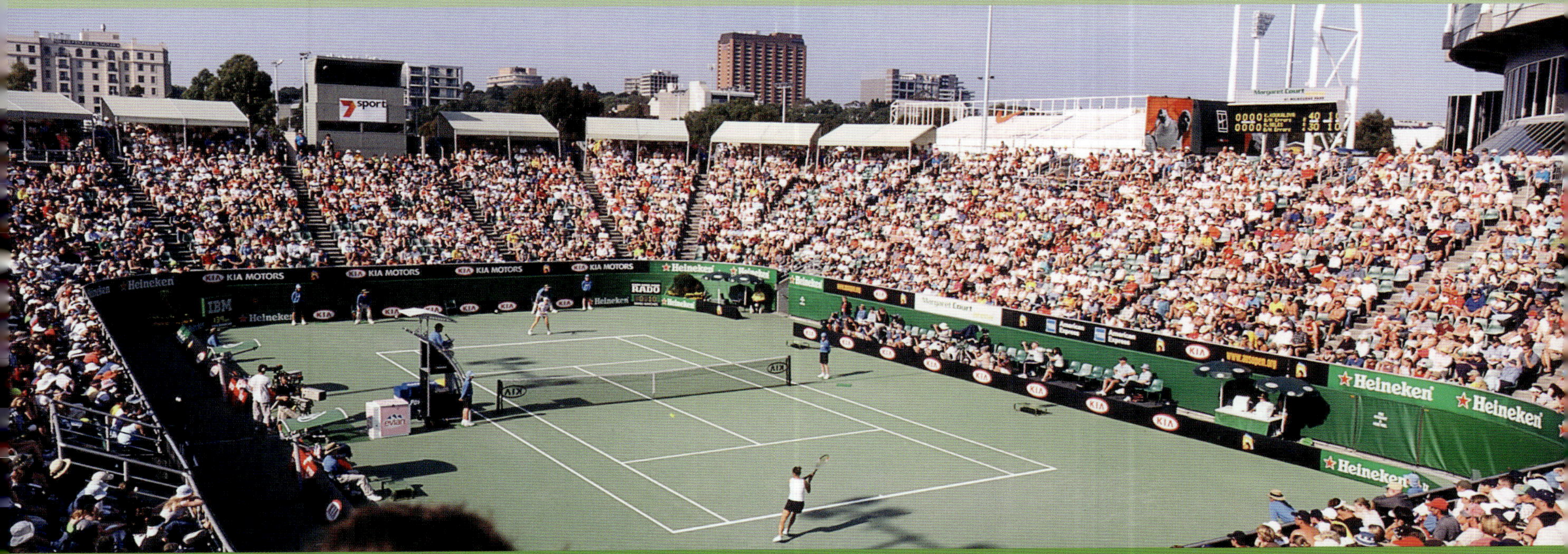

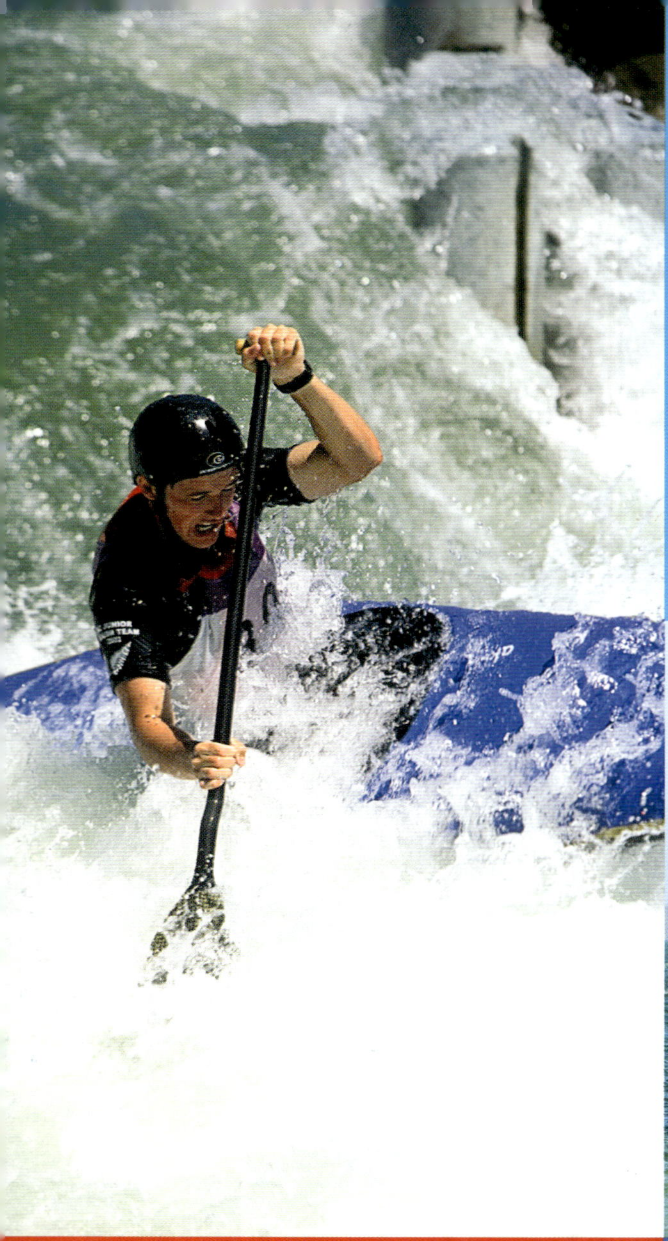

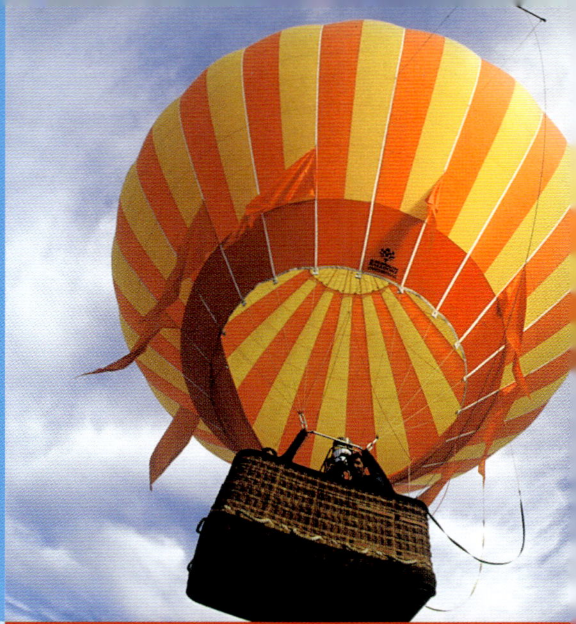

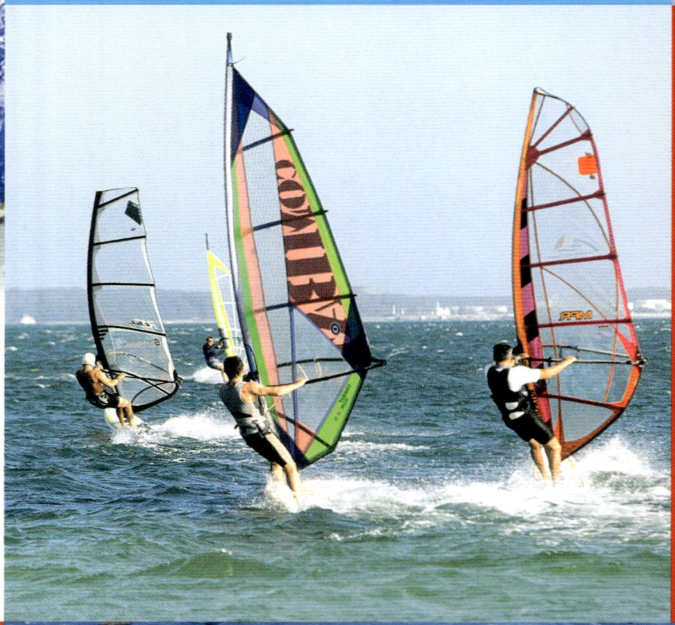

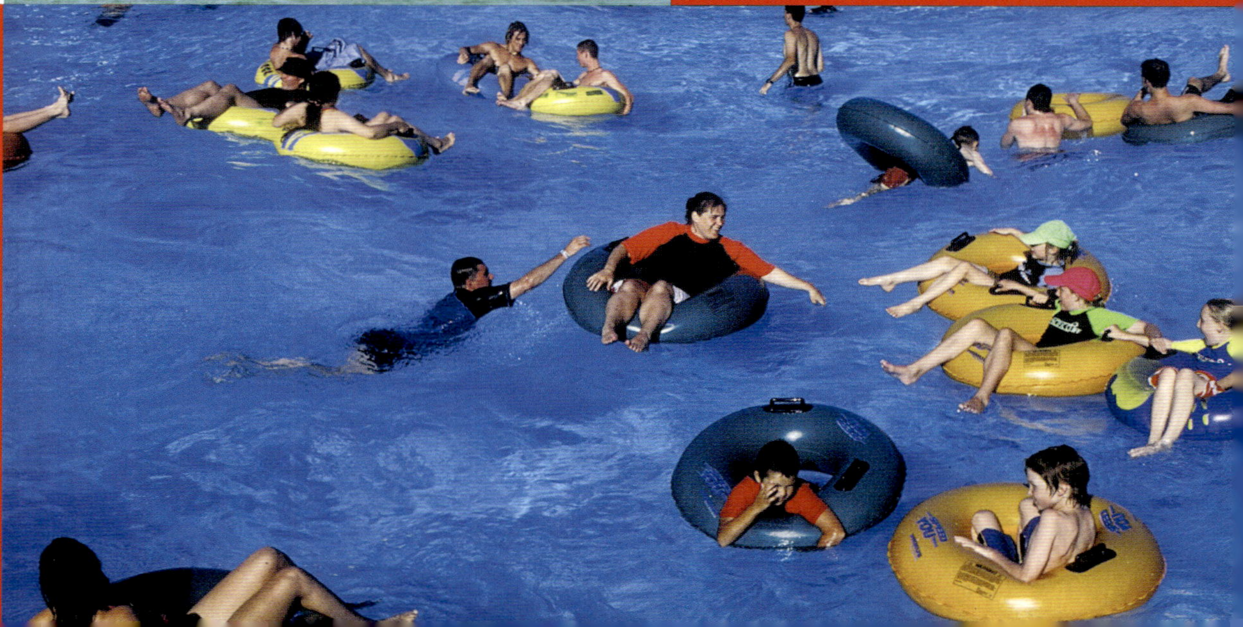

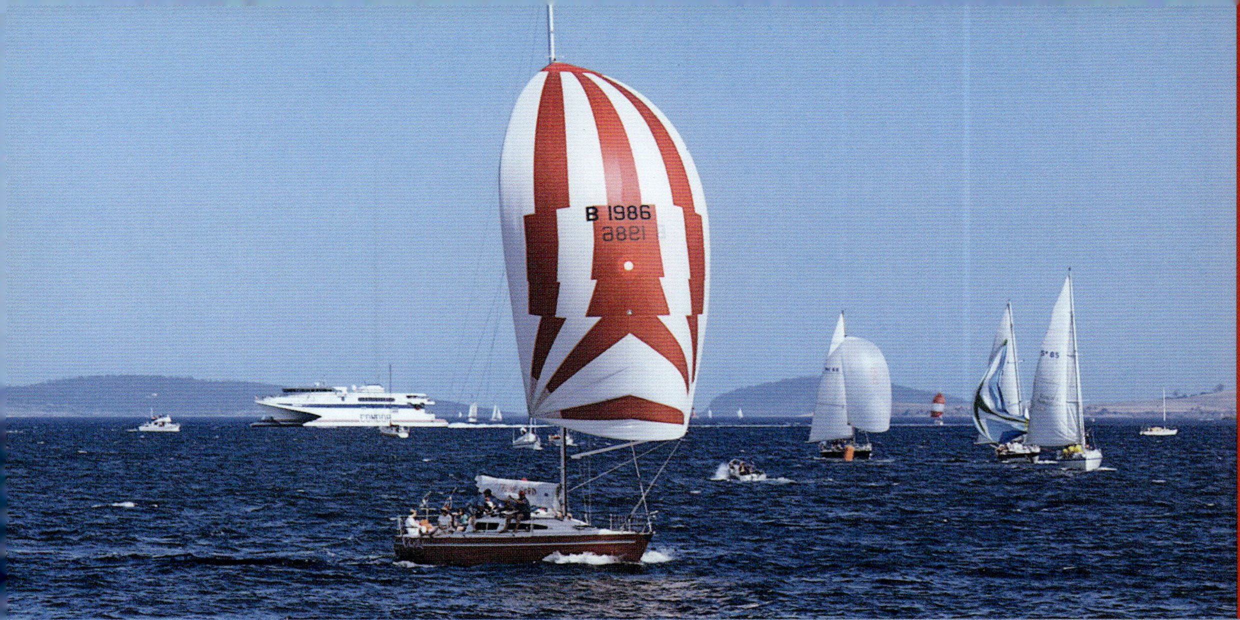
B 1986
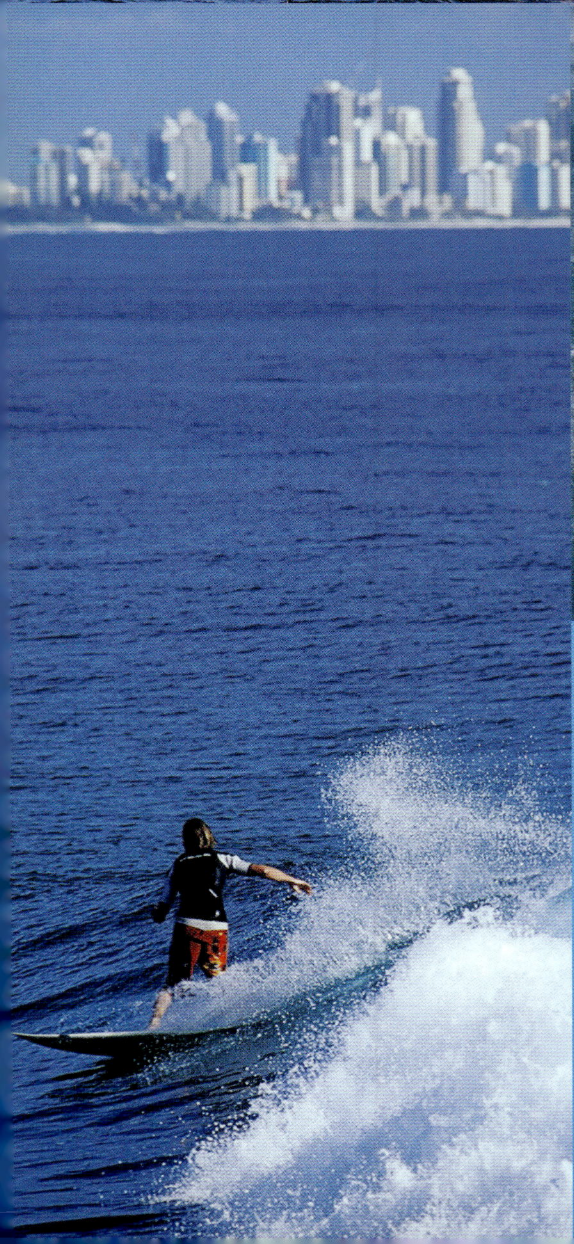
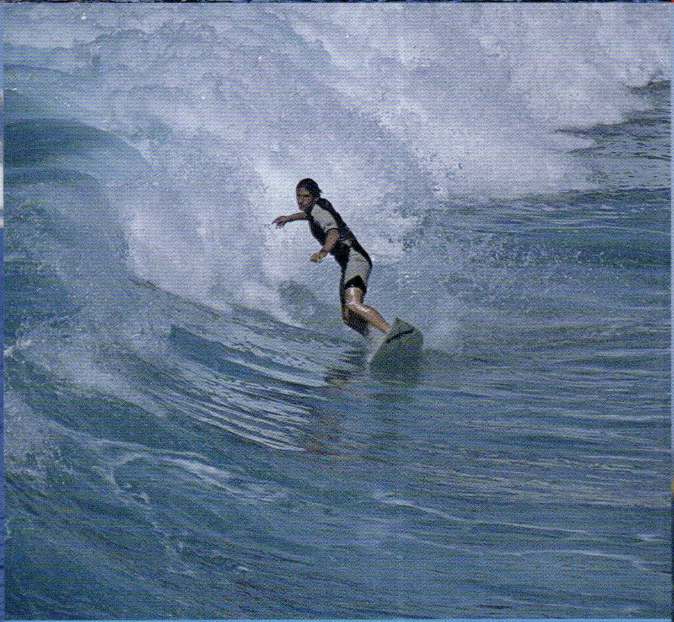
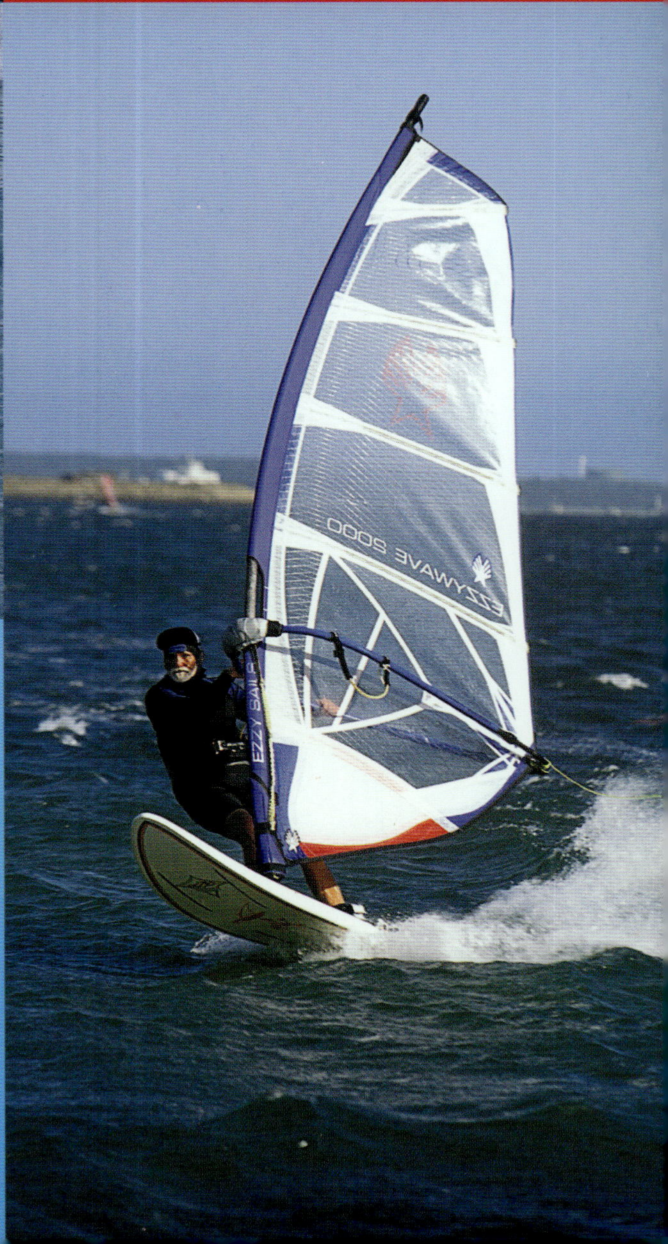

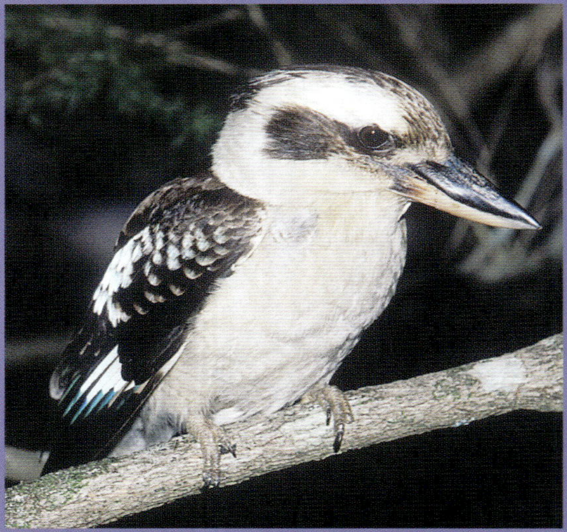

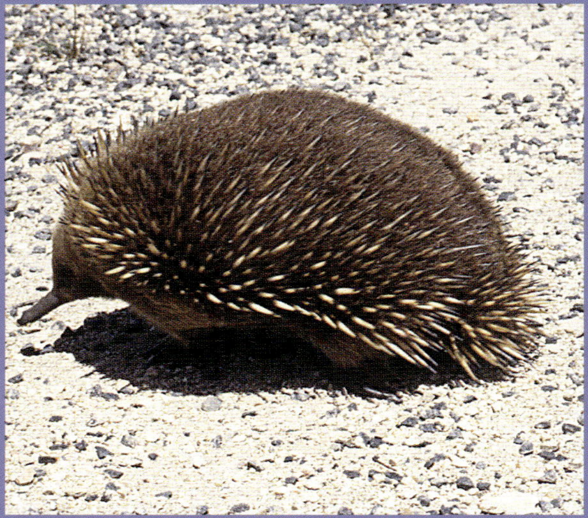

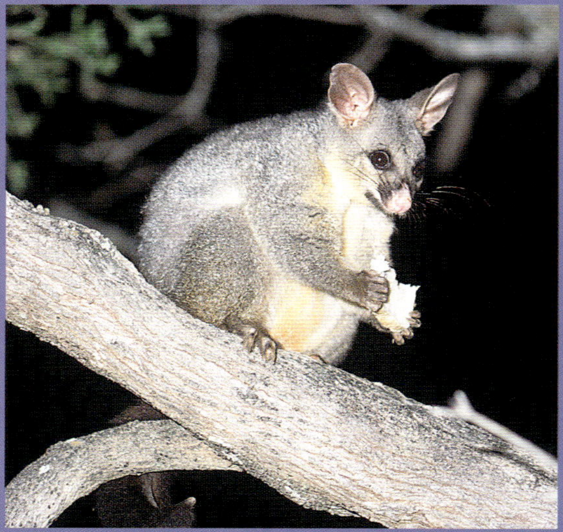

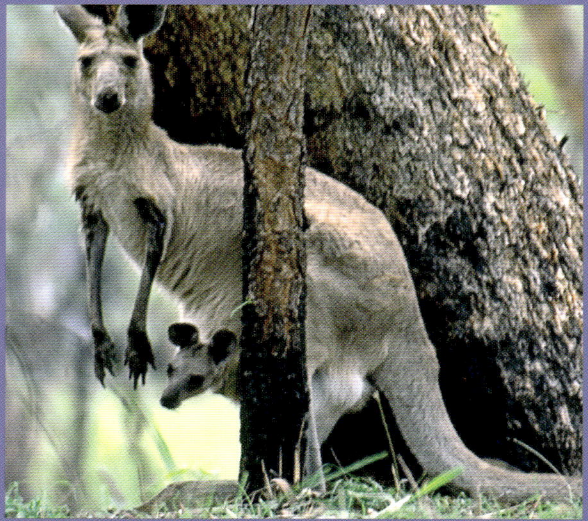

Few countries can boast such a weird and distinctive native fauna as Australia. Isolation from other land masses over millions of years has produced species that are wonderful, sometimes seriously odd, and often highly dangerous. Kookaburras (top left), possums (above left), koalas, and kangaroos are some of the amazing species that make up wildlife in Australia. Some mammals, like the echidna (top right) and the platypus are so extraordinary they have their own unique scientific classification—the monotremes.

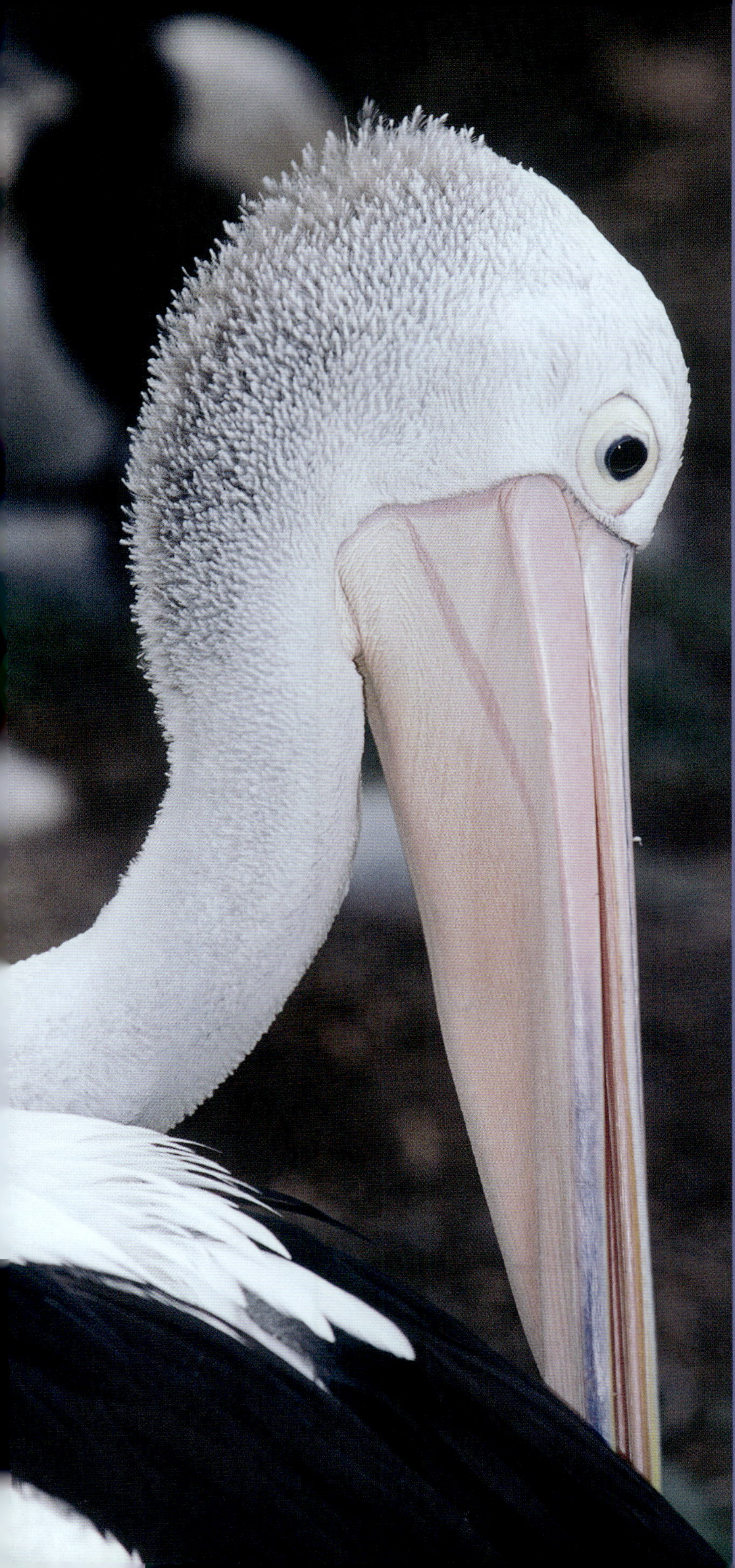

FUR & FEATHERS

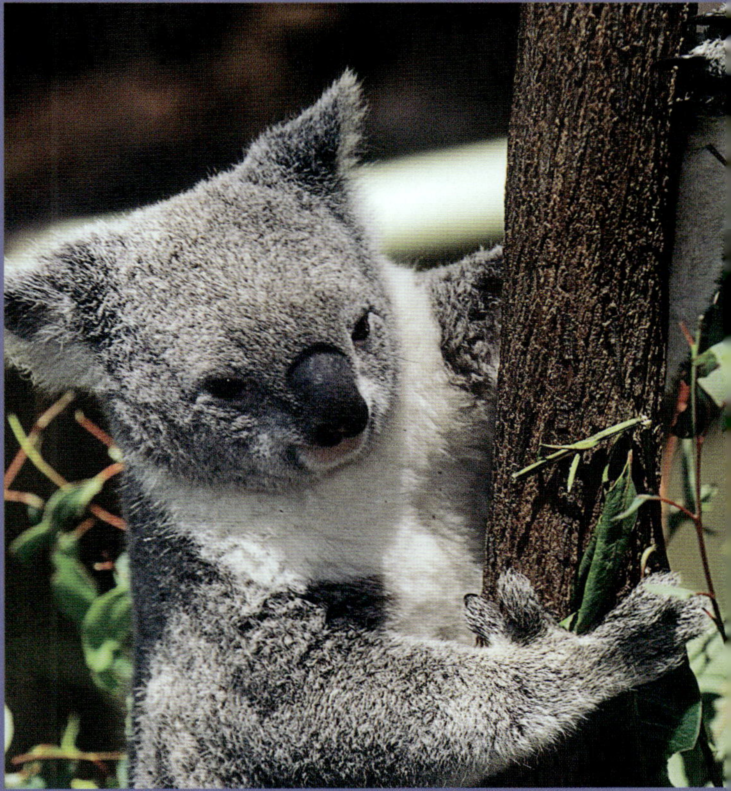

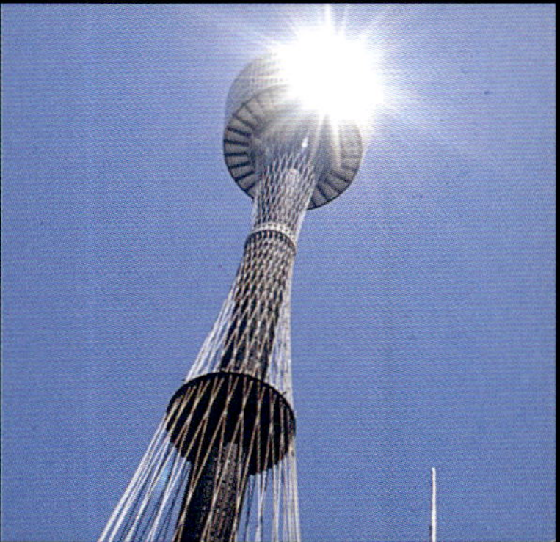

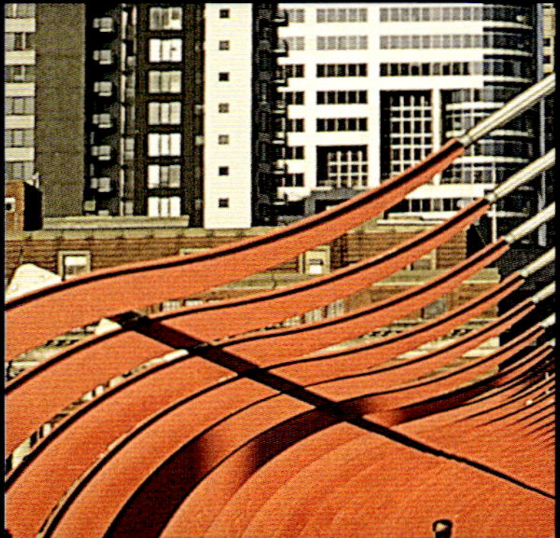

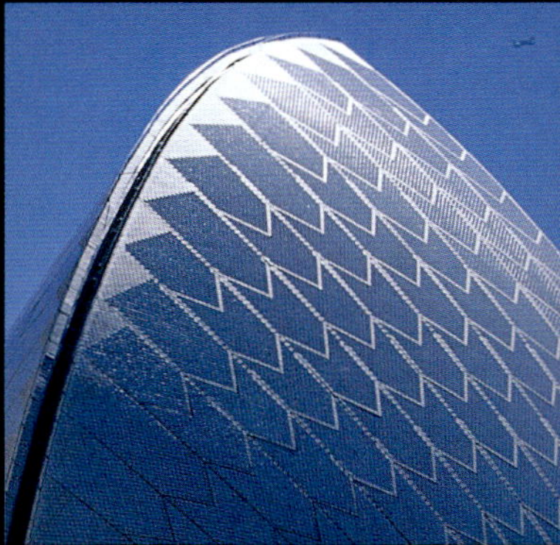

CTURE 3

COLORS OF AUSTRALIA: ARCHITECTURE

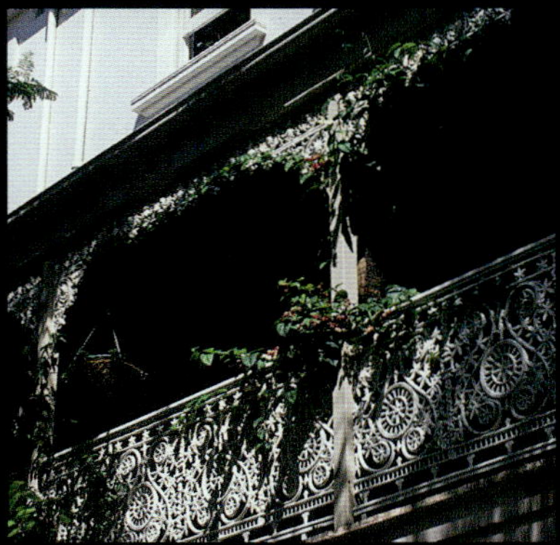

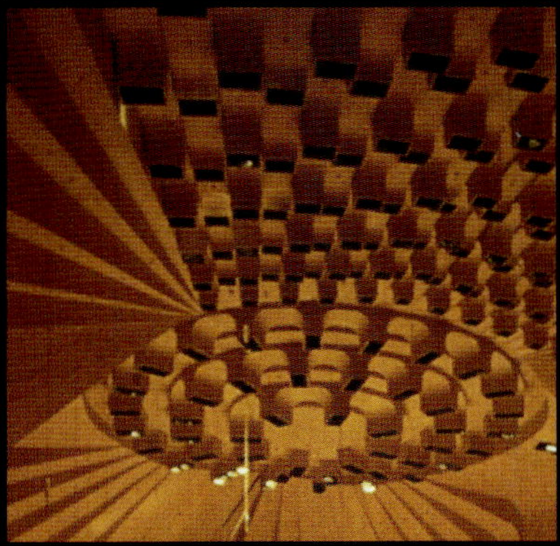

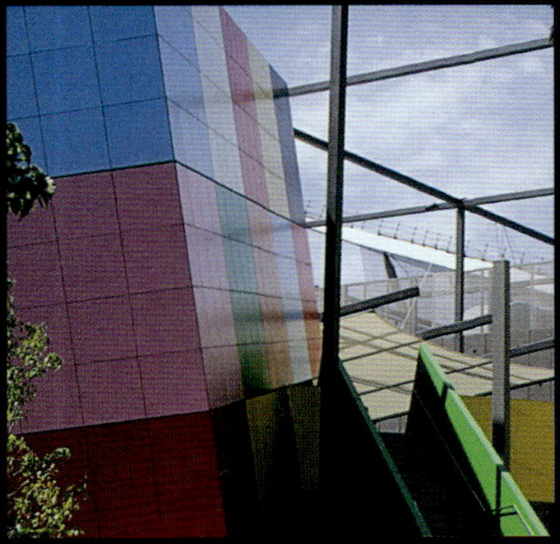

REACH FOR THE SKY

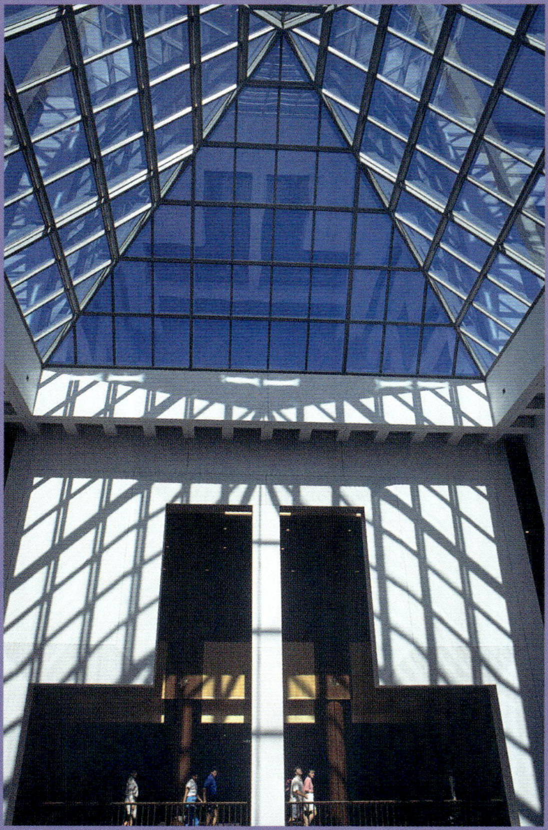

Australia's modern architecture is as breathtaking as it is inspiring. The vaulted glass roof and galleries around which visitors may walk within New Parliament House, Canberra (above), illustrate an openness that is welcoming and refreshing.

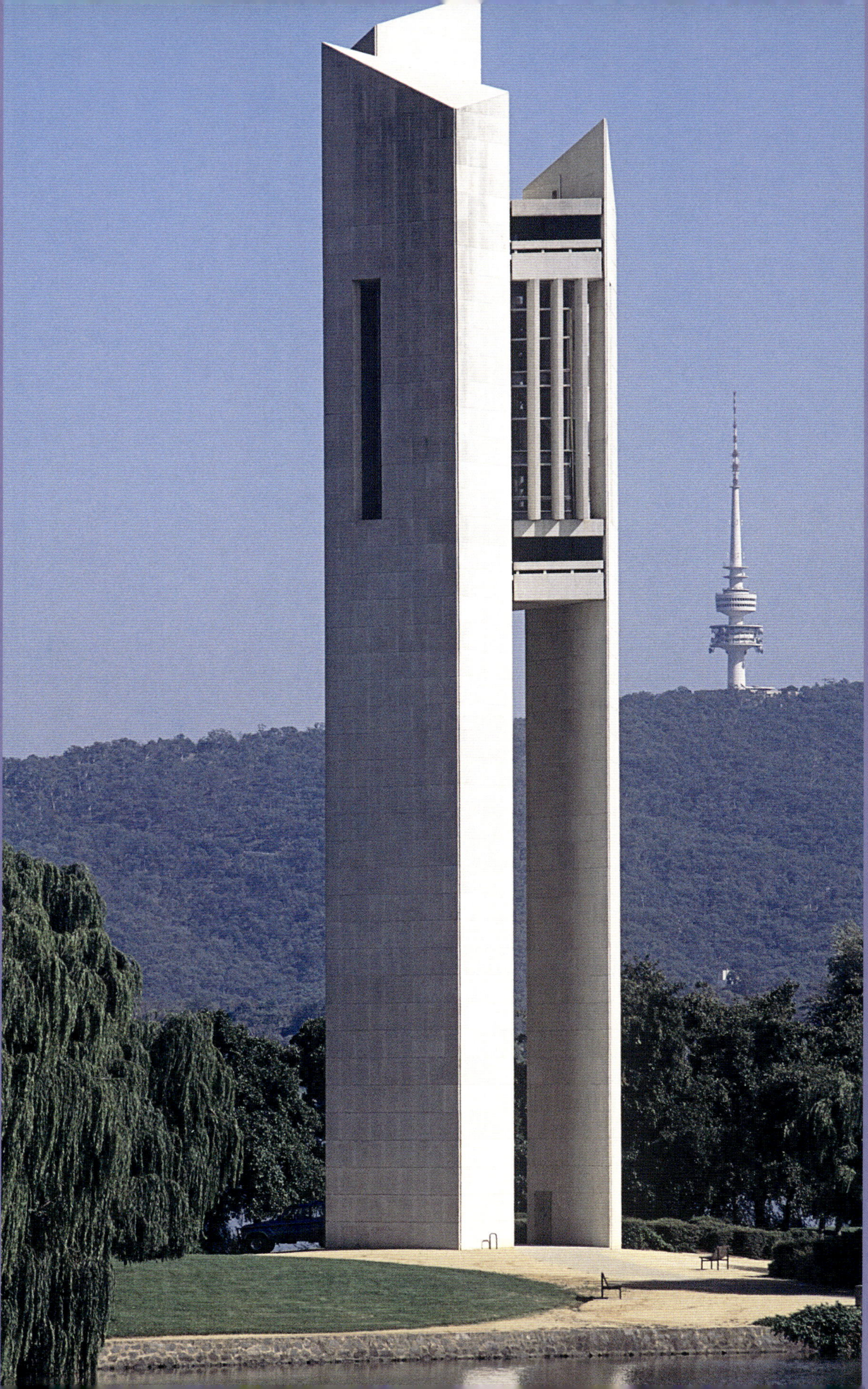

Forty years ago, Robin Boyd, the influential Australian architectural critic, described what he termed "the ugliness of bad conscious design" as Australia's worst failing. So what would he think of Australian architecture today?

During the architectural boom of the late 1990s, the creative vigor was palpable, confidence soared, and the entire nation became endowed with a new sense of architectural independence, one that more often betrays the personal aspirations of its creators than a unique sense of place.

Familiar icons adorn city skylines, while elsewhere towering glass structures that reflect the skies warmly embrace the modest, low-level colonial-style buildings in one of the most startling architectural juxtapositions imaginable—and it works, wonderfully well. Old and new stand fittingly side by side, leaning on each other for companionable support, and at the same time, defining the extremes of Australia's limited historical and architectural spectrum.

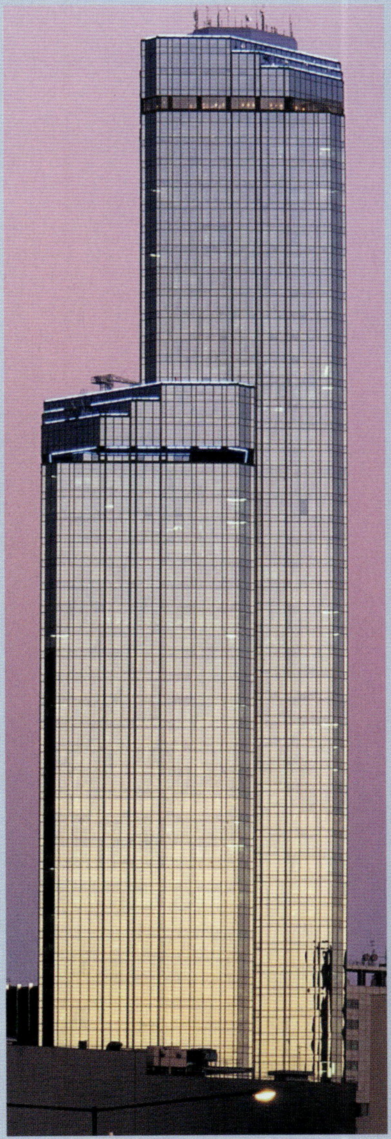

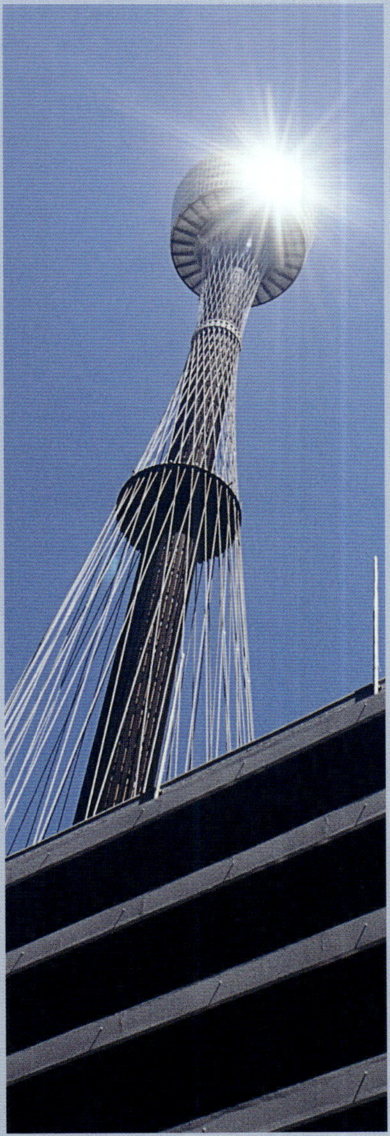

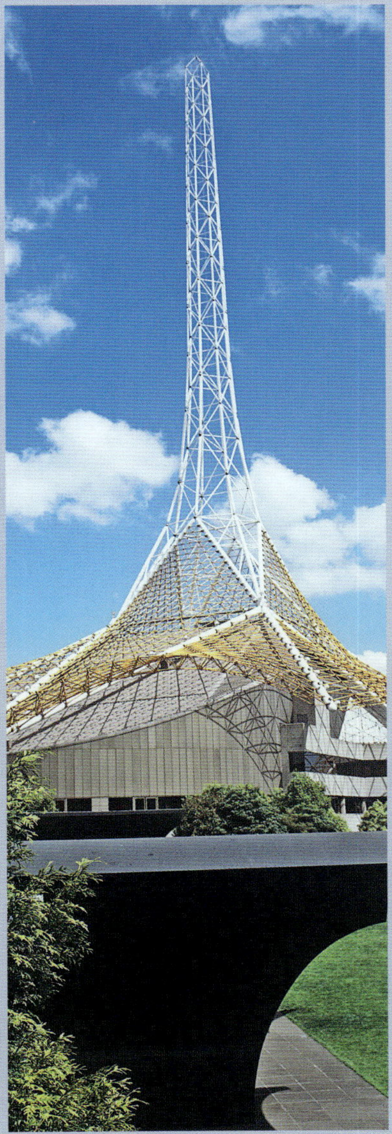

The Carillon Tower (left) on Lake Burley Griffin in central Canberra was gifted by the British government in 1963 and contains fifty-three bells ranging in size from 15lb to 6 tons; in the background is the Telstra Tower, which has a stunning view over the city.

Rialto Towers, Melbourne (above left) is the tallest reinforced concrete structure in the southern hemisphere and is well known for its unique design and glass facade. Right in the heart of the Sydney central business district (CBD) rises the 1,000ft Sydney Tower (above center), a distinctive, highly visible landmark, and the city's tallest structure. The Arts Centre, Melbourne (above right), is the flagship of the performing arts in Victoria. Its iconic spire locates the performing arts at the heart of Melbourne's civic and cultural precinct.

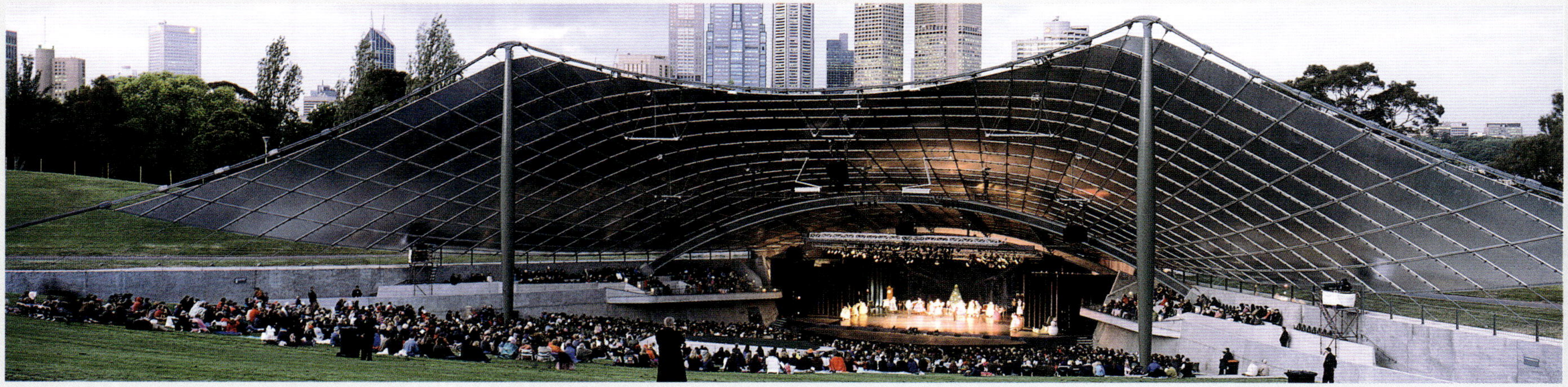

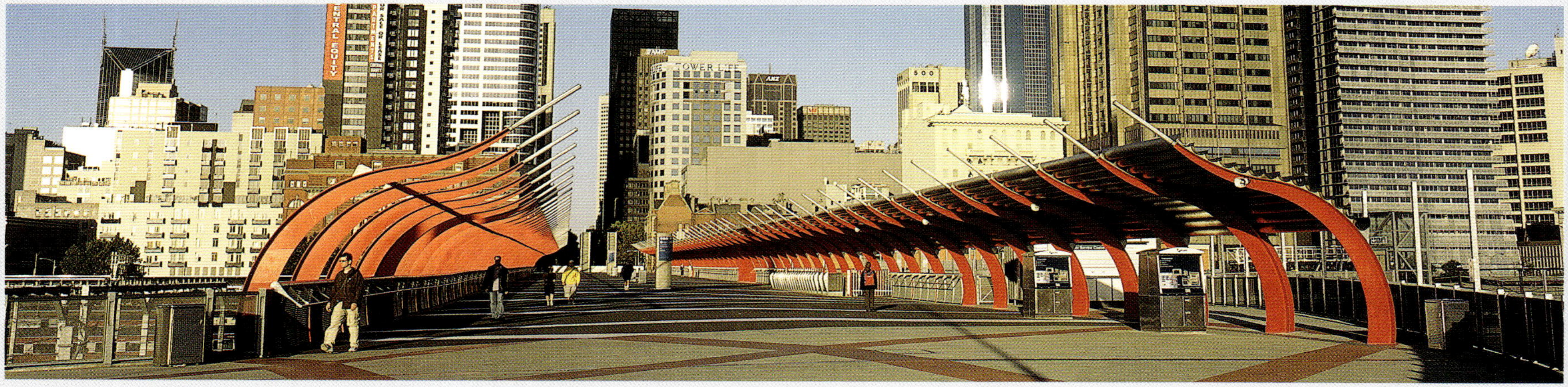

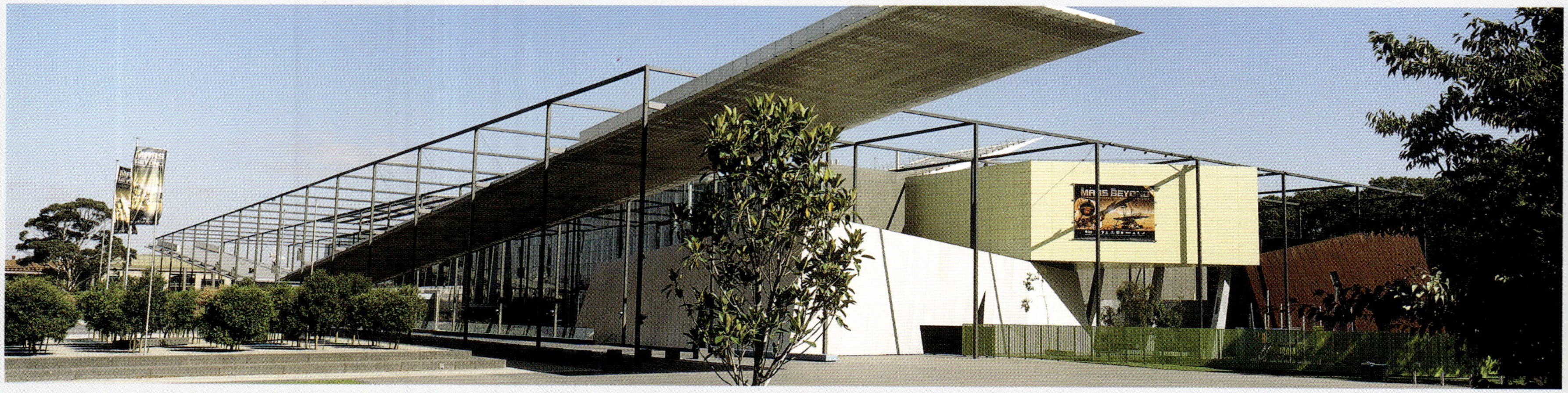

Set in the Kings Domain Gardens, Sydney, the Myer Music Bowl (top) is a popular summer venue that hosts everything from Summerdayze dance festival to Dame Kiri Te Kanawa. Bourke Street extension footbridge (center) in Melbourne's Docklands precinct typifies the best bold and imaginative Australian design concepts. Completed in 2000, Melbourne Museum (above) became the largest museum not only in Australia but in the southern hemisphere. Birrarung Marr Park (right) is on the southern edge of Melbourne's central business district.

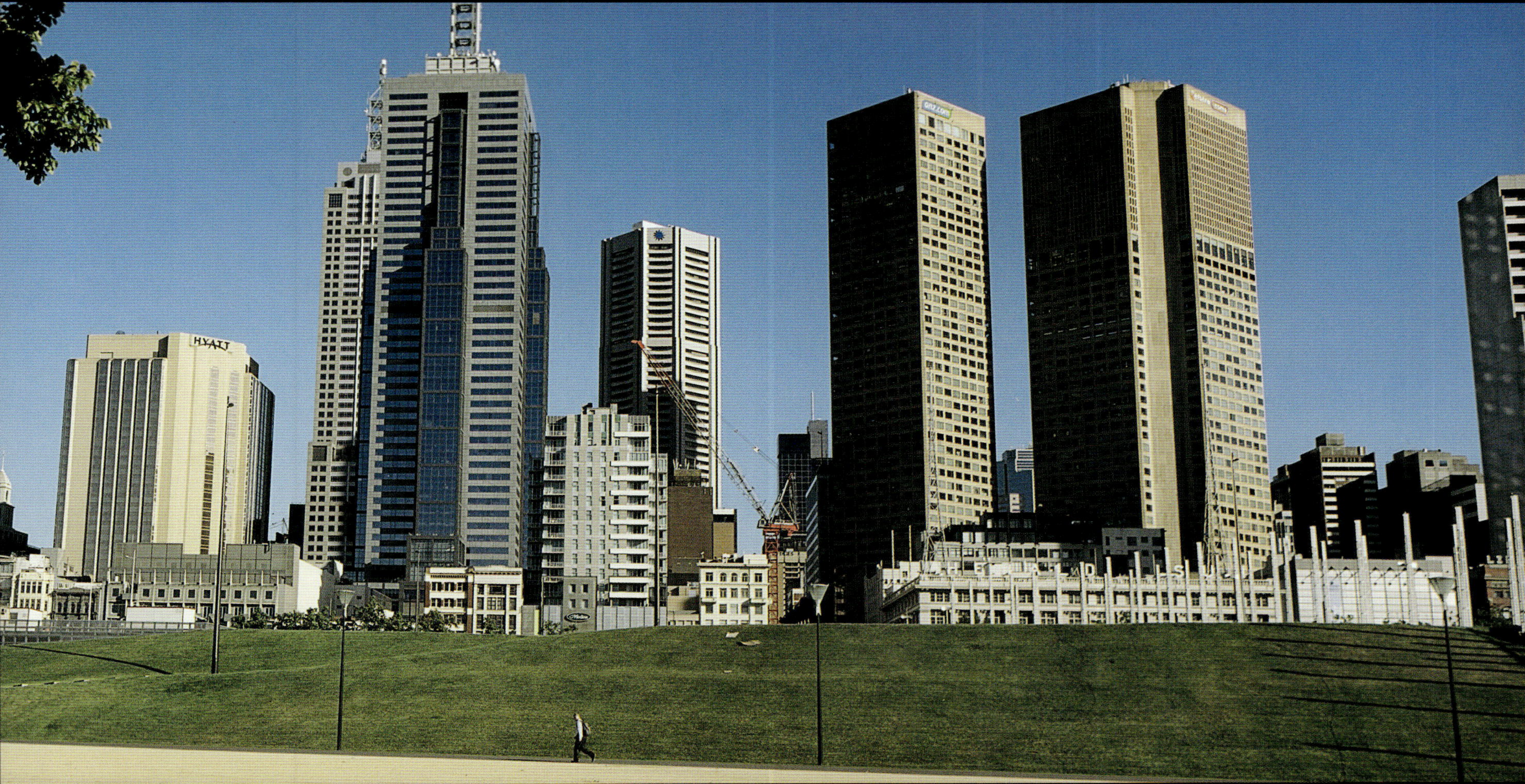
HYATT

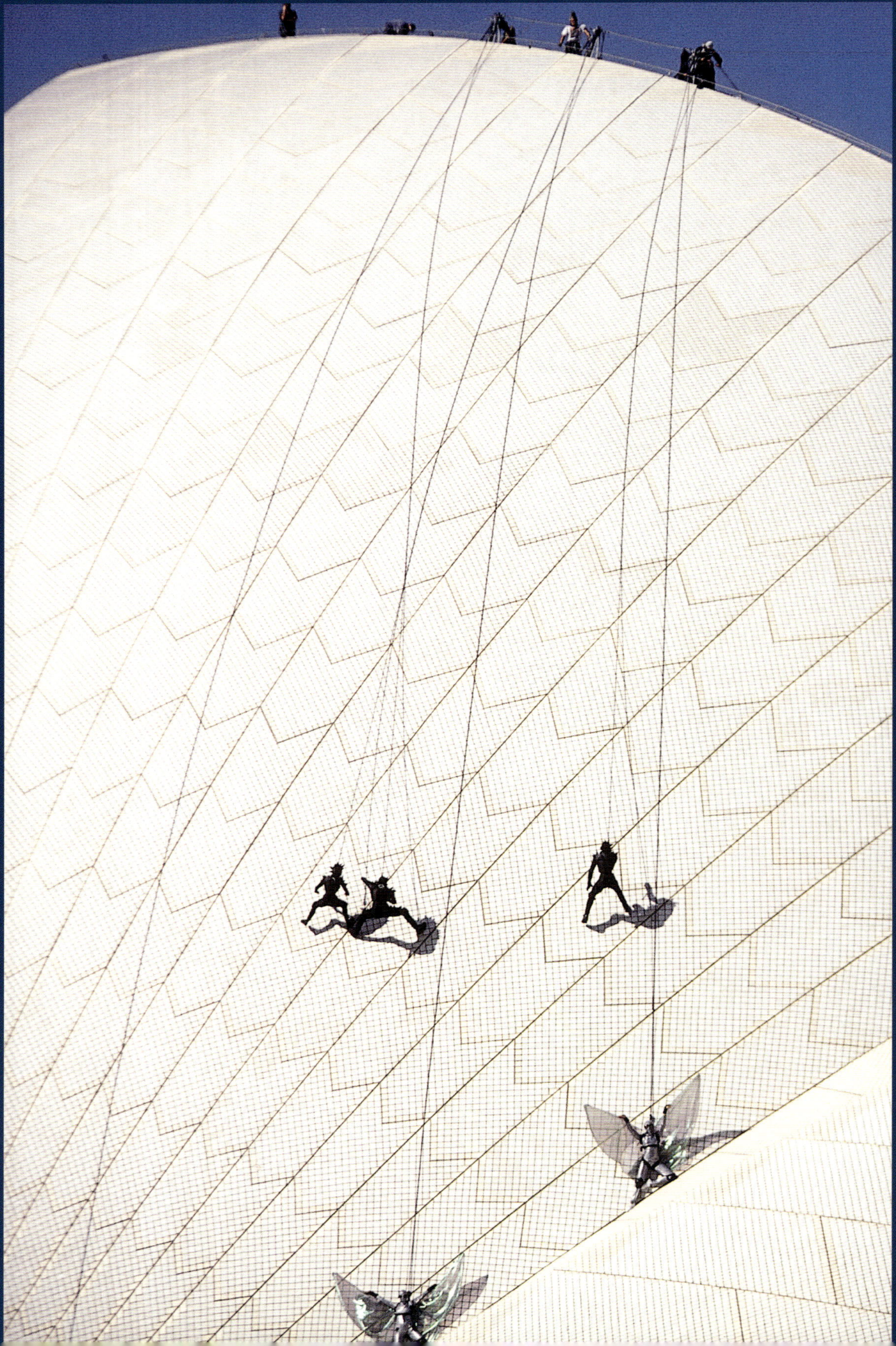

AN ICON IN FULL SAIL

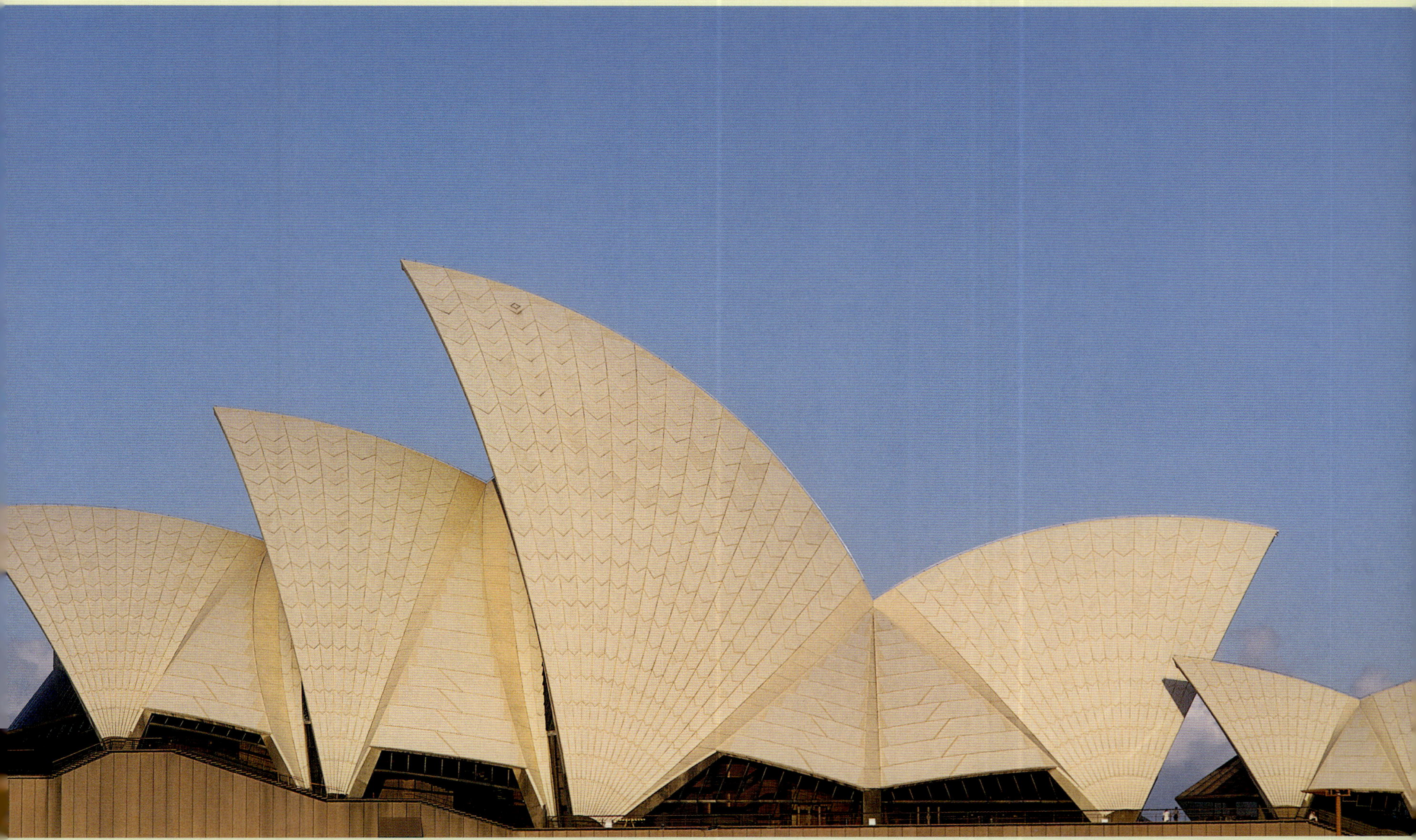

As part of its twenty-fifth birthday celebrations, four people abseiled down one of the sails of Sydney Opera House, surely the world's most instantly recognizable structure. It is one of the busiest performing arts centers in the world, averaging around three thousand events each year with audiences totaling up to two million. In a typical year, the Sydney Opera House presents theater, musicals, opera, contemporary dance, ballet, and every form of music from symphony concerts to jazz.

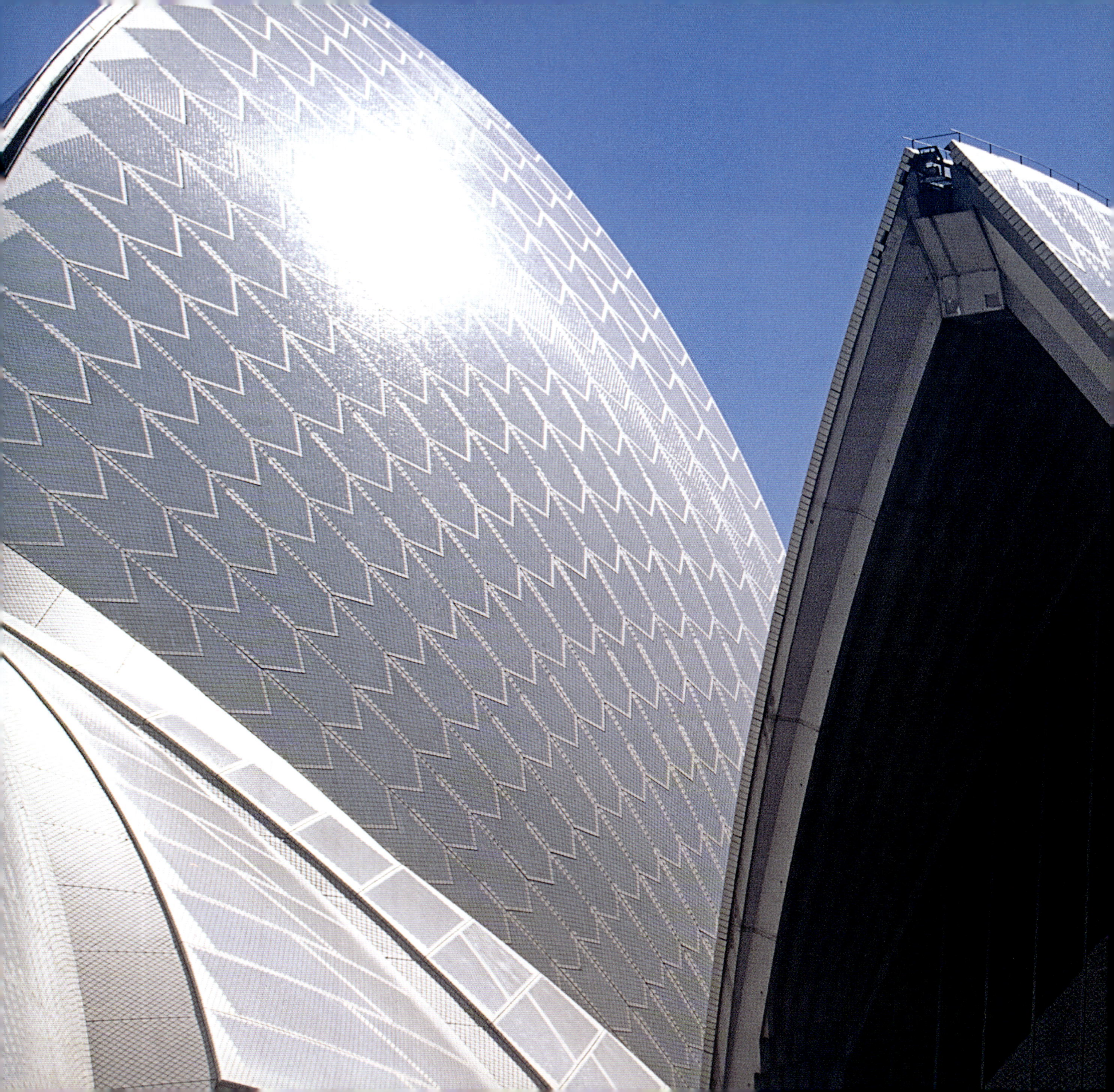

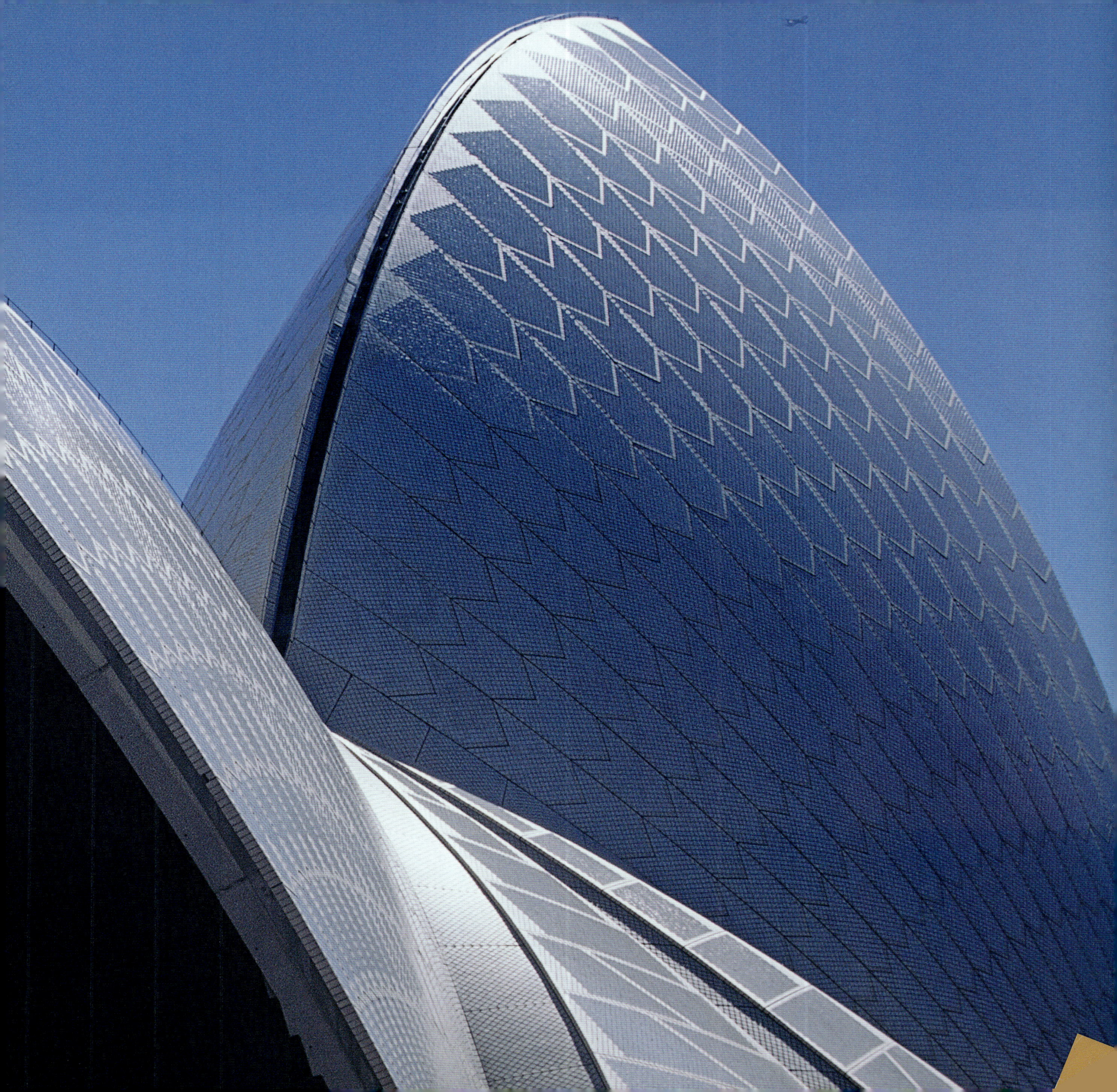

COLONIAL STYLE

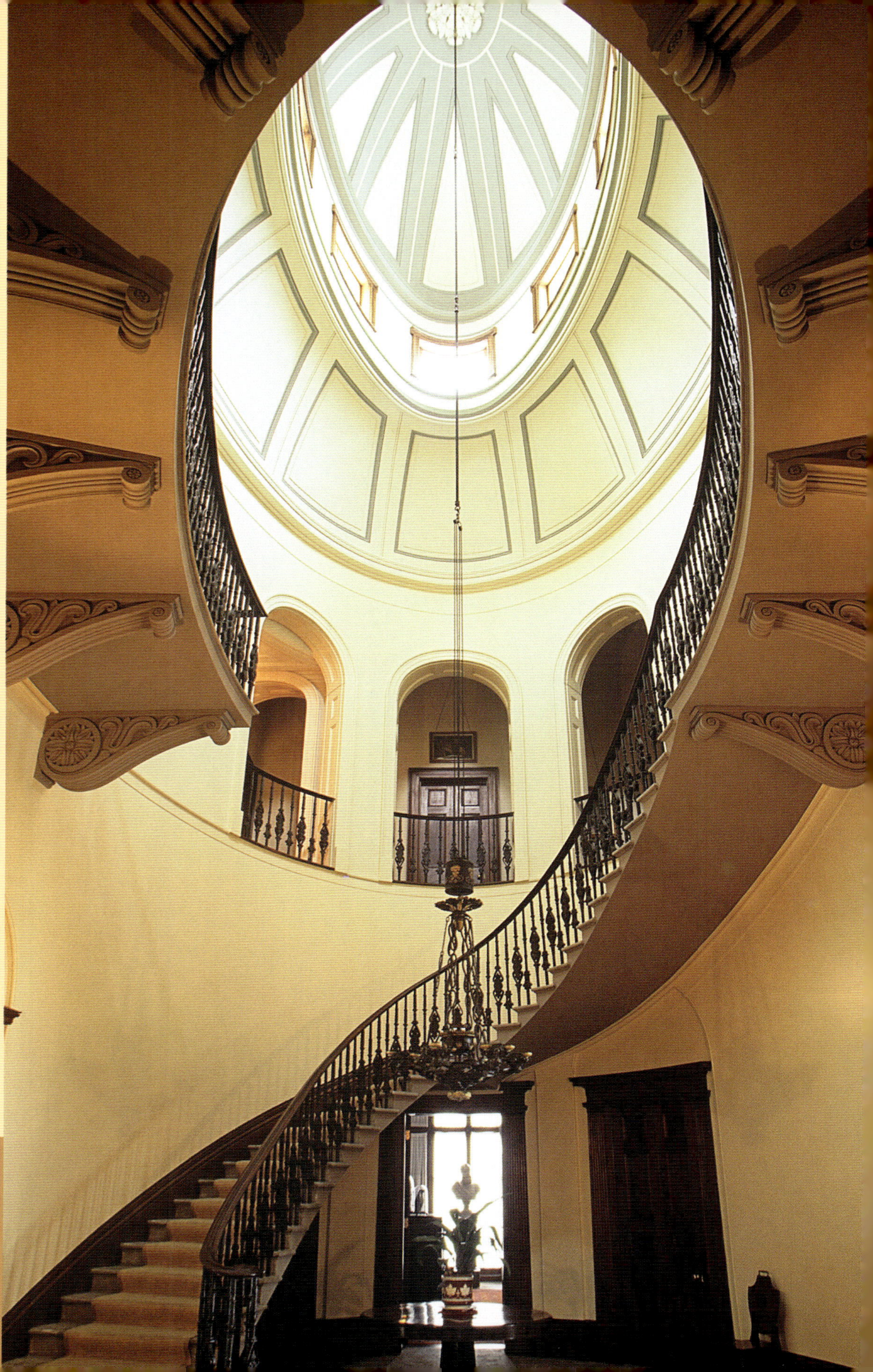

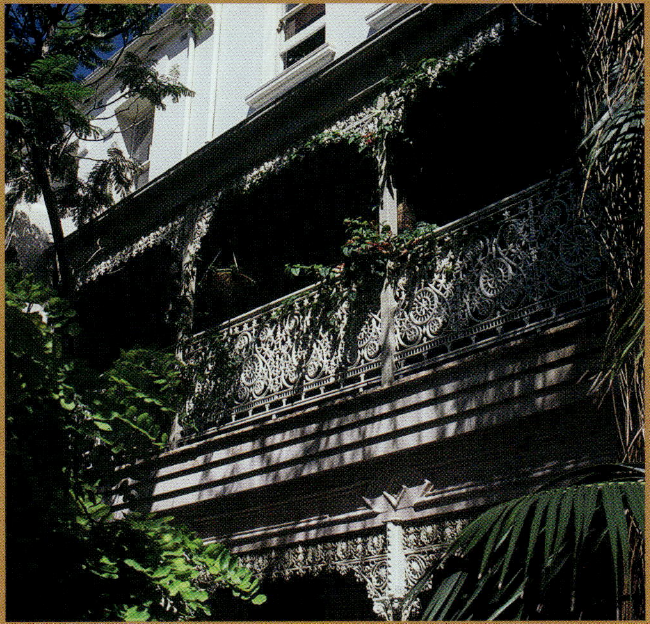

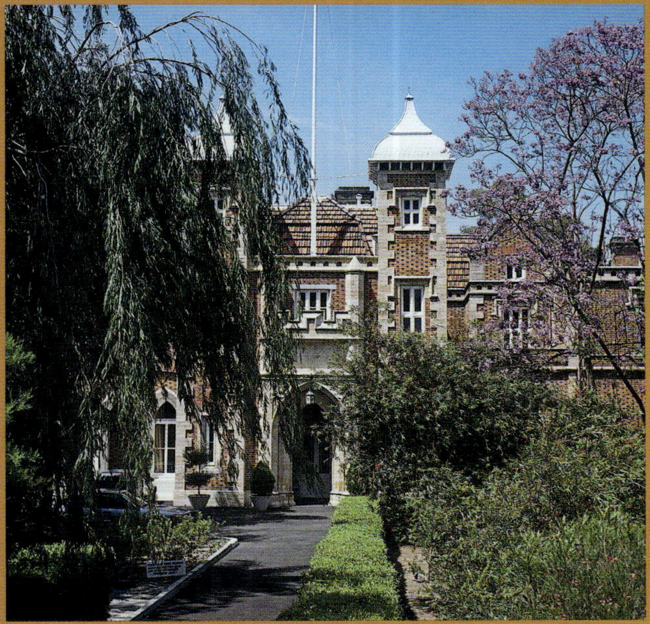

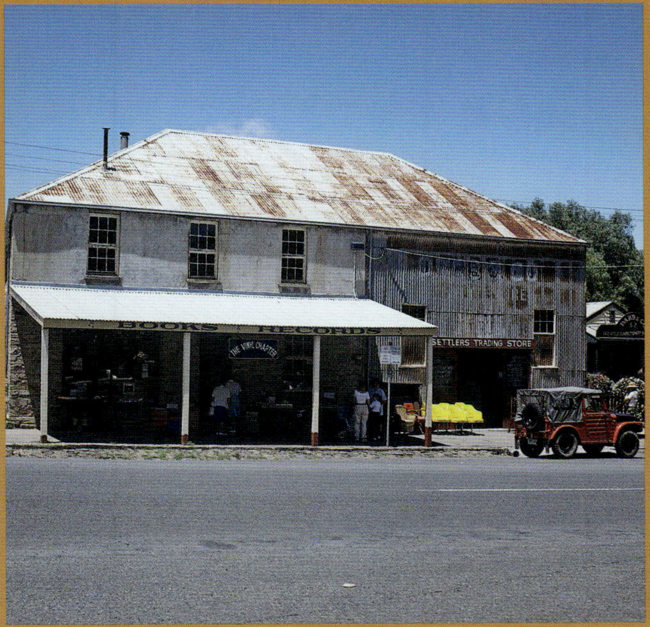
SETTLERS TRADING STORE

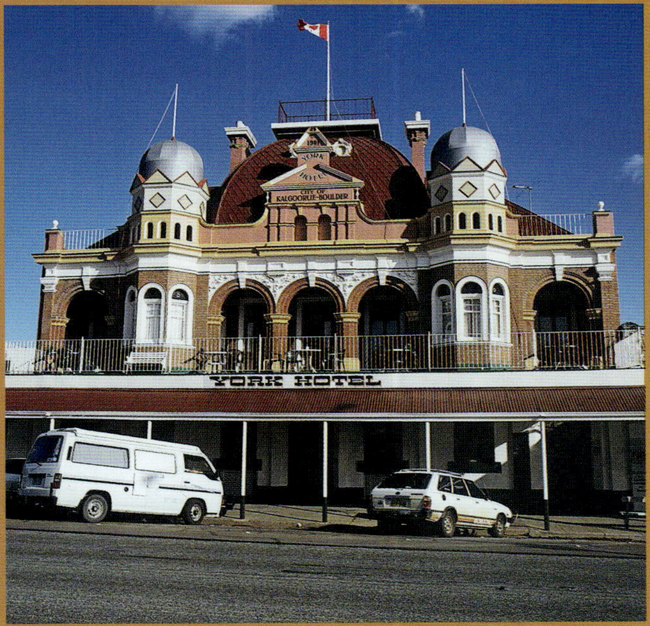
YORK HOTEL

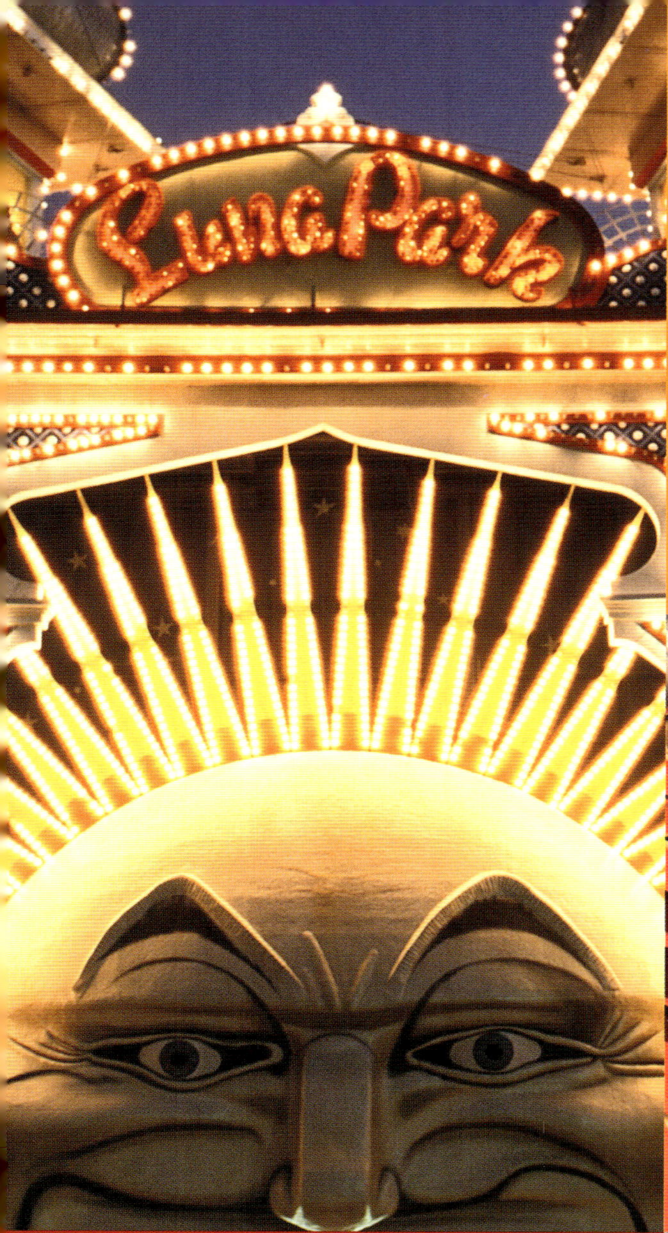
Luna Park

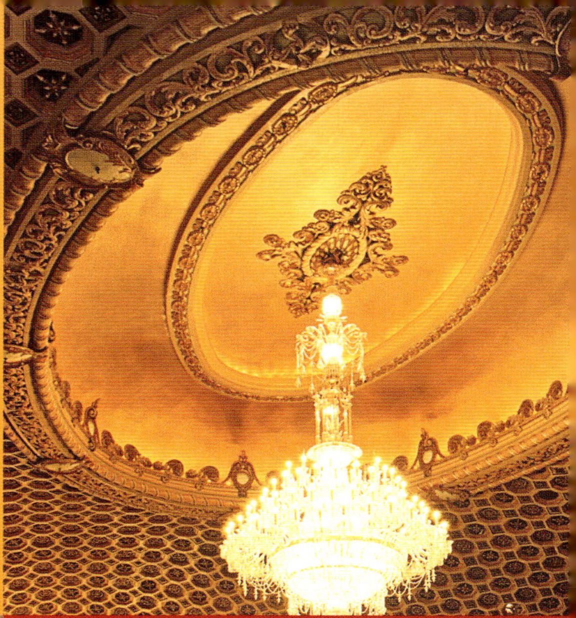

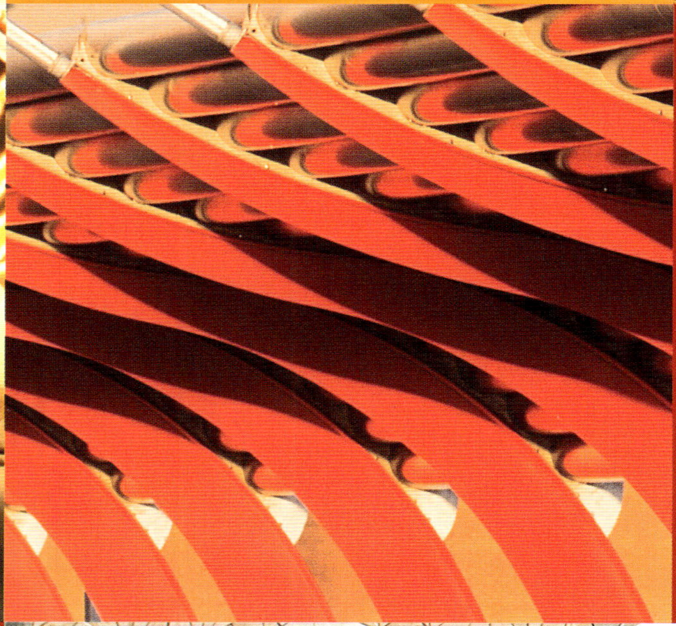

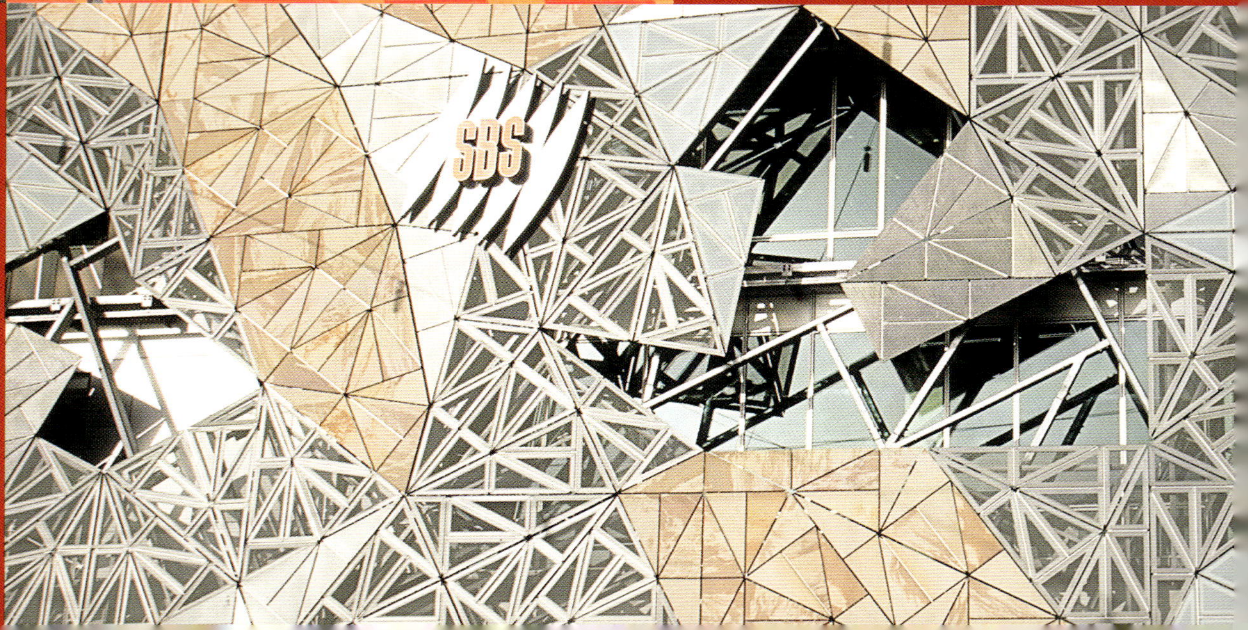
SBS

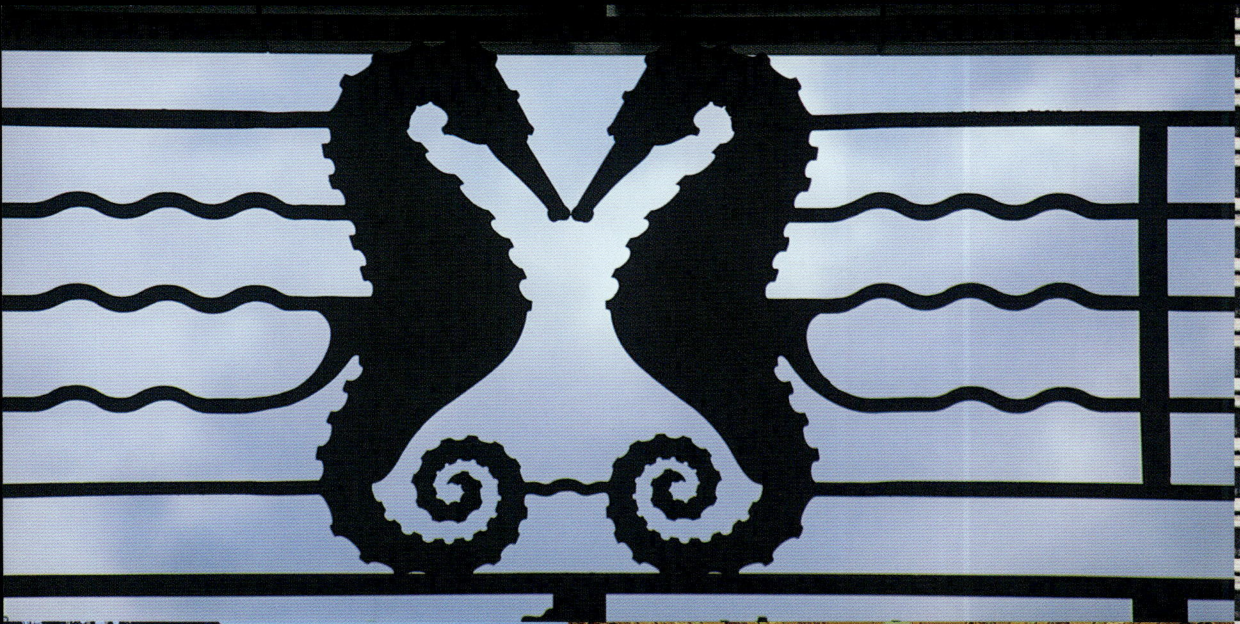
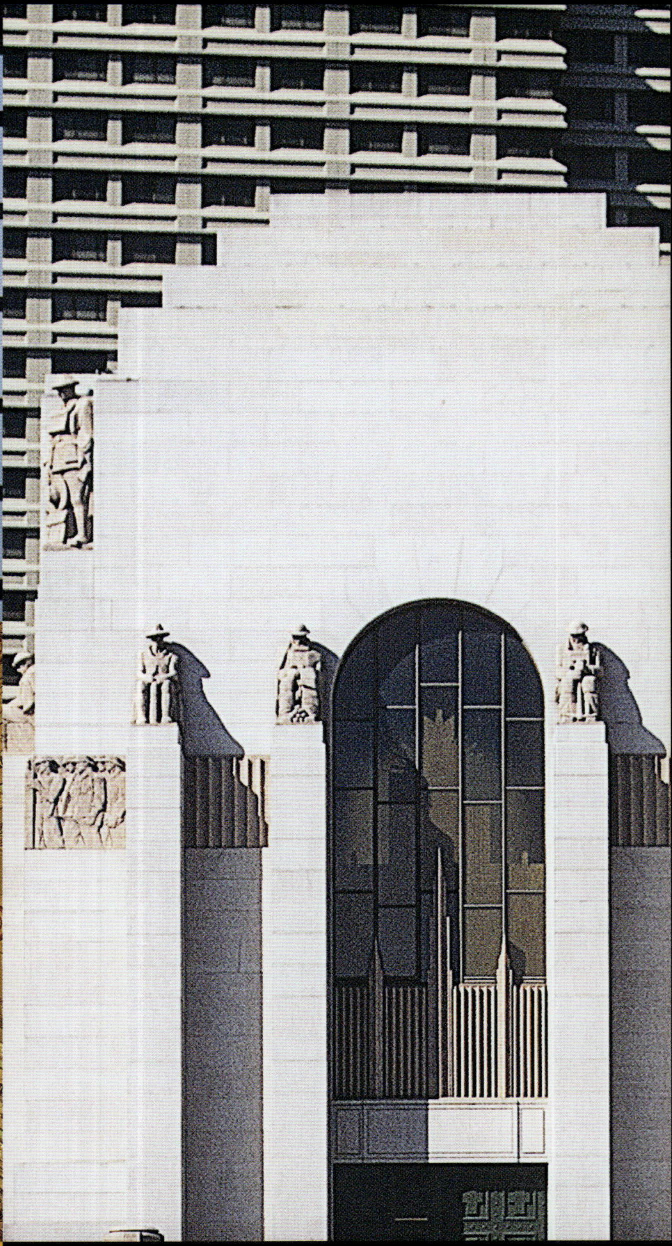
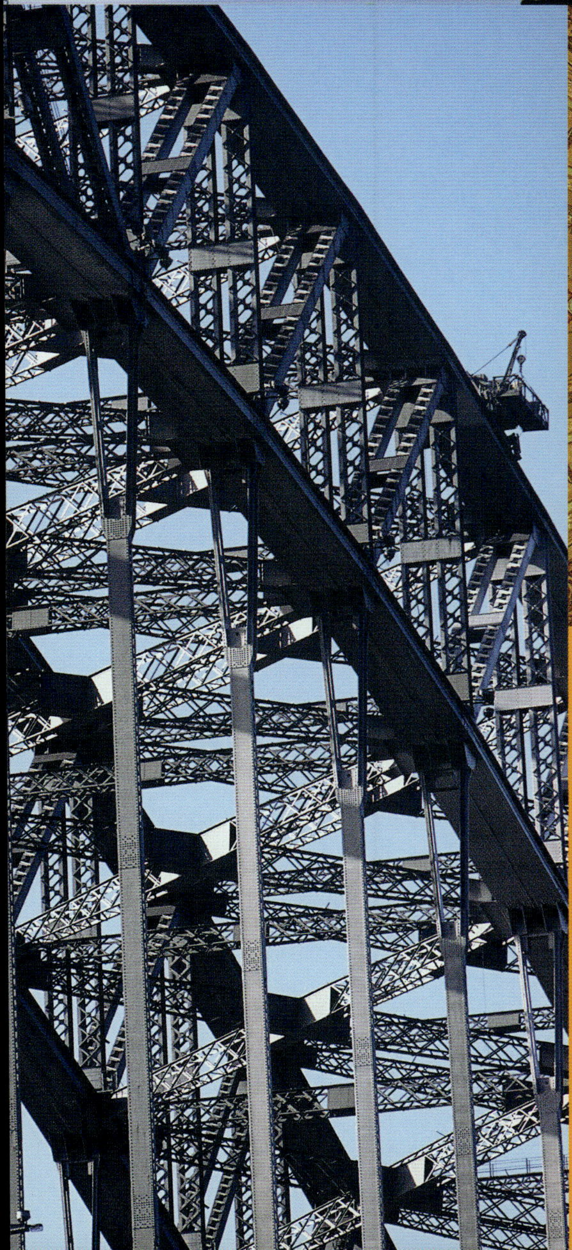
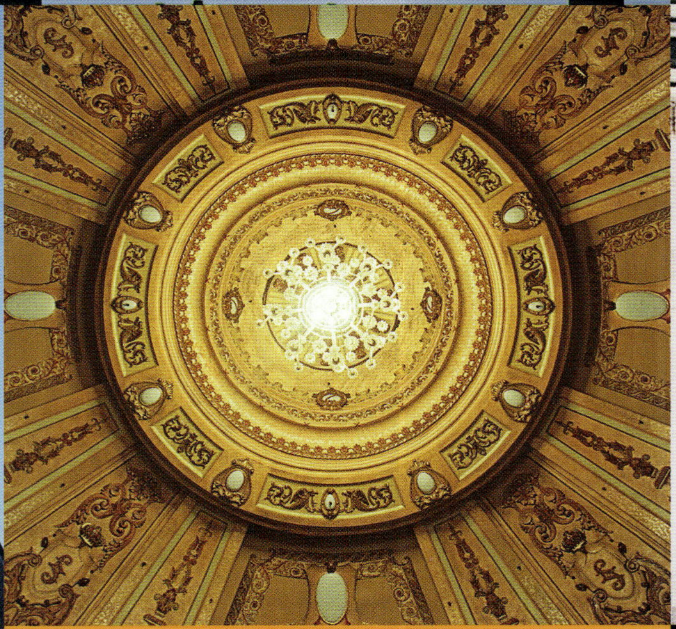
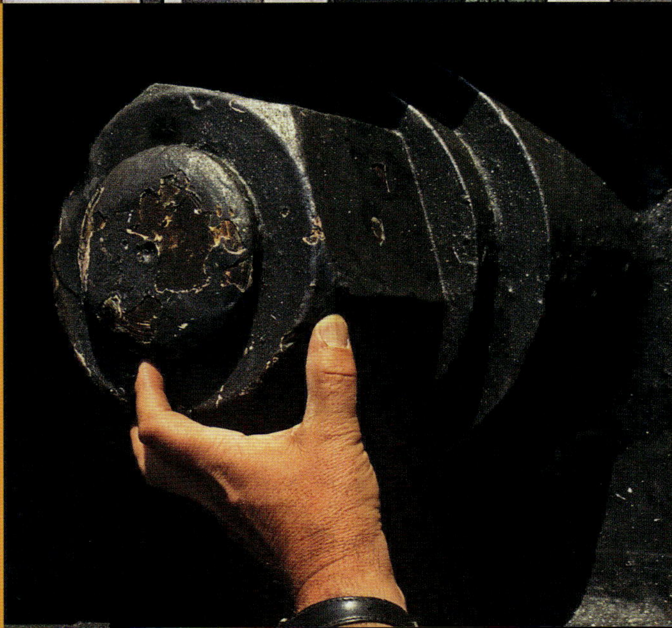

SPACE WITHIN

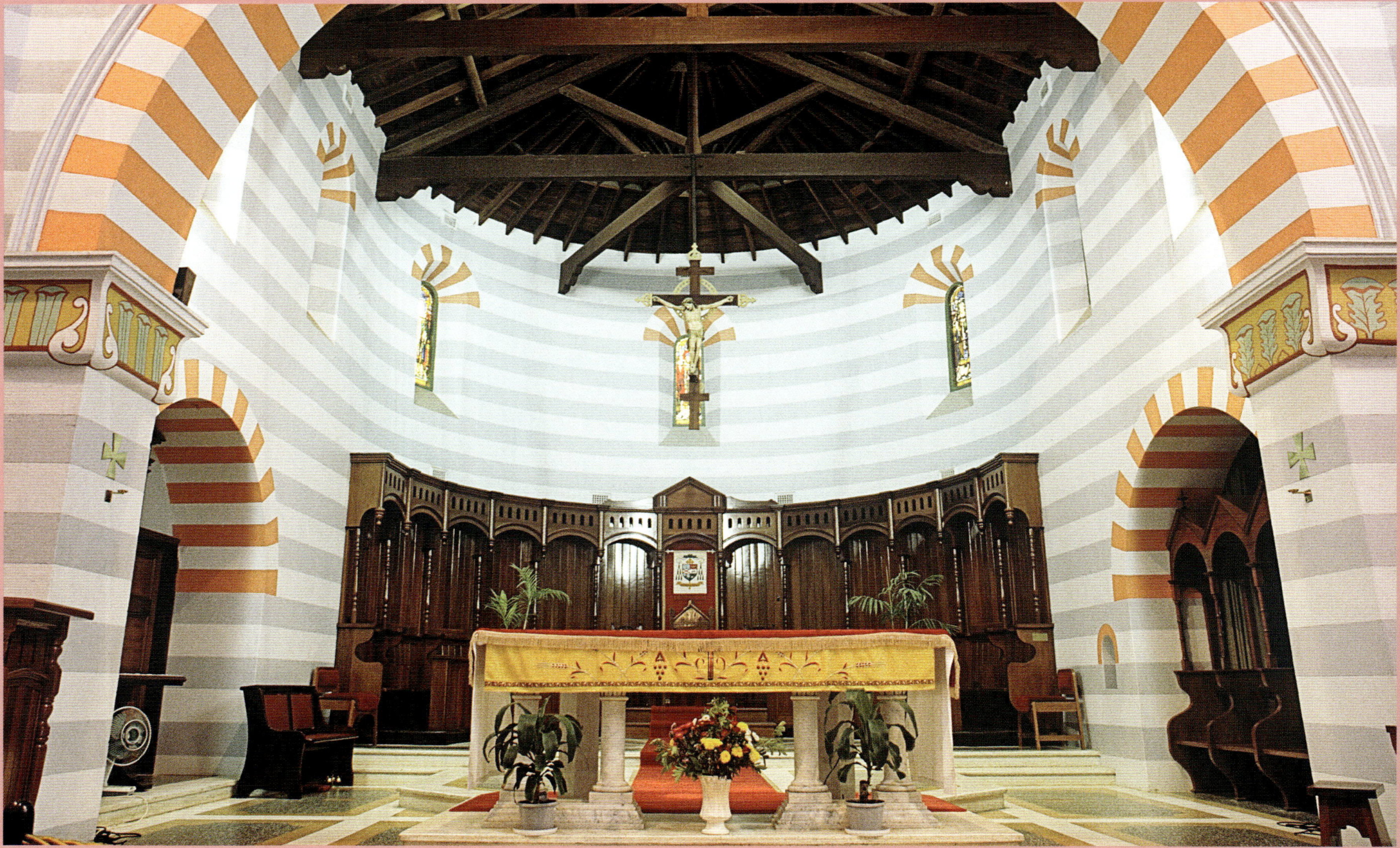

The Byzantine-style interior of St Francis Xavier Cathedral (above) in Geraldton, Western Australia, designed by Monsignor John Hawes, reflects a readiness to break away from traditional ideas.

It is a far cry from the classical, spacious, vaulted roof of St Paul's Anglican Cathedral, Melbourne (right), and the imaginative interior of the concert hall in the Sydney Opera House (far right).

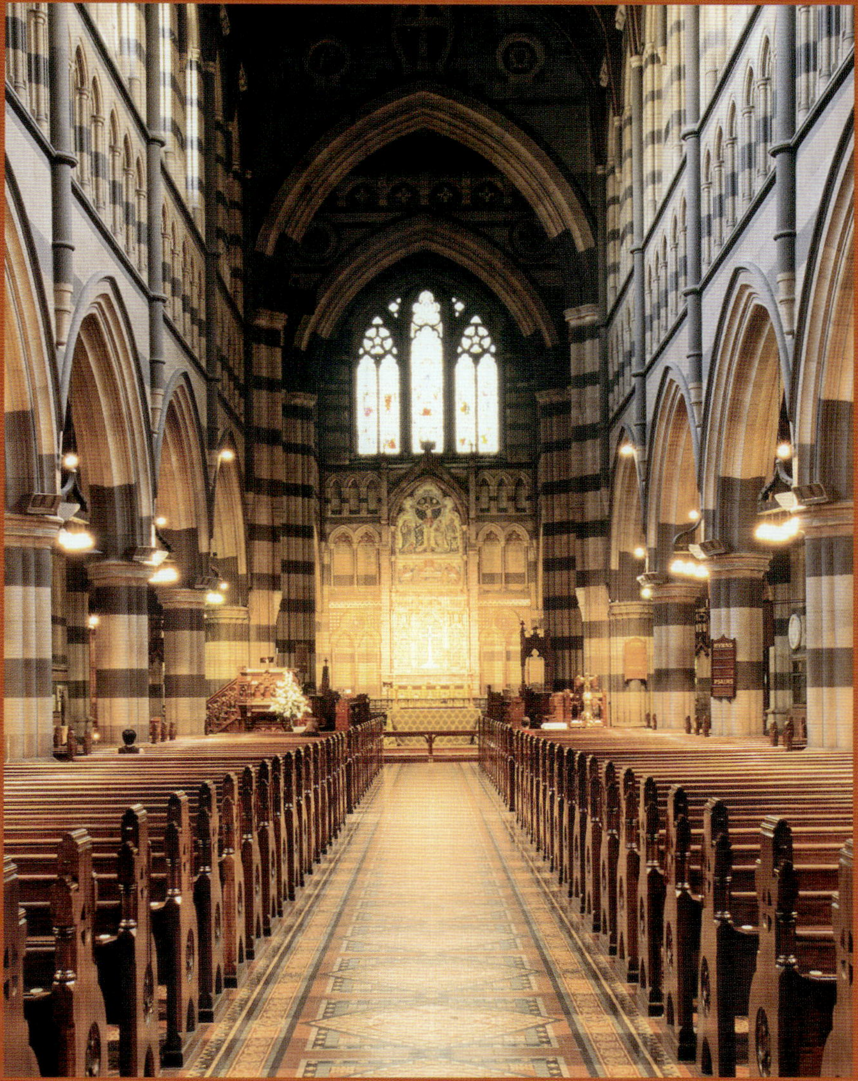

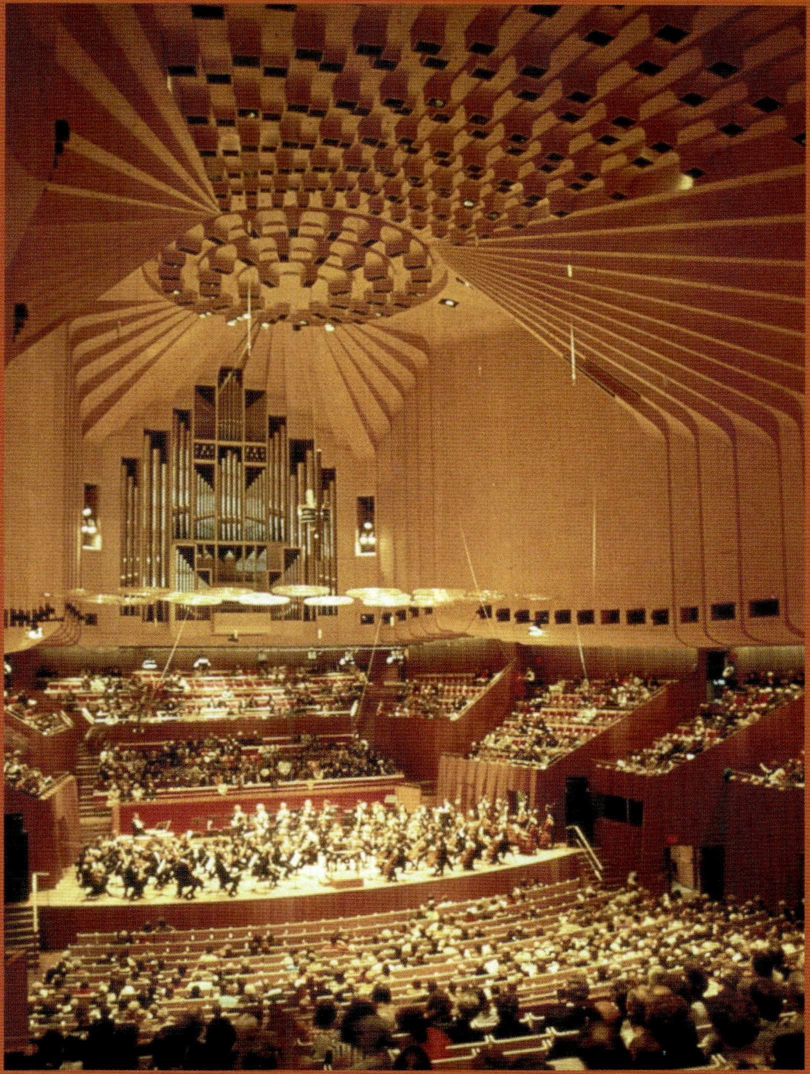

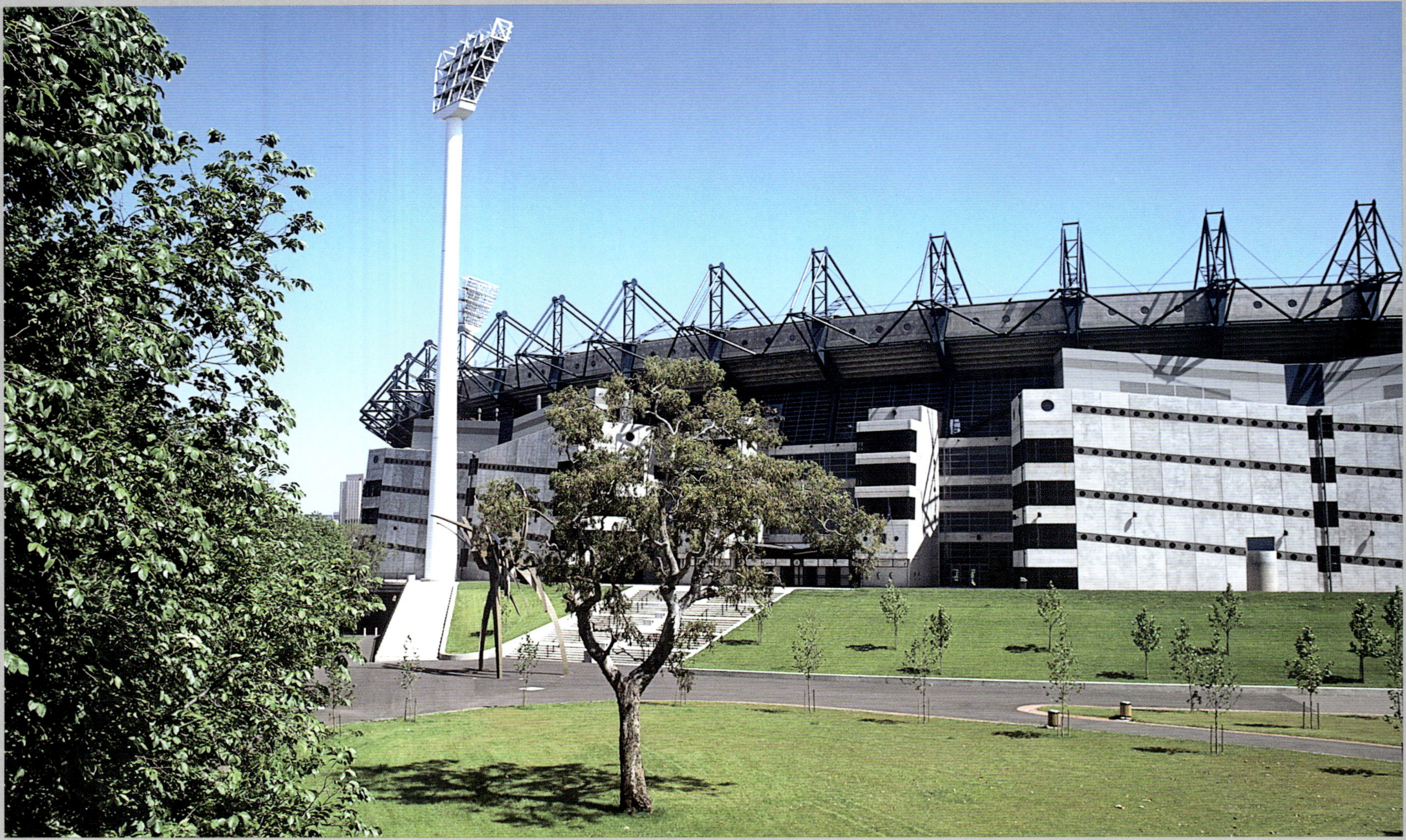

It is always a good policy to expect the unexpected in a country where architectural imagination is virtually off the leash. Melbourne Cricket Ground (above) is Australia's sporting hub, yet these days its title is somewhat misleading, as football dominates the ground during winter, while only a handful of international cricket matches are played there in summer. Carlton Gardens Children's Garden (top right) is situated outside the Melbourne Museum. "Echoes of Paris", or the Pyramid, Sydney Tropical Center, is part of the Royal Botanic Gardens (bottom right).

The National Gallery of Victoria (far right) displays a collection of works by European and Australian artists of the nineteenth and twentieth centuries, as well as Aboriginal art.

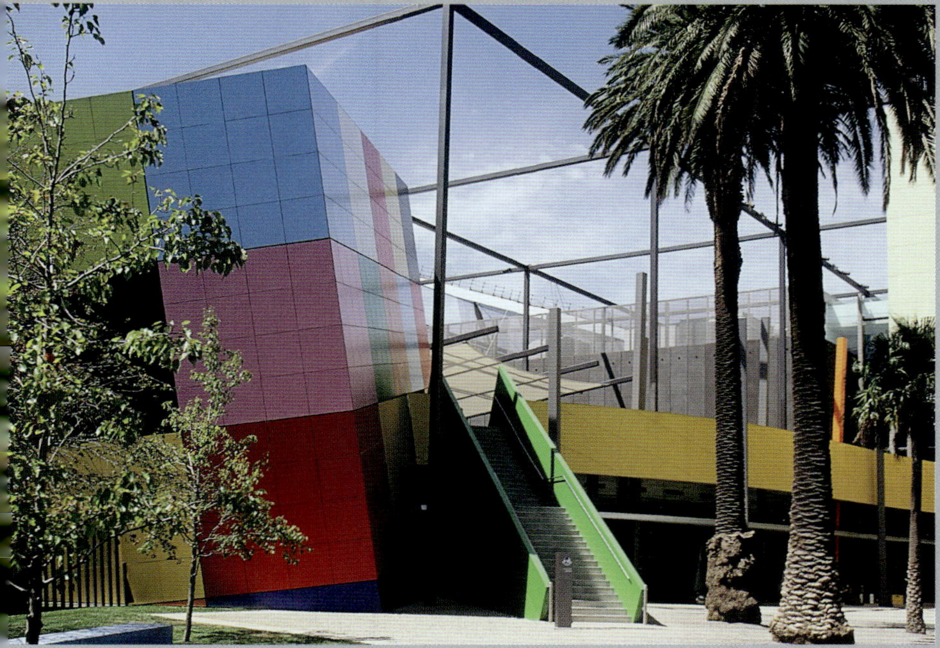

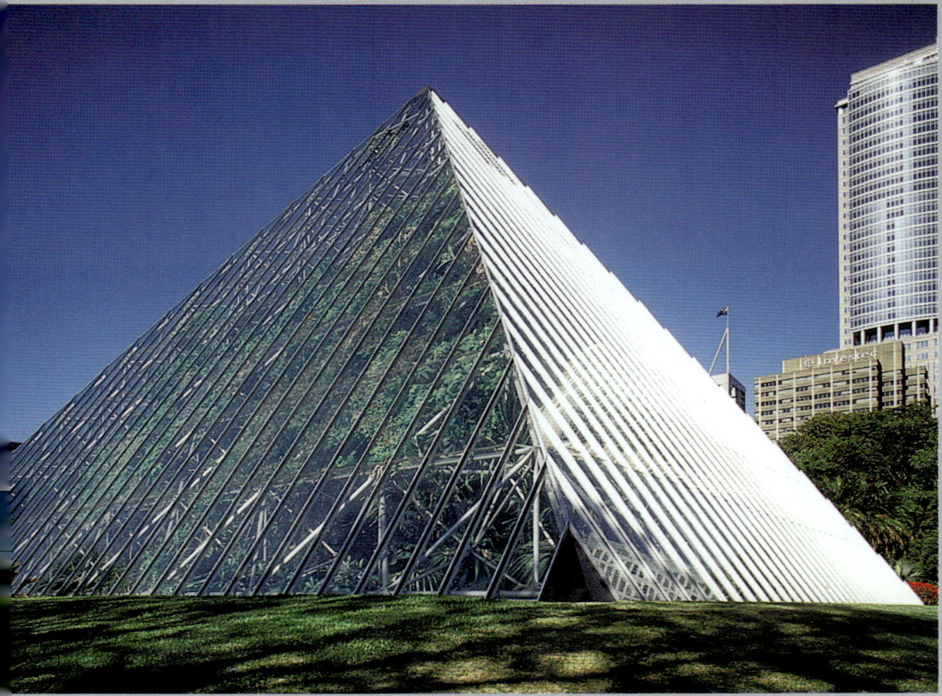

CONTEMPORARY DESIGN

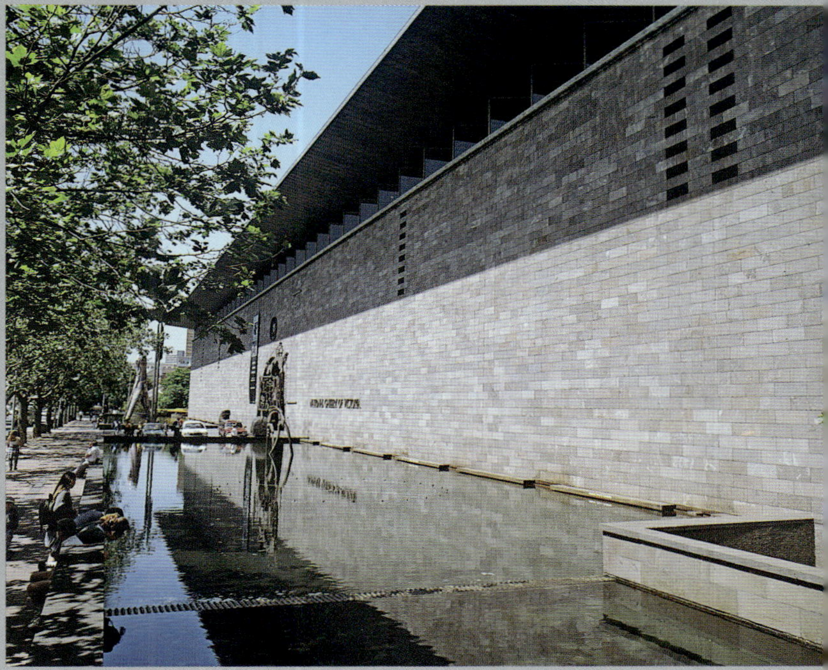

& VIEW

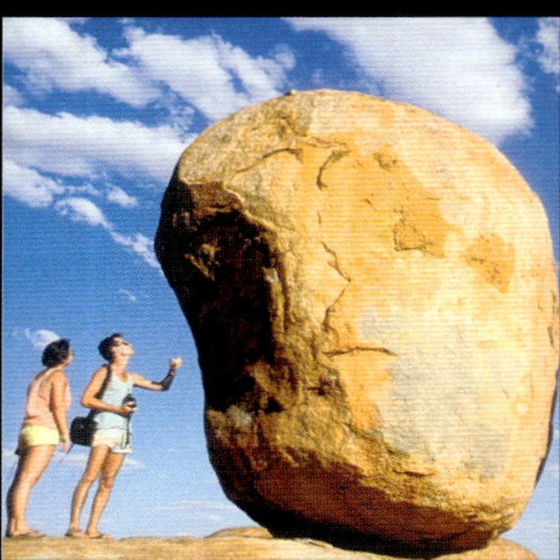

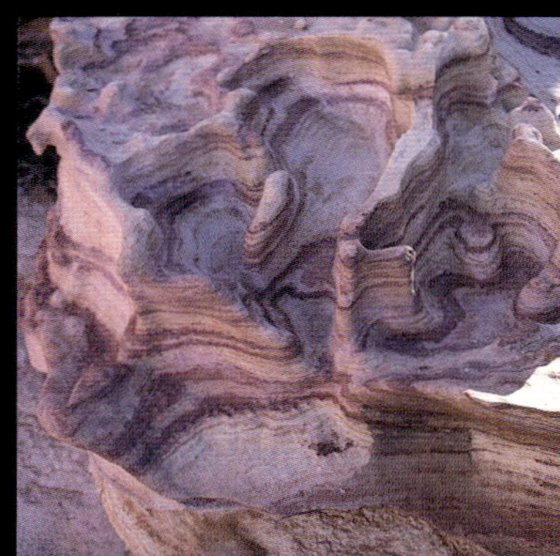

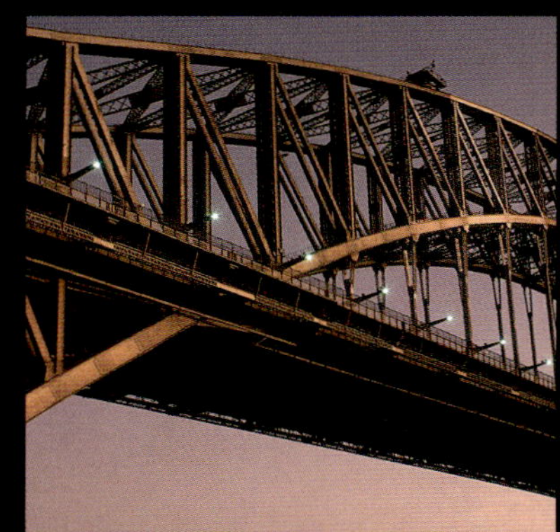

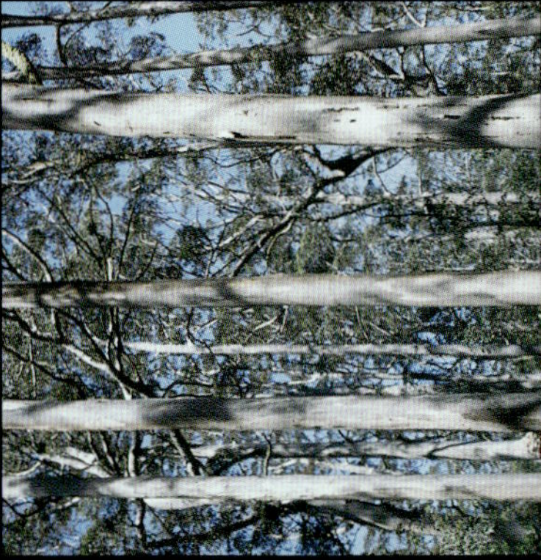

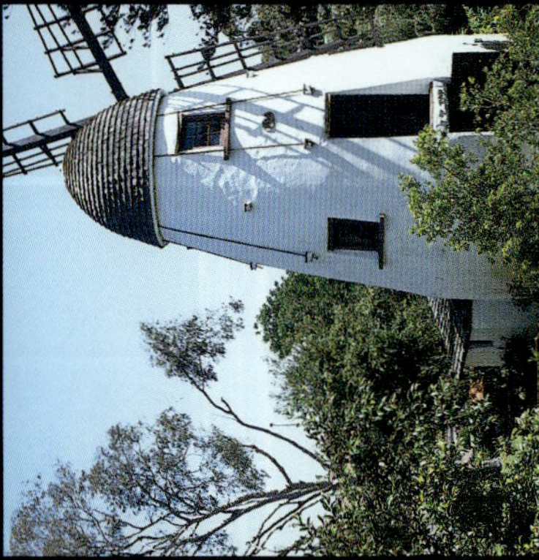

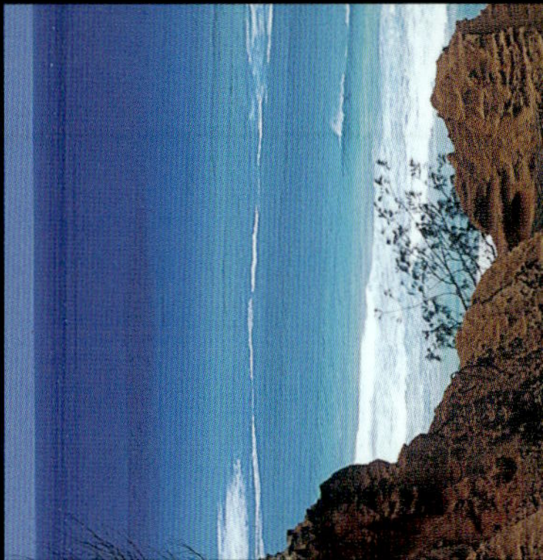

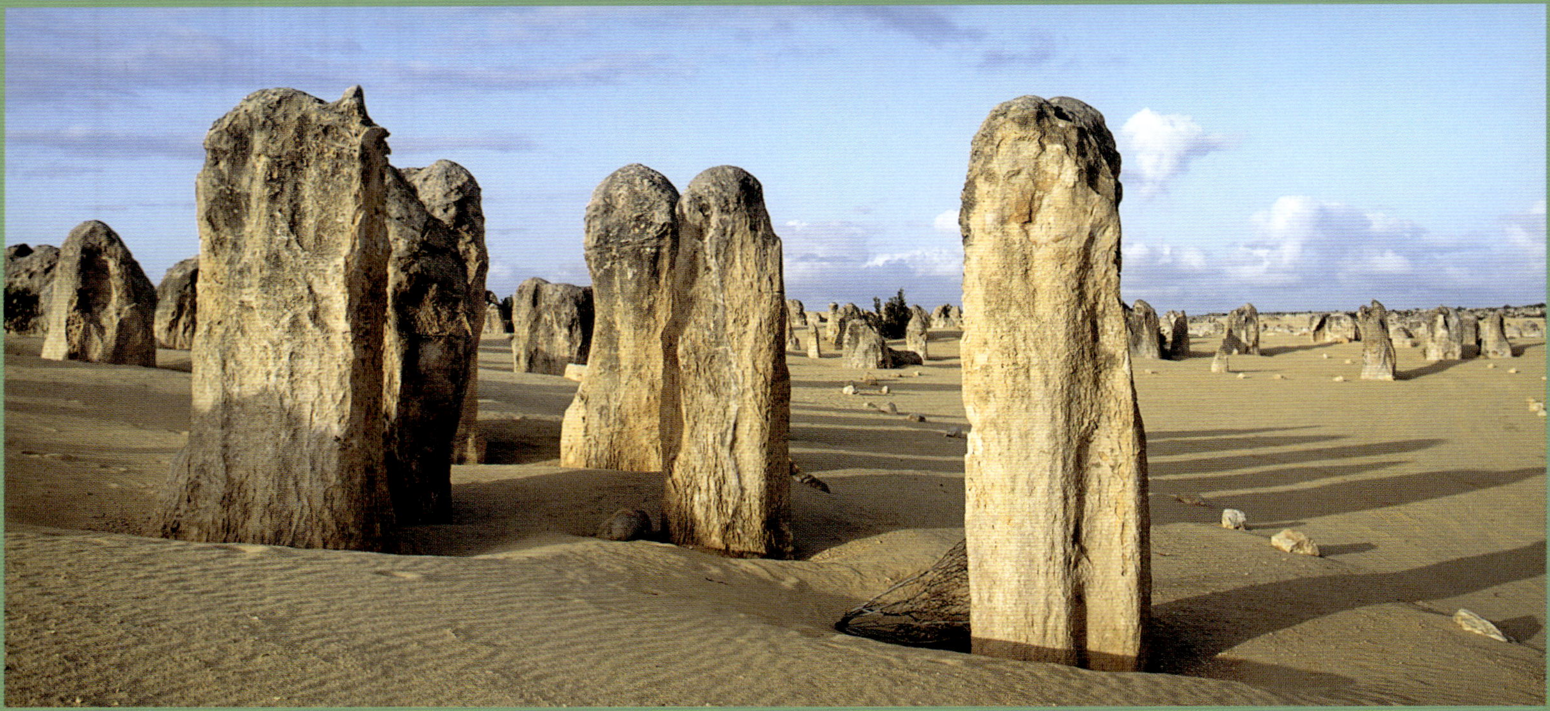

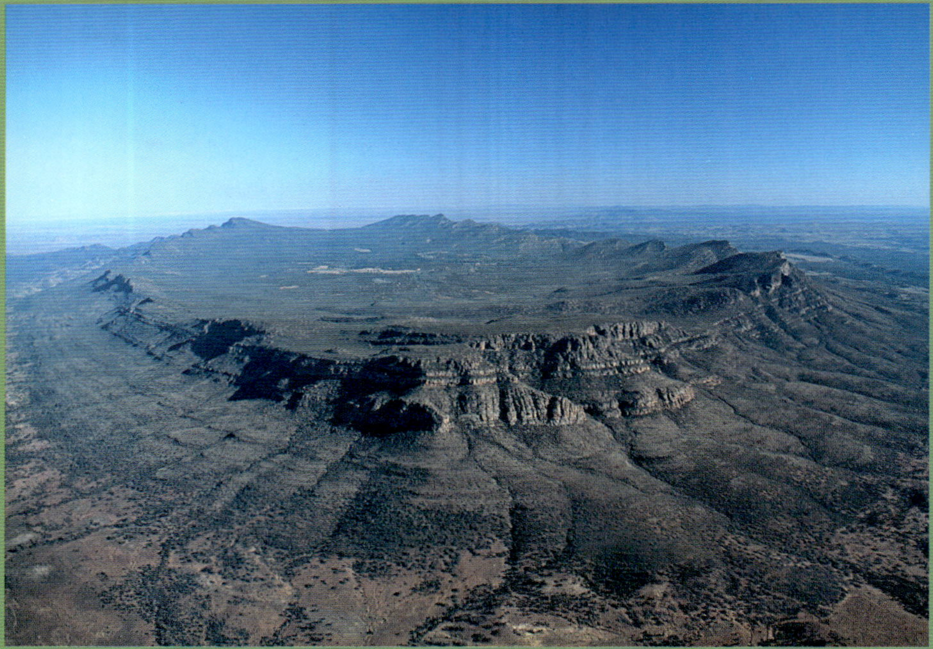

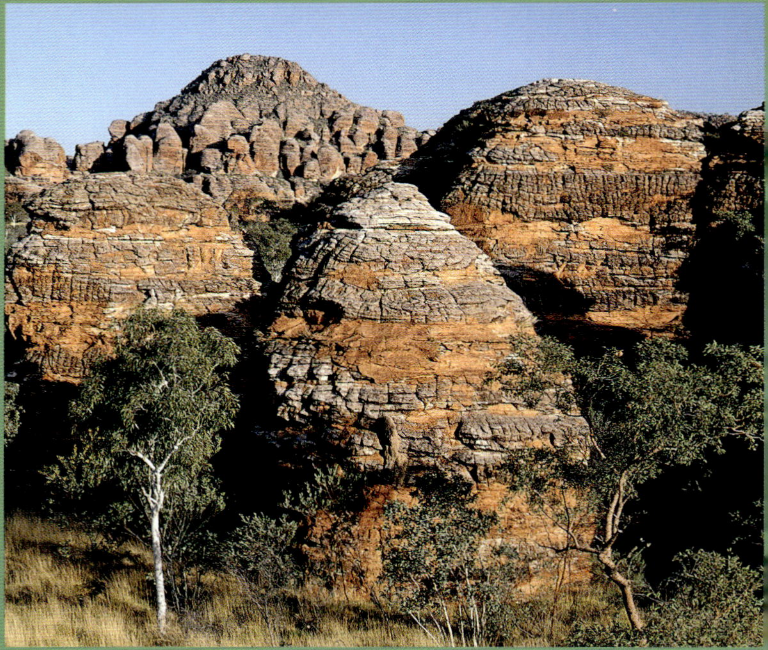

In a country the size of Australia, diversity in almost all things is to be expected, but the country's menu of natural landforms is staggering in its variety and beauty. The Pinnacles Desert in Western Australia (top) was created by the agents of erosion in a manner not dissimilar to the Bungle Bungles (above right) and the Devil's Marbles (opposite bottom left). One day, thousands of years from now, they will crumble to sand, and then rival the colorful sands of Fraser Island (far right). The natural amphitheater at Wilpena Pound (above left) in the Flinders Range of Southern Australia, is another matter. This remarkable rock basin has been venerated by Aboriginal people for fifteen thousand years. And few people complete a trip to Australia without visiting its most famous icon, Uluṟu (Ayers Rock, opposite and next page).

NATURE'S LANDMARKS

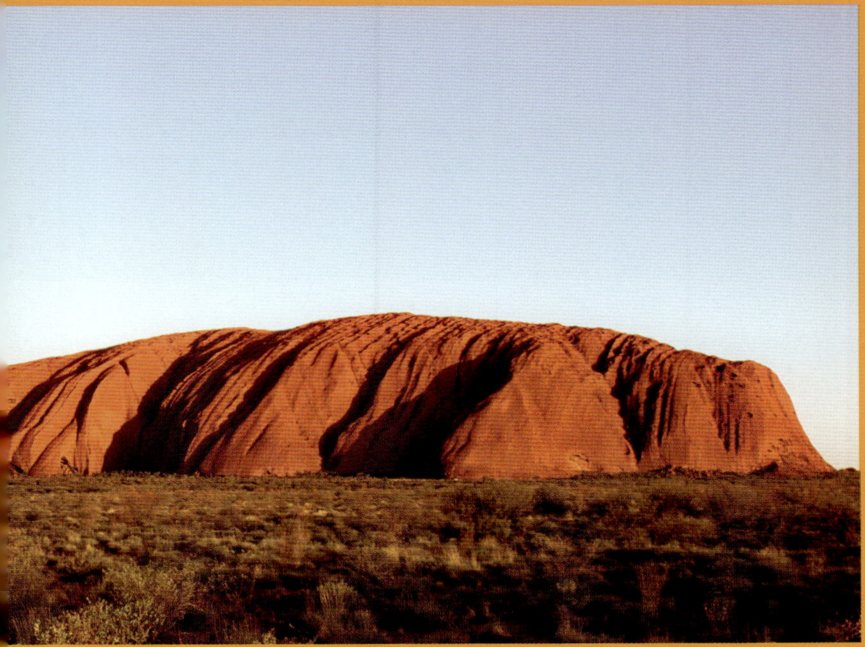

Hundreds of miles of searing red-sand landscape dominate Australia; roads and rail tracks run arrow-straight for hours at a time with little to penetrate the endless spread of salt bush, spinifex, mulga, and desert oak. Elsewhere, rainforests are lush green oases from the far north of Queensland to the far south of Tasmania.

Uluṟu (Ayers Rock) is paramount among Australia's natural landmarks, but is rivaled for grandeur by Watarrka (Kings Canyon) and Kata Tjuṯa (the Olgas). North of Perth, the Nambung National Park offers the bizarre Pinnacles Desert; south of Tennant Creek, the Devil's Marbles, considered by the local Aborigines to have been eggs laid by the Rainbow Serpent during the Dreamtime, simply bewilder the mind. The tranquillity of Rainbow Valley near Alice Springs, the confusion of the Bungle Bungles, the great sand dunes, the endlessly twisted and torn rock landscapes, the stromatolites at Hamelin Pool, all spell out that the finest artist of all is Nature.

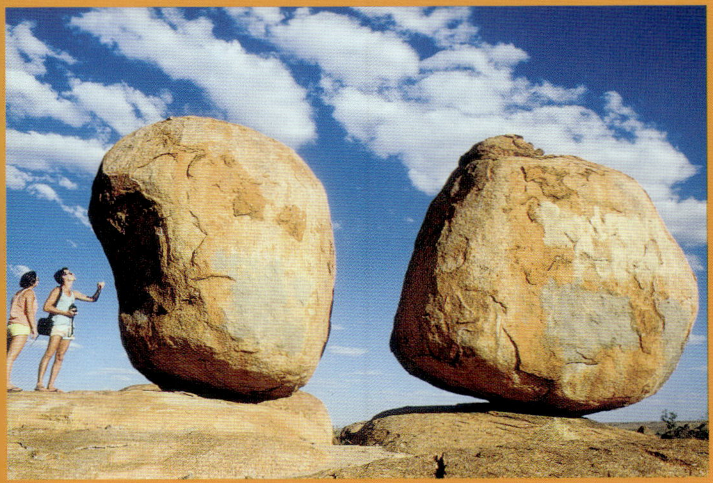

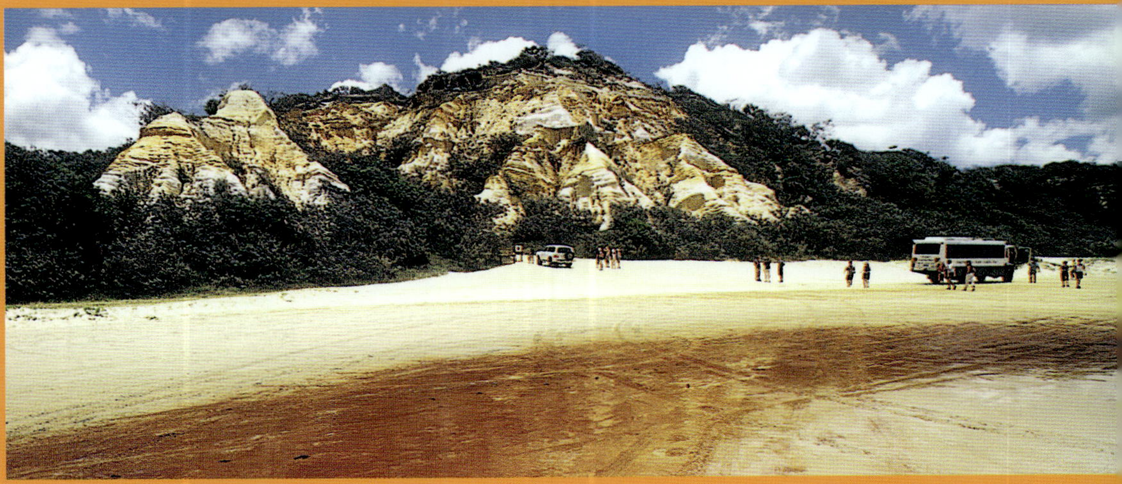

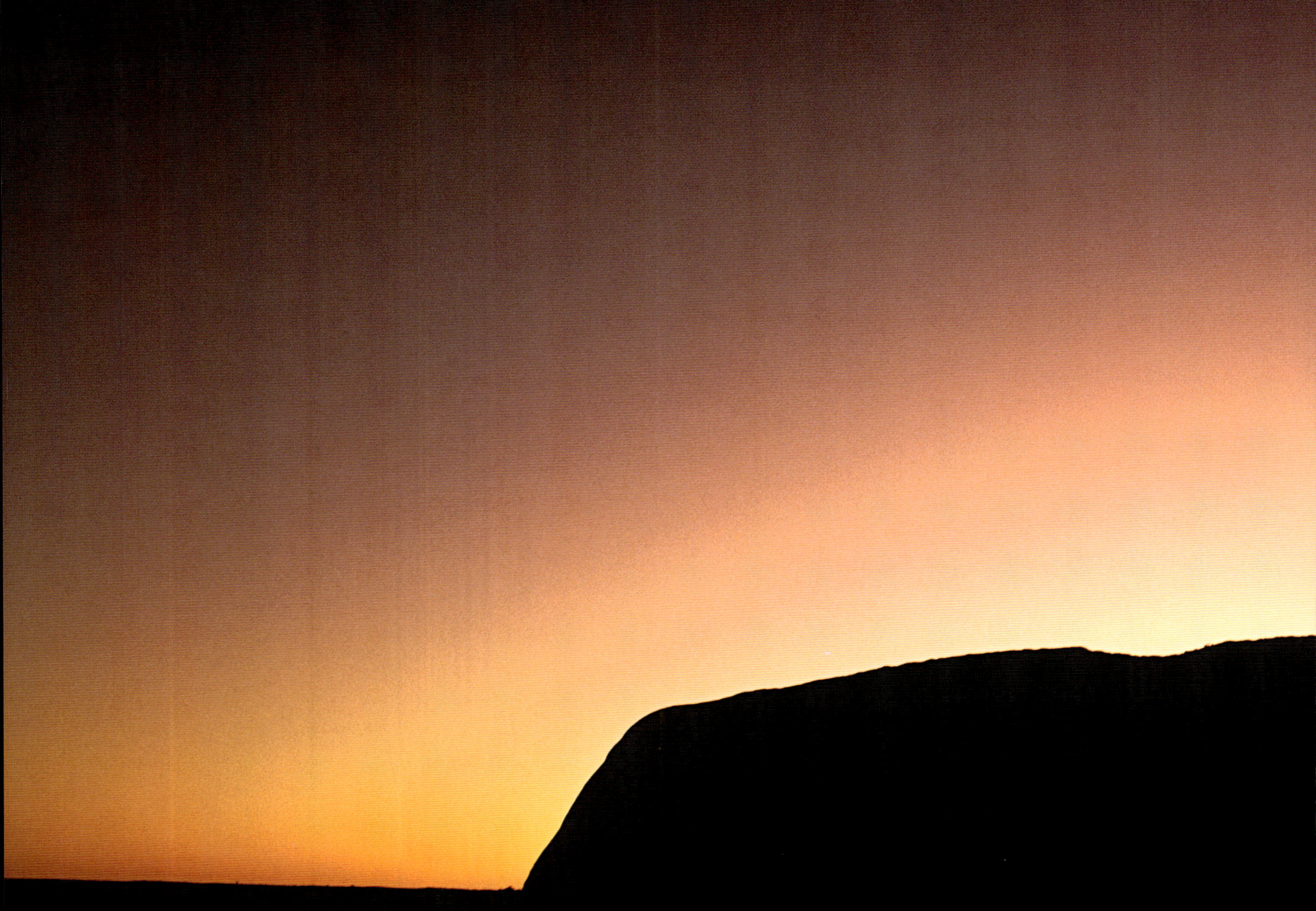

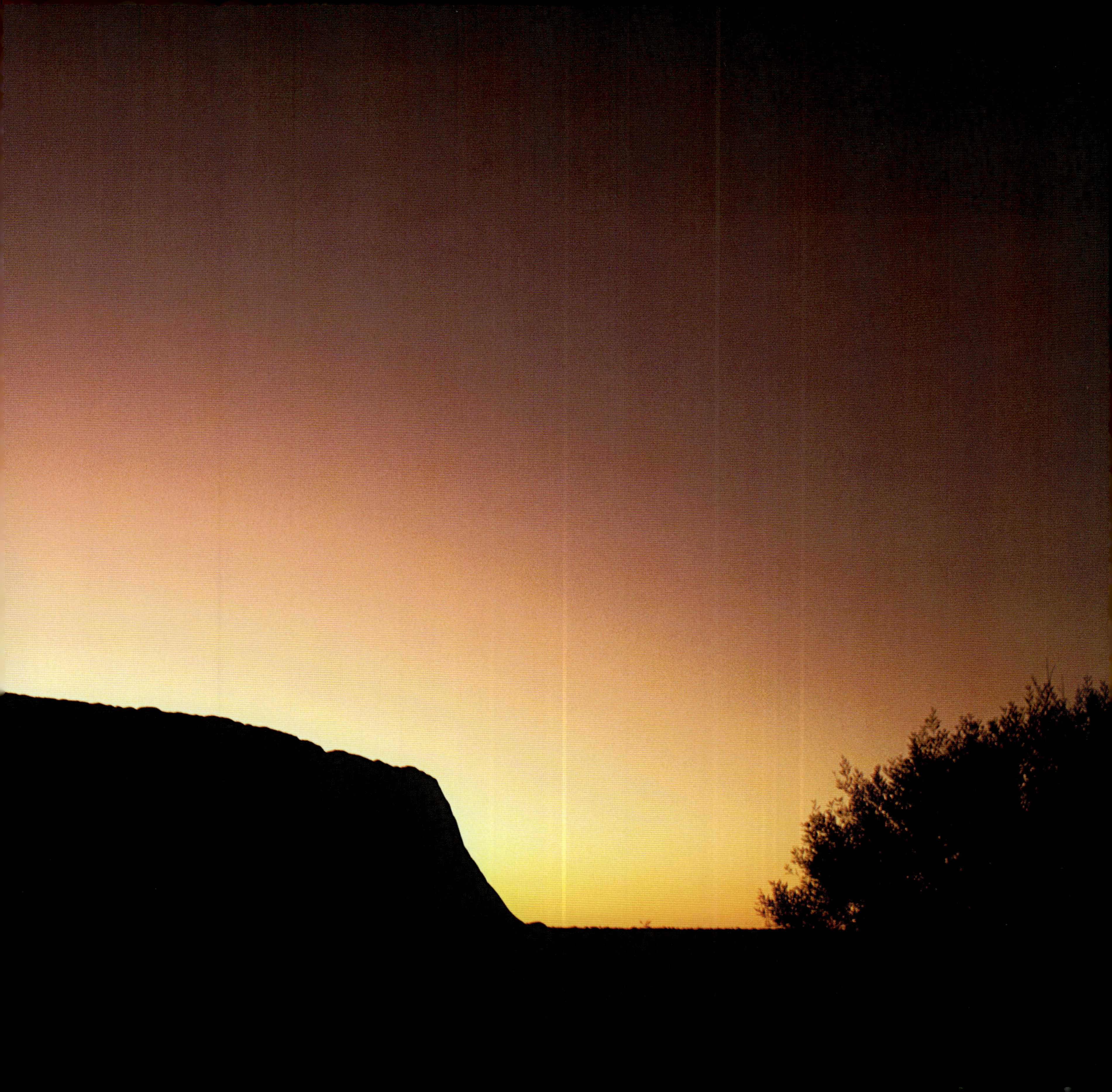

UNIQUE LANDSCAPES

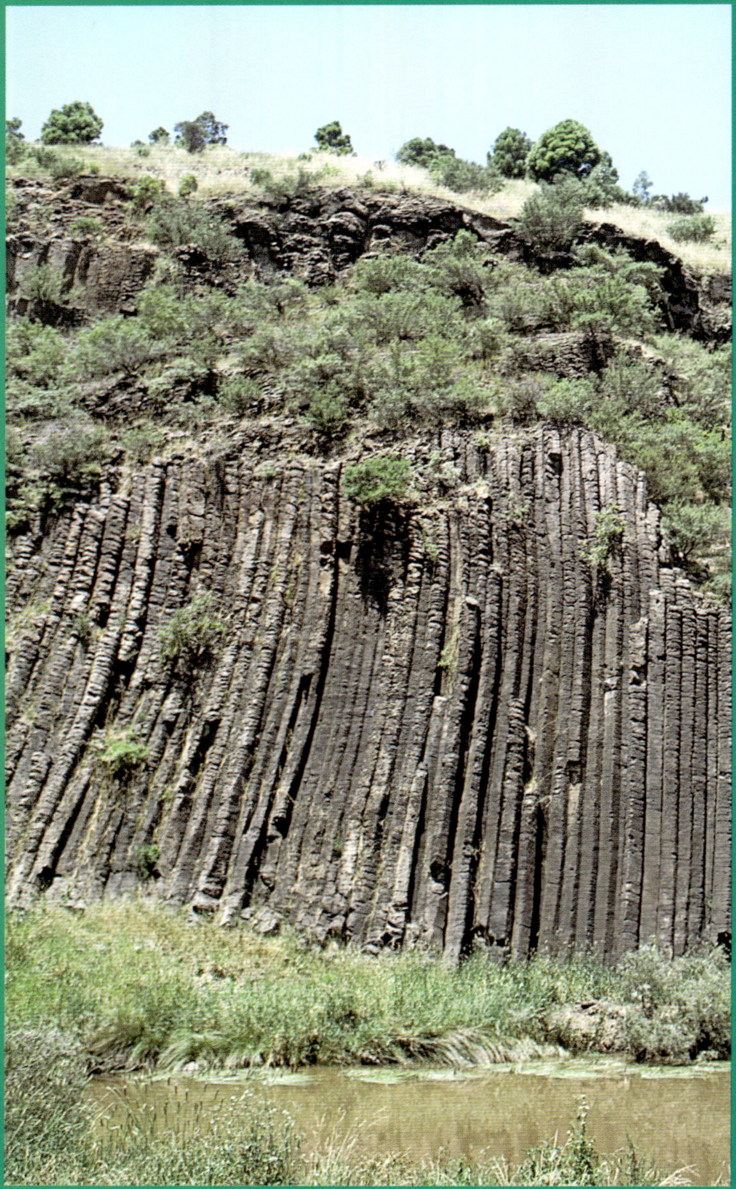

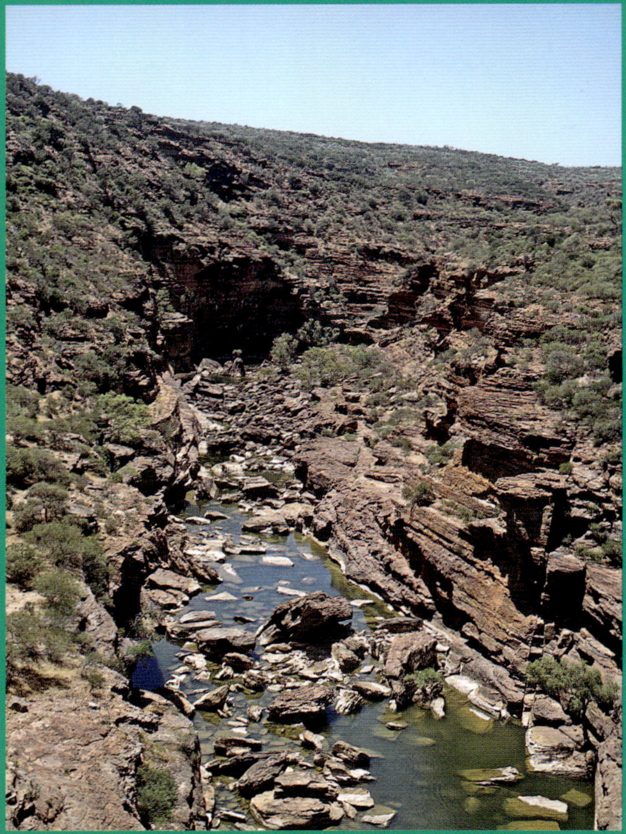

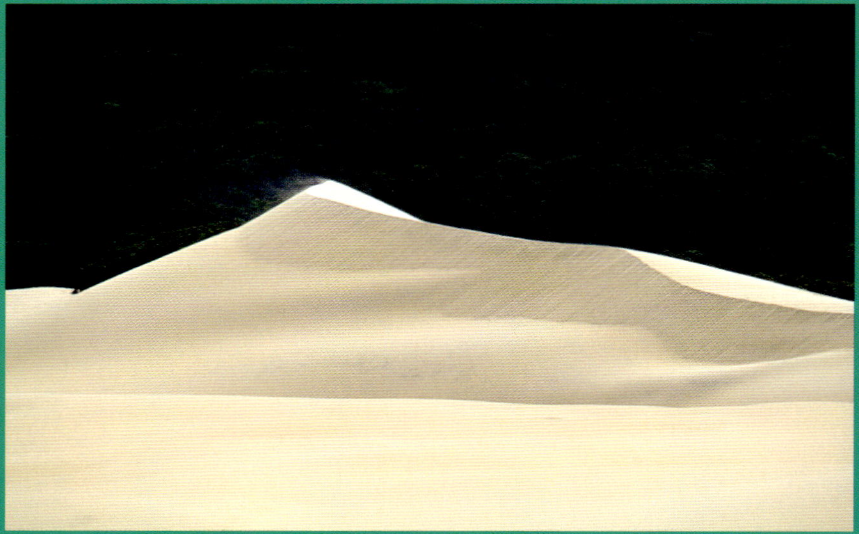

Eroded rock gives the impression of organ pipes in the Organ Pipes National Park, Melbourne, contrasting sharply with the less permanent Knife Blade Sand Dunes of Fraser Island. What makes Murchison Gorge (above, top right) so special is its sheer size; the red and white banded rocks throughout most of the river gorge were deposited as tidal flats four hundred million years ago. At Hamelin Pool, Shark Bay, the domelike rock formations or stromatolites (opposite, top left) to give them their proper name, were built by microscopic living organisms called cyanobacteria, similar to the earliest forms of life on earth. But with so much of the country uninhabited, it is commonplace to encounter limitless skies and desolate landscapes, rugged ski country, and swirling rock formations like those in Rainbow Valley, Alice Springs (far right).

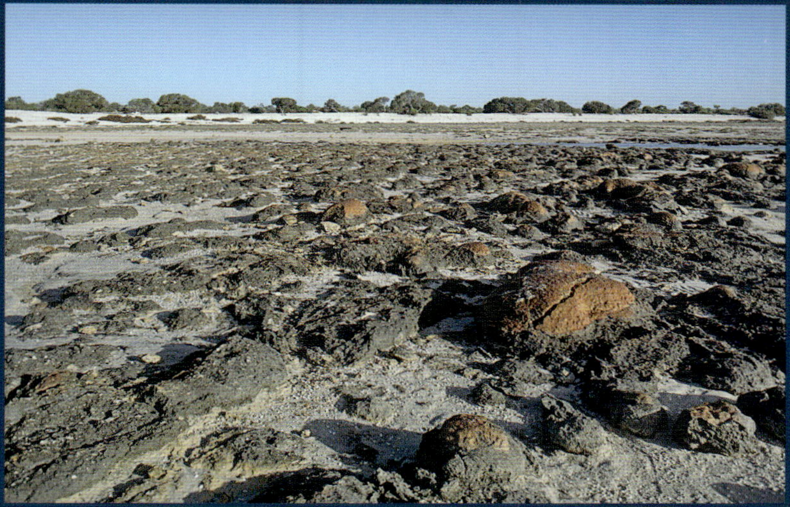
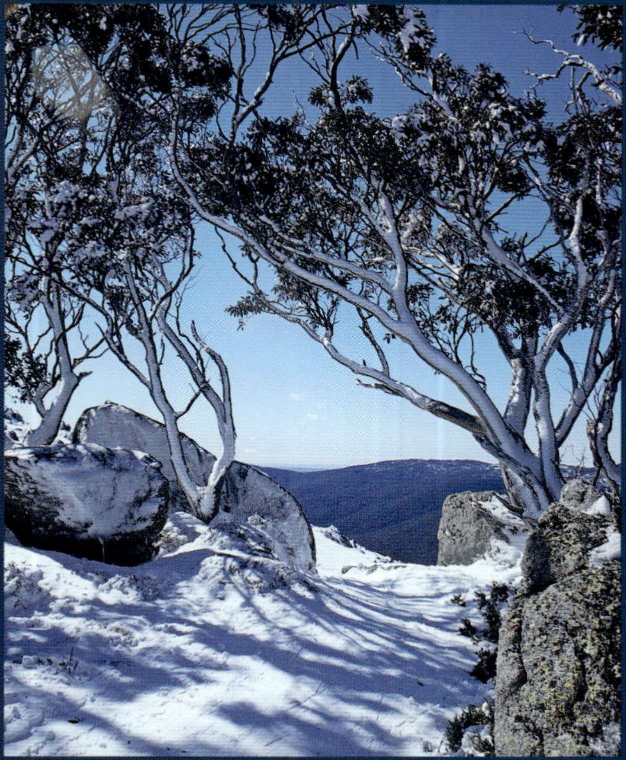
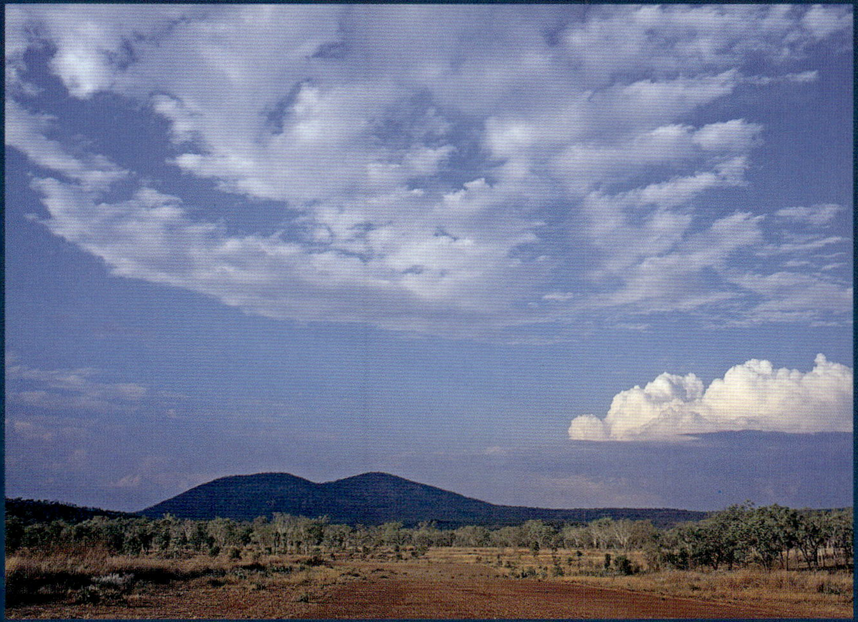
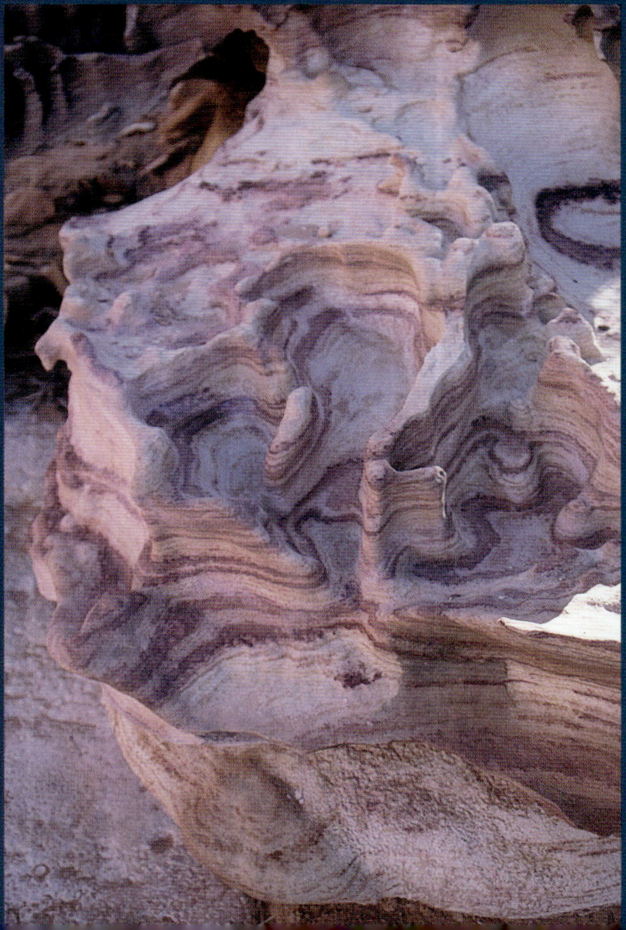

HARBOUR BRIDGE

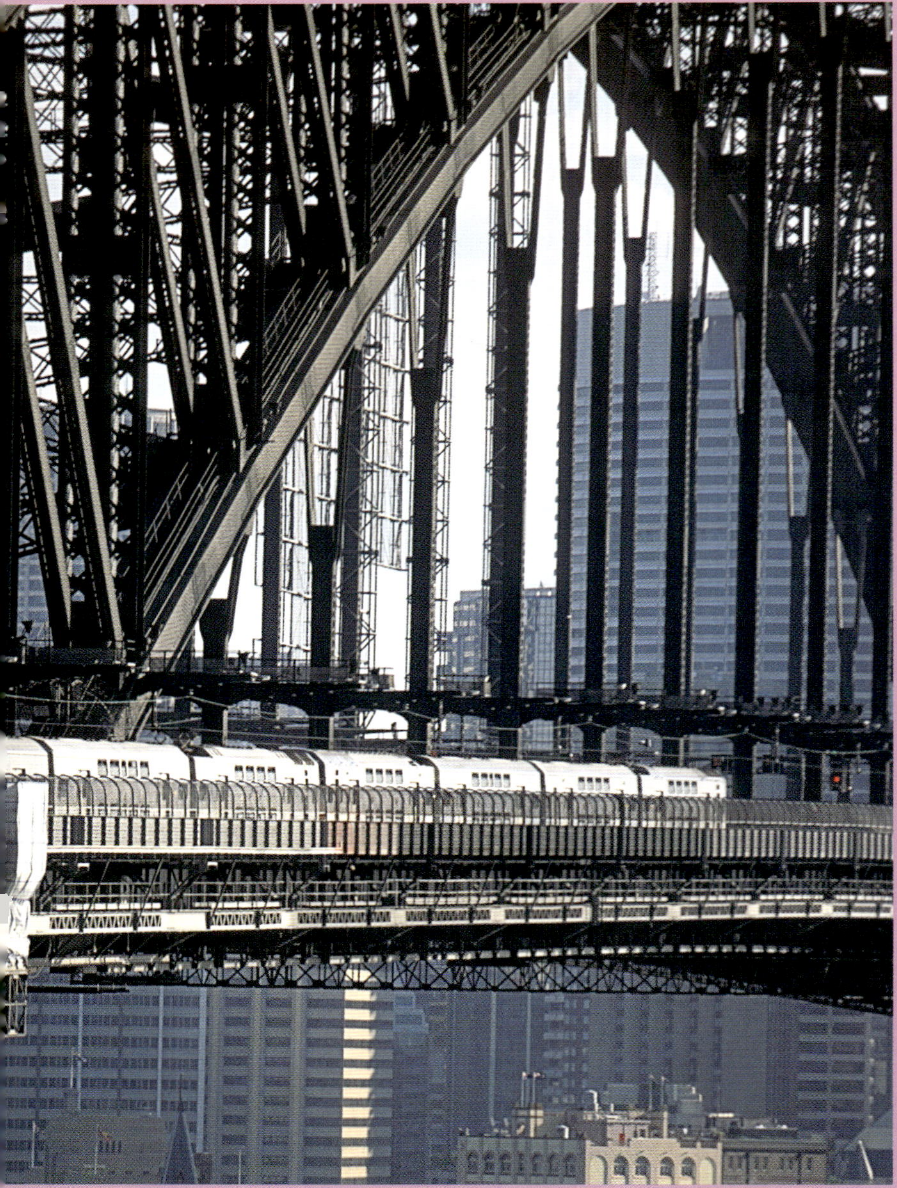

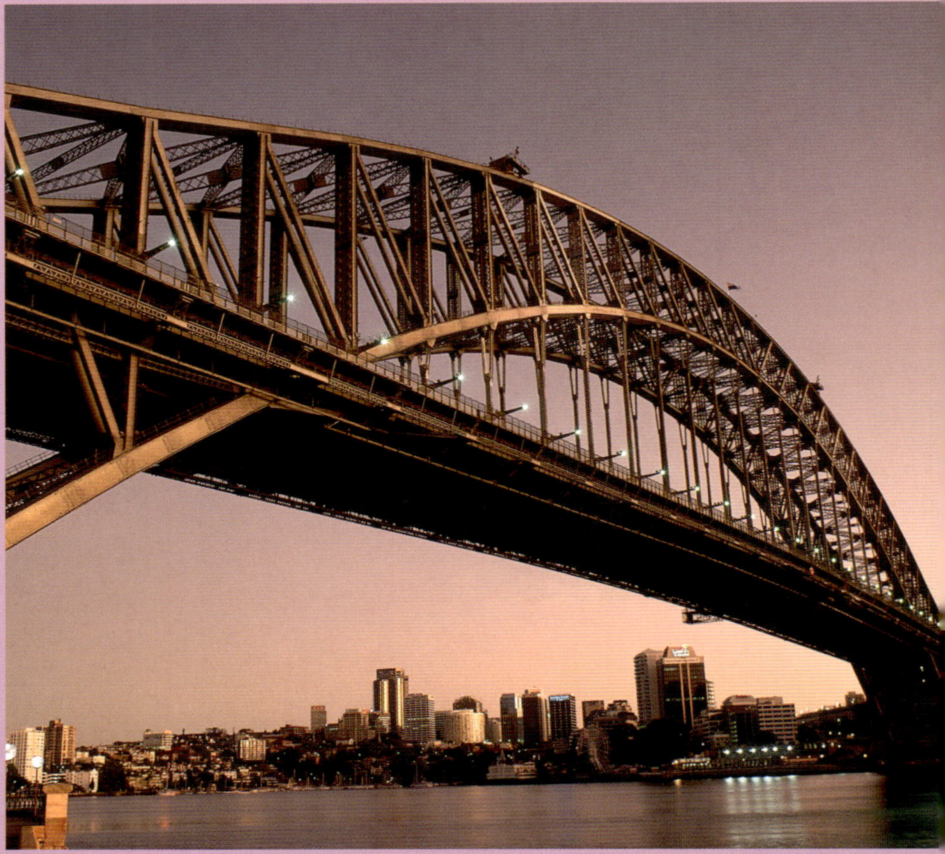

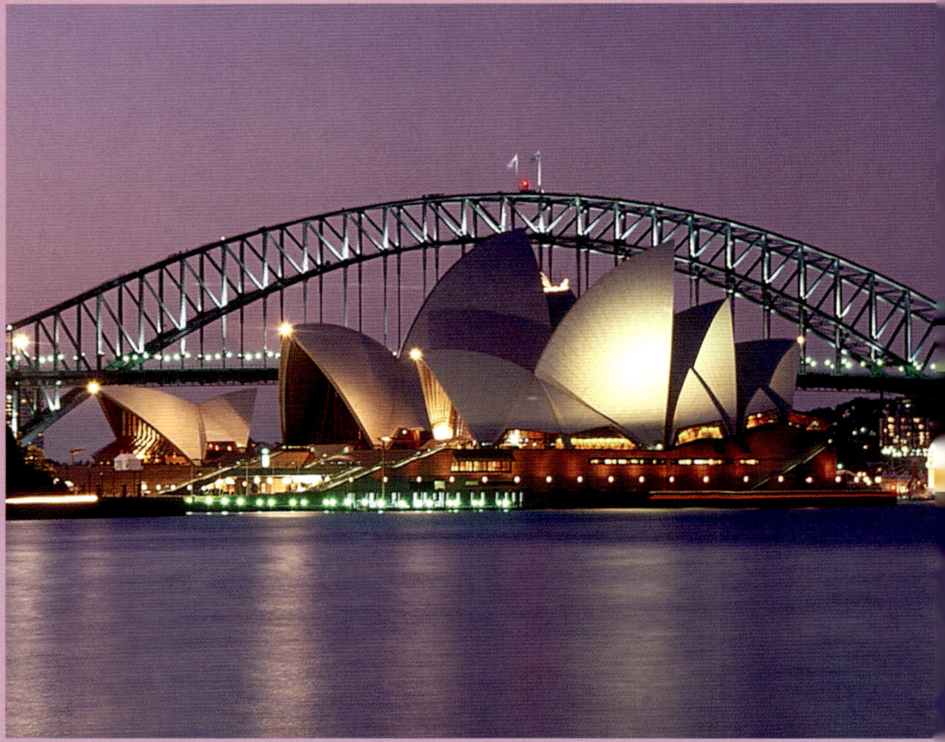

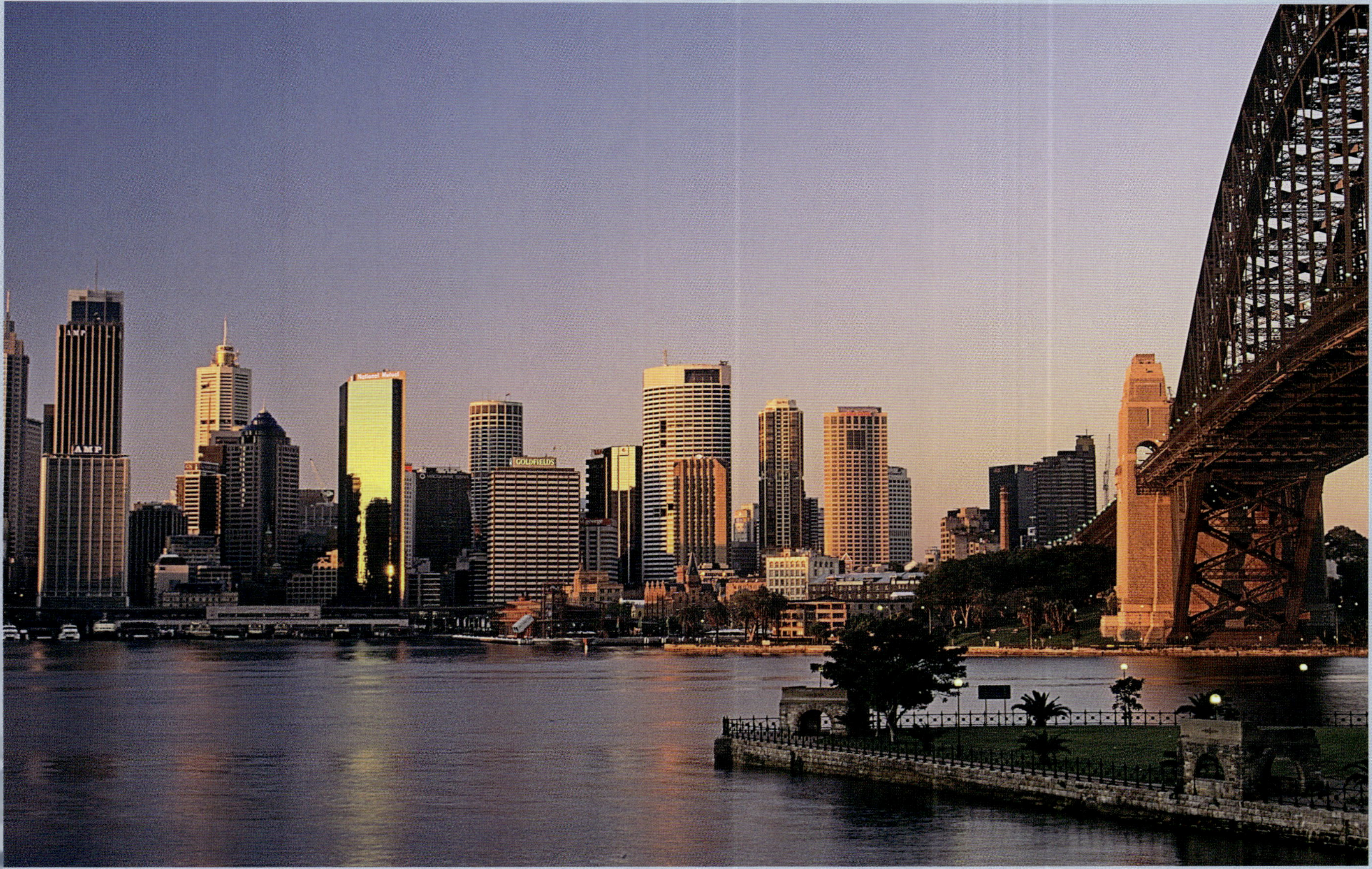

Sydney Harbour Bridge is the world's largest (but not longest) steel arch bridge and has become a world-renowned symbol of Australia, affectionately known as the "Coathanger." Construction fell to the firm of Dorman Long and Co. Ltd. of Middlesbrough in England, and began on July 28, 1923, ultimately employing approximately 1,400 people. The bridge finally opened in March 1932. When the arch was joined at 10pm on August 19, 1930, north and south Sydney were at last permanently linked. The length of the arch span is 1,650ft, and the height above sea level at the top of the arch is 440ft. The construction used around six million rivets, some weighing as much as 8lb and measuring more than 15 inches in length. The total weight of the steelwork is 58,202 US tons. By any standards this is a monumental construction, and today you can take an organized tour across the very top of the bridge.

COASTAL WATERS

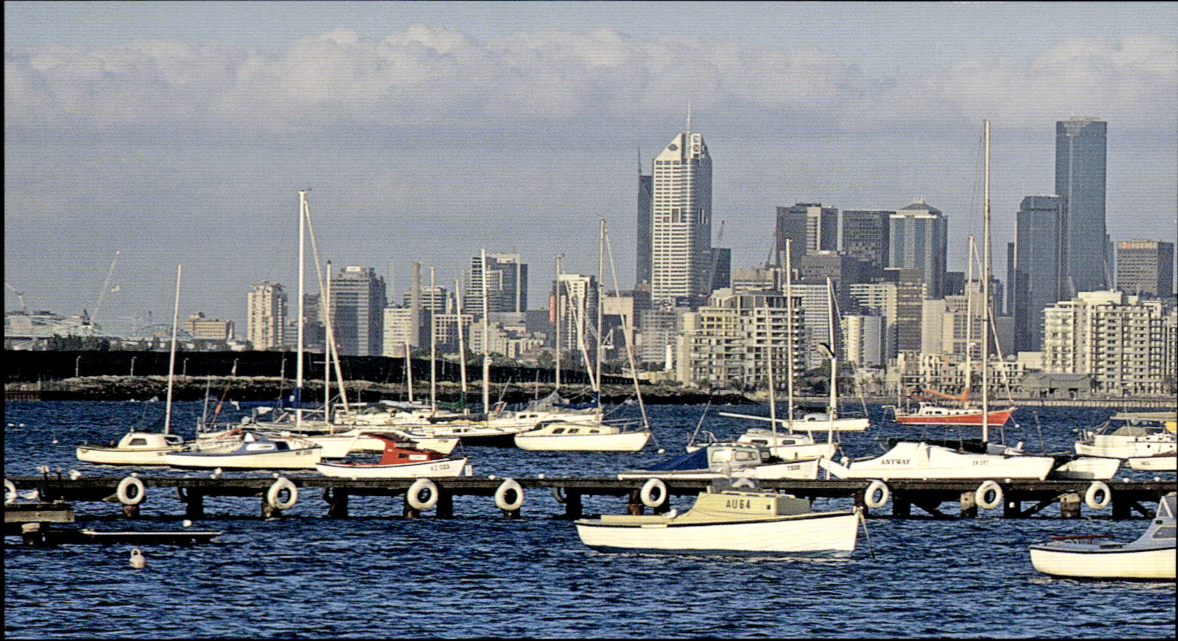

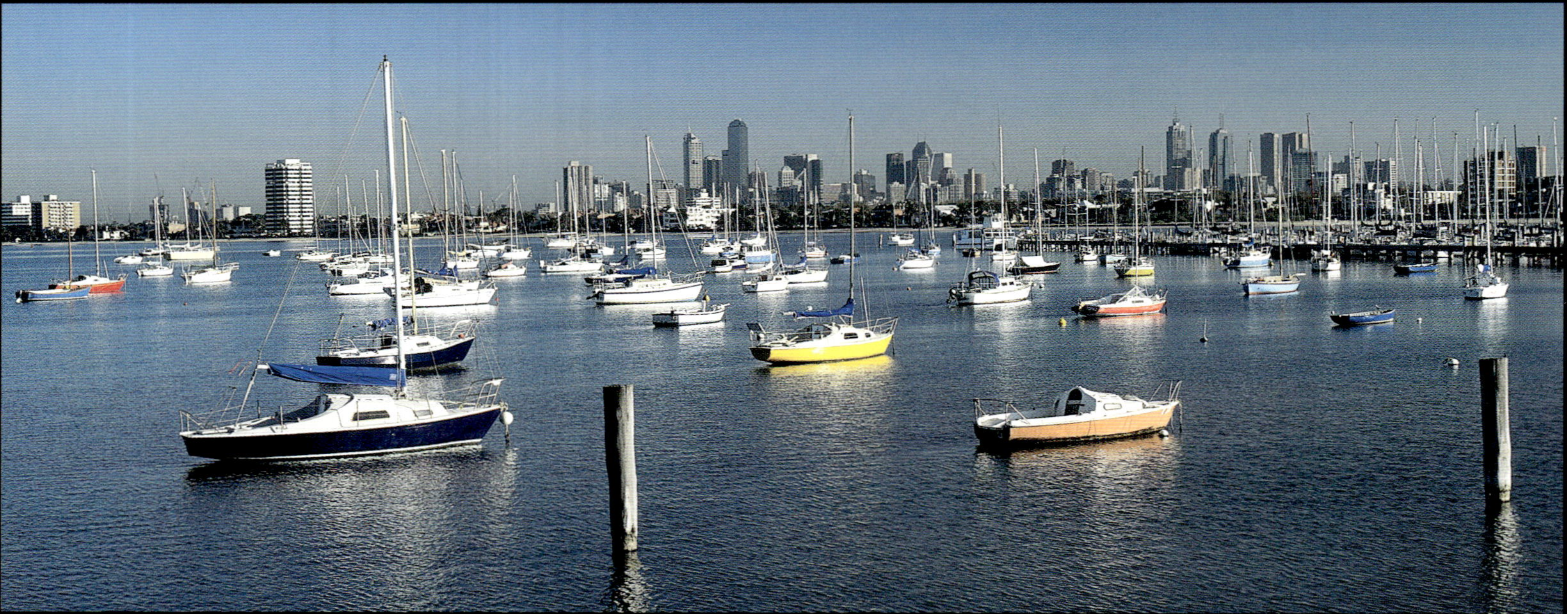

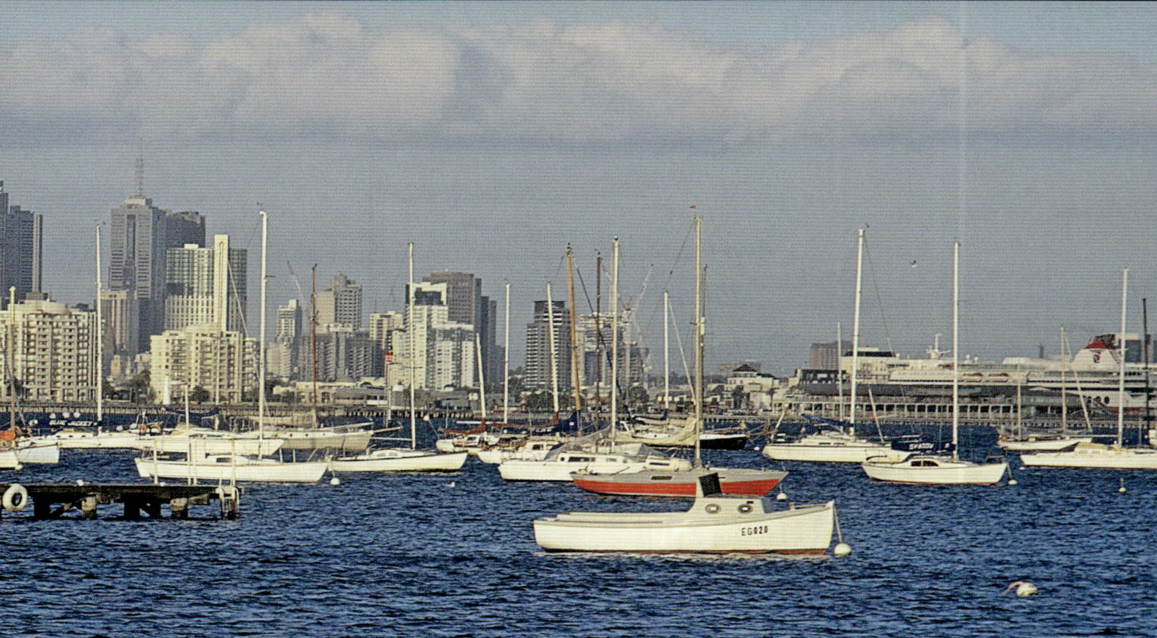

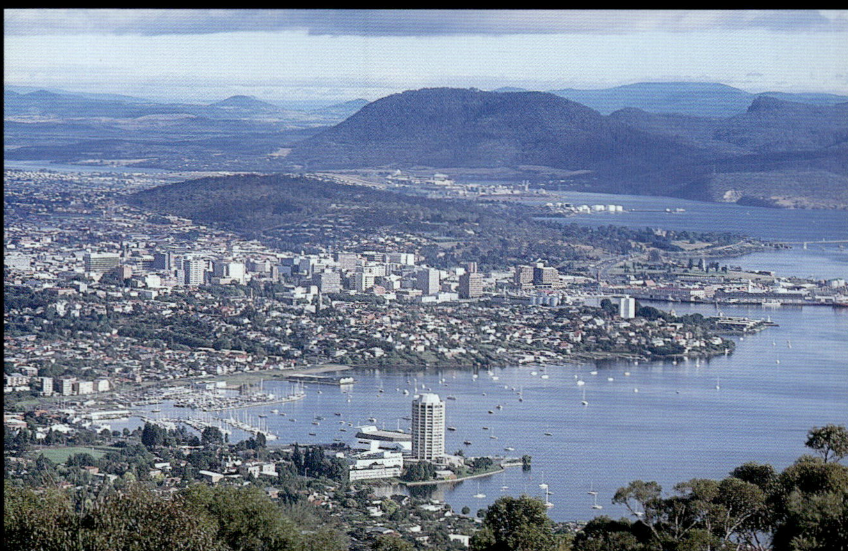

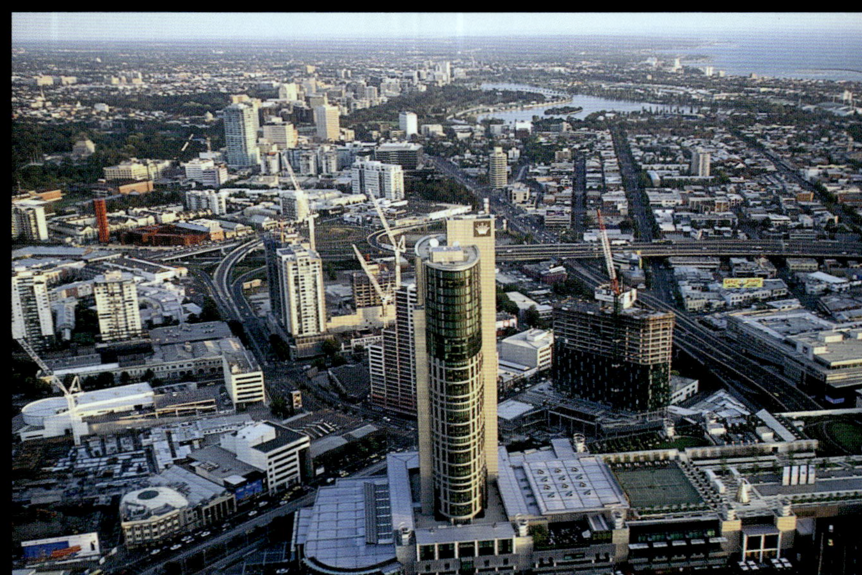

Above: Hobart, the capital of Tasmania.
Right: Looking towards Bayside in Melbourne.
Next pages: Cape Wollamai, Melbourne (top left), the Red Canyon, Fraser Island (top center), the Twelve Apostles, Victoria (bottom left), and eroded coast near Kalbarri, Western Australia (far right).

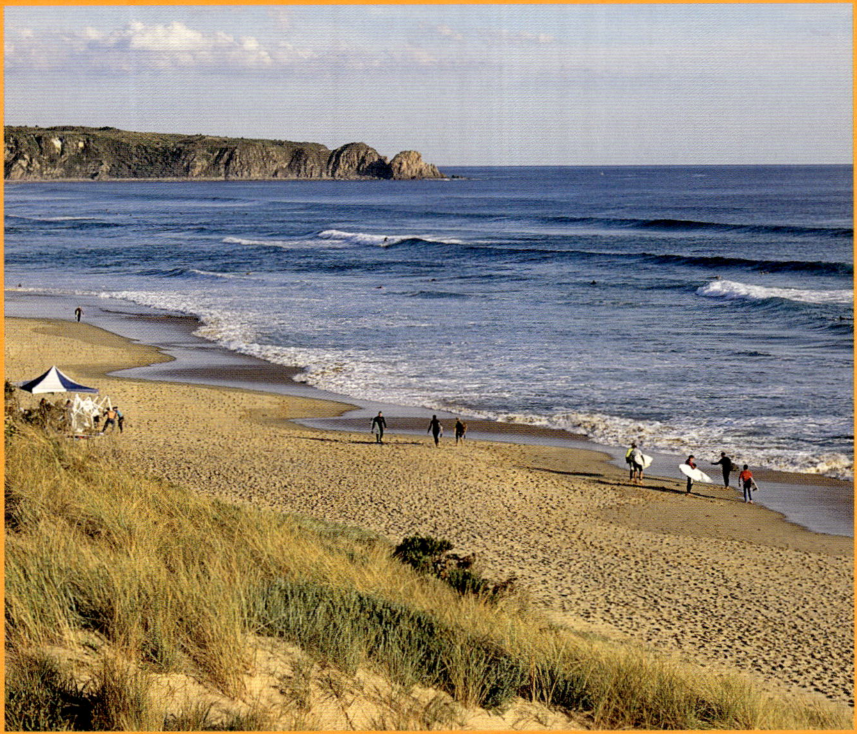

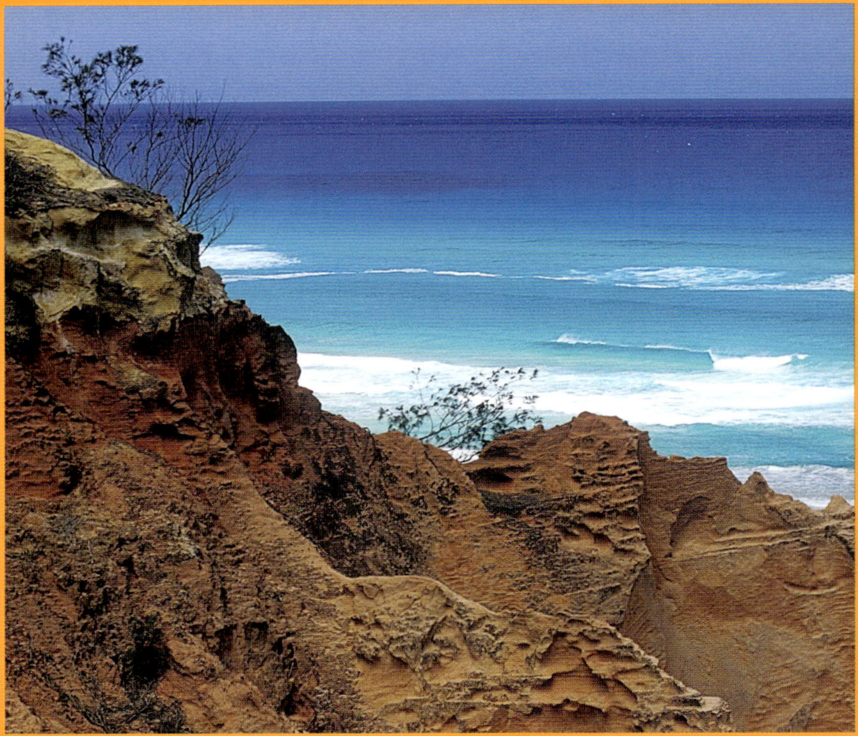

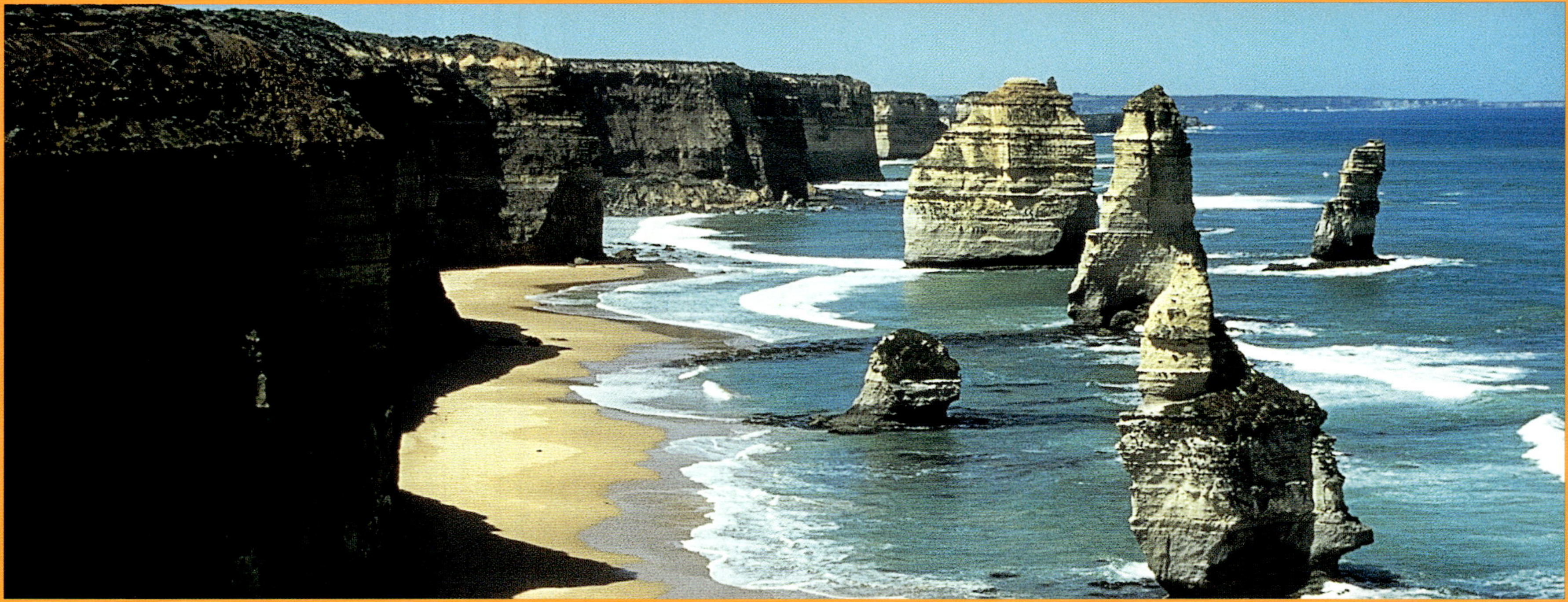

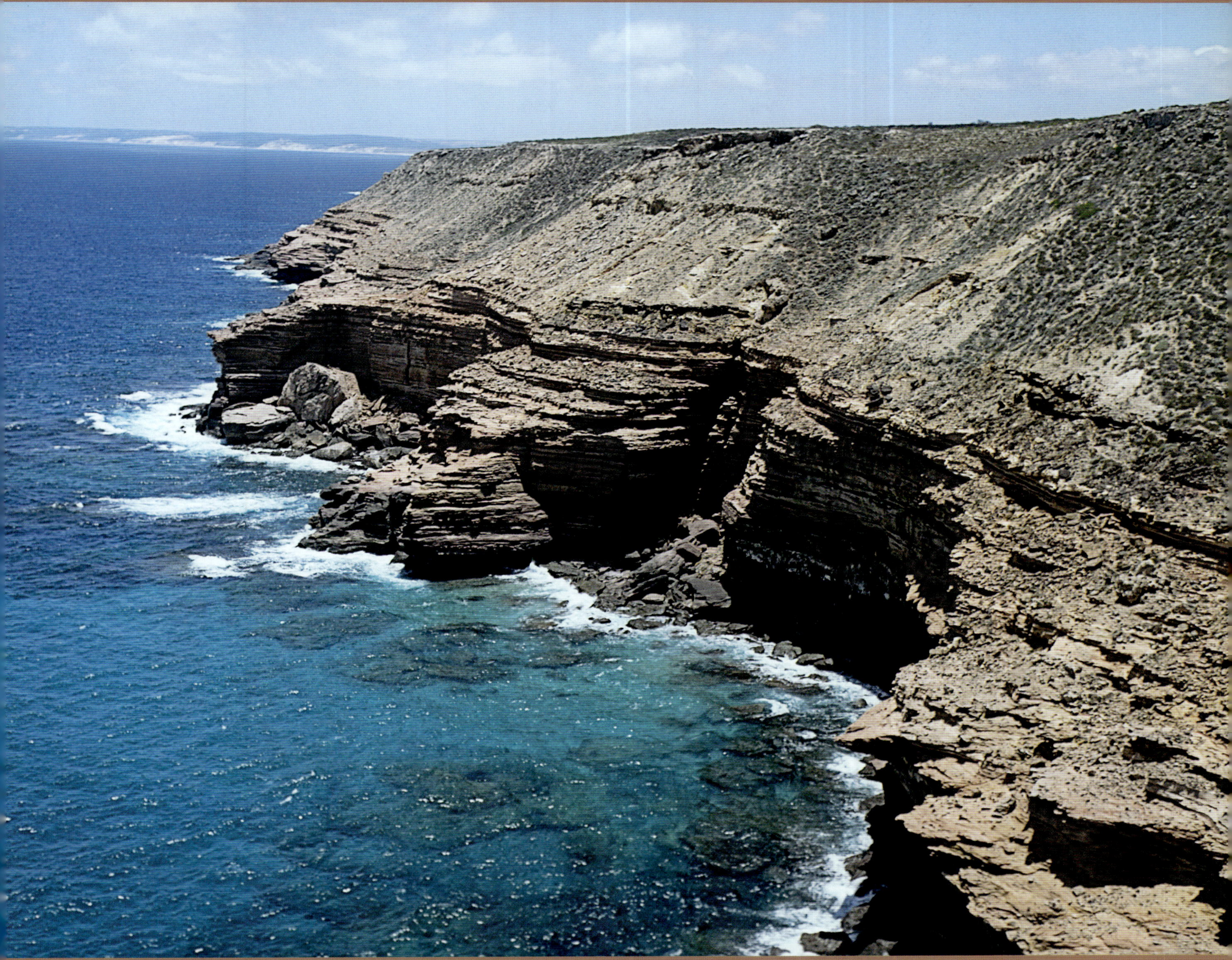

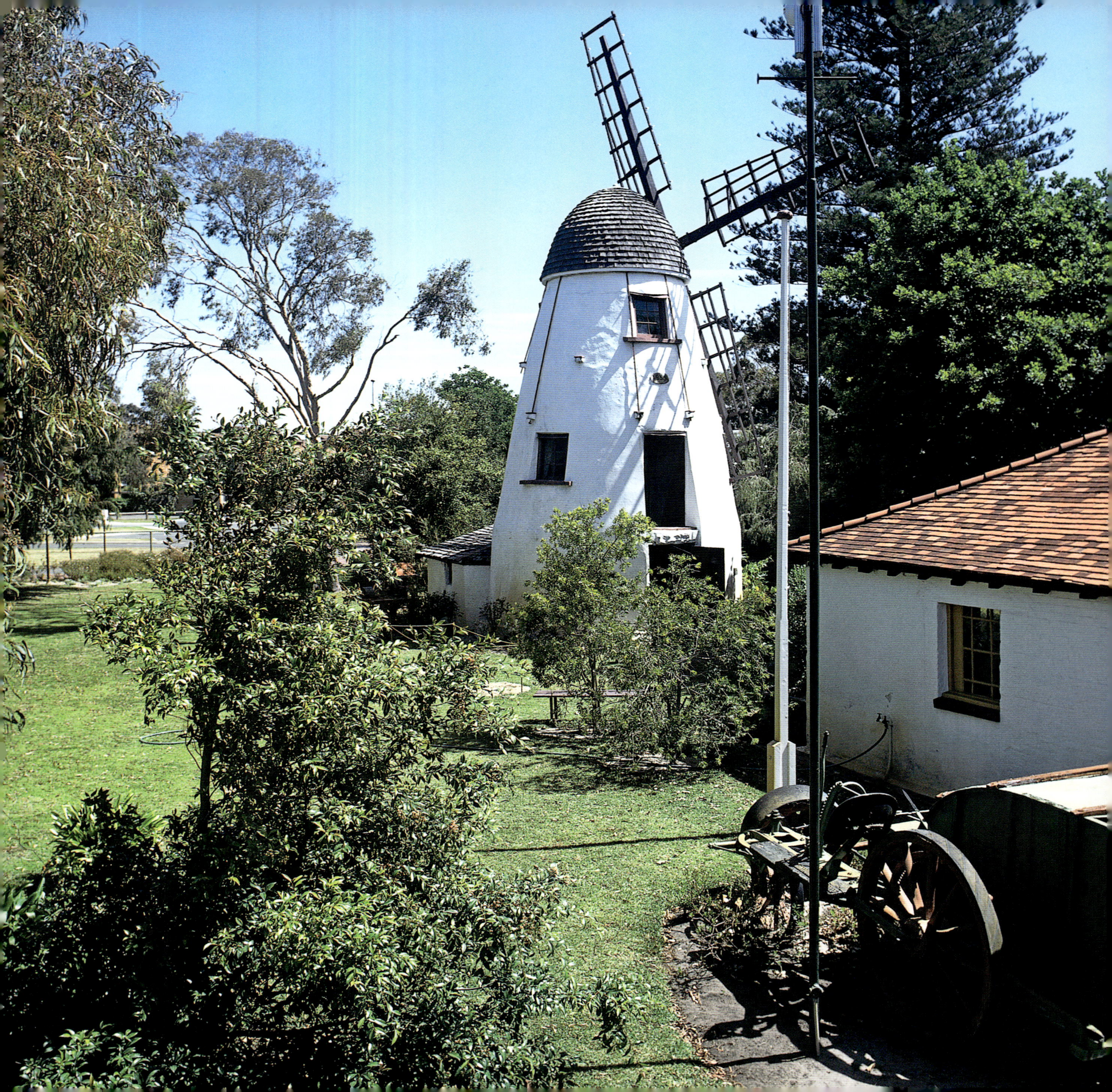

EARLY DAYS

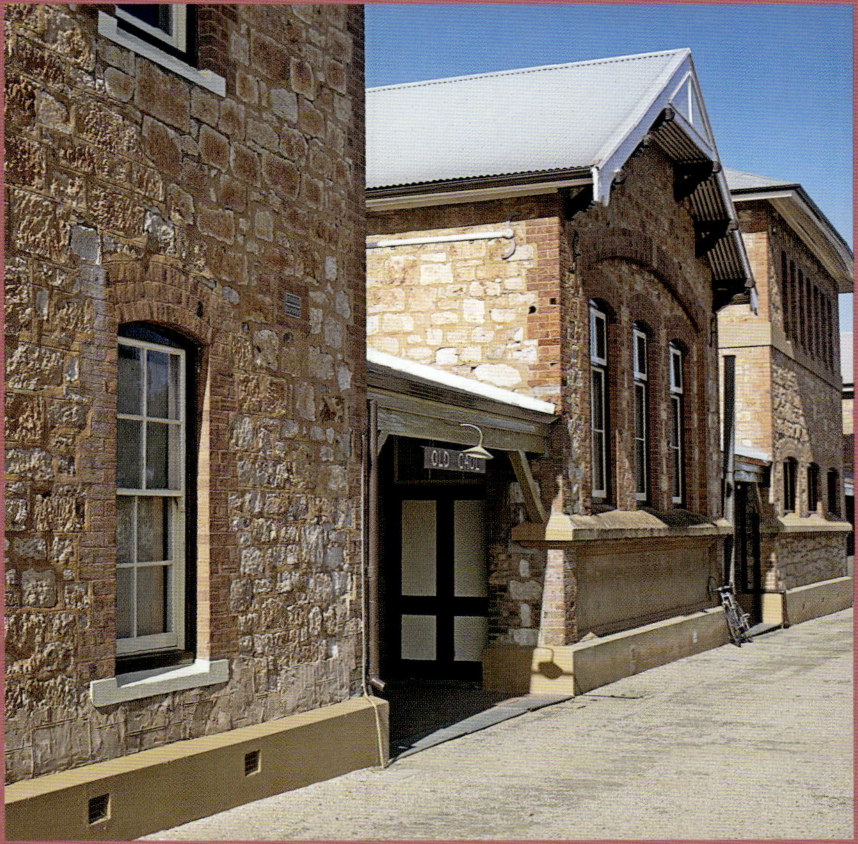

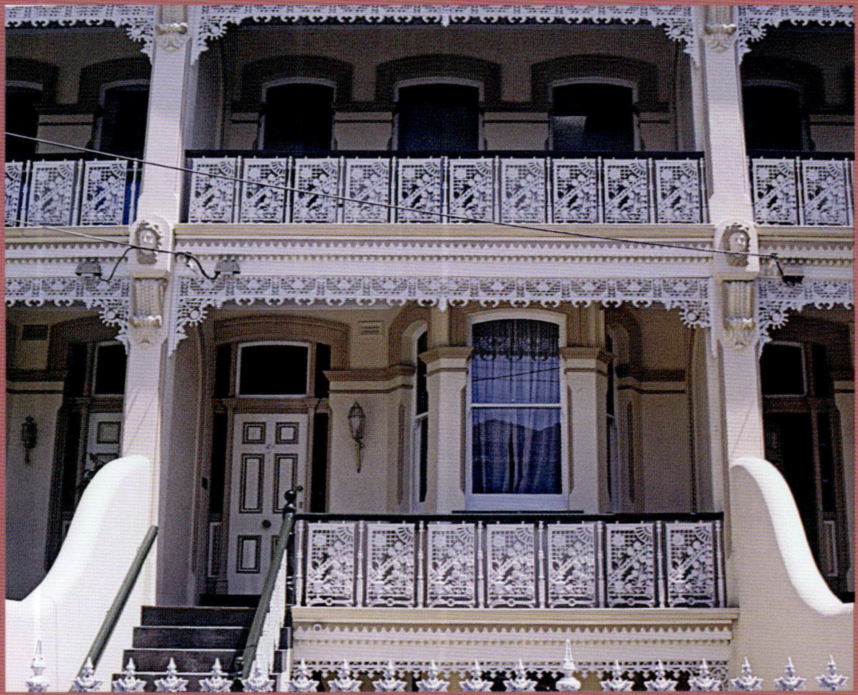

"Old" is a relative term when applied to Australia. The continent is certainly old, but "The Early Days" of civilized society are almost within living memory. This old flour mill (left) on Mill Point on the south side of Narrows Bridge, Perth, was built in 1835, by a miller named Shenton, and is one of the oldest buildings in Australia. Terraced houses in suburban Melbourne display decorative frontages of Melbourne "lace" (cast-iron work), typical of the nineteenth century. The Old Gaol at Coolgardie, in Western Australia, owes its existence to the discovery of gold at nearby Fly Flat in September 1892. During the seventy years of its existence this mining claim recovered more than 500,000 ounces of the precious yellow metal. Before the gaol was built prisoners were simply chained to a tree to await trial.

UNDERGROUND

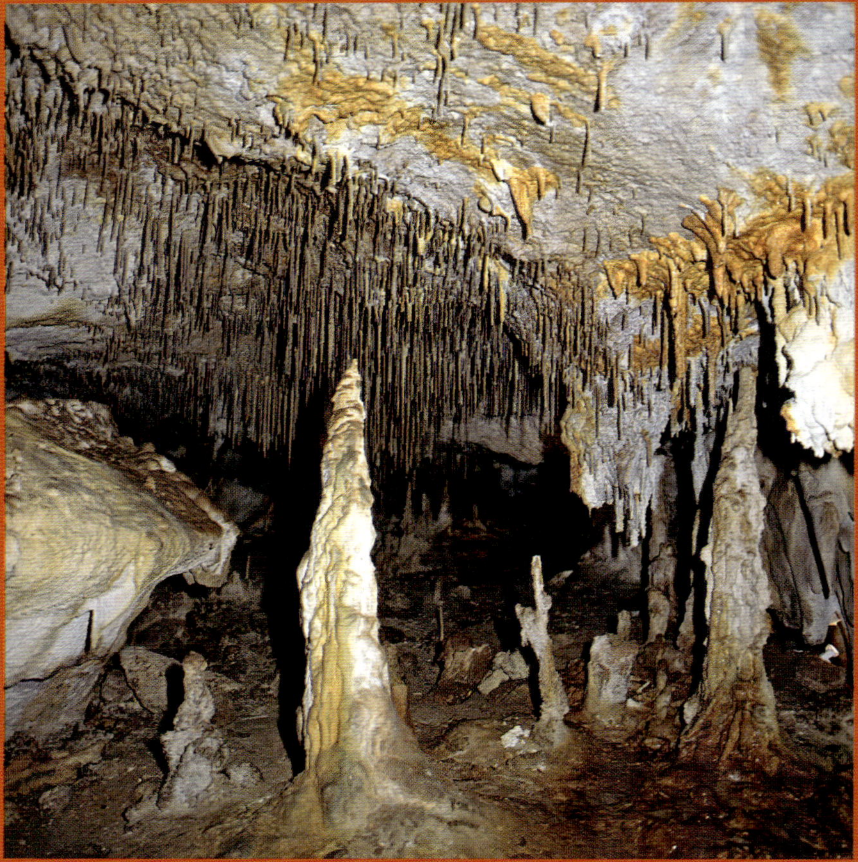

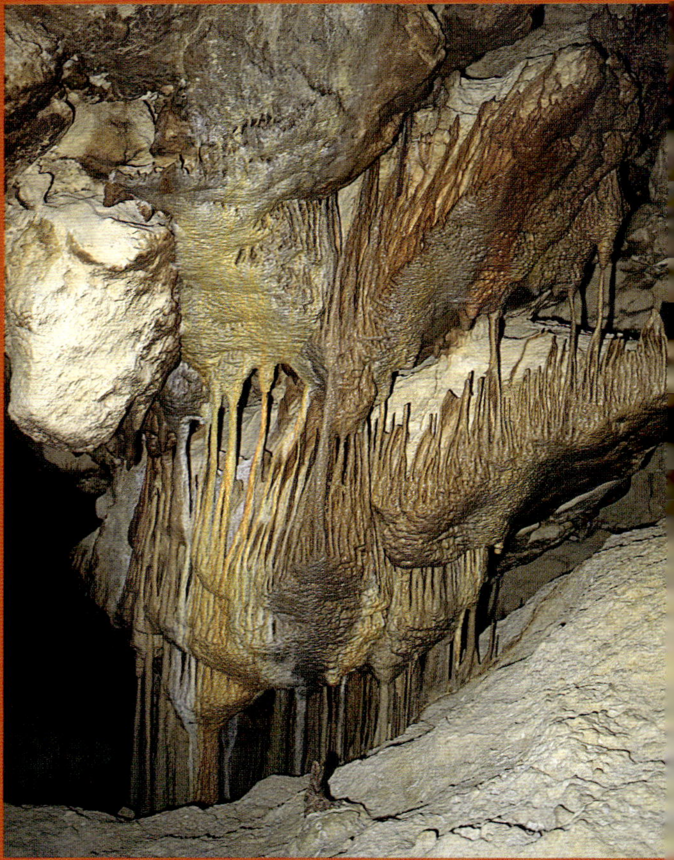

Naracoorte, famed for its world-class limestone caves (above), is located on the Keith to Mount Gambier Road, southeast of Adelaide. Equally impressive are the extensive cave systems of Margaret River in Western Australia (opposite). For well over a century travelers have come to witness the vast tunnels, fossil remains, and brilliant crystaline formations found the length and breadth of the Leeuwin-Naturaliste Ridge.

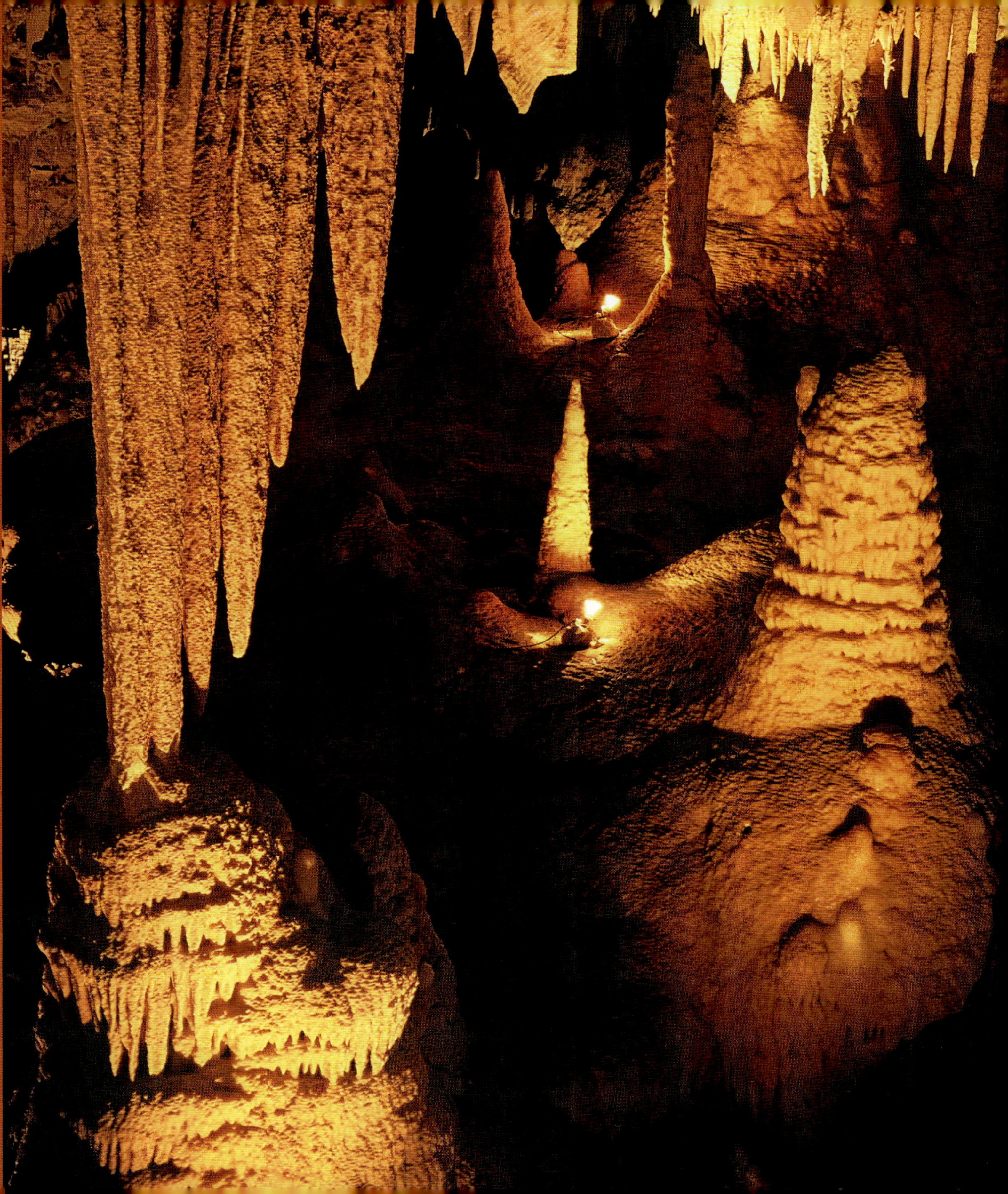

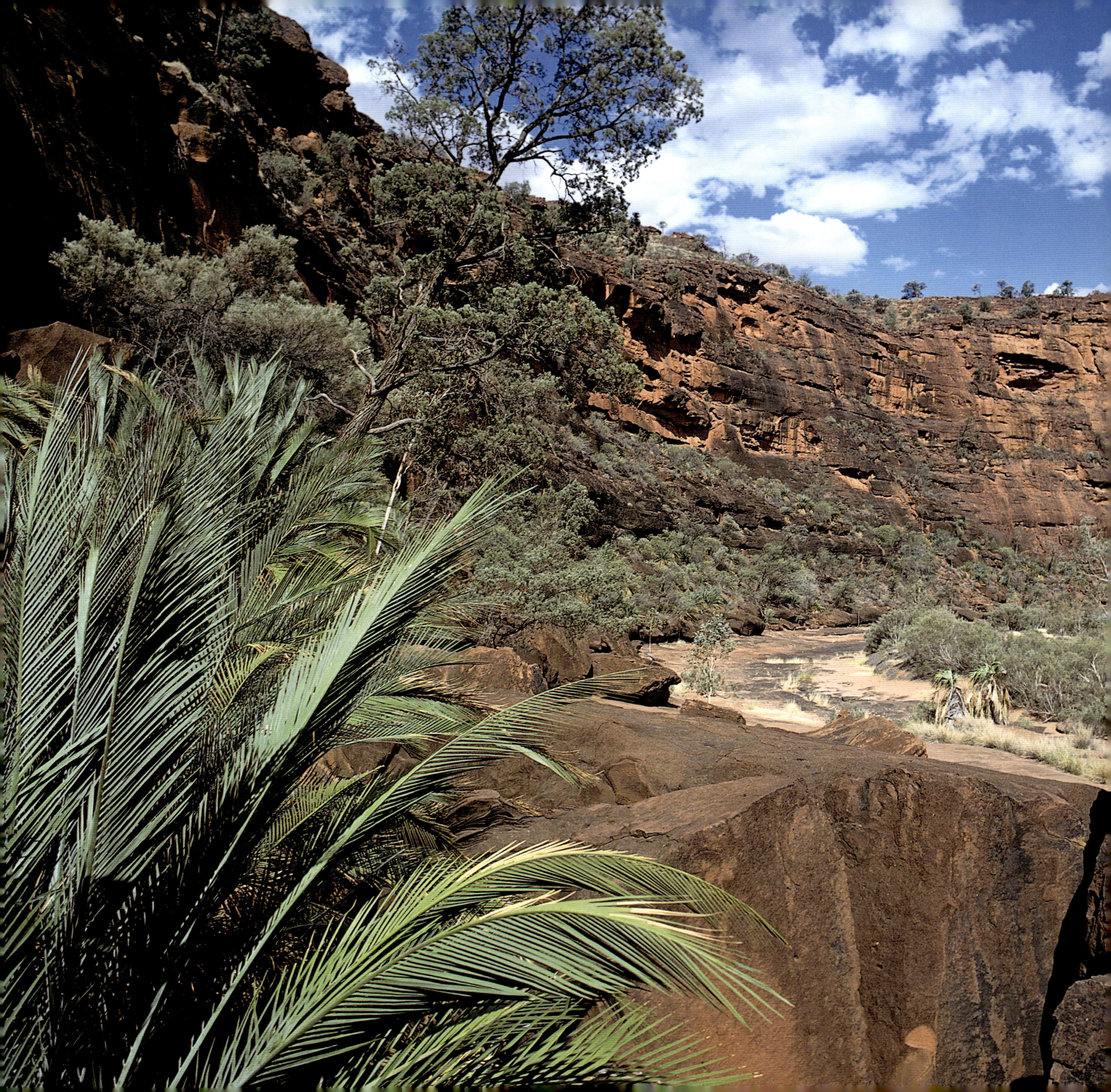

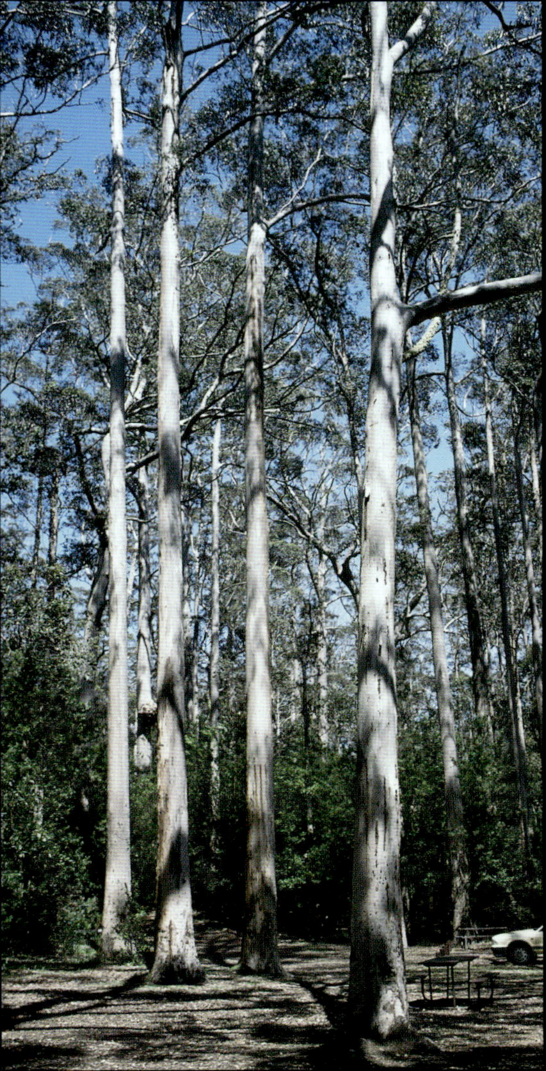

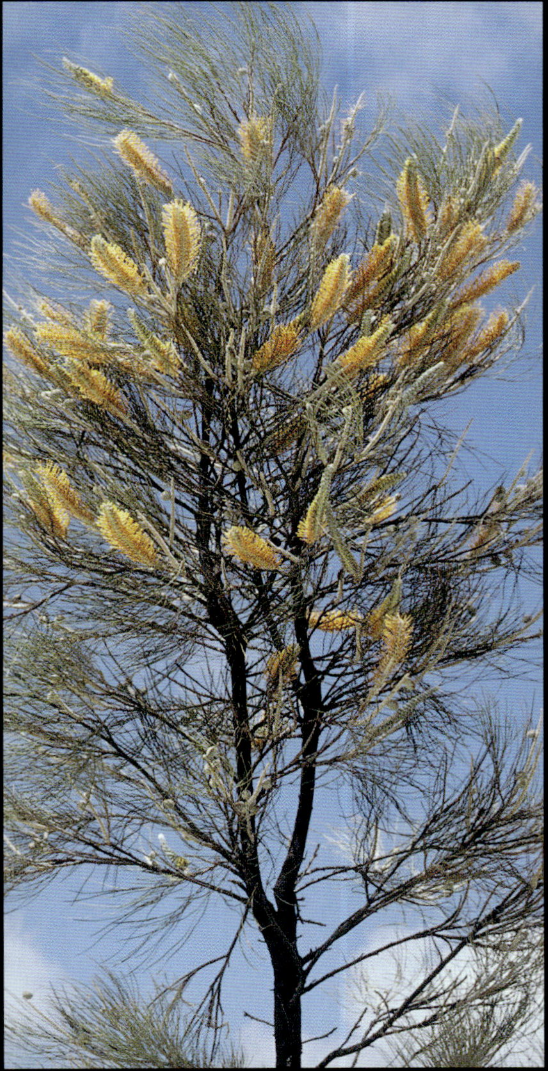

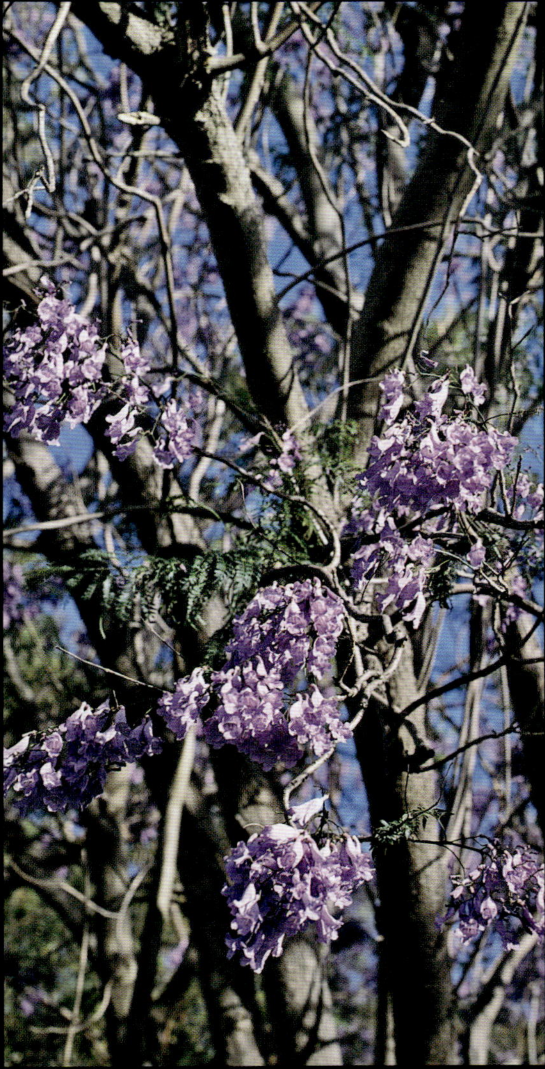

Flame tree, ghost gum, grass tree, Cootamundra wattle—the list of Australian trees is long, and probably still growing. There are more than six hundred species of gum tree alone. Cycads (opposite) are a group of very primitive plants that look like palms. They are "living fossils," a group of plants that reached its highest point of evolution in the Mesozoic Period (about two hundred million years ago), yet remains abundant today. Australian trees and shrubs are naturally tough. They do well in harsh, dry, salty conditions, and in poor soils—they have no choice.

ART, CULTUR & STYL

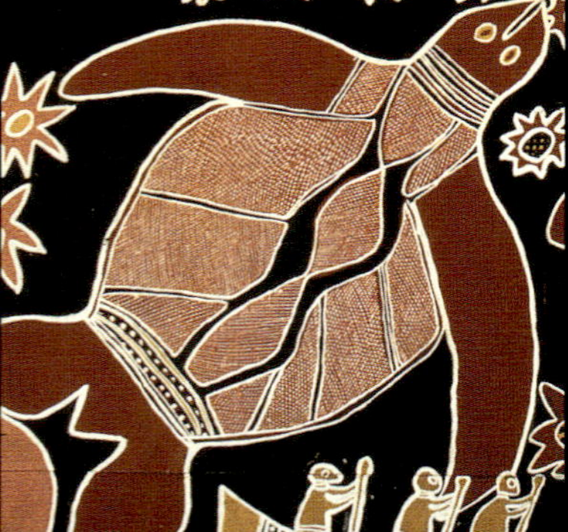

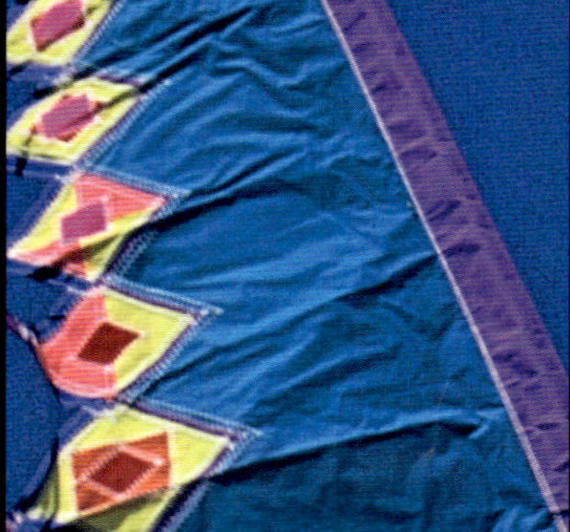

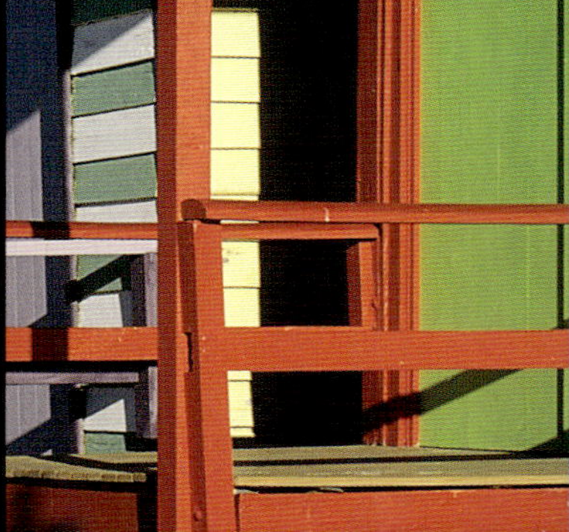

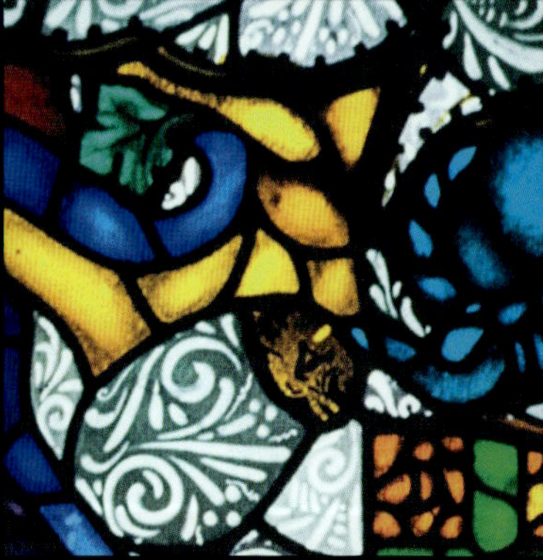

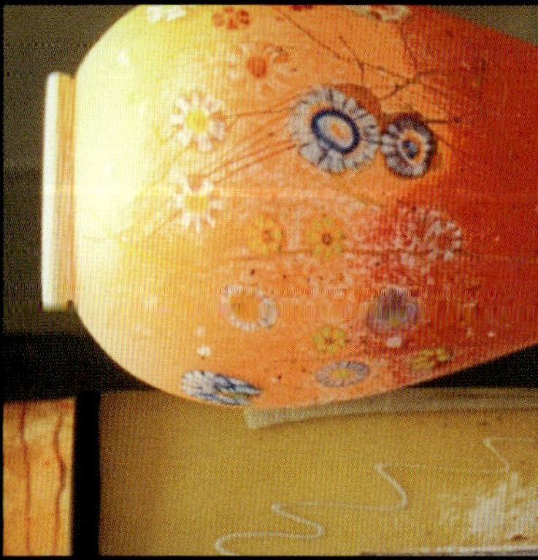

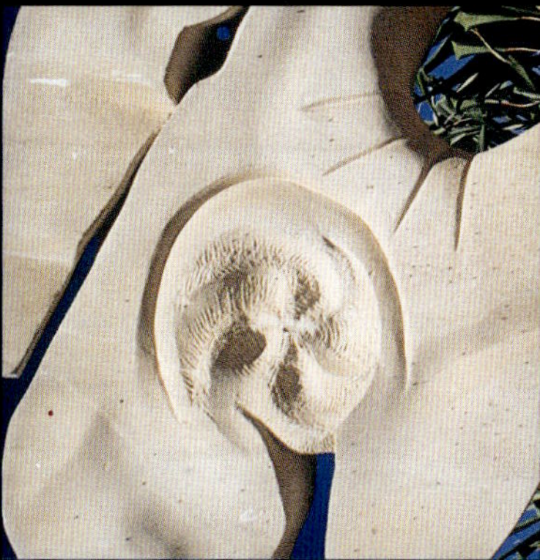

ABORIGINAL ART ROCKS

Dating back more than fifty thousand years, Australian aboriginal paintings are the world's oldest form of art. They are also the most complex, a synergy of ideas that weaves history, mythology, and the geography of the land into one whole. Founded on such a pedigree, it is not surprising that contemporary Australian artists, free from the influence of European traditionalists, sought and developed their own styles. Sidney Nolan, one of the country's finest artists, commented: "I wanted to paint the great purity and implacability of the landscape. I wanted a visual form of the 'otherness,' of the thing not seen." His art was "a confused mix of landscape, animals, and Aboriginal culture, with a kind of Bible overtone."

This pursuit of identity hallmarks the culture of Australia, its style, its uniqueness; it is an underlying thread binding a new nation. Whatever it is, wherever it comes from, it will be adopted and adapted and made Australian. And it will be done with pride.

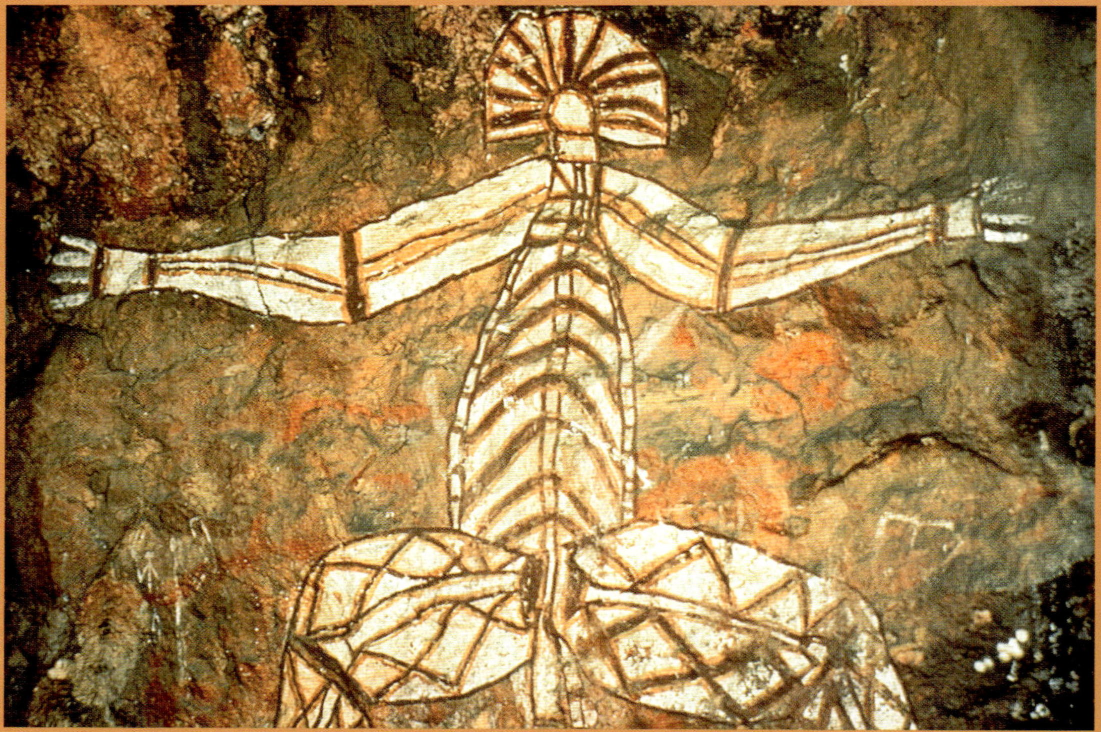

Aboriginal rock art is five times older than the Egyptian pyramids. It is art with a purpose; it is about story telling, myths, rituals, and magic, where the artist describes their Dreaming, the story of creation, their beliefs, and their spirituality. The basis for this art is the strong relationship between the ancestral beings of the "time before time," the Dreamtime, with the landscape and every living creature. Some Aboriginal engravings and paintings are so old that it is impossible to know who made them, why they were made, or what their true meaning might be.

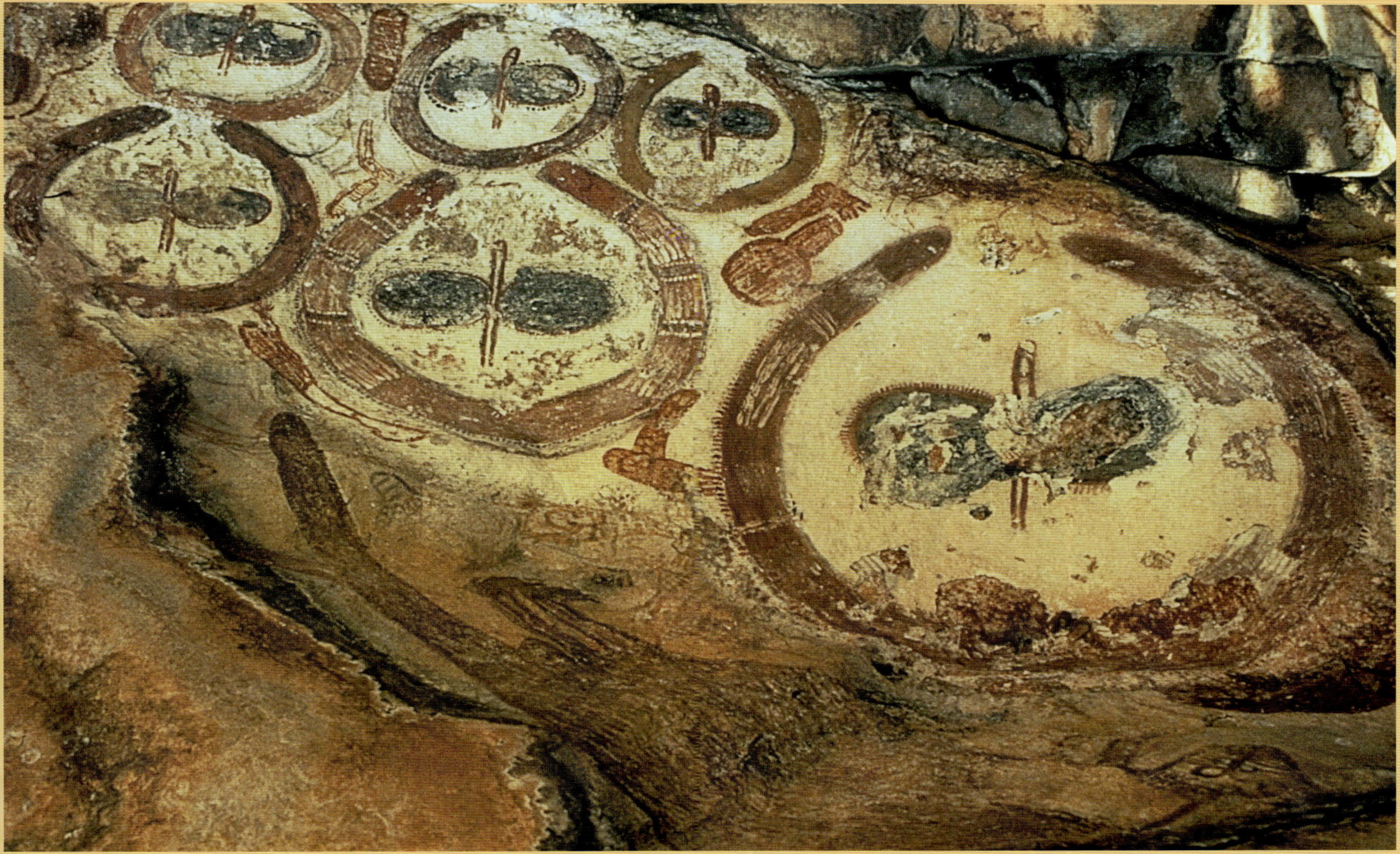

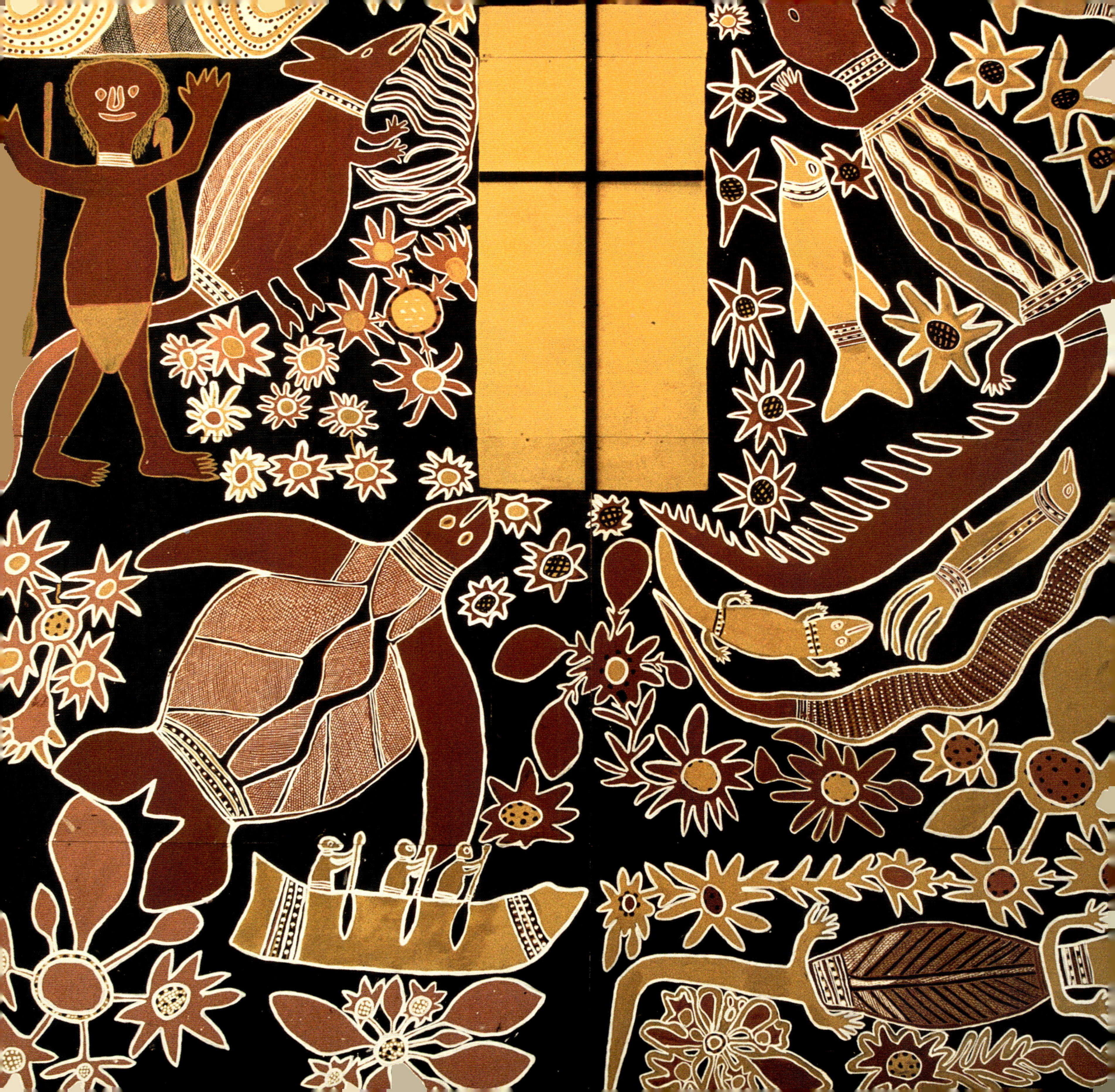

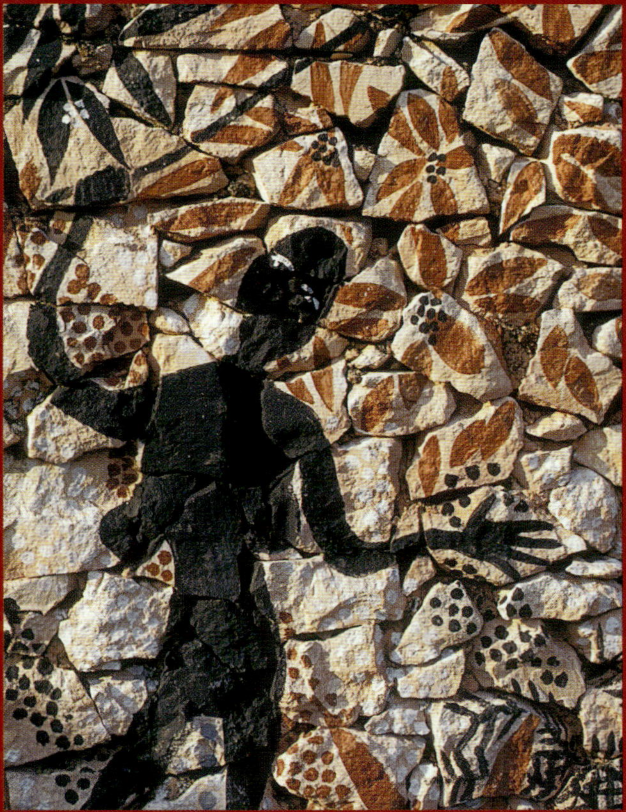

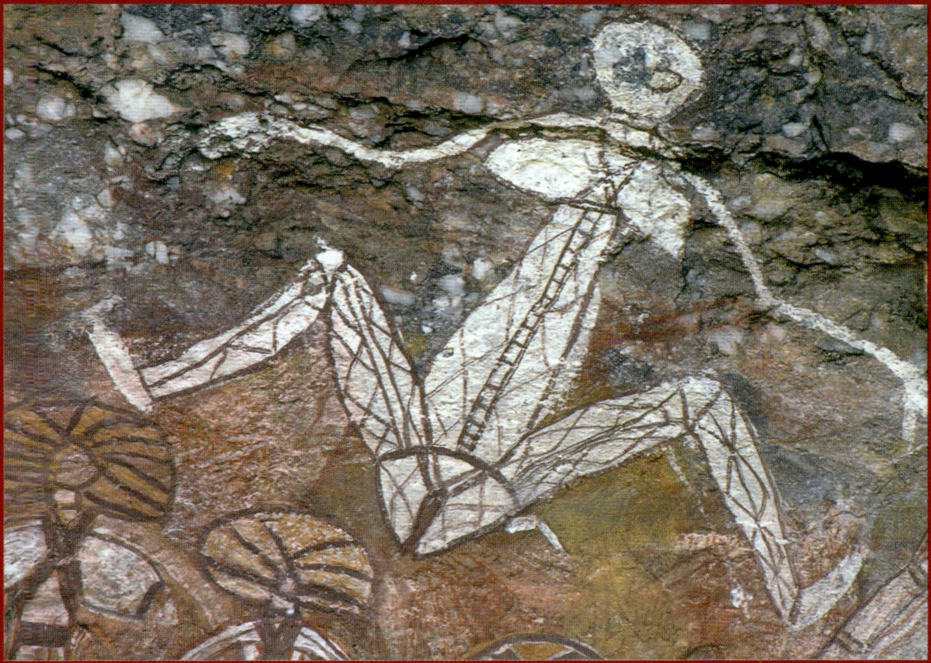

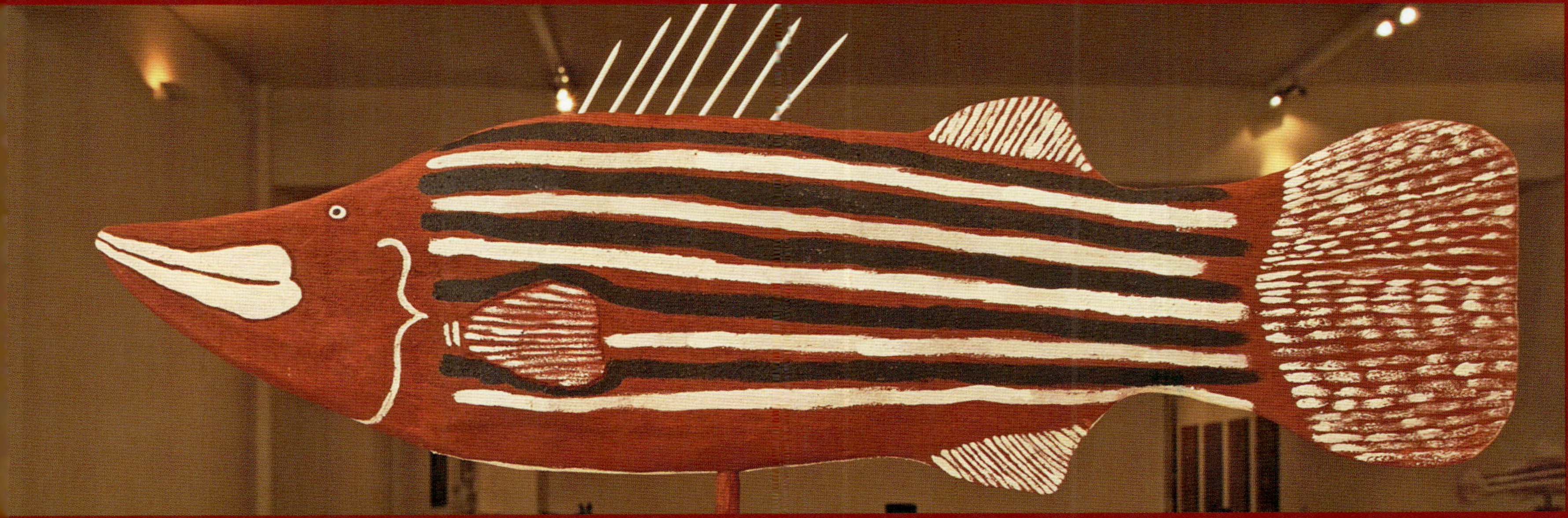

KITSCH COLOR

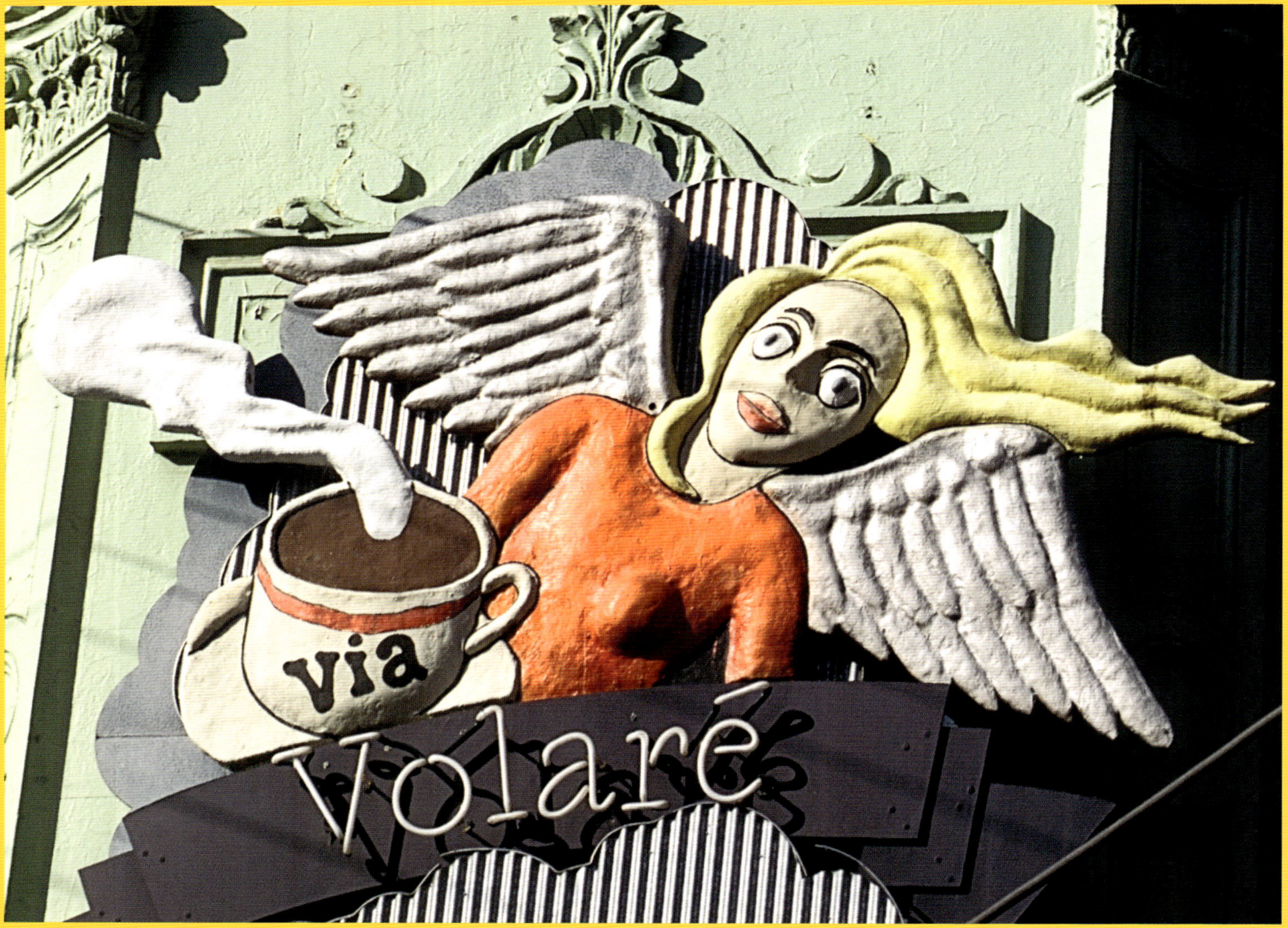

Color is everywhere; color is beautiful. Brunswick Street, Fitzroy, Melbourne is famous for its funky streetscape, retro fashion, and Bohemian lifestyle. Humor is never far from the surface of everything, as many street signs and posters illustrate.

Opposite: A colorful kite from the festival organized to celebrate the tenth anniversary of the Mount Annan Botanic Gardens, Sydney.

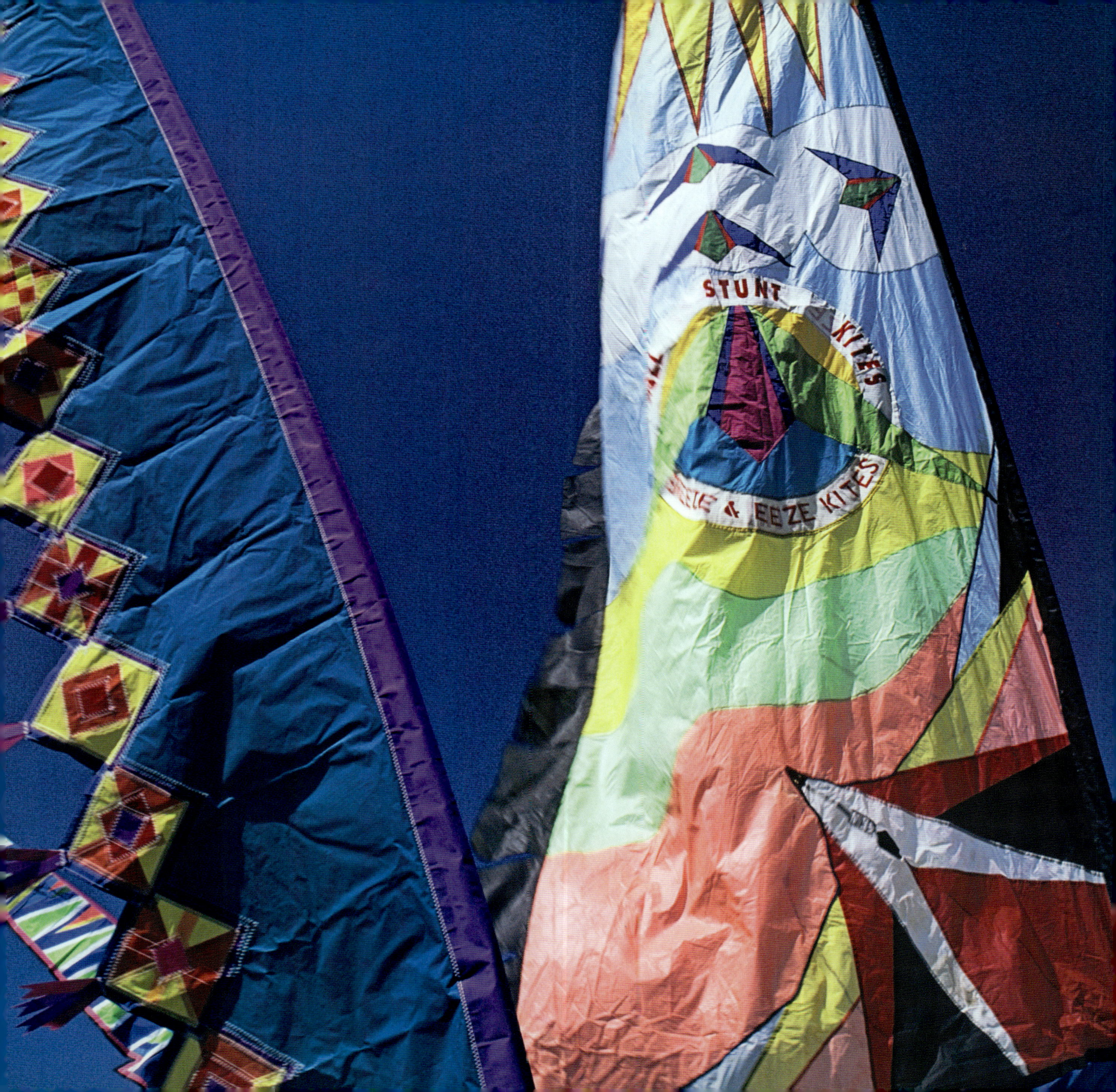
STUNT
KITES
KITES

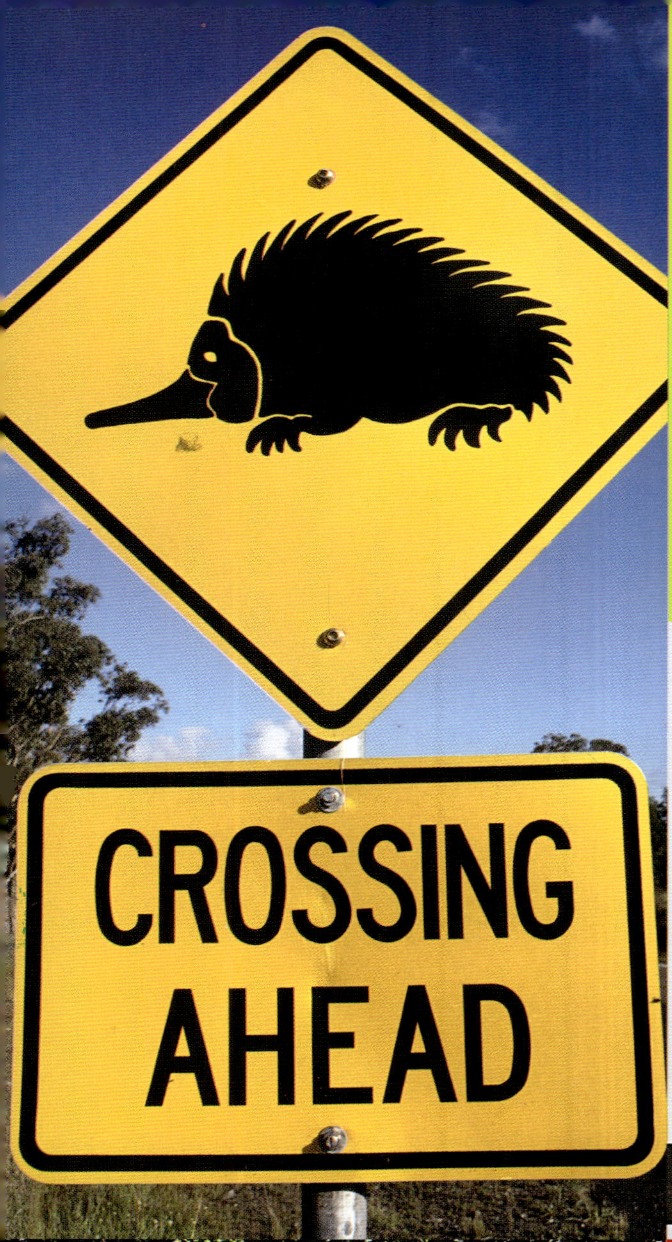
CROSSING
AHEAD

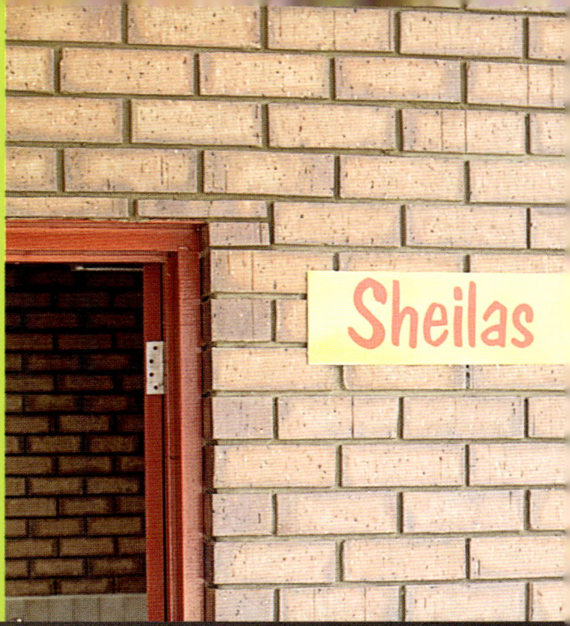
Sheilas

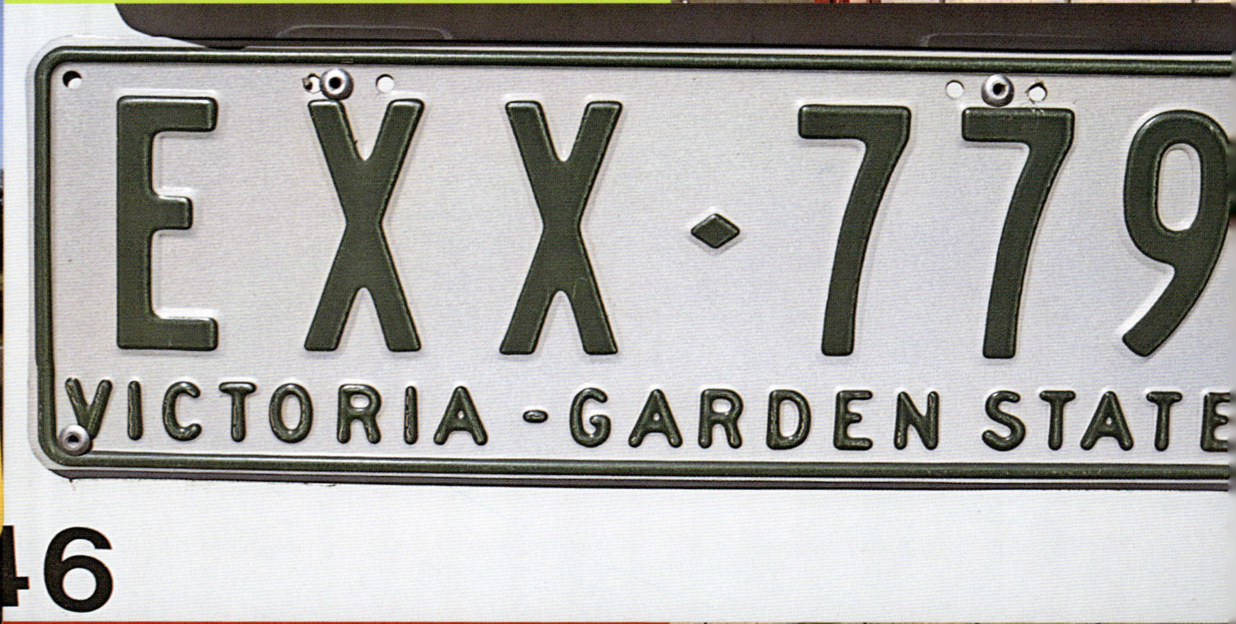
EXX·779
VICTORIA - GARDEN STATE

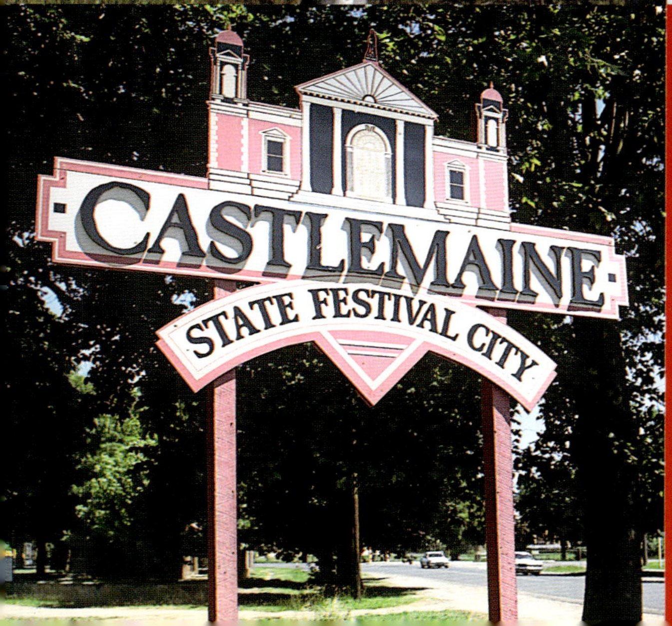
CASTLEMAINE
STATE FESTIVAL CITY

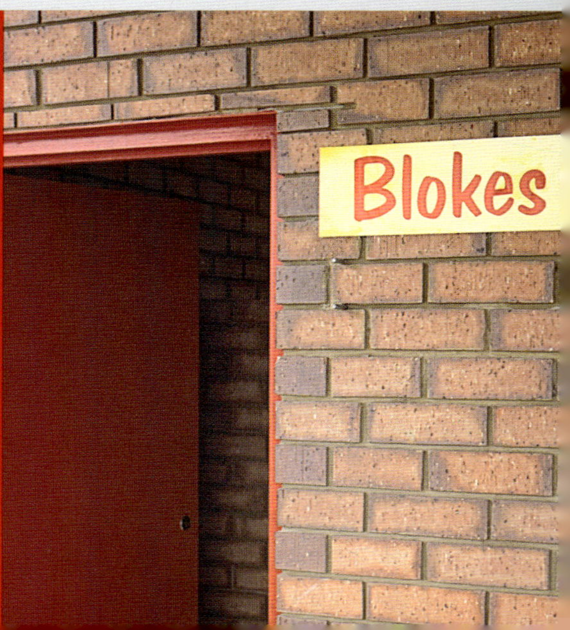
Blokes

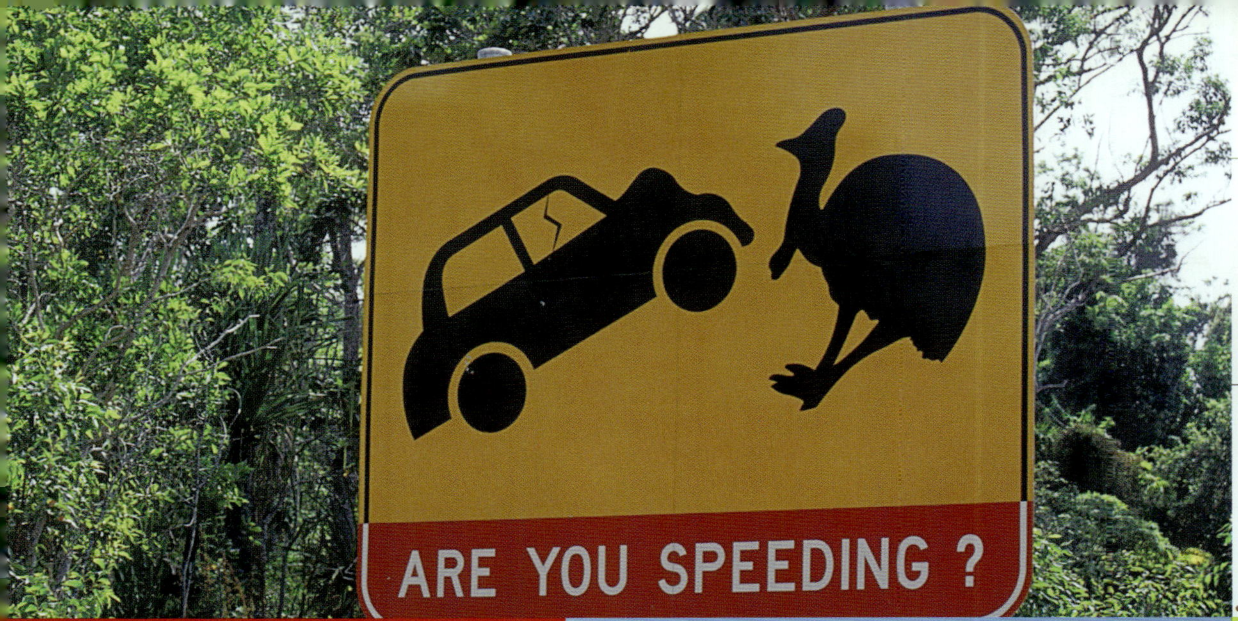
ARE YOU SPEEDING ?

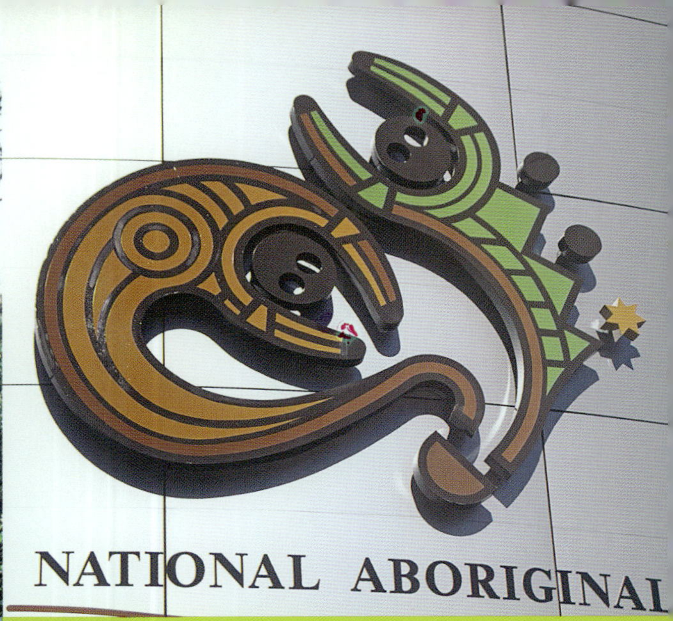
NATIONAL ABORIGINAL

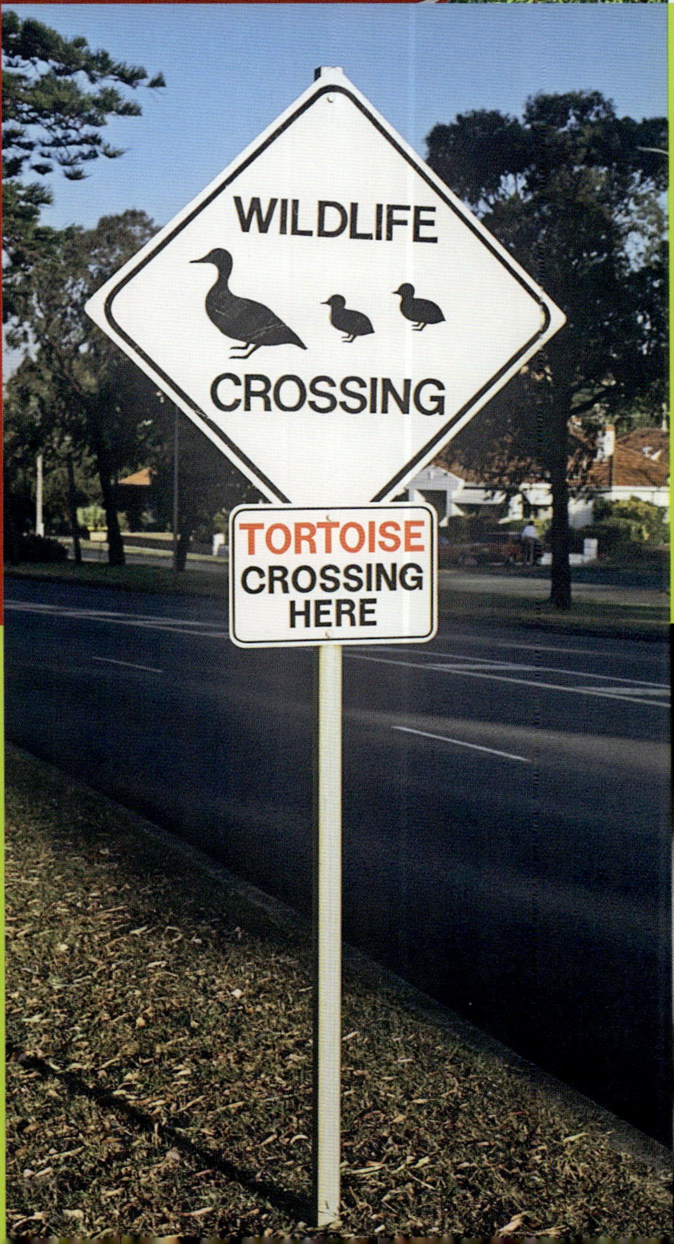
WILDLIFE
CROSSING
TORTOISE
CROSSING
HERE

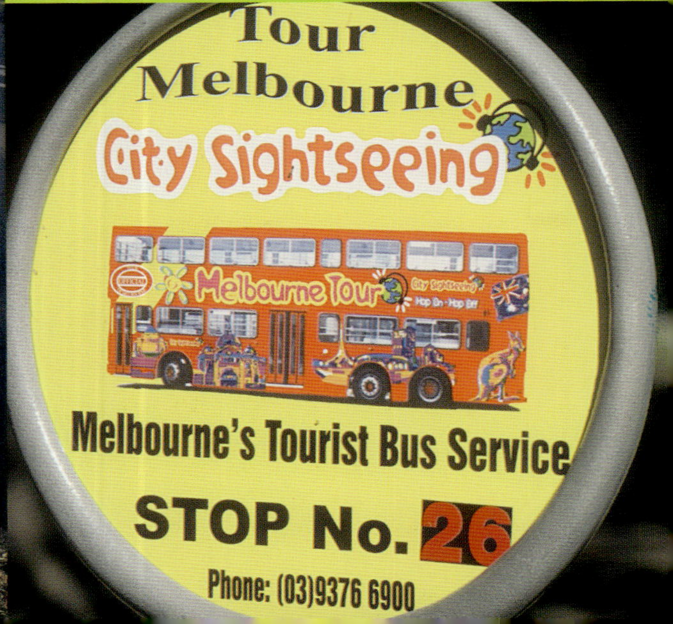
Tour
Melbourne
City Sightseeing
Melbourne Tour
Melbourne's Tourist Bus Service
STOP No. 26
Phone: (03)9376 6900

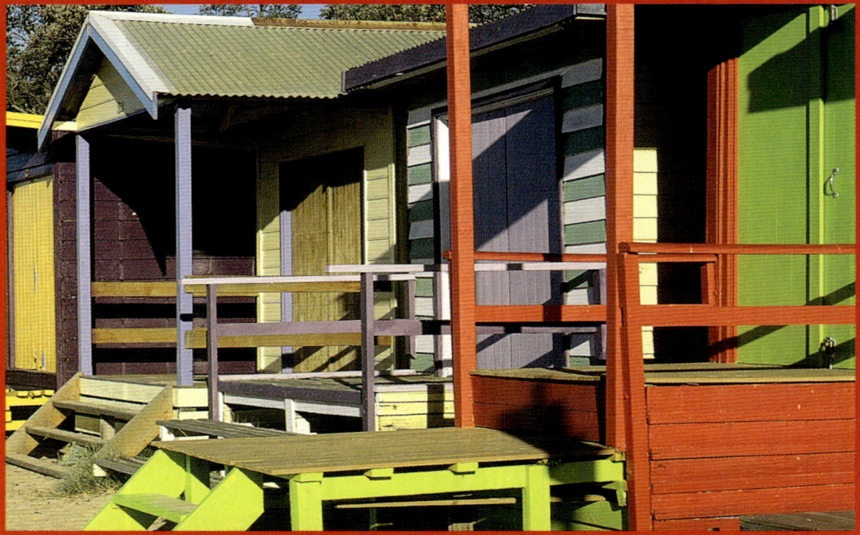

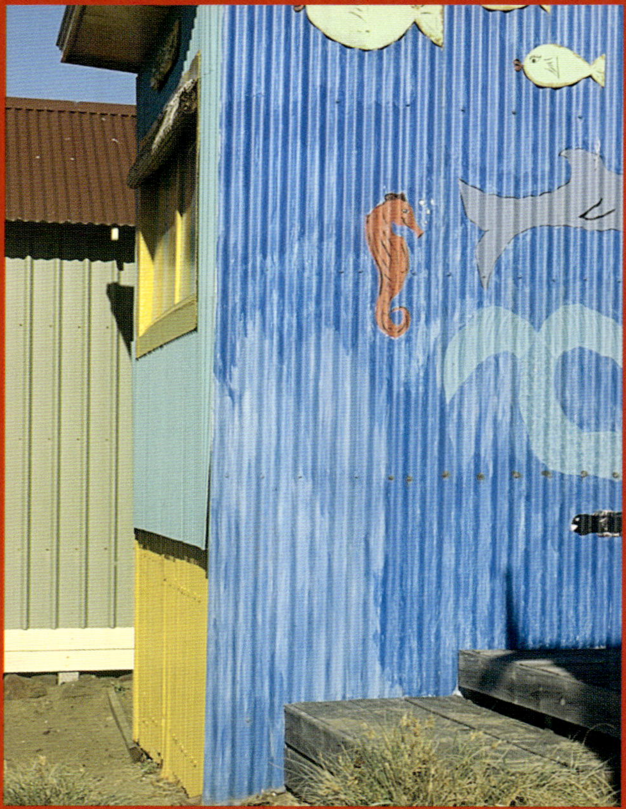

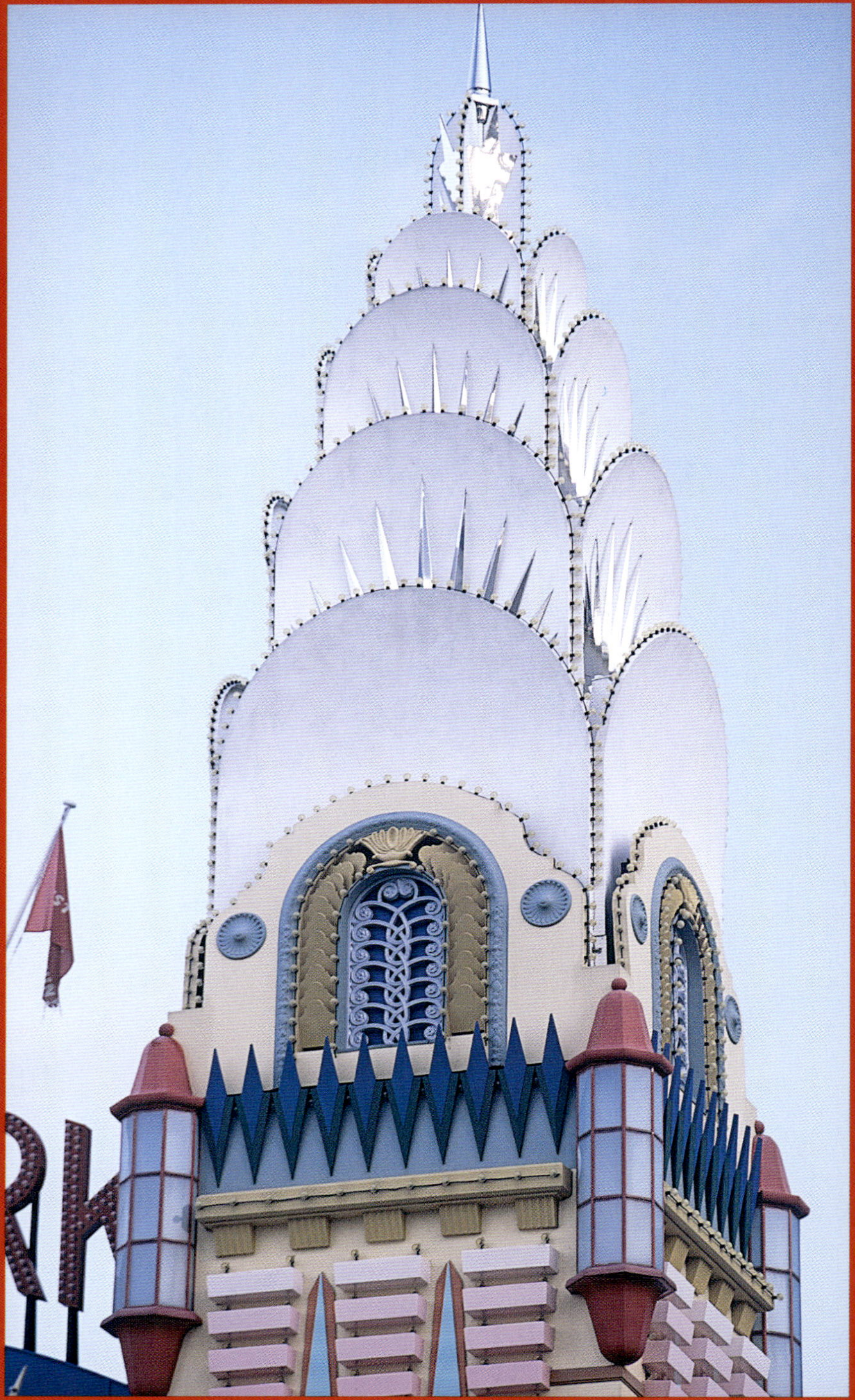

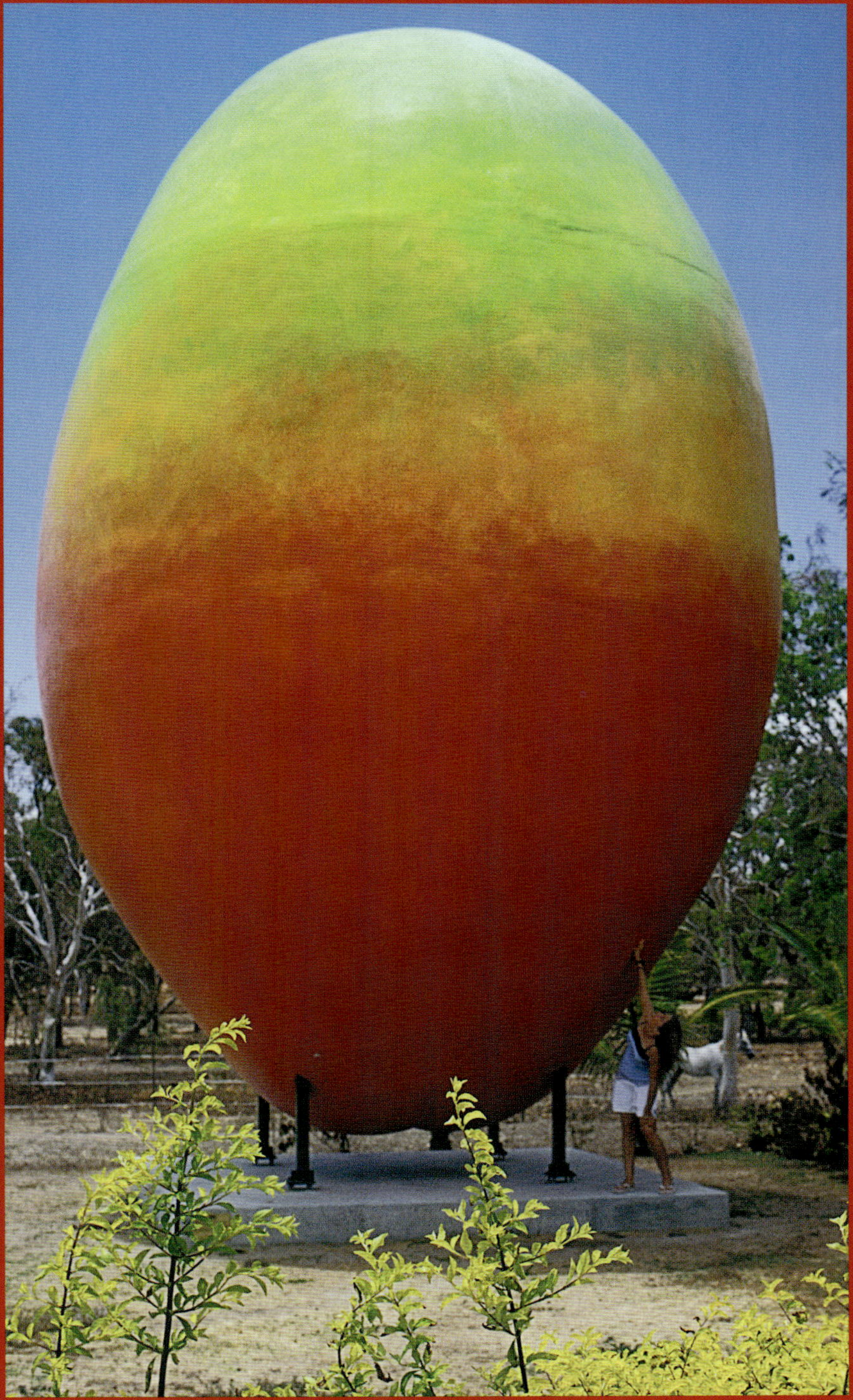

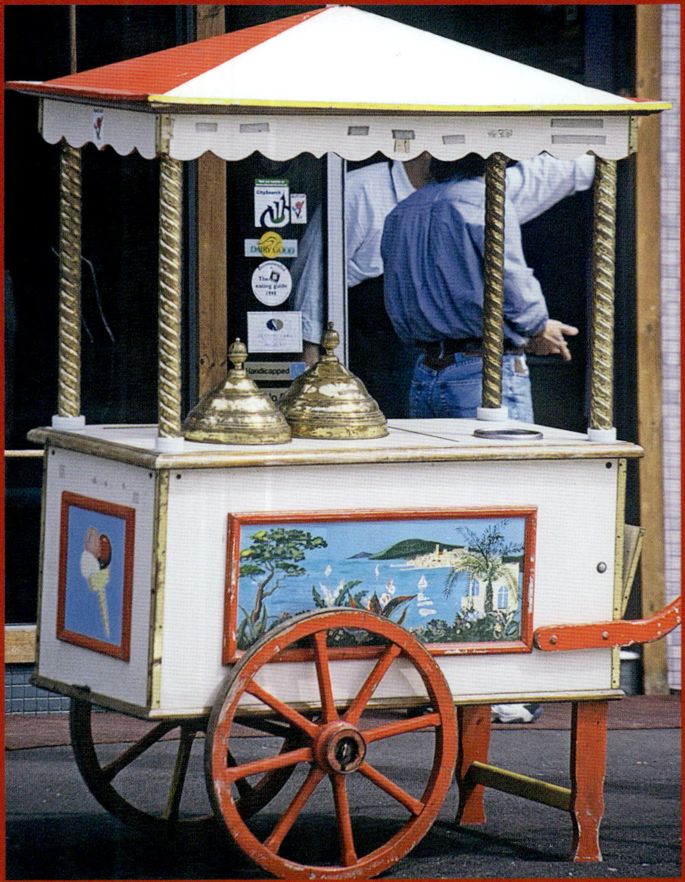

STREET SCENES

The Australian determination not to take life too seriously has resulted in a countrywide series of "Big" things, like the Big Mango in Queensland; others include an avocado, a banana, a cow, guitar, merino sheep, yabby (crayfish), oyster, figure of Ned Kelly, windmill, and the Big Lobster on the Princes Highway, Kingston, which actually houses a restaurant. It is a challenge to visit them all. Color gets everywhere, among beach huts on the Mornington Peninsula, Melbourne; in Luna Park, Sydney; even in a simple ice cream vendor's cart. Next page: Community street mural in Melbourne.

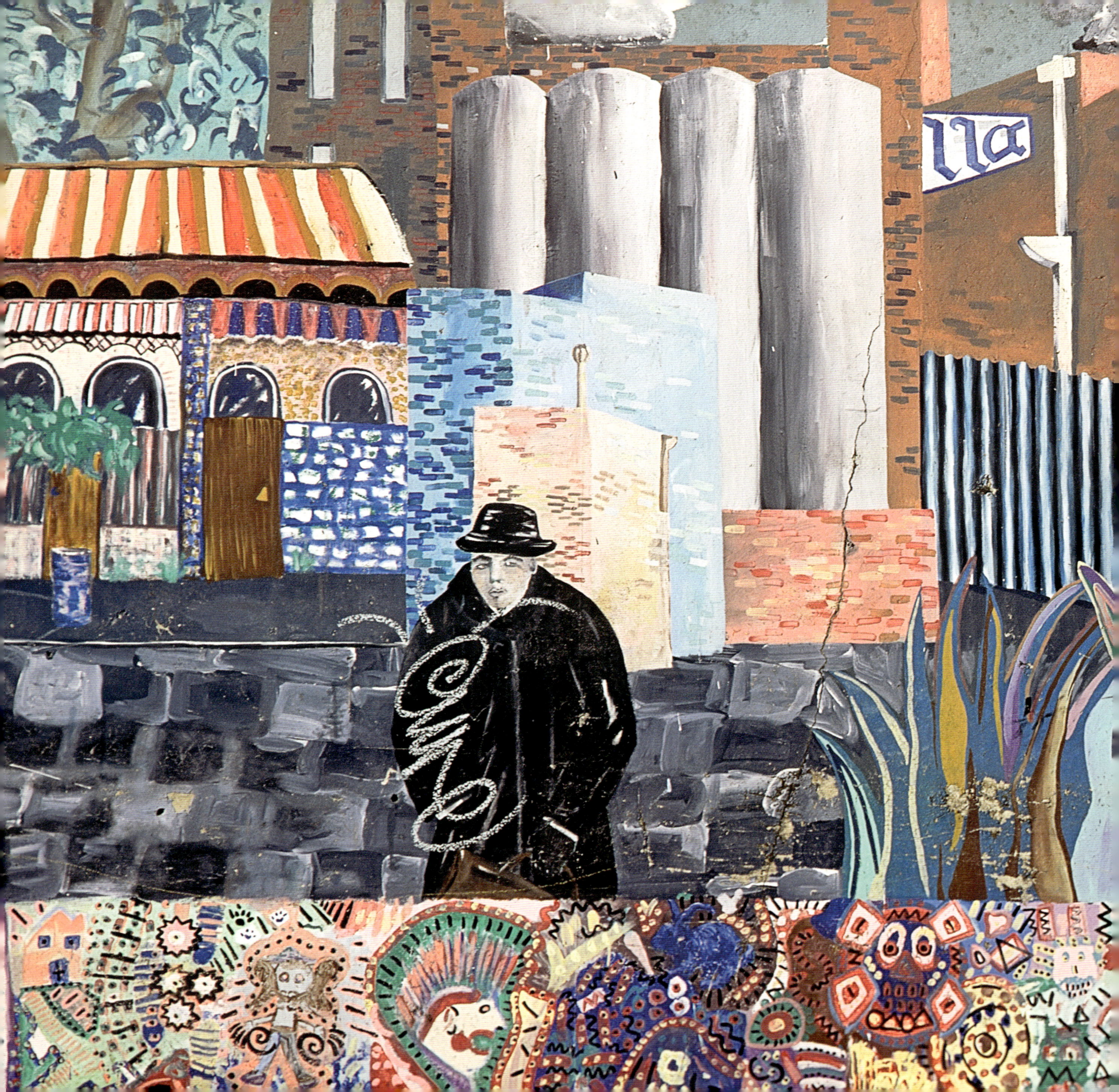

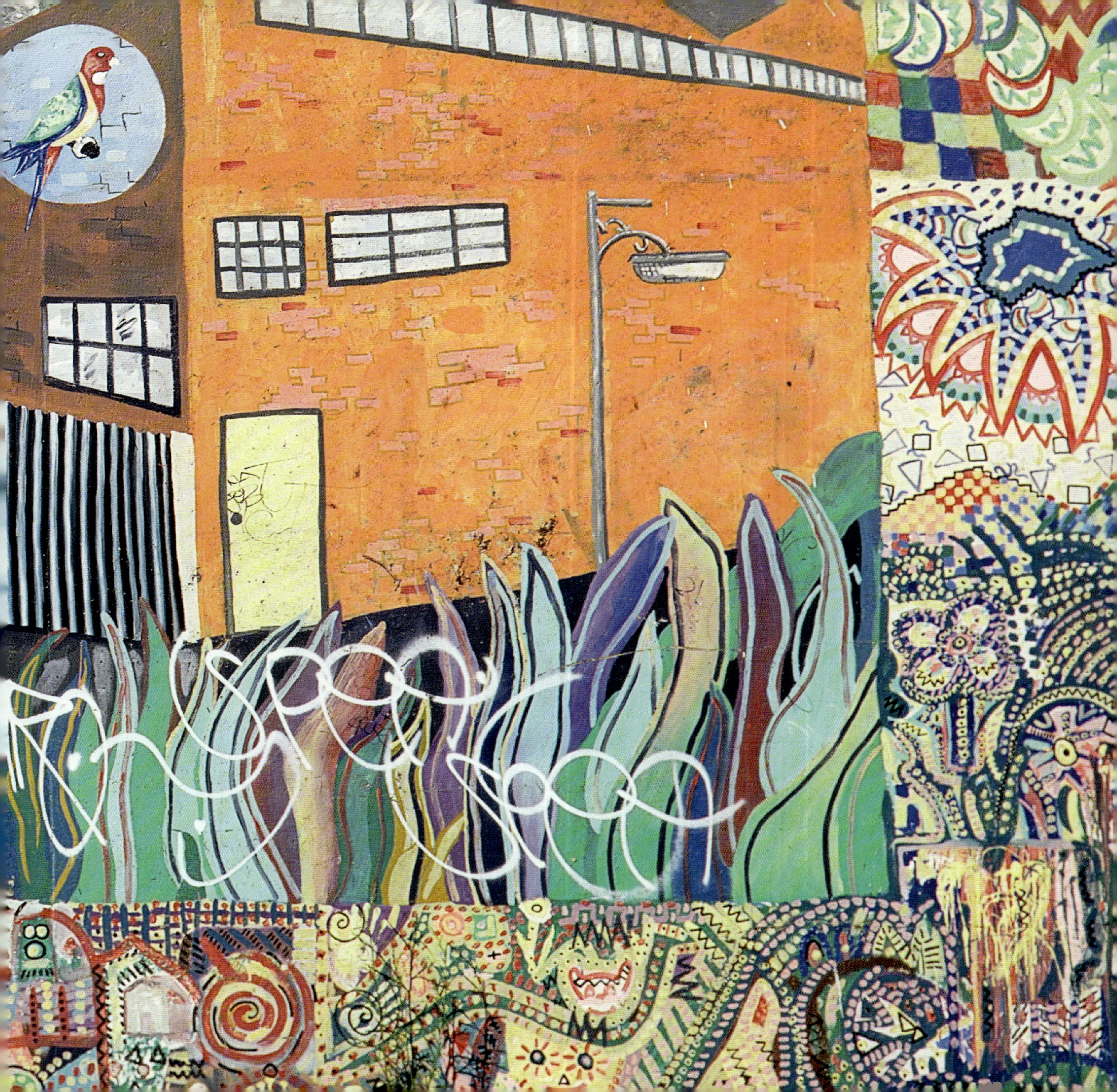

SCULPTURE

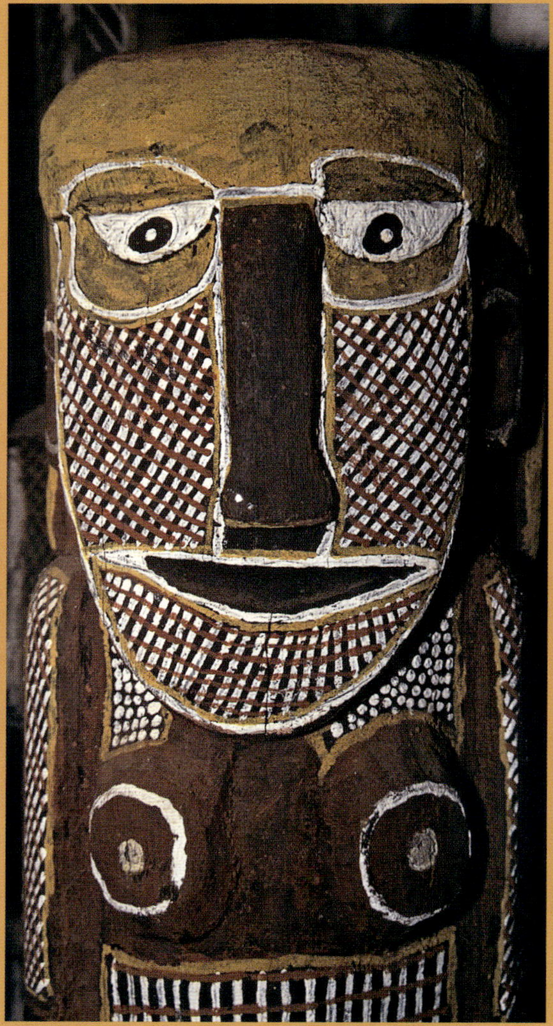

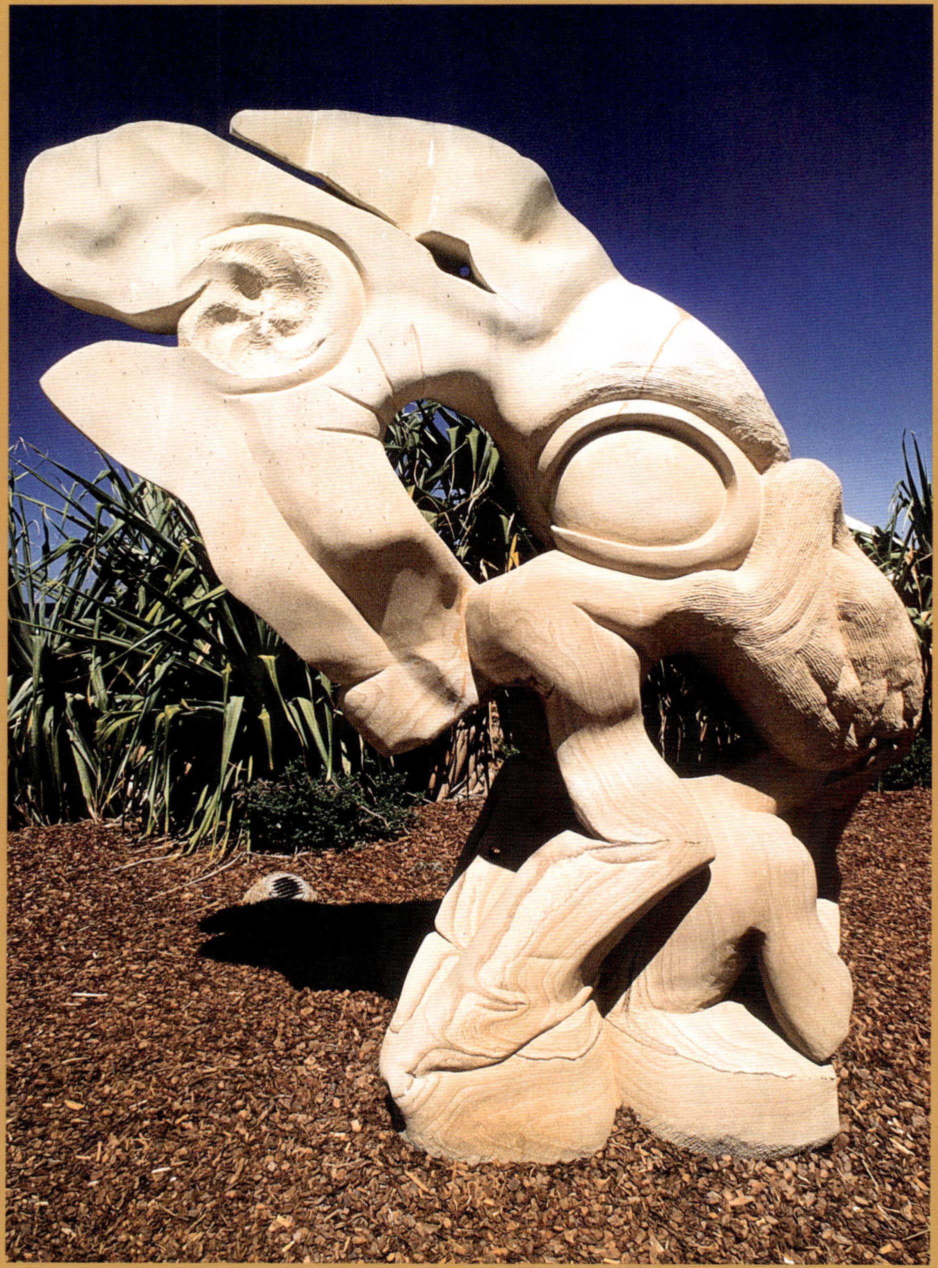

Sculpture is part of everyday life in Australia, and found in many places, including streets, public squares, buildings, parks, and gardens. Sculptors use stone, wood, metal, resin, and plastics to create anything from small art objects to large-scale works that become powerful landmarks.

As in any country, sculpture takes on many forms, from the conventional statue of Captain Cook outside his cottage in Fitzroy Gardens, Melbourne, to the more esoteric ironwood figure from the Manyallaluk Aboriginal Community and the group sculpture at the Docklands Area in Melbourne.

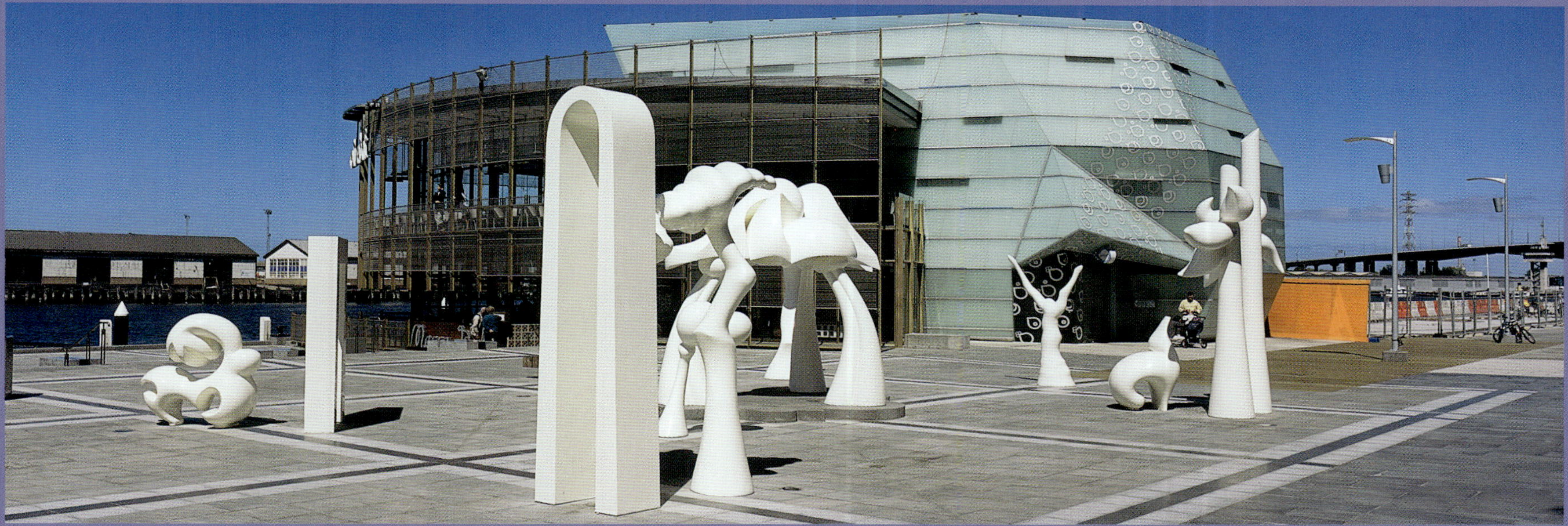

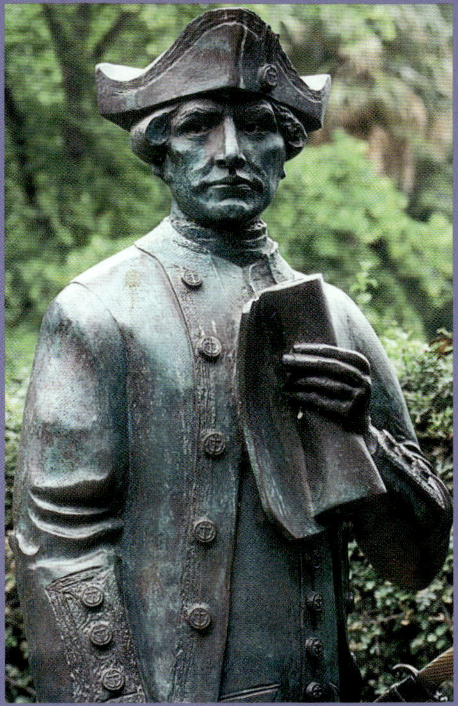

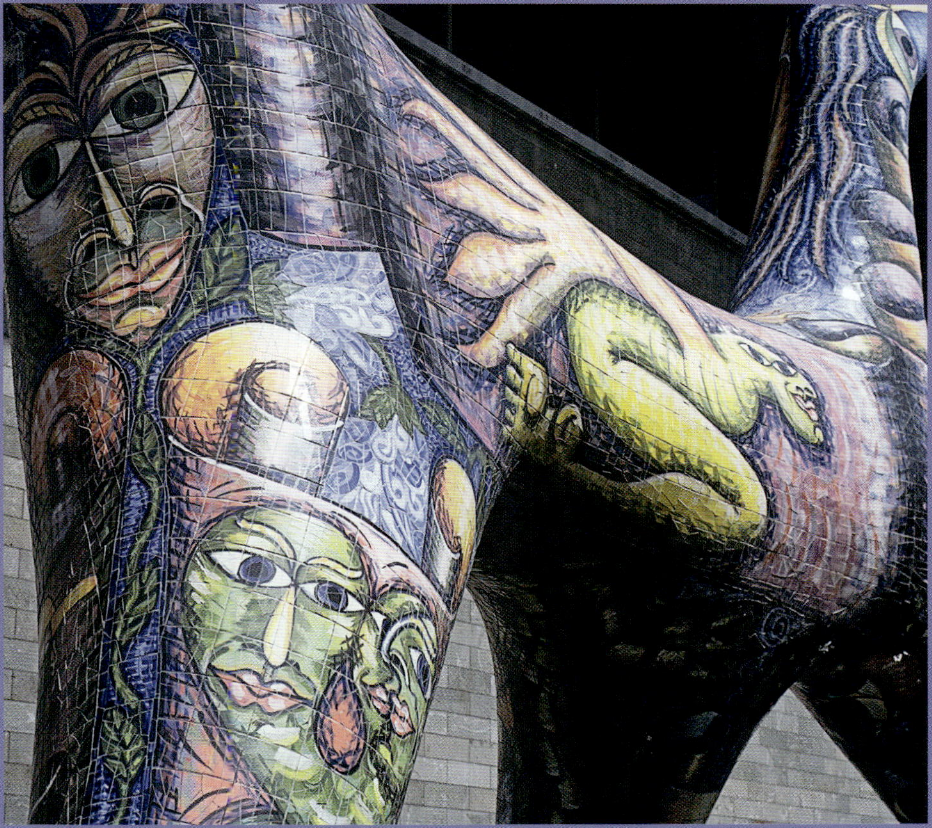

RETAIL THERAPY

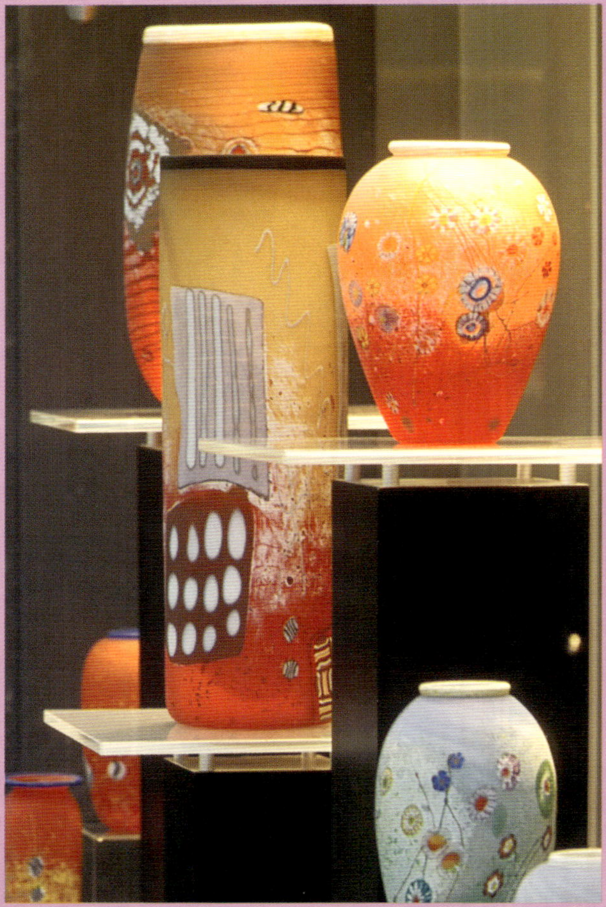

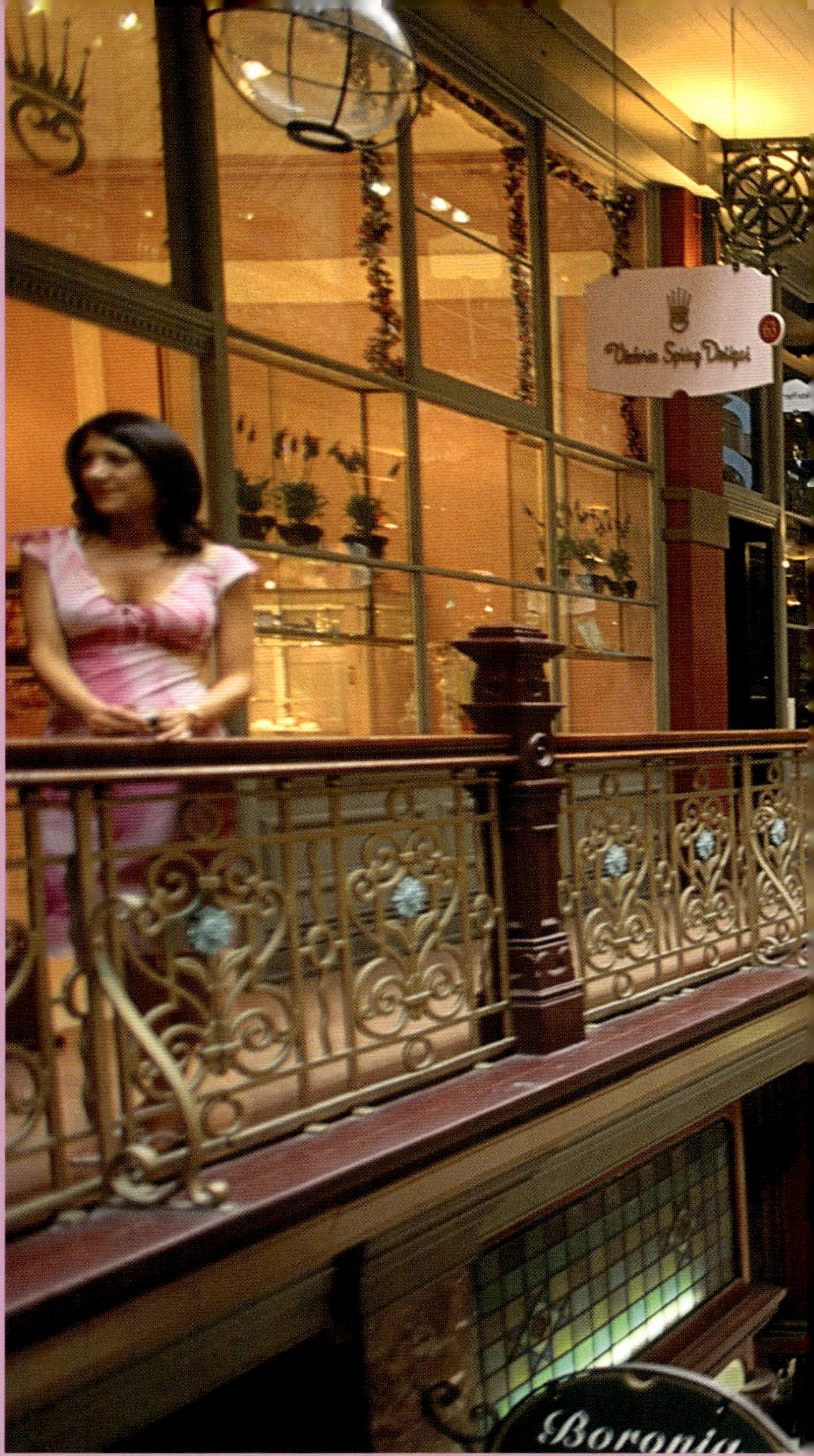

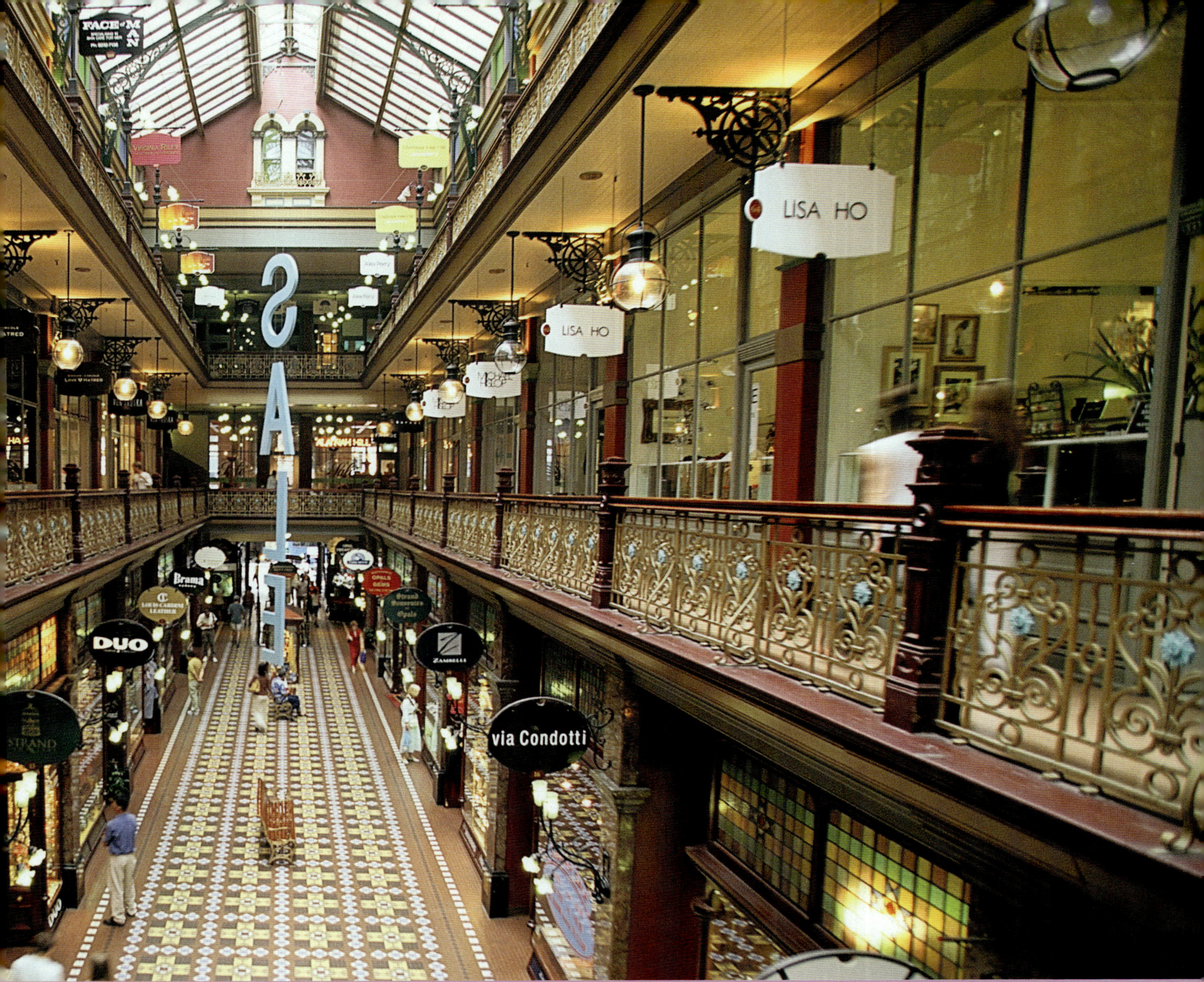

All the principal cities of Australia, and some smaller towns, too, have plenty of scope for retail therapy. Ornate, double-decker arcades lined with everything from trendy boutiques to barber shops are a world within a world, like the Pitt Street Mall in Sydney (above), or the Makers Mark Gallery, in Collins Street, Melbourne, which features the work of some of Australia's finest jewelers, glassmakers, and woodworkers.

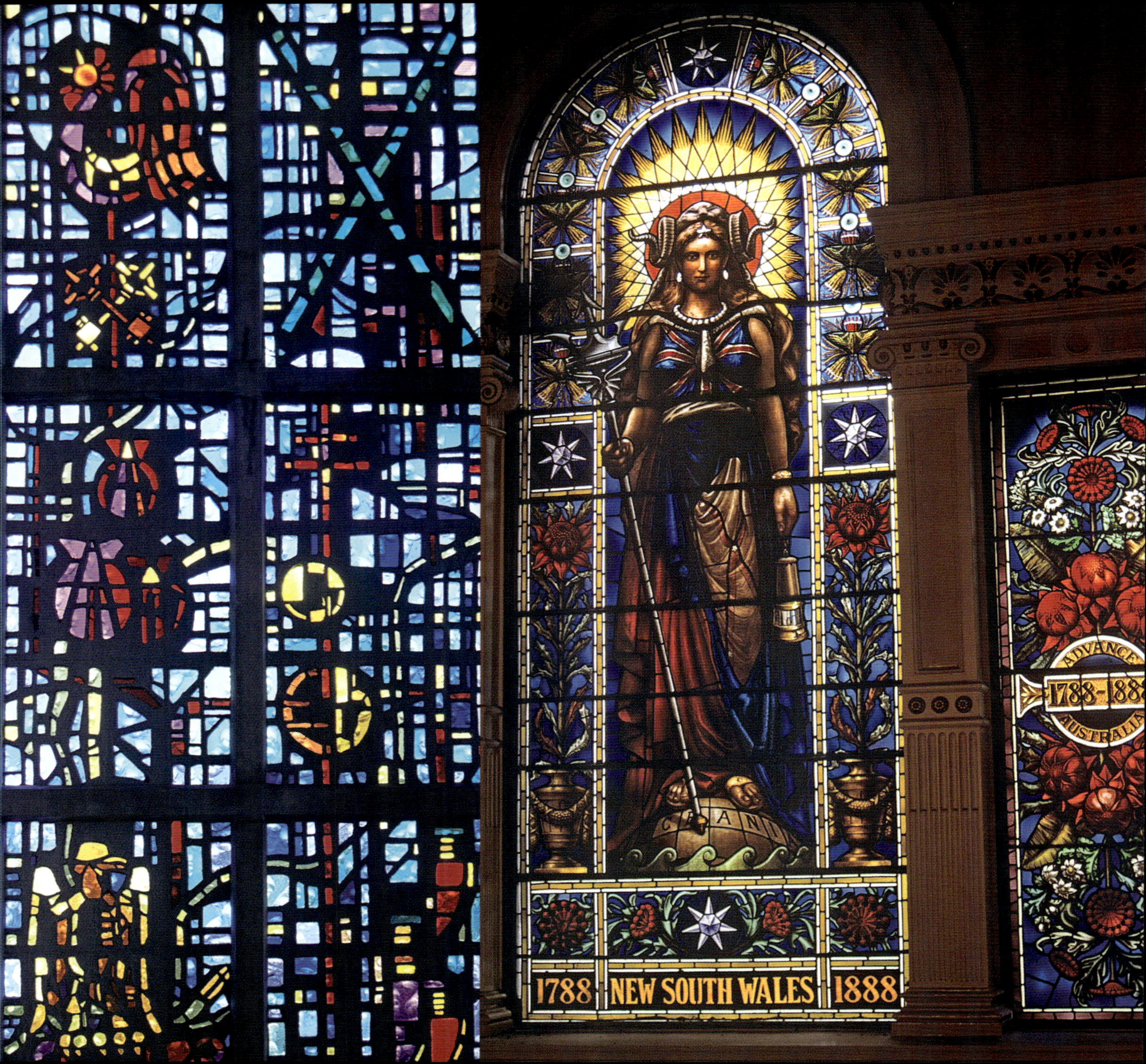

…s, stained glass is probably the …estionably beautiful and …windows, notably in religious …a story. They are an early form …e sponsor of the window, and …ories for those unable to read.

Opposite: The sun streams through a stained-glass window in the State Library, Sydney.

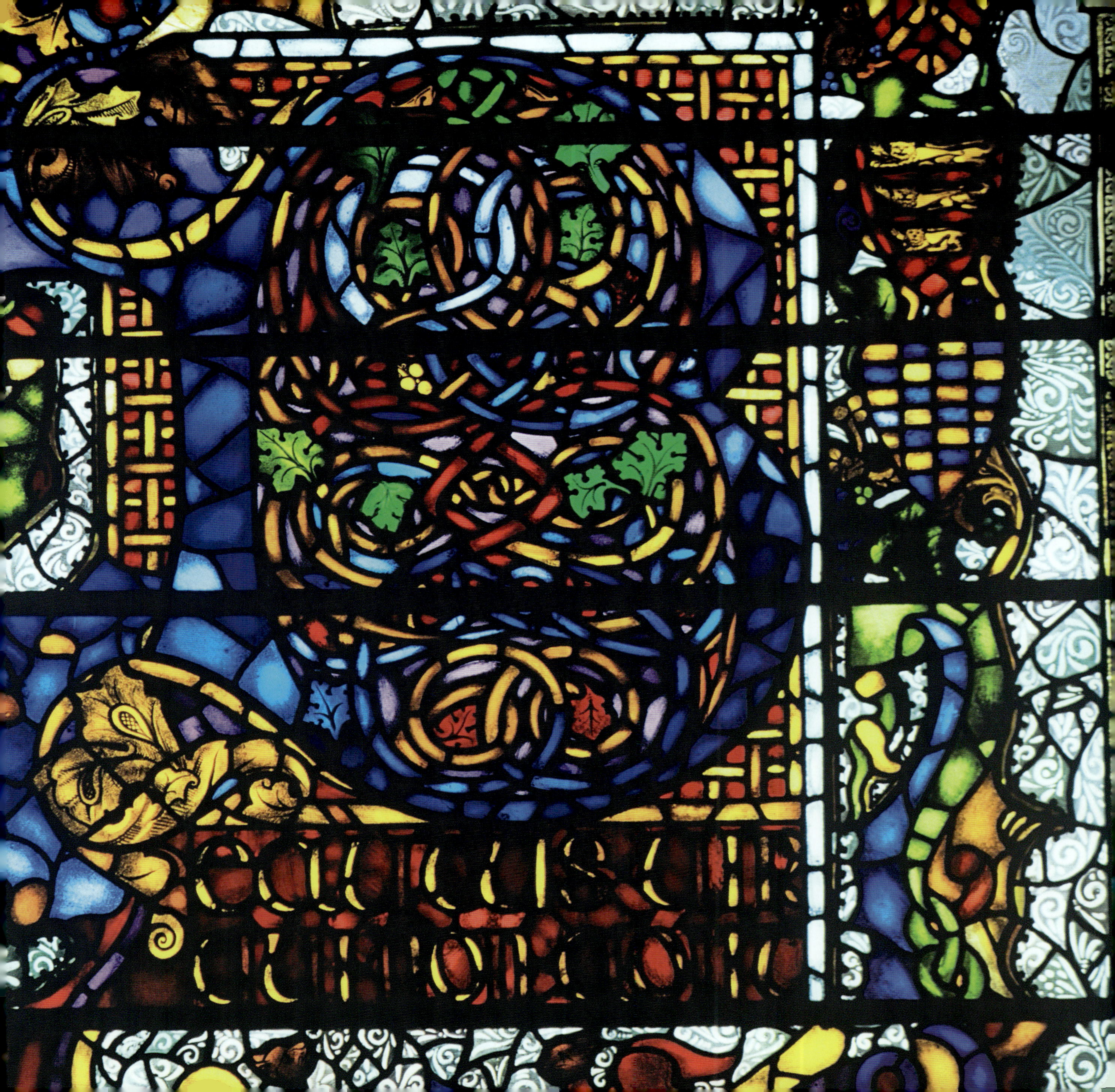

LIGHT &
REFLEC

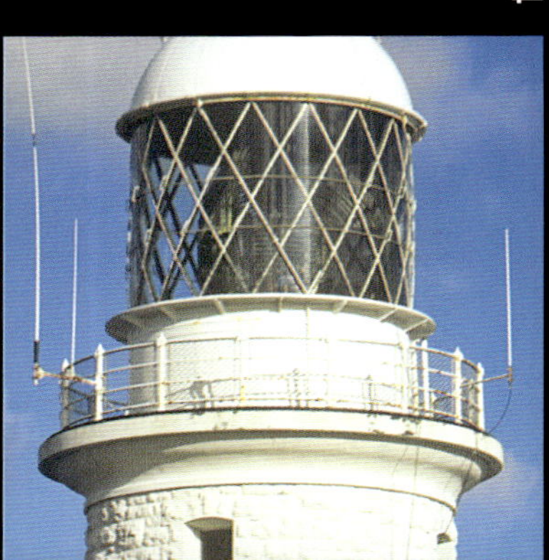

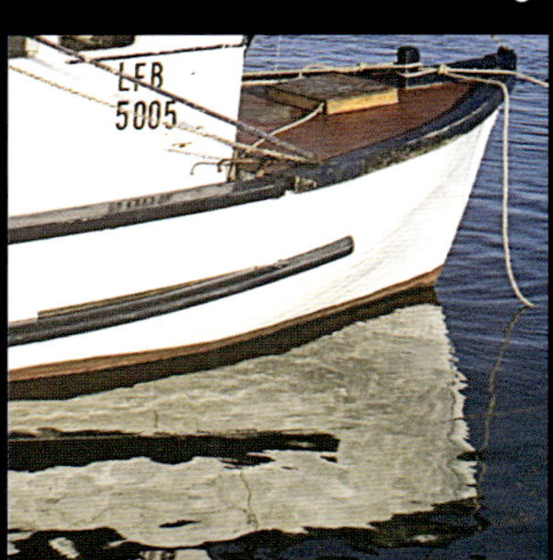

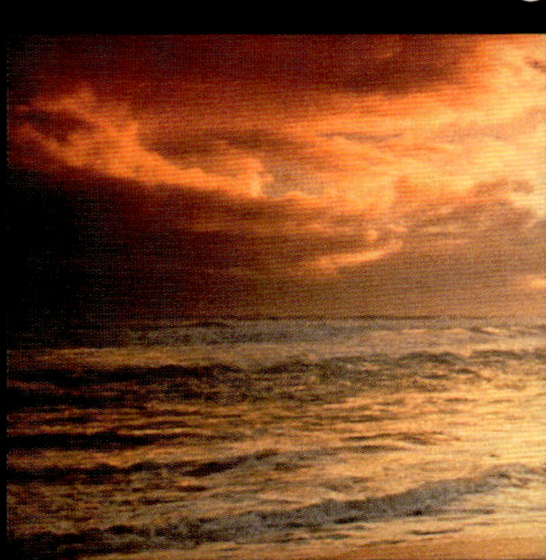

6

COLORS OF AUSTRALIA: LIGHT & REFLECTIONS

ONS

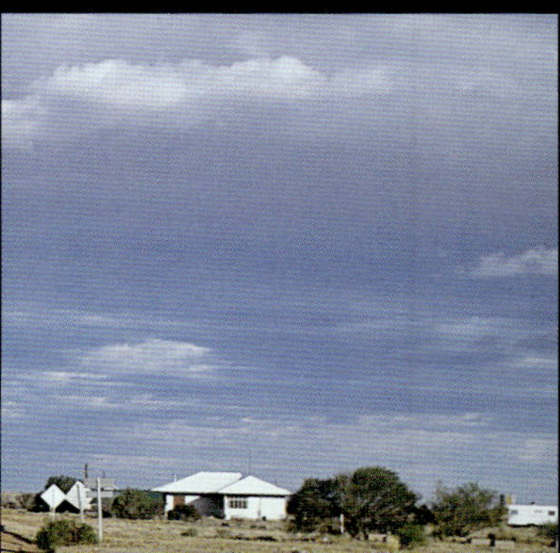

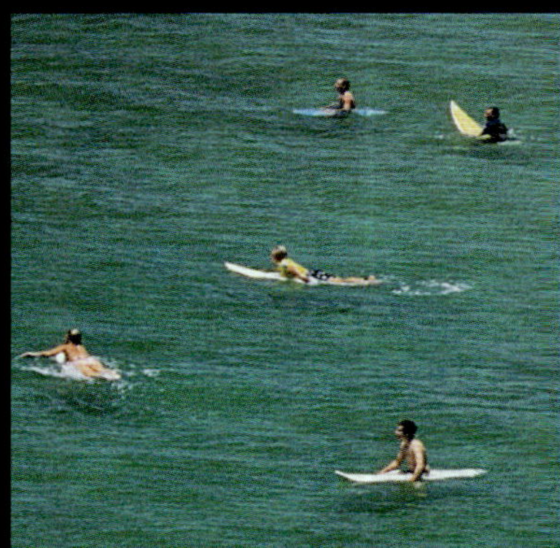

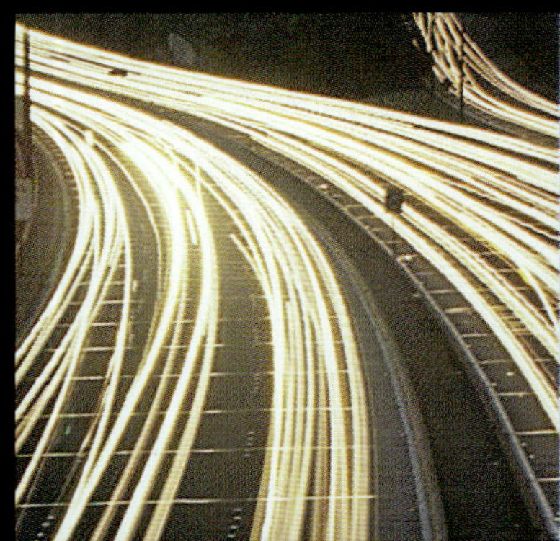

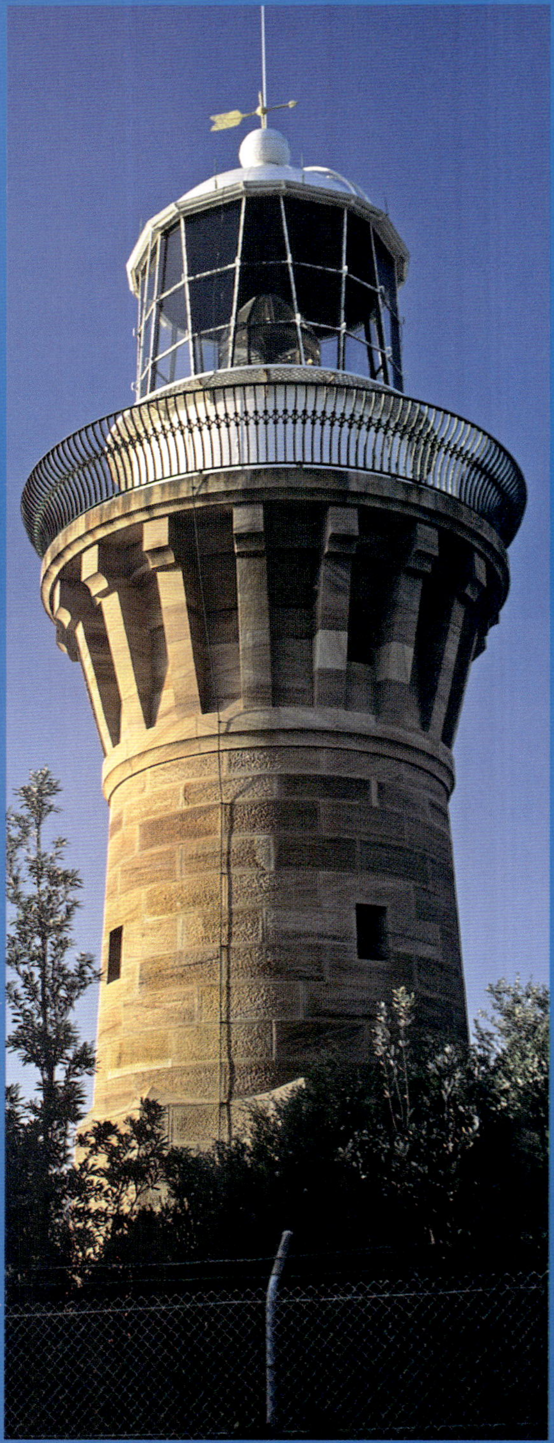
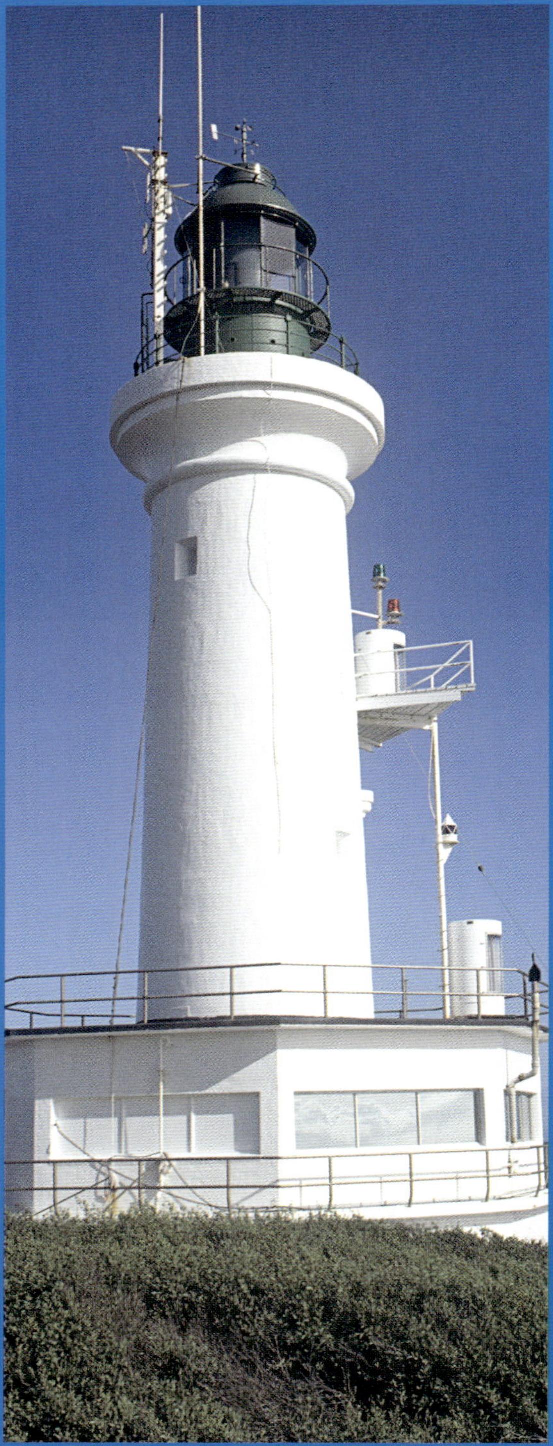
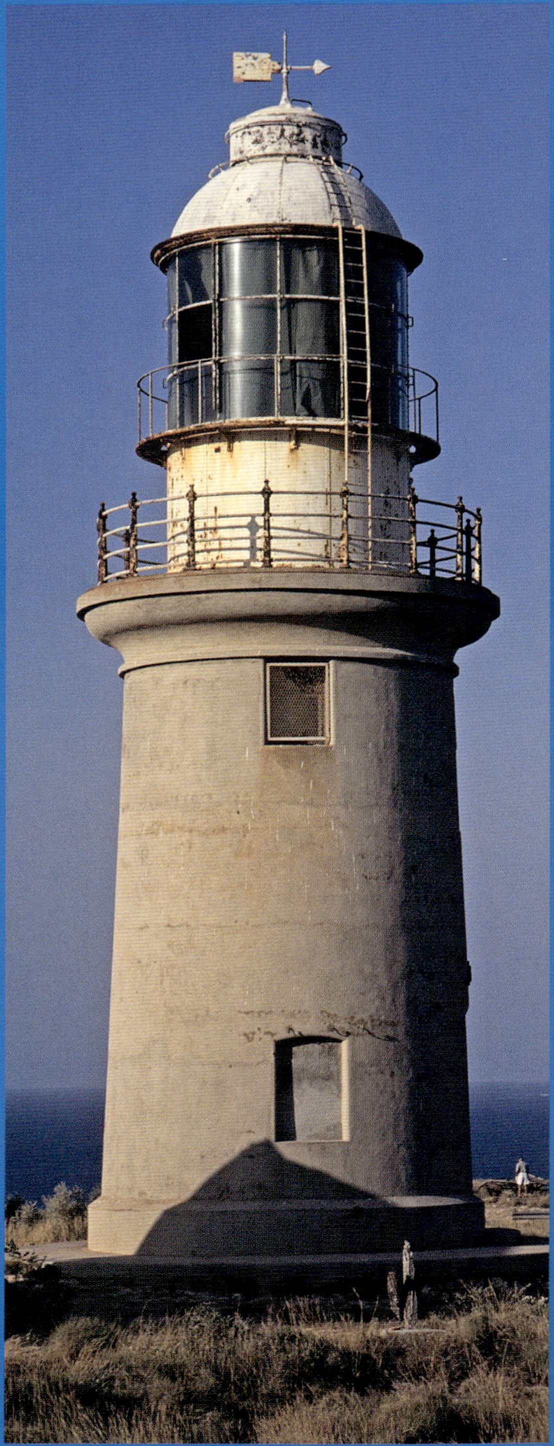

LIGHTHOUSES

Every dawn, every sunset, every star-strewn night sky seems only to beautify the brilliant, colorful face Australia shows to the world. Nowhere is this better exemplified than out in the desert, in the endless Outback, where magnificent skies are a daily round and roads sail ahead into a distant shimmering lake of heat haze. Still waters reflect those skies, a chiaroscuro blend of light and shade that makes the heart ache and the spirit rejoice.

Sunlight bounces from rock faces and towering buildings alike, penetrating the pure waters of the coast, adding luster, bringing life and light into every corner of the land. Buildings reflect in windows, shadows frame angled light, cities of light illuminate the darkness of night and mark man's presence around the edges of this island continent. And in a quiet park corner, a lone black swan is mirrored in the reedy water of a pool.

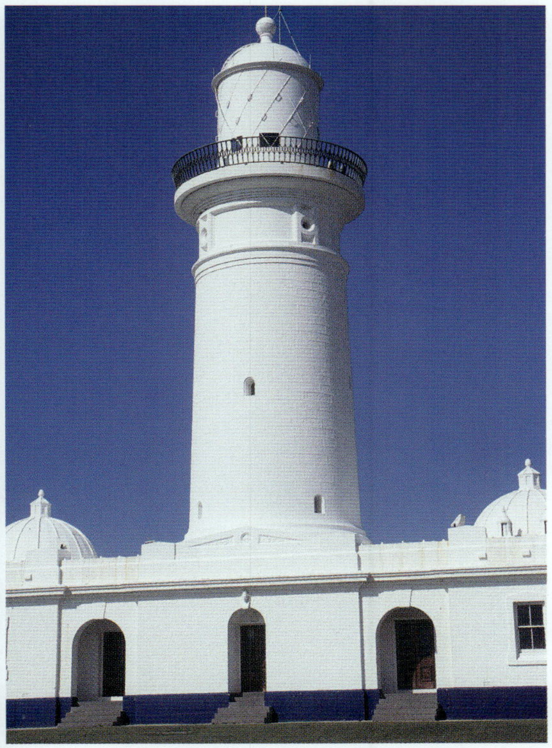

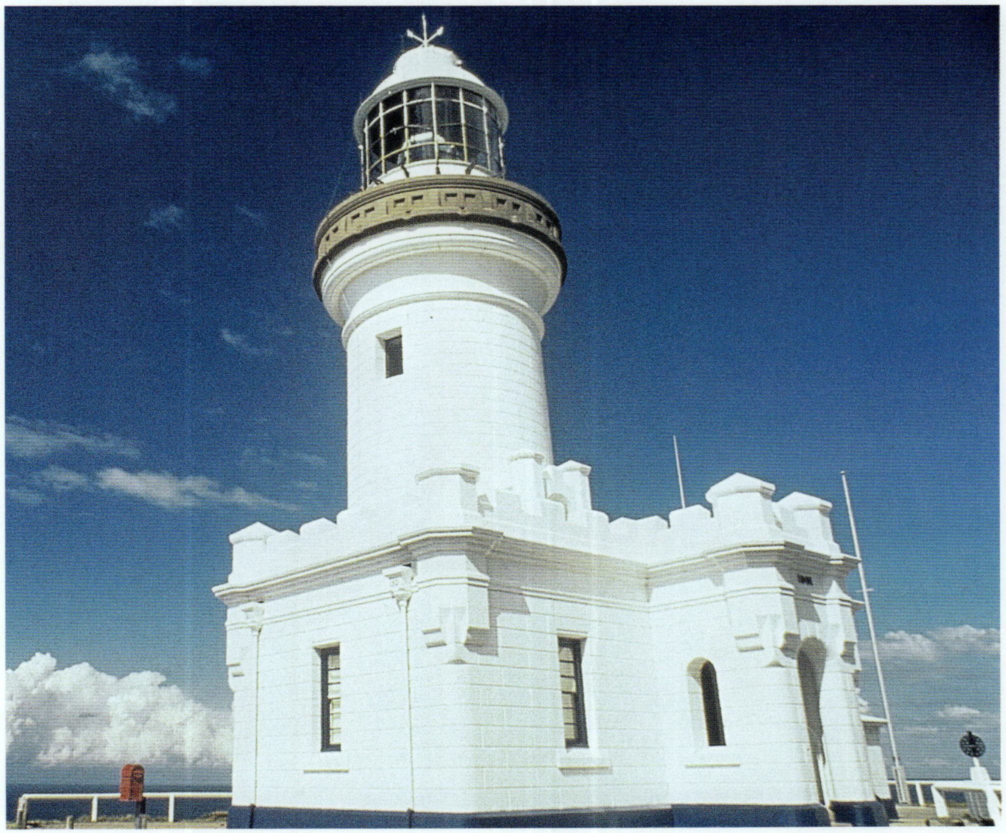

Lighthouses are unique, romantic, and an intimate part of Australia's maritime heritage. They have inspired and are admired by many. Whether it's their distinctive architecture, their splendid isolation, or the romantic associations they conjure, almost everyone has a soft spot for lighthouses.

Australia's coastline of 29,000 miles is home to more than 350 of them, all erected over the past 200 years. The last manned lighthouse was Maatsuyker Island in Tasmania which remained so until December 1995. Most lighthouses now belong to the various State Parks and Wildlife Services.

MIRROR IMAGE

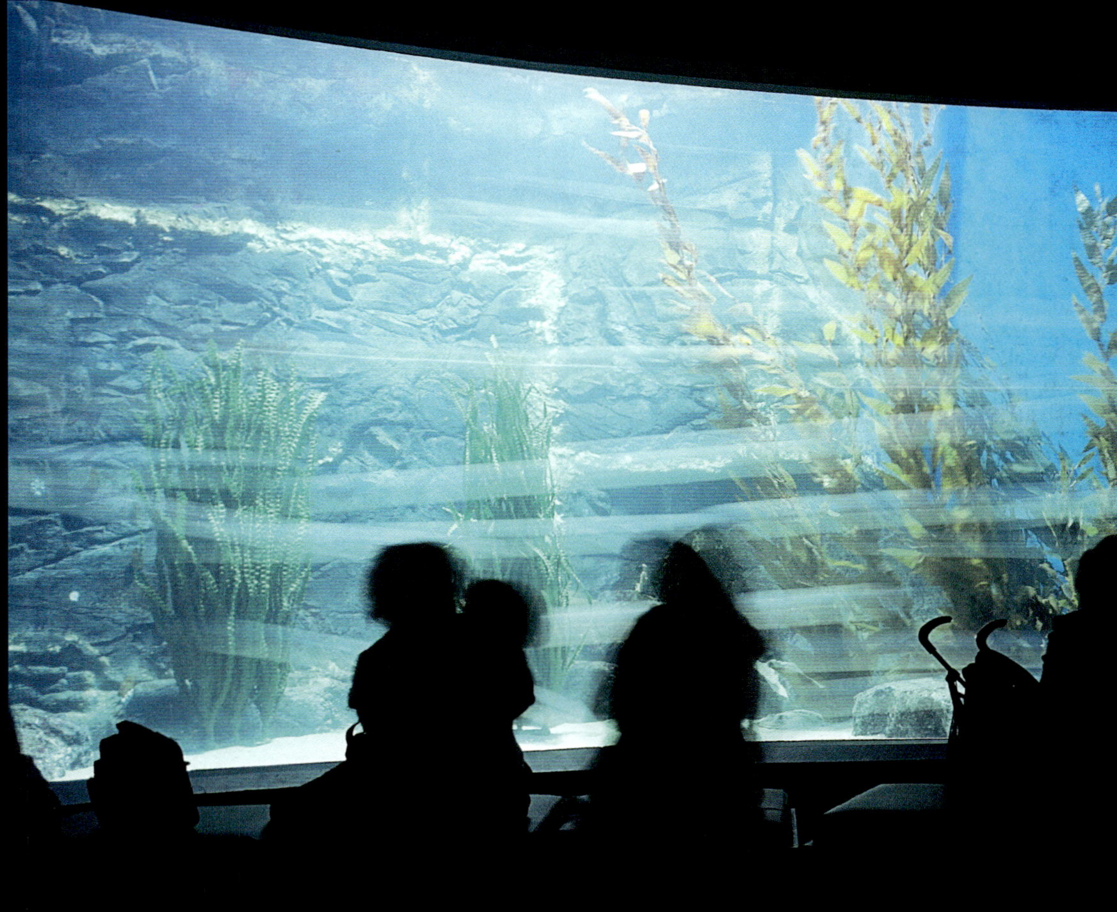

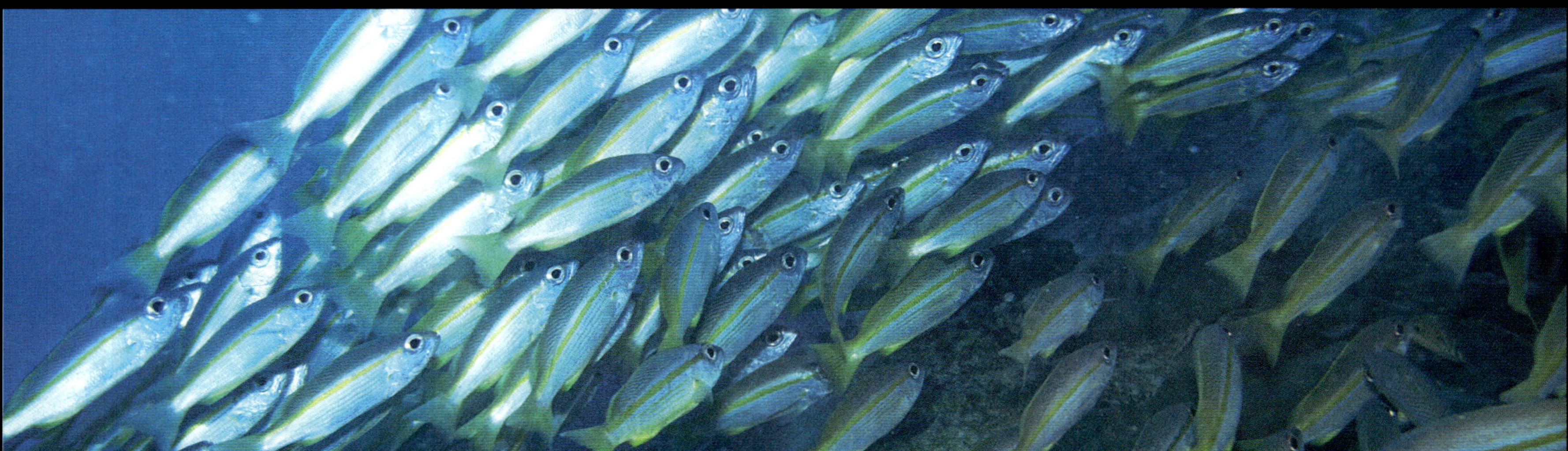

With such clear waters and invariably rich blue skies, clarity and reflections abound across Australia, whether in the Yarra River Fishbowl in the Melbourne Aquarium; the sight of shoals of fish off the Muiron Islands, Exmouth, or simply a South Wales, which is famed for its crayfish, rock lobster, and, best of all, oysters.

Next page: Melbourne Aquarium and Kings Bridge viewed from across Yarra River.

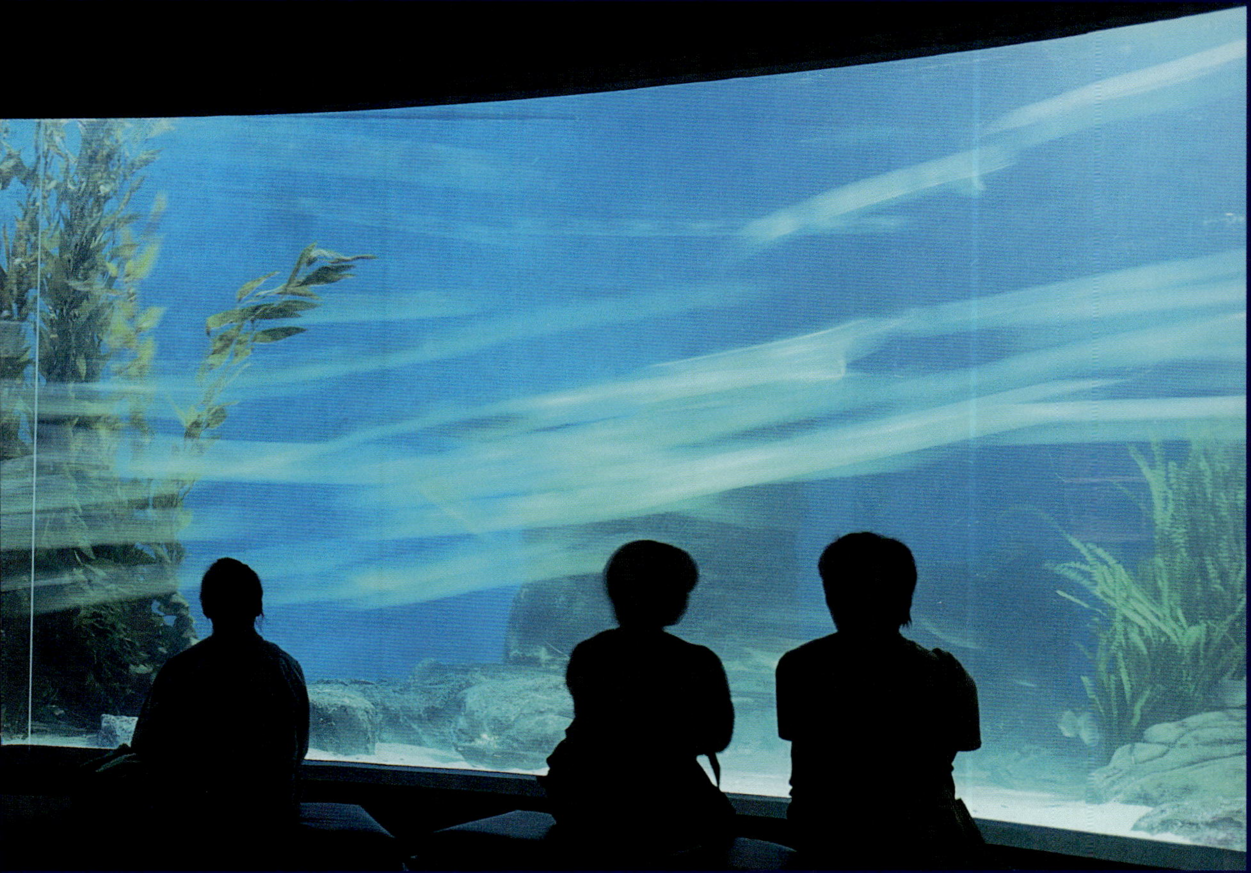

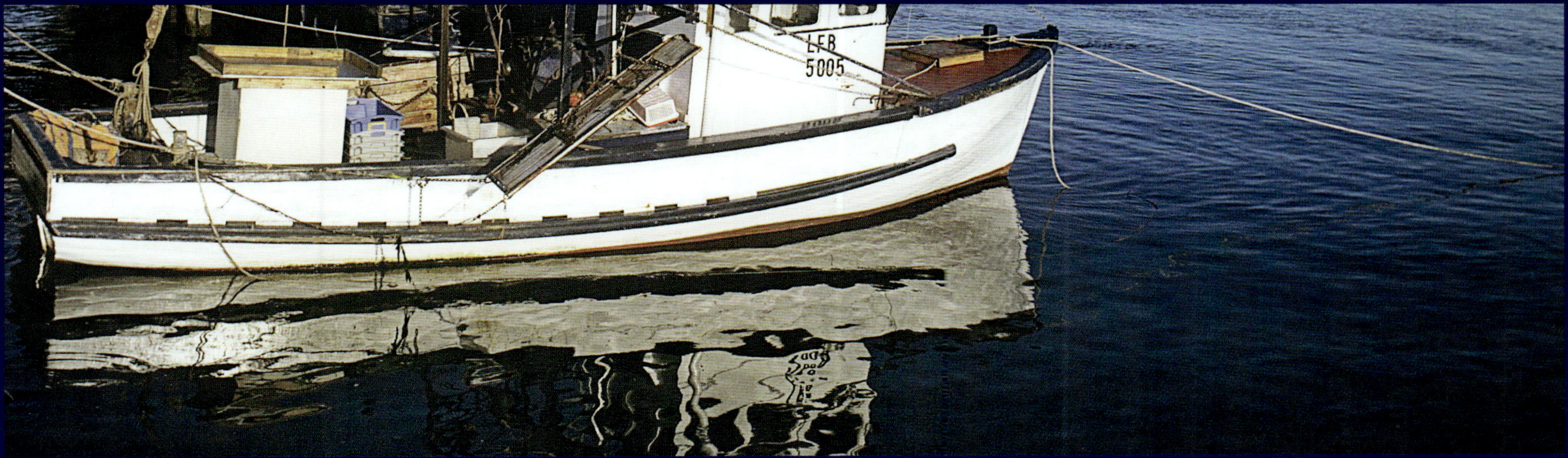
5005

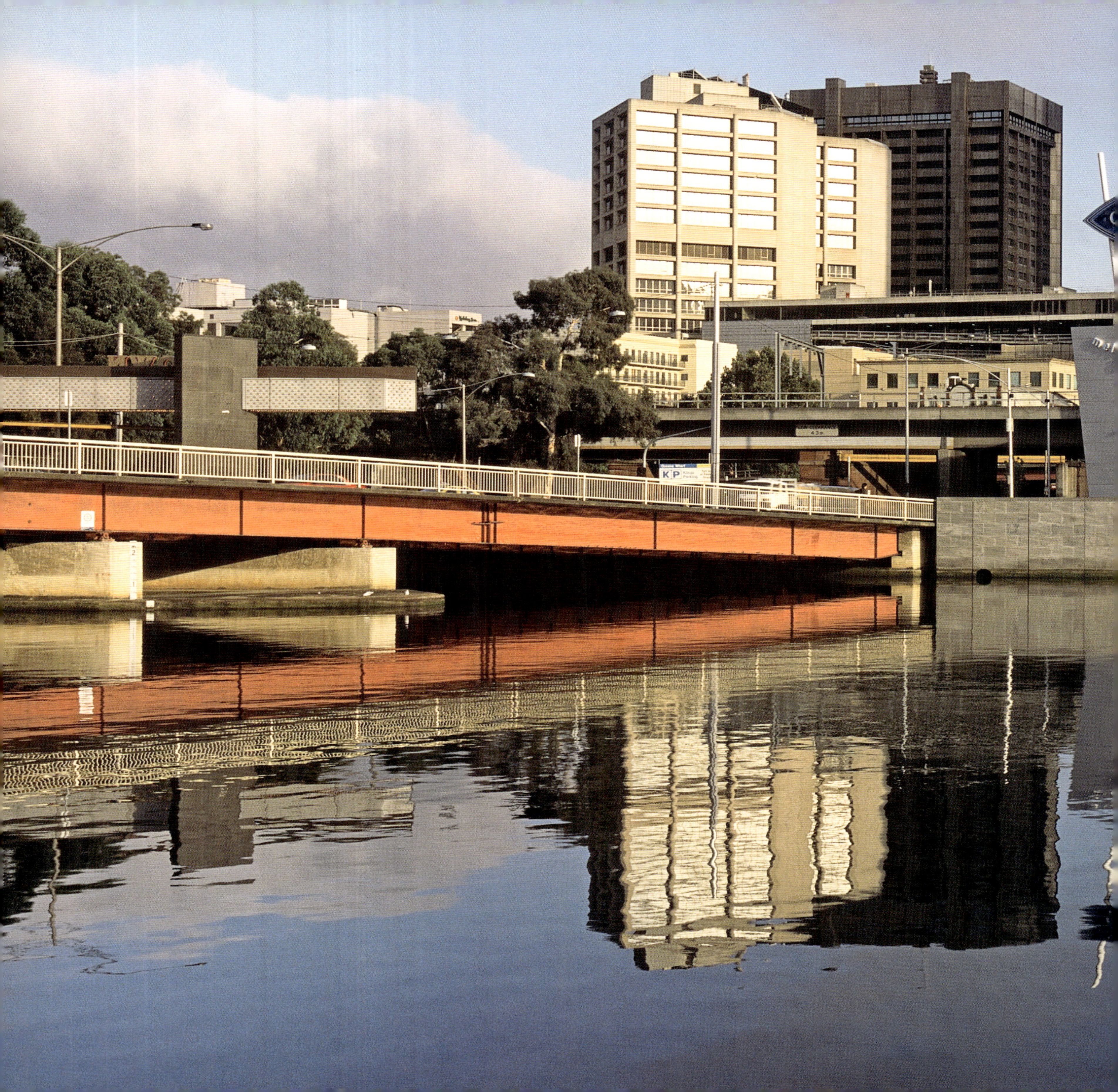

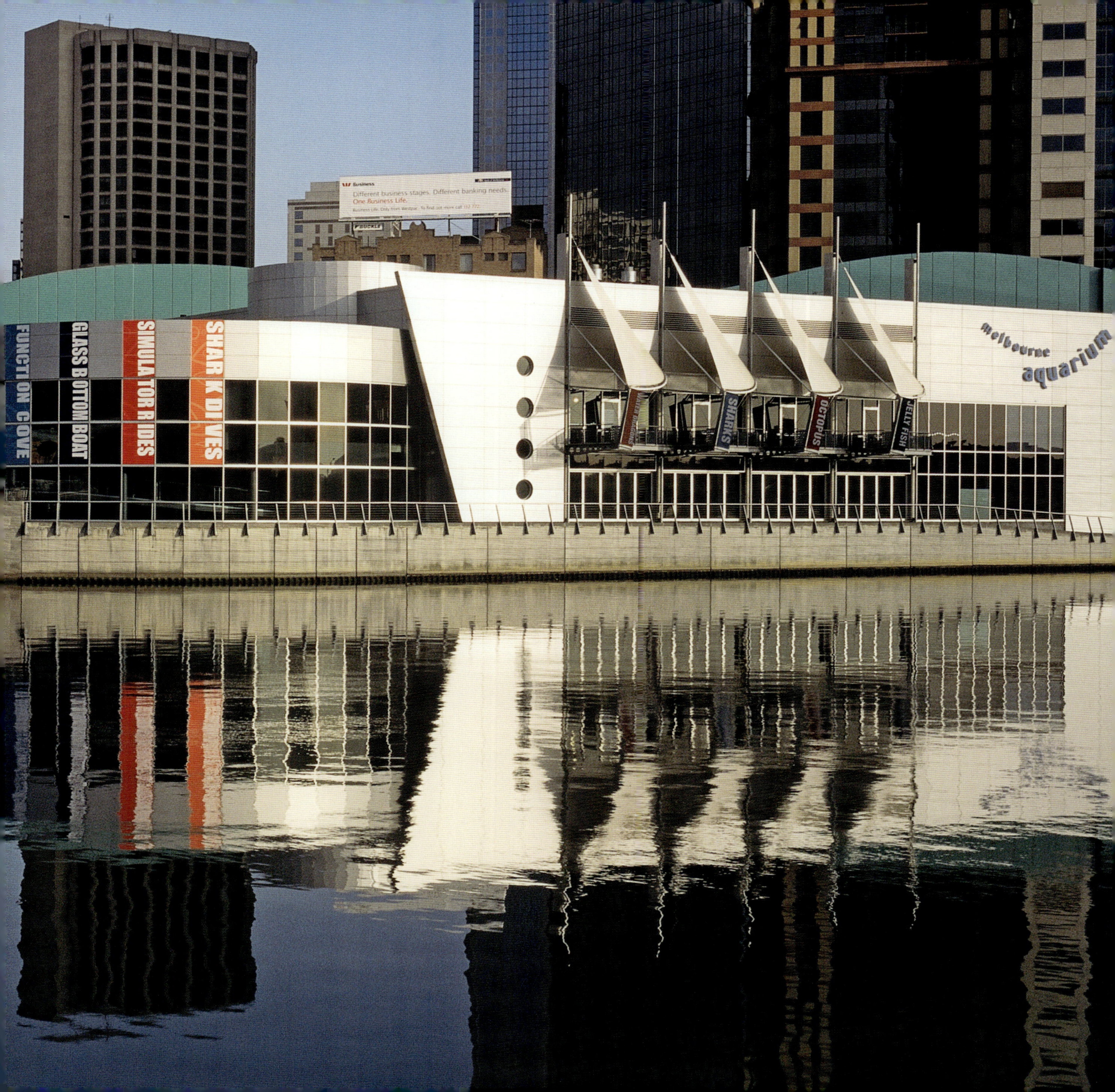
Business
Different business stages. Different banking needs.
One Business Life.
FUNCTION COVE
GLASS BOTTOM BOAT
SIMULATOR RIDES
SHARK DIVES
SHARKS
OCTOPUS
JELLY FISH
melbourne
aquarium

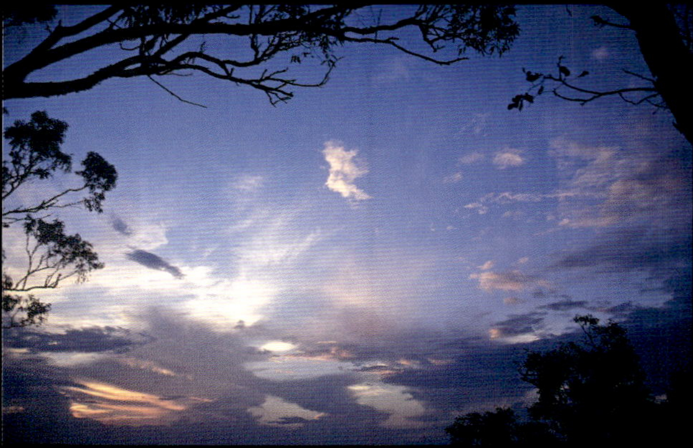

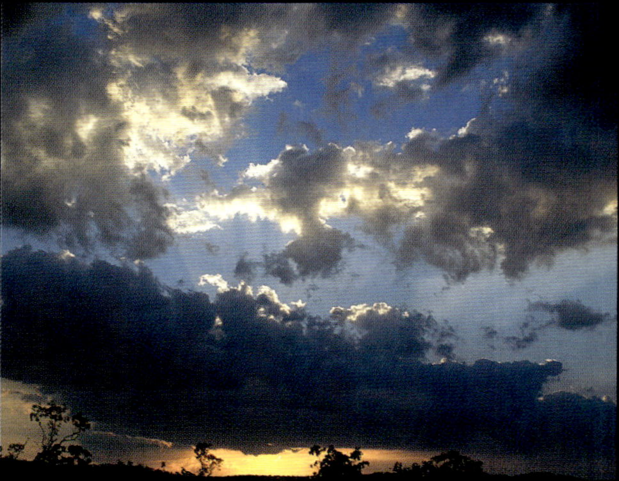

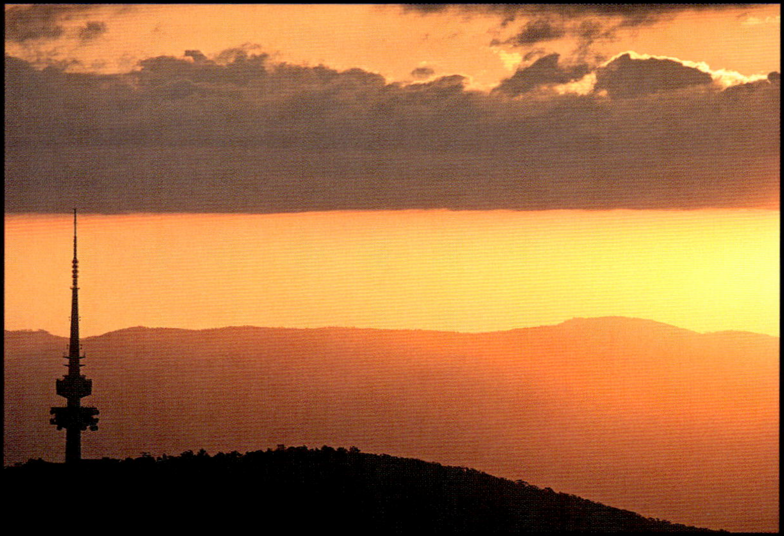

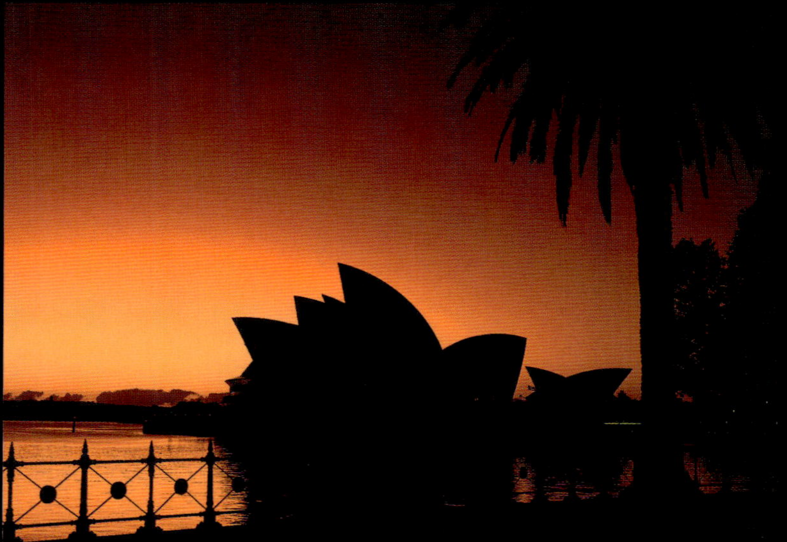

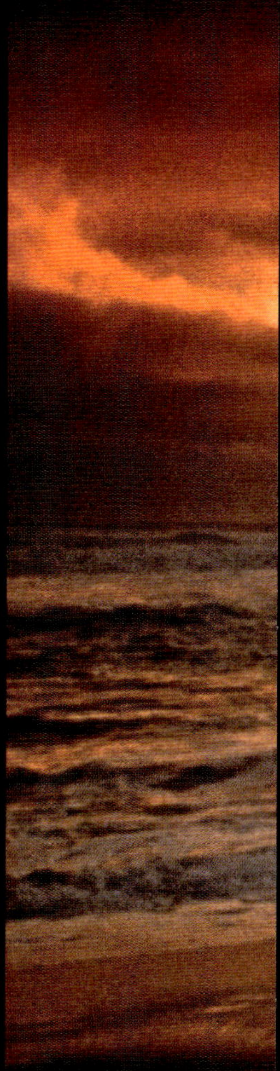

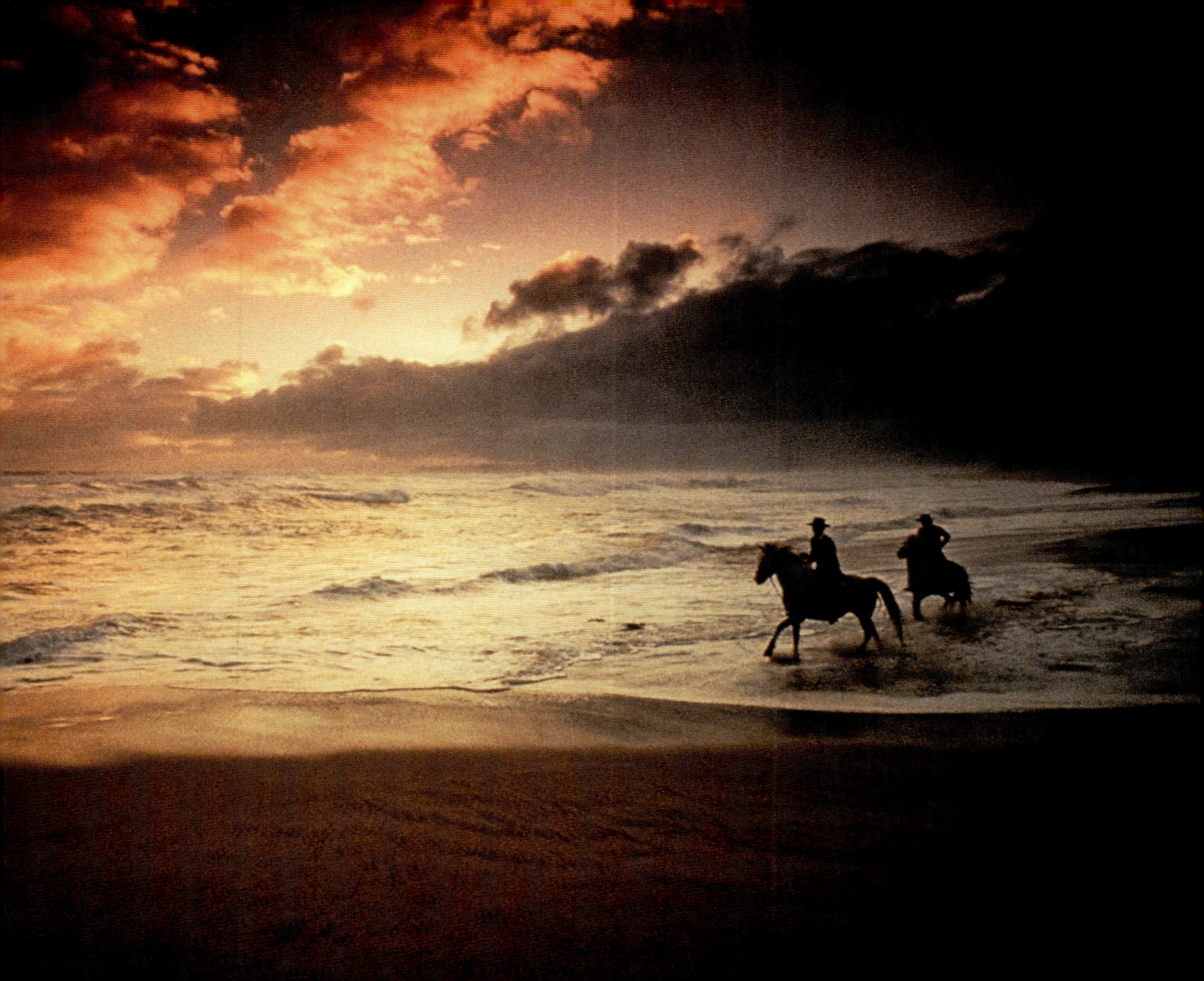

At dawn and sunset, Australia's skies put on a magical show. It is tempting to believe it is all intentionally orchestrated for the benefit of visitors, but, of course, it is simply Nature doing what Nature does best.

The setting sun highlights the silhouettes of landmarks like Canberra's Telstra Tower and the Sydney Opera House, and horse-riders on the beach at Cape Otway, Victoria.

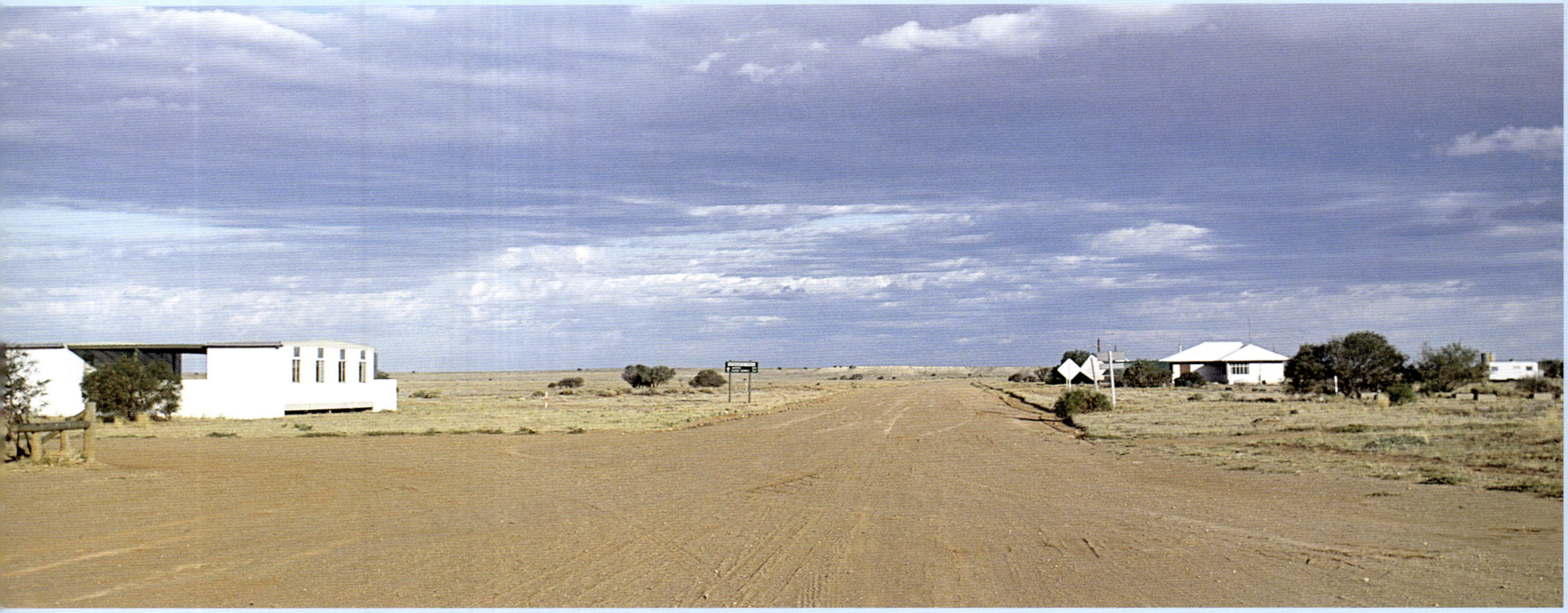

BIG SKIES

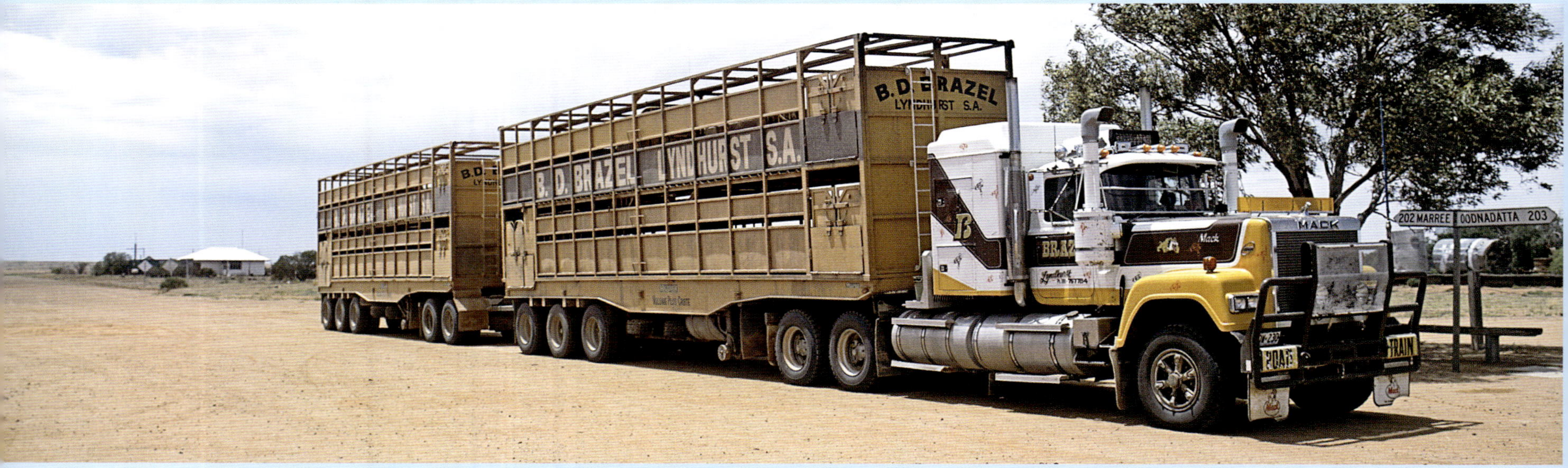

In the Outback everything is dwarfed by the immense skies, often threatening and dark as bad weather brews, but more often displaying great canopies of cerulean blue.

Here, endless vistas drift to shimmering horizons, road trains plough a dusty furrow, lonely pubs beckon weary travelers, and signs warn of floodways—bone dry in all but the wet season.

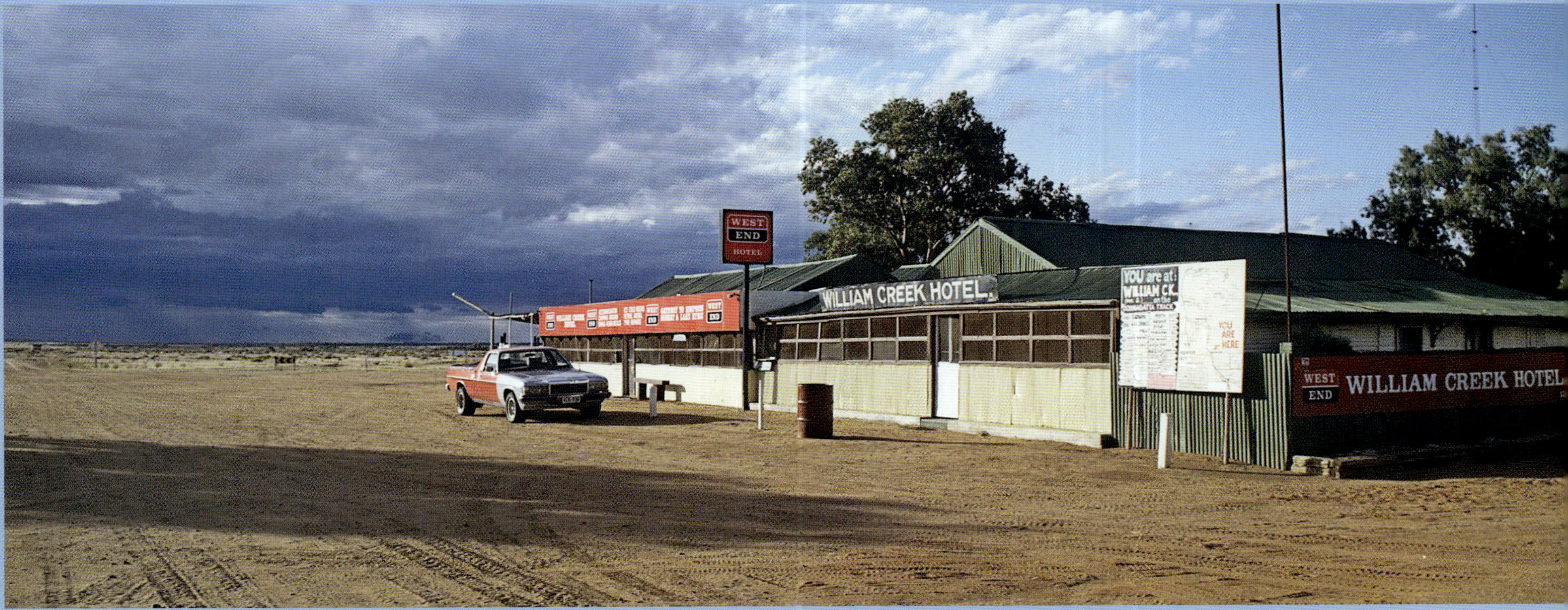
WEST END HOTEL
WILLIAM CREEK HOTEL.
YOU are at WILLIAM CK.
YOU ARE HERE
WEST END
WILLIAM CREEK HOTEL

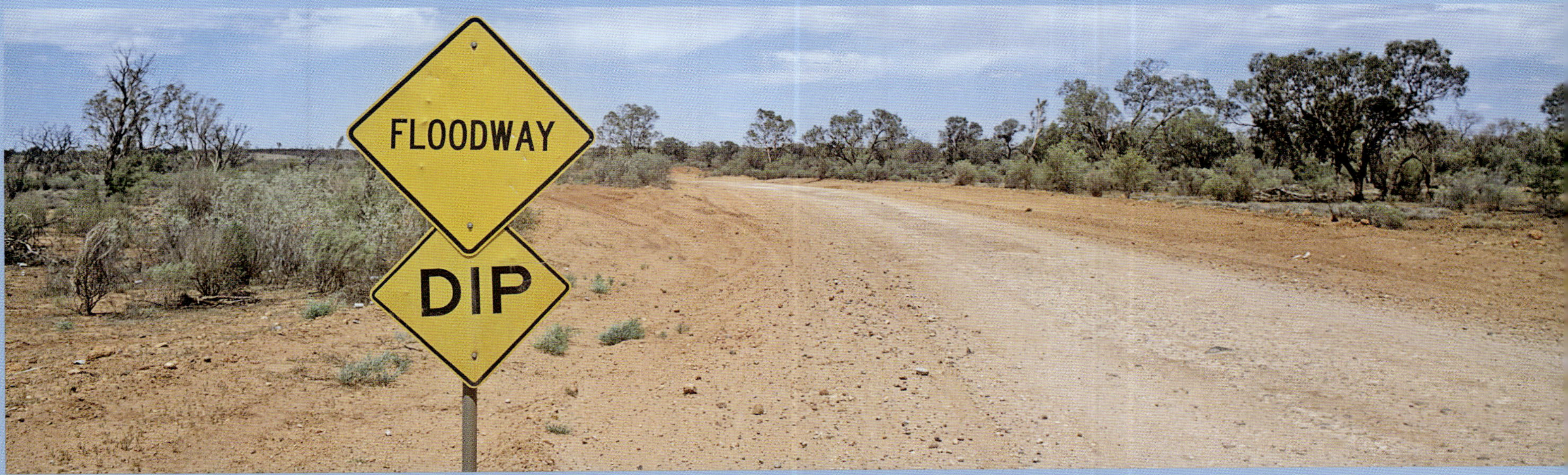
FLOODWAY
DIP

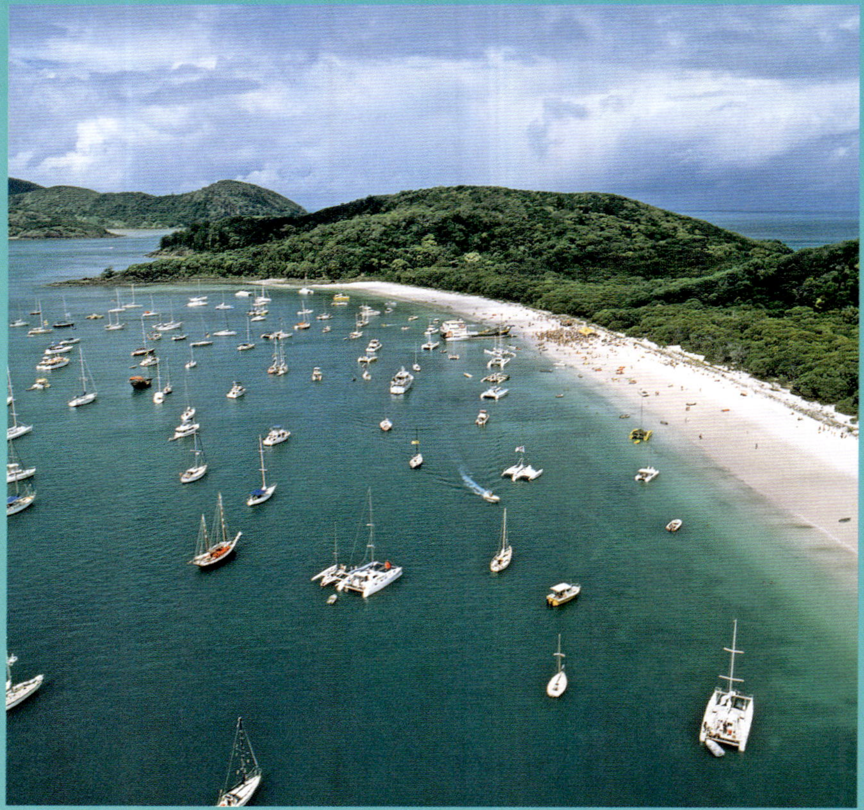

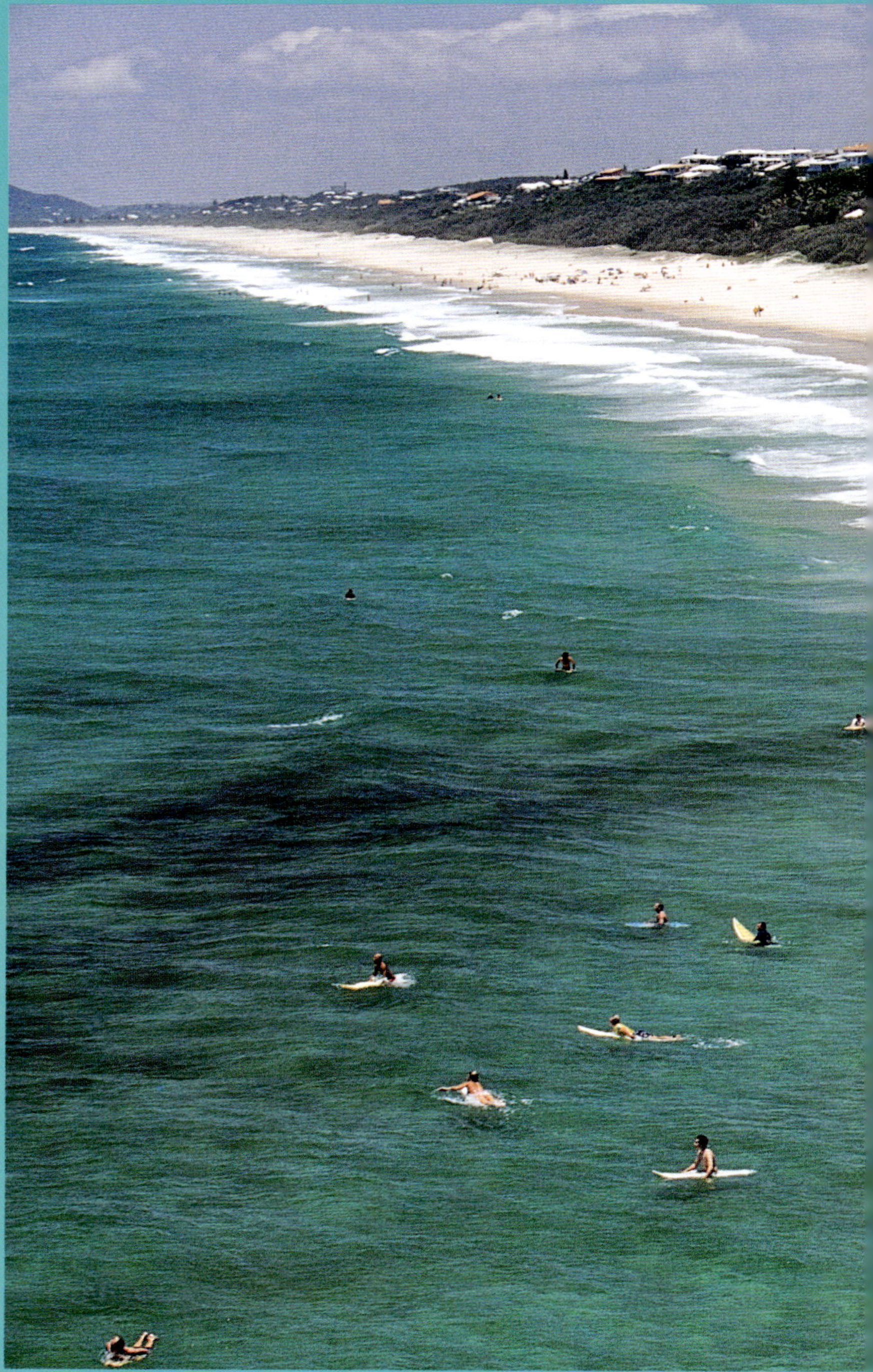

CALMER WATERS

An assortment of pleasure boats moor in the azure blue water of the Great Barrier Reef (above). With many Australians living a brief drive from a beach the country is the home of beach culture.

Sunshine Beach at Sunshine Coast, Noosa, is a popular surfing location, while the tree ferns and myrtle beech trees around Triplet Falls in Otway State Forest offer a more relaxed view of things.

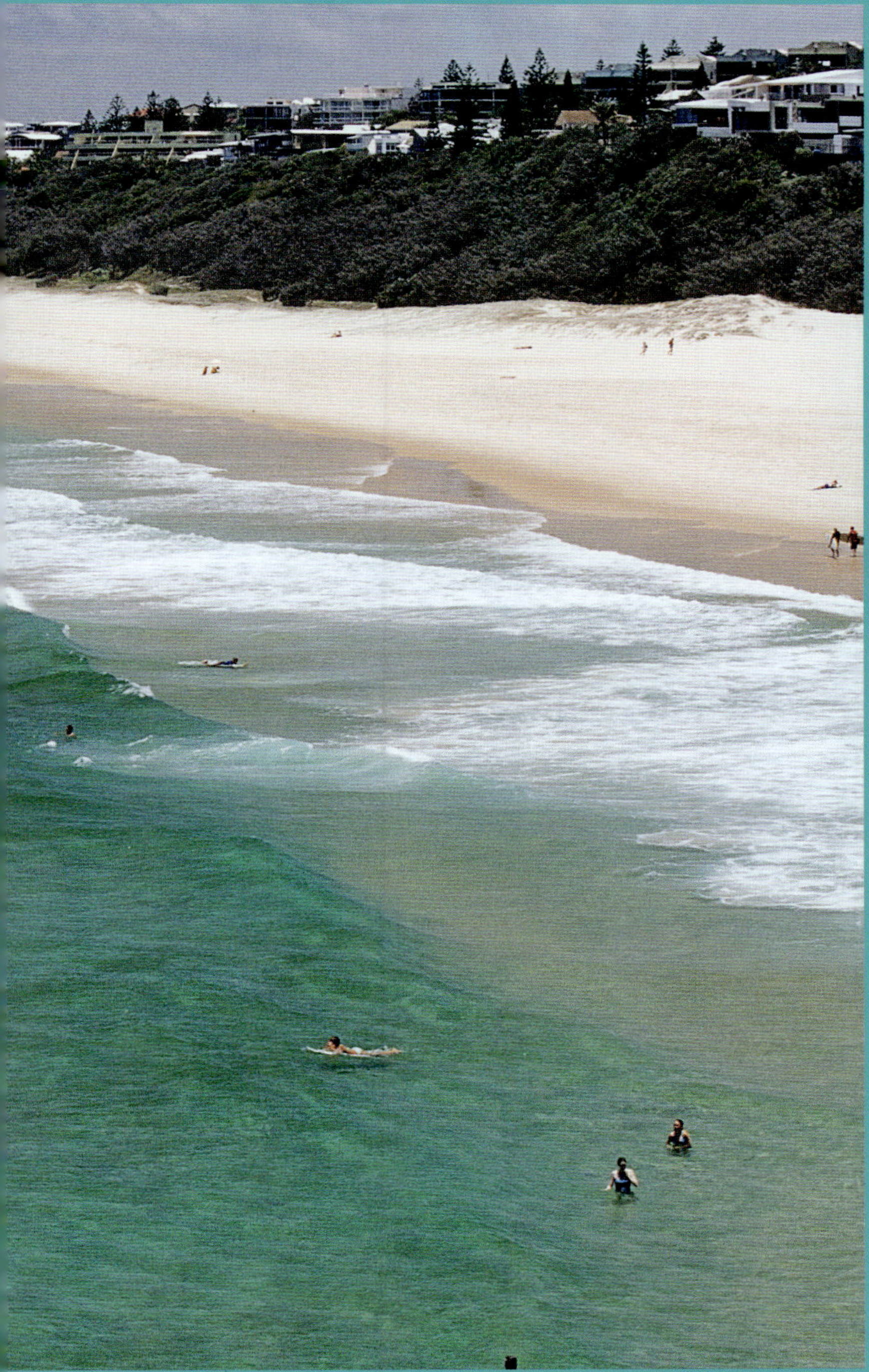

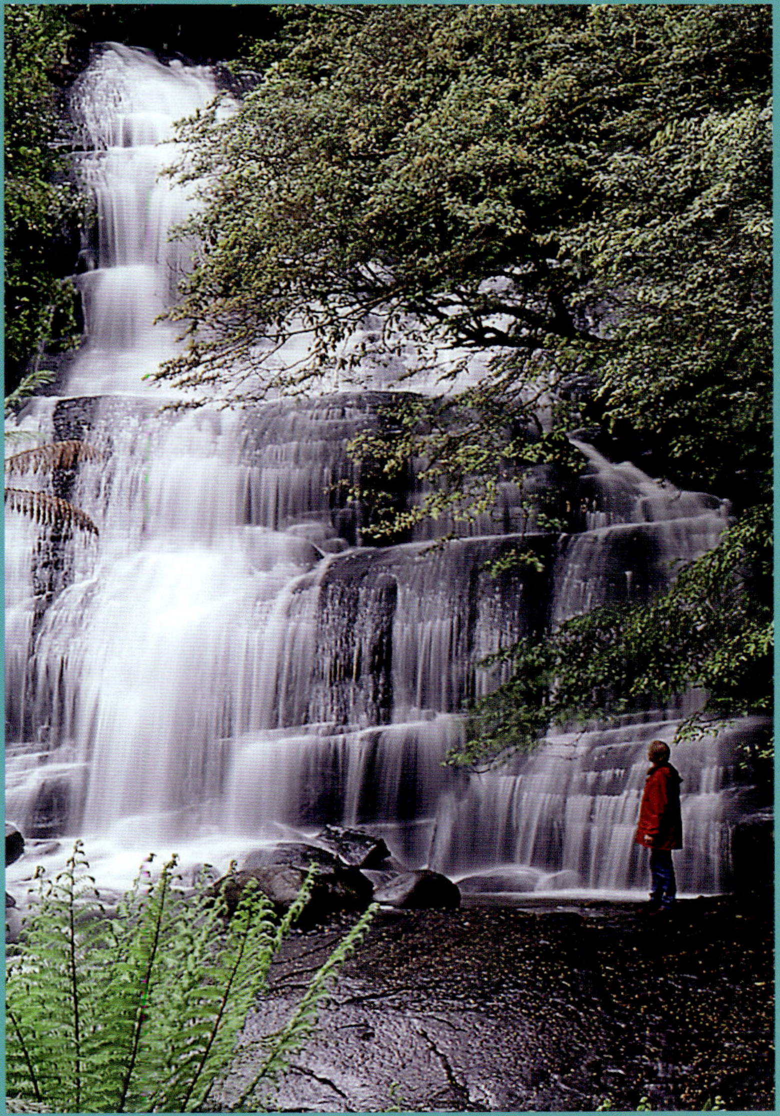

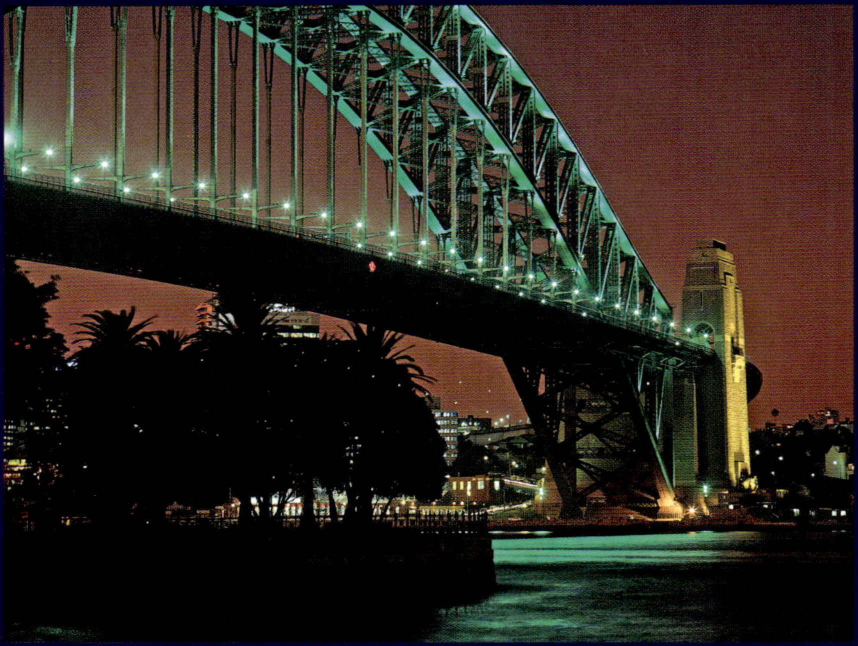

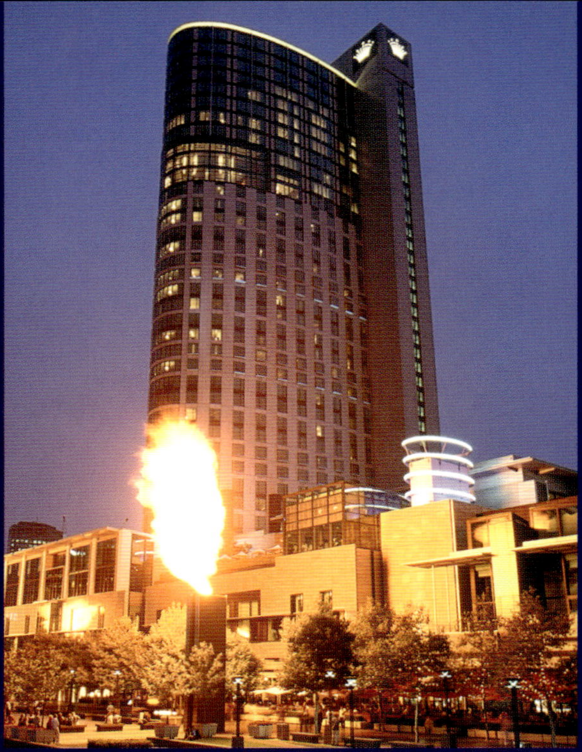

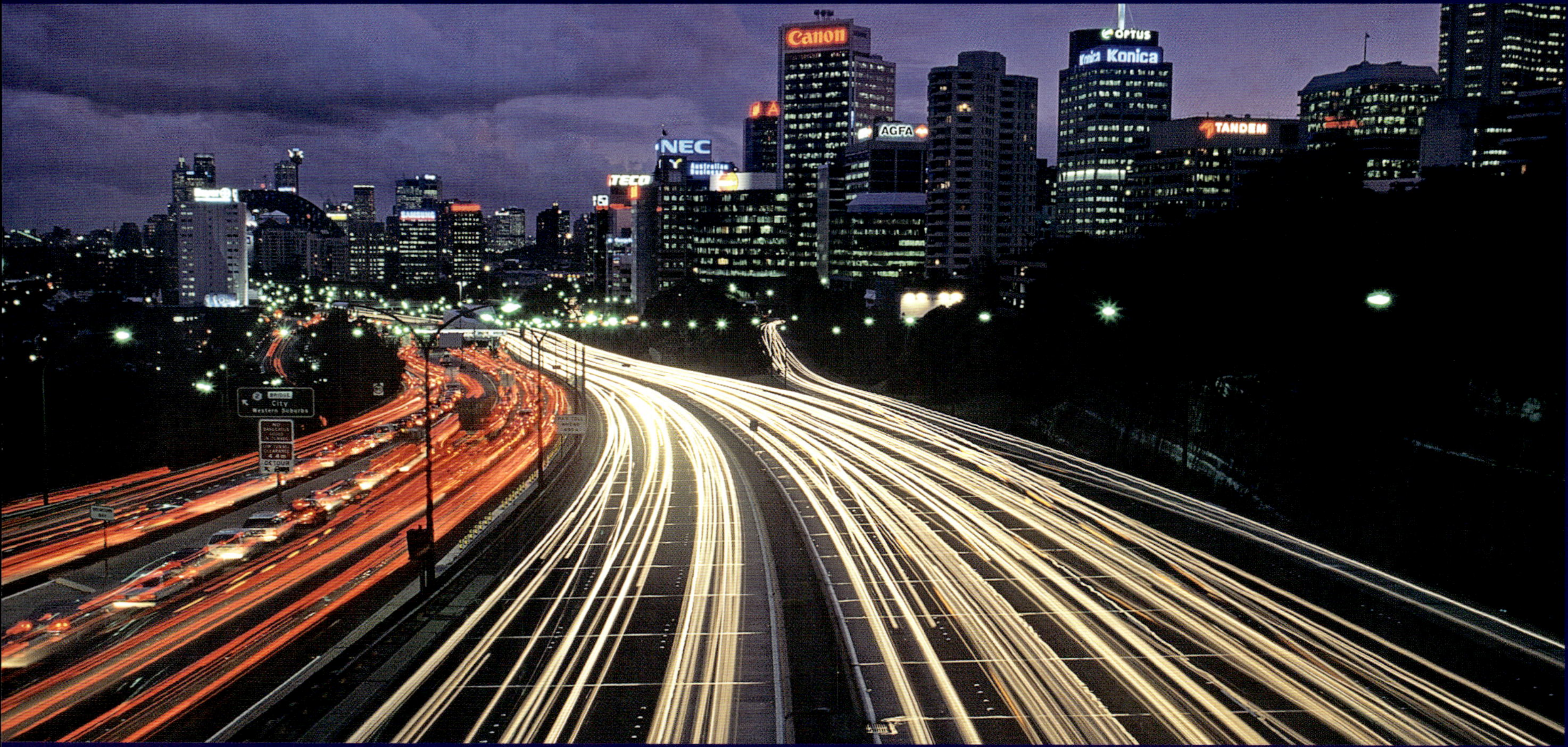
Canon
OPTUS
Konica
NEC
AGFA
TANDEM

CITY LIGHTS

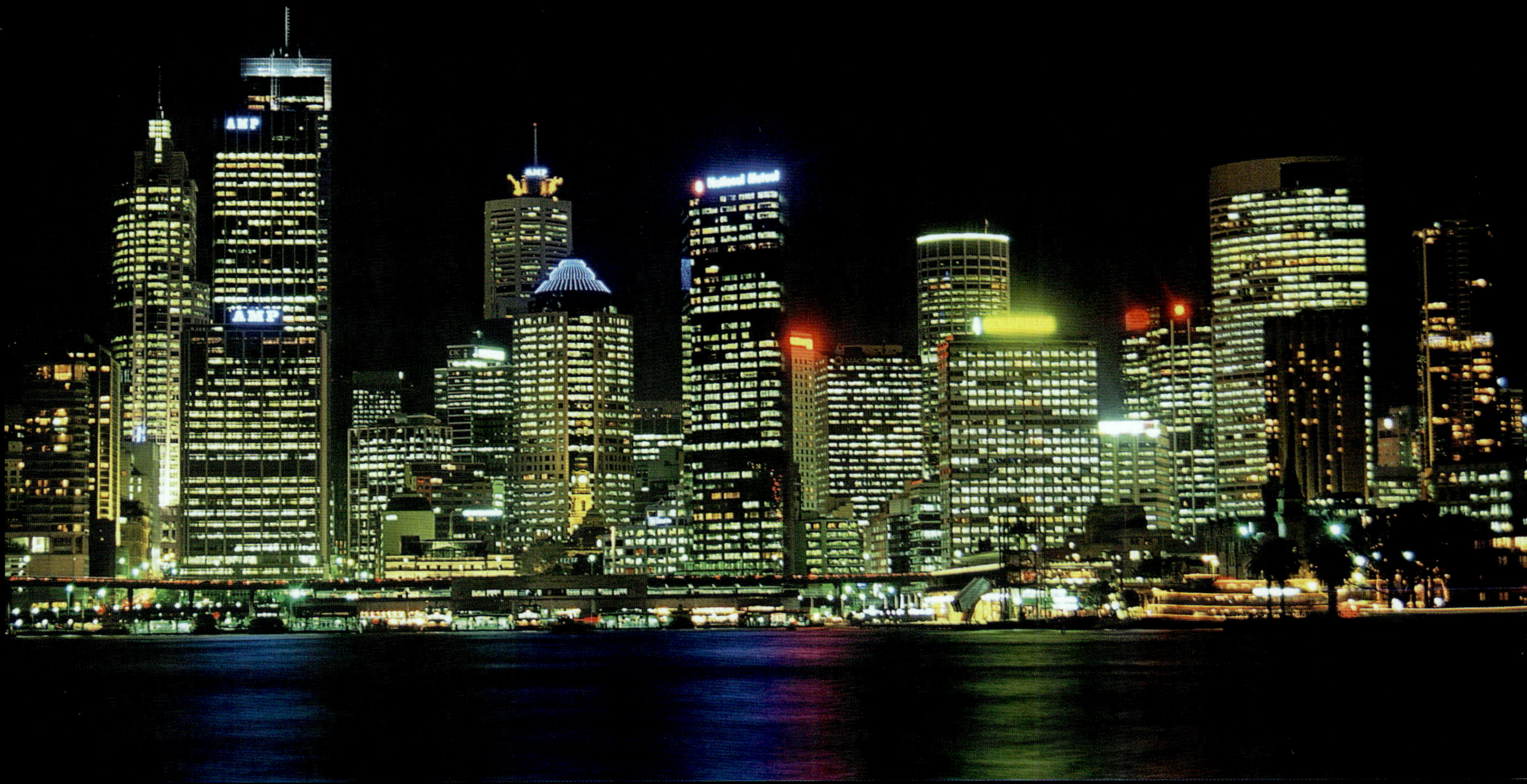

During the day, Australia is at work. At night, the cities come alive beneath myriad lights. Sydney Harbour Bridge (top left) is illuminated at night, as are many buildings such as the Crown Towers Hotel in Yarra Promenade, Melbourne. A time-delay exposure of the main roads leaving Sydney's Harbour Bridge means the cars' rear lights and headlights form continuous lines of light. Above: Gleaming lights of Sydney's Central Business District, seen from Milson's Point.

TIME & MOTION

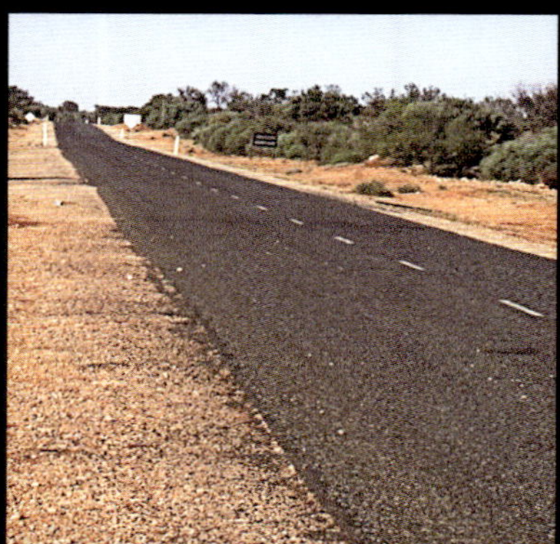

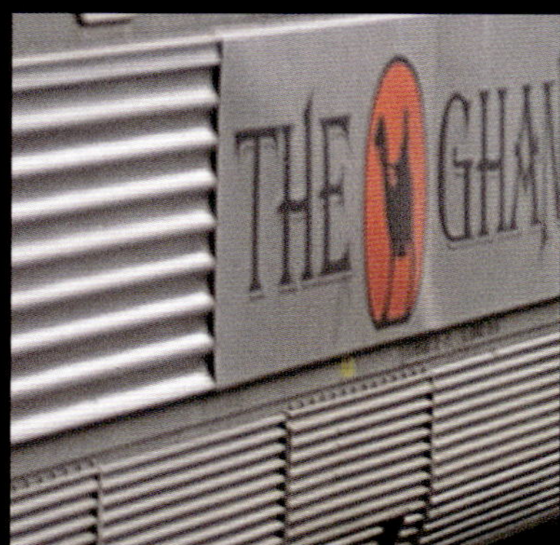

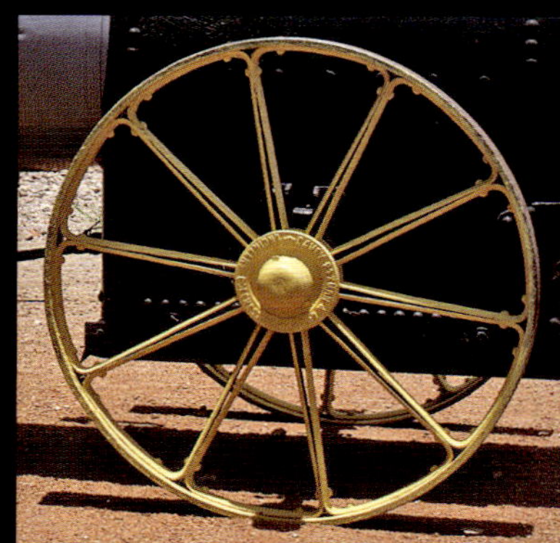

7

COLORS OF AUSTRALIA:
TIME & MOTION

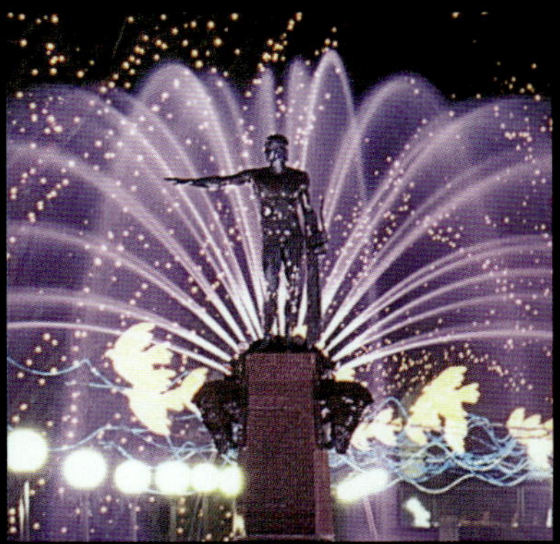

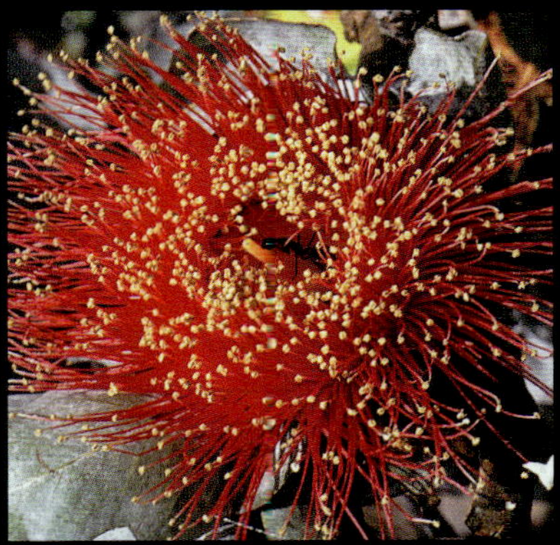

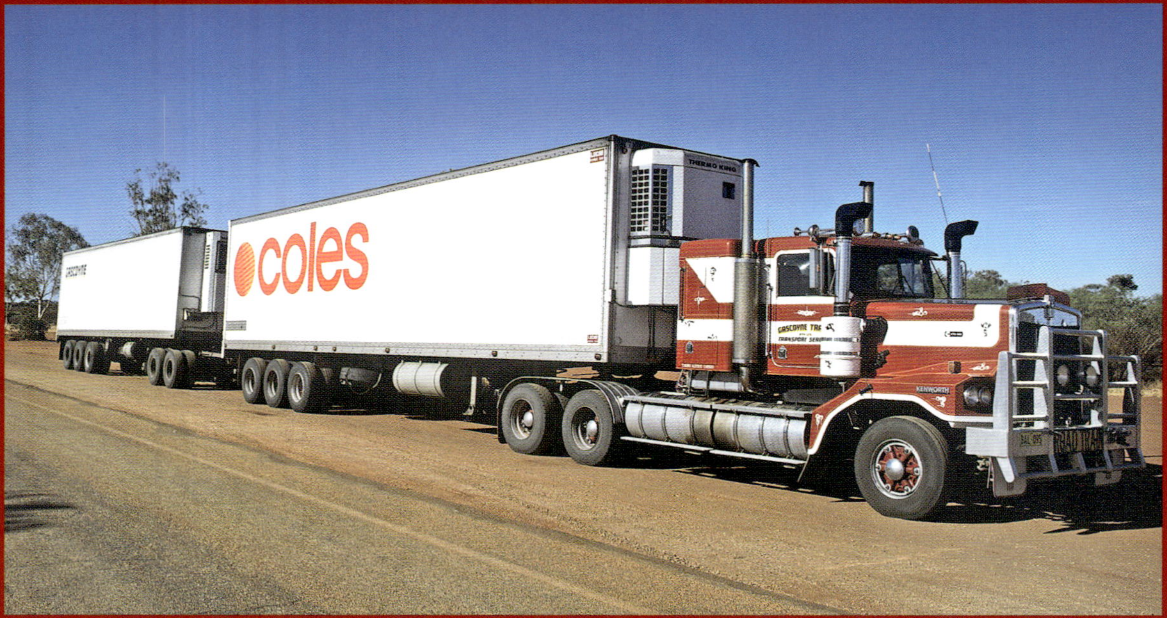
coles

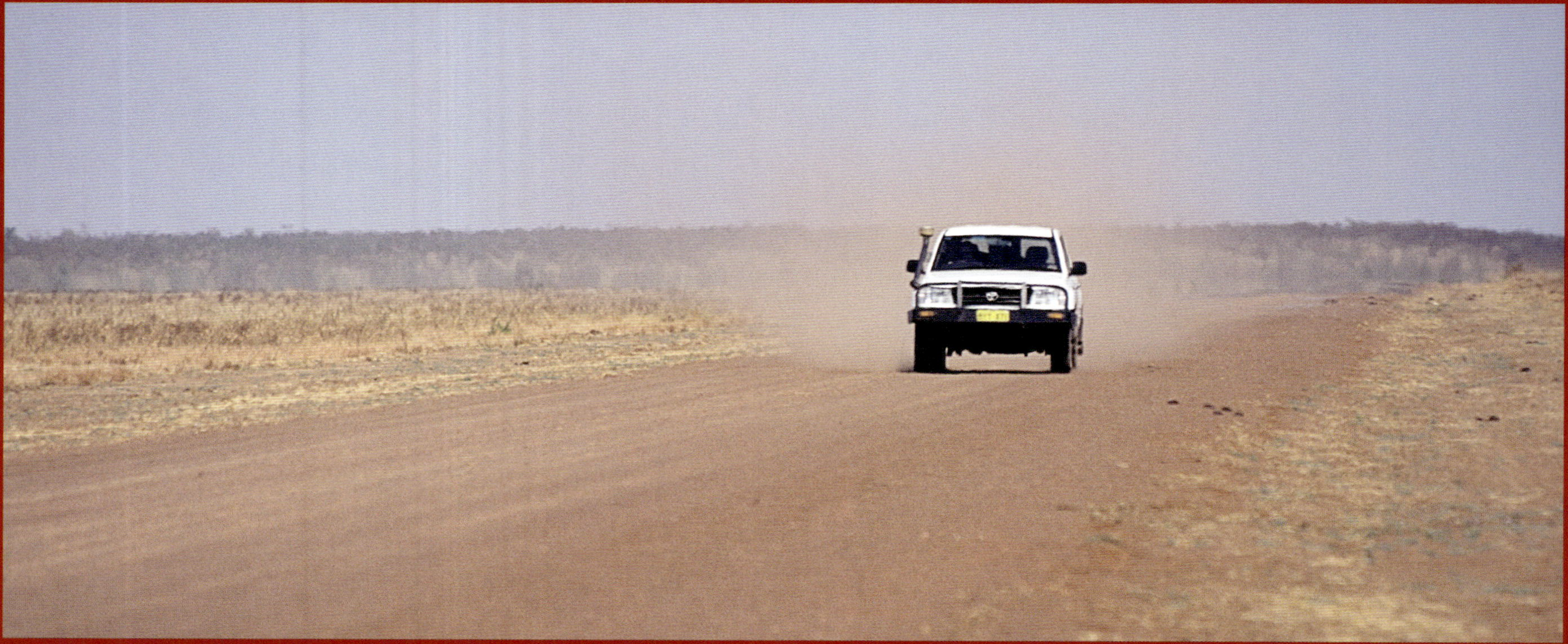

THE LONG DRIVE

By land, sea, and air, Australia is circumscribed, but only just. The train leaving Darwin for Adelaide is a mile long and takes three days to reach its destination; the train that sets off west from Sydney, bound for Perth is arguably longer. Some rail journeys include sightseeing tours en route, to break the monotony.

You can make five flights from London to Paris in the time it takes to fly across Australia; you surrender hours, maybe days of your life to make the journey. Try this by road, and the days slip by in a haze, dodging road trains and animals alike, stopping off at roadhouses where dingoes stand on the piano and "sing," where "mateship" prevails, and Outback people spin their own webs of legend and intrigue.

You feel free in Australia, free from tension, free from ill will, free from pressure or control. "Going bush" is not just an Aboriginal trait, it's a modern state of mind.

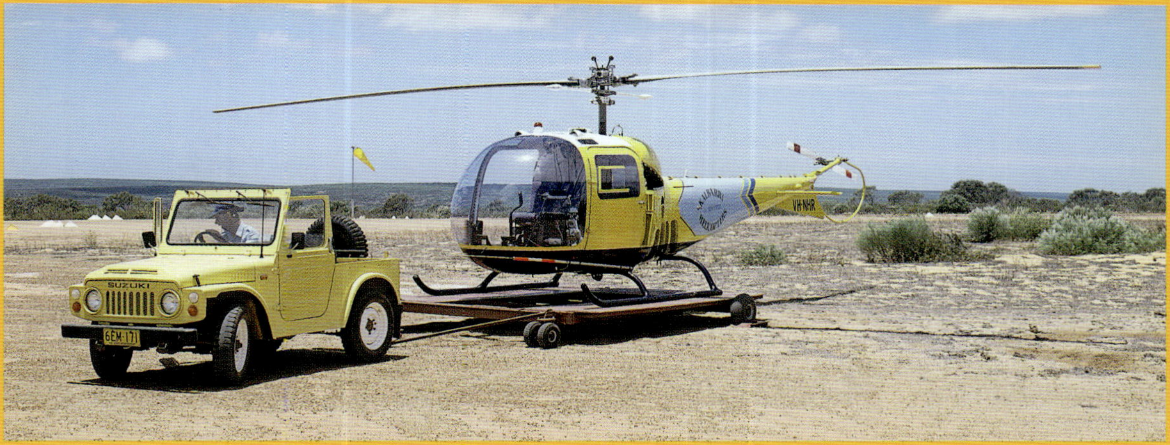

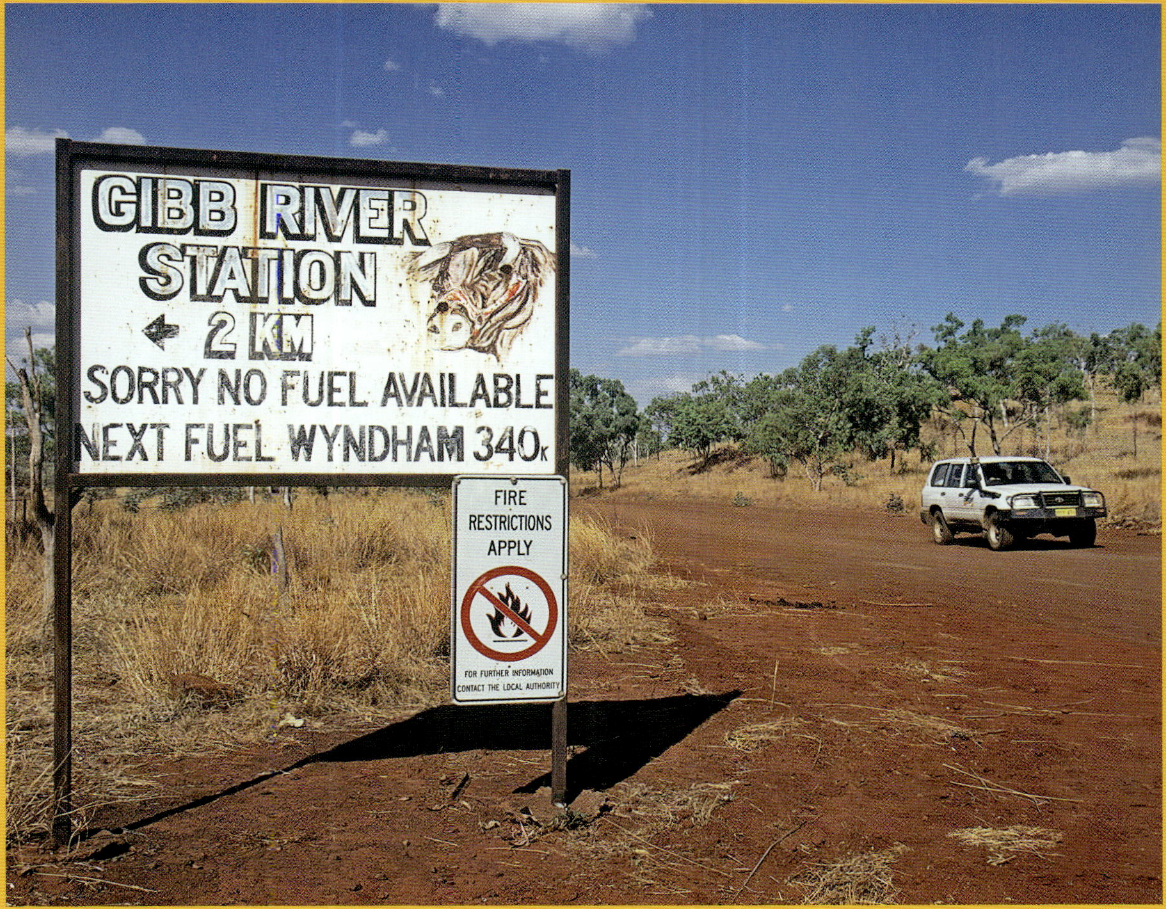

The Australian Outback road train (top left) is a grand thing, the biggest and heaviest road freight vehicle in the world. These brutes deliver more than 650 horse power and gobble fuel at an alarming rate.

In central Australia, many roads are no more than gravel or corrugated, compressed sand that only four-wheel drive vehicles can be certain to survive. Helicopter and jeep tours are common ways for visitors to explore the Outback.

The Gibb River Station sign, rather apologetically declares its lack of fuel; for passing motorists the next stop is Wyndham, Kimberley, and 340 kilometers is 212 miles—a long way if you are running on empty.

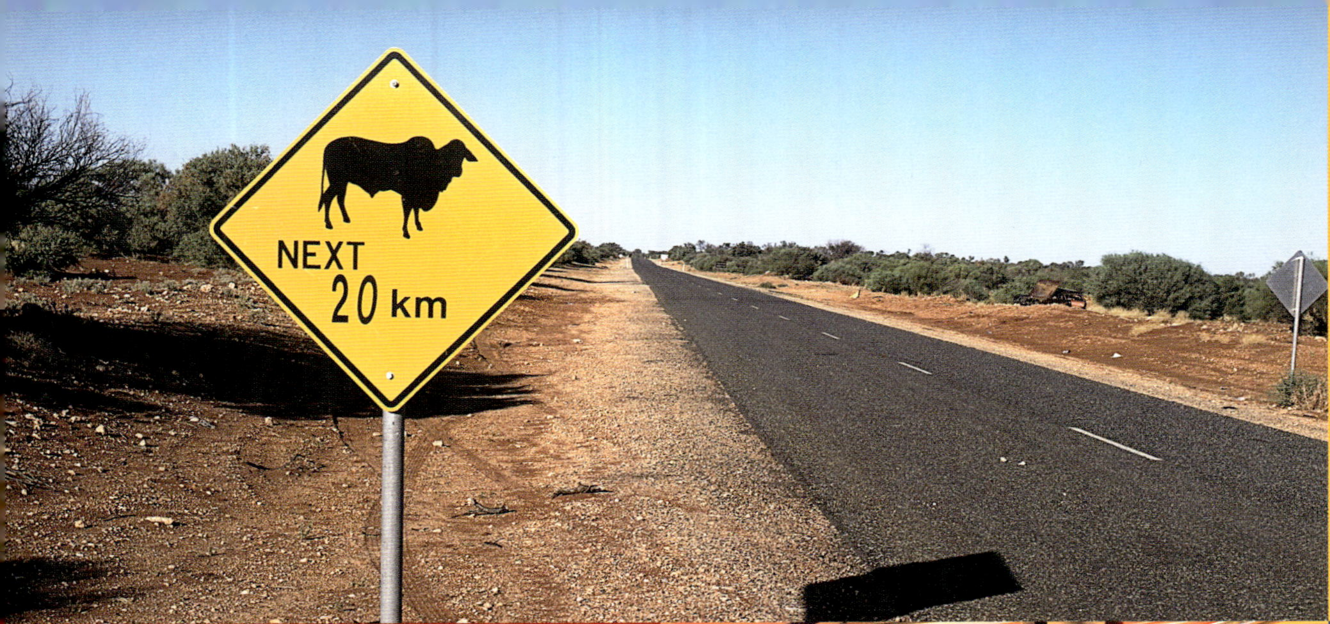
NEXT
20 km

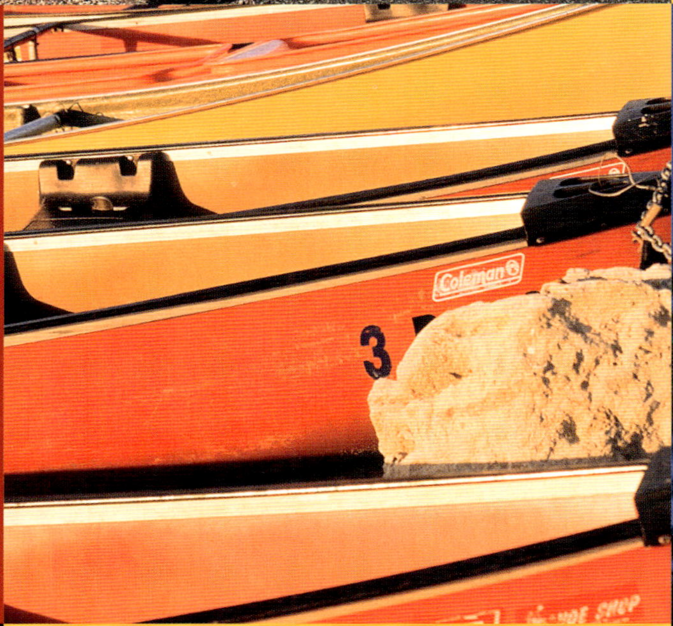
Coleman
3

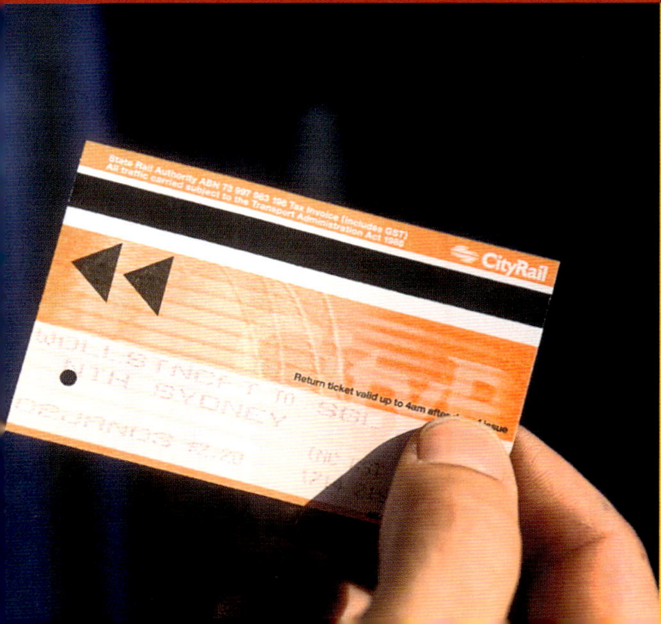
CityRail

STOP 9
THE SYDNEY EXPLOR

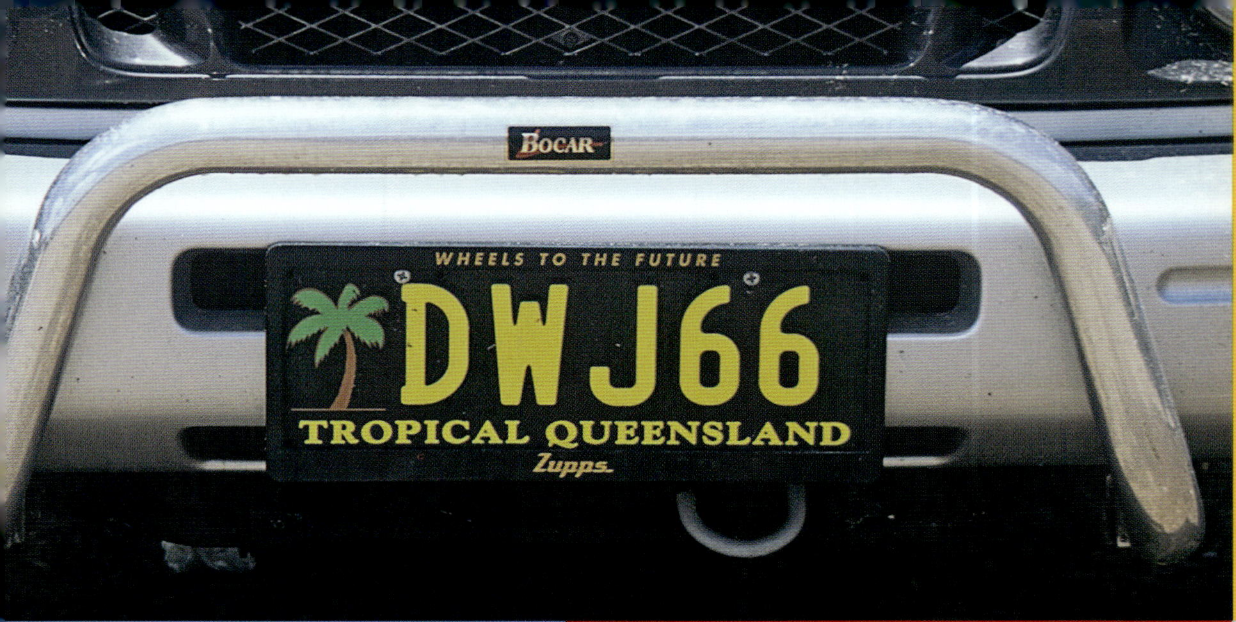
BOCAR
WHEELS TO THE FUTURE
DWJ66
TROPICAL QUEENSLAND
Zupps

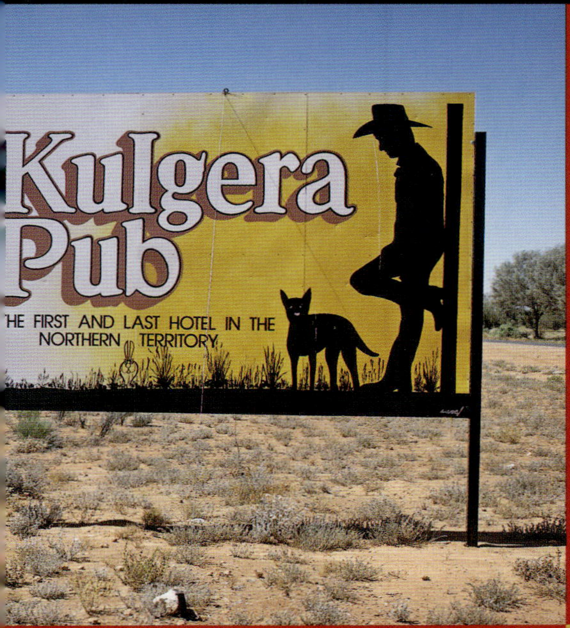
Kulgera
Pub
THE FIRST AND LAST HOTEL IN THE
NORTHERN TERRITORY

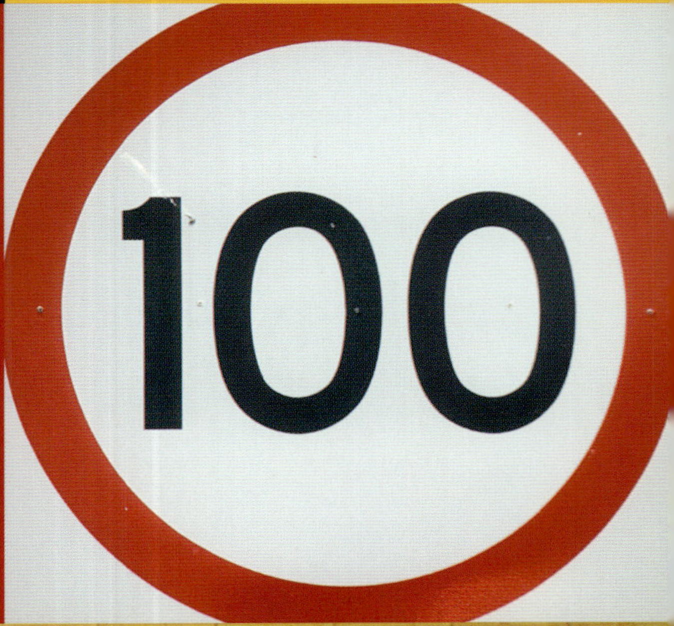
100

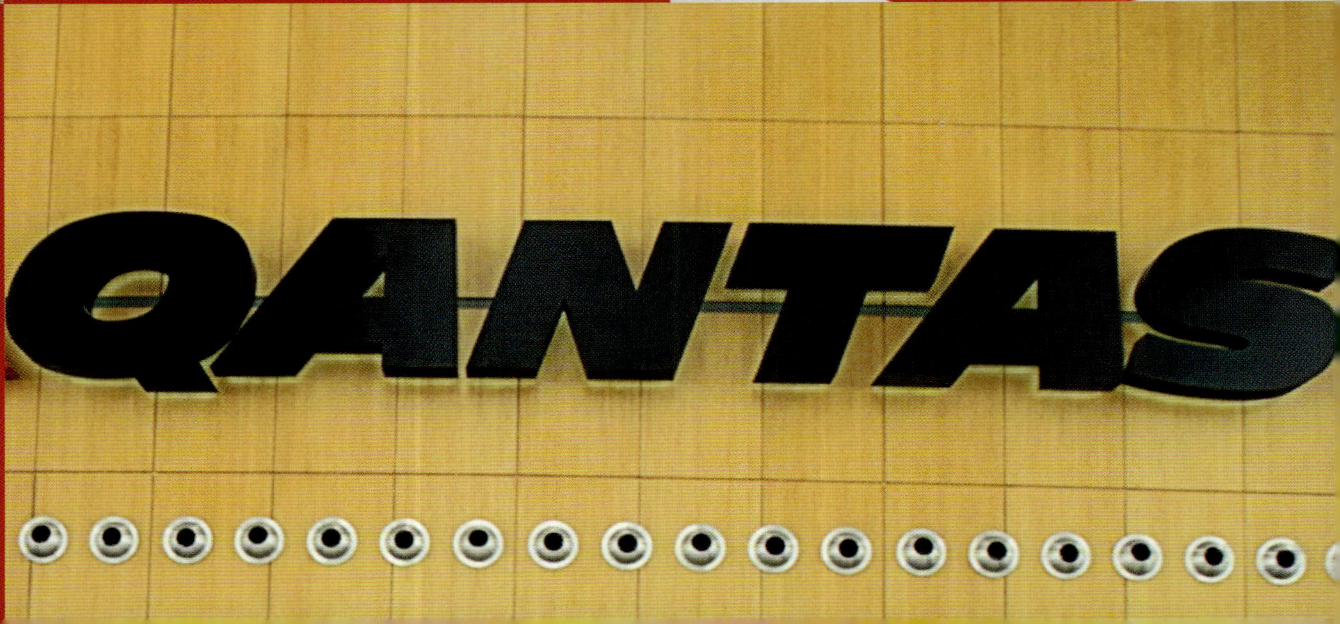
QANTAS

ON THE MOVE

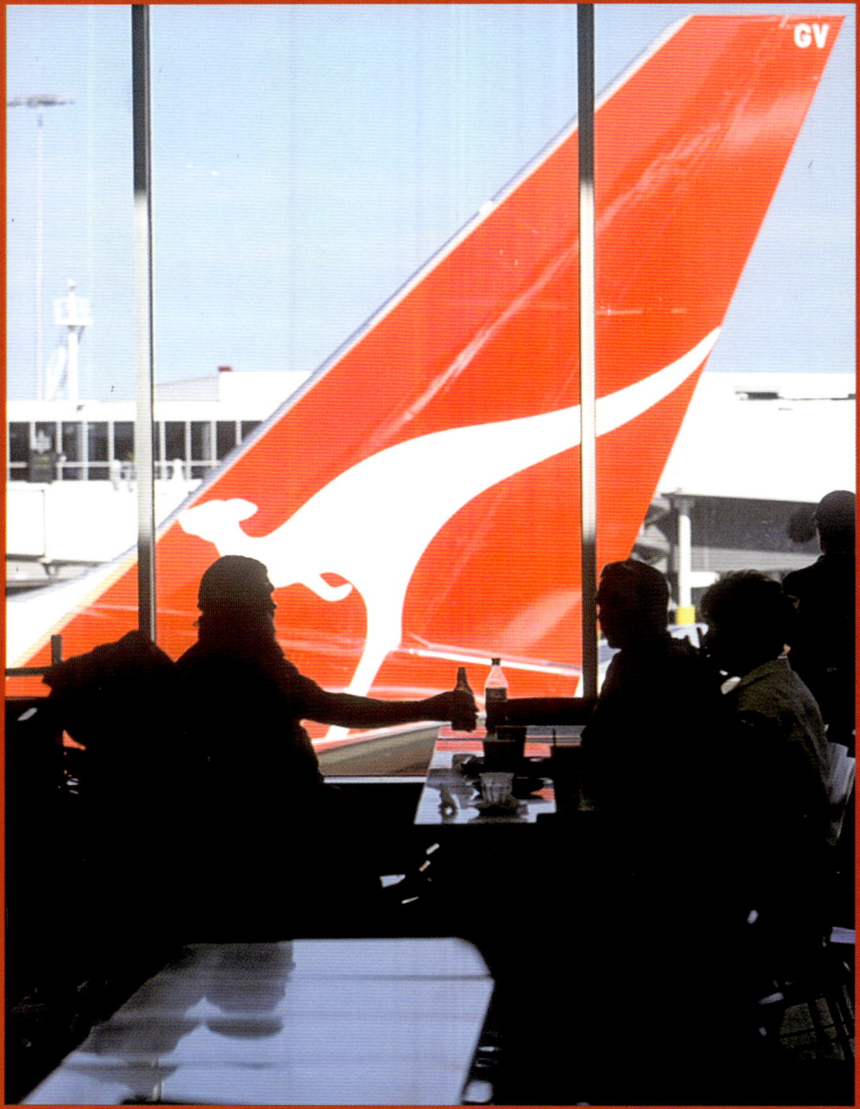

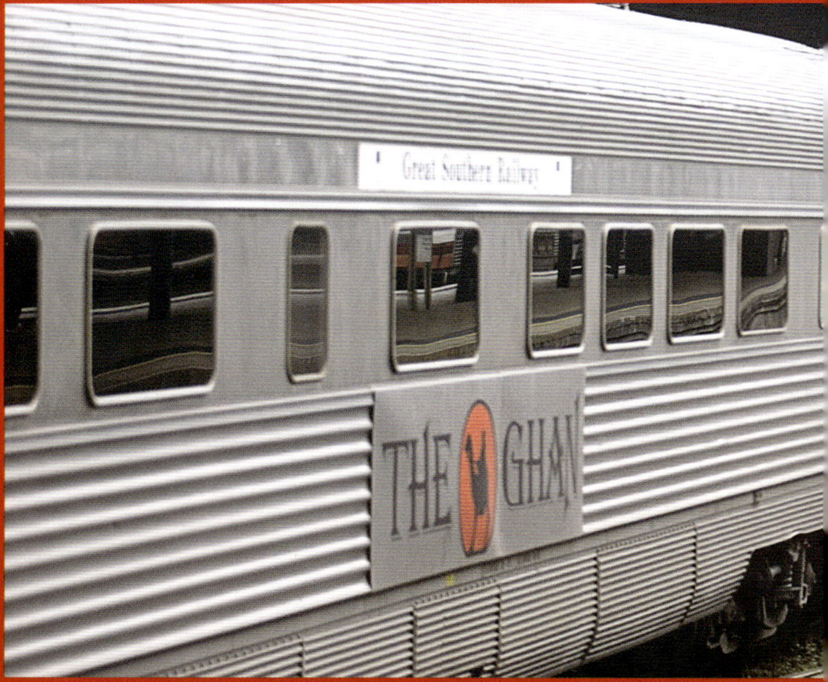

Air and rail are the best means of coping with Australia's great expanses. The national airline Qantas, is being challenged by low-cost Virgin Blue. For a relaxed and stylish rail journey, the Ghan travels from Darwin to Adelaide, and the Indian-Pacific from Sydney to Perth via Adelaide.

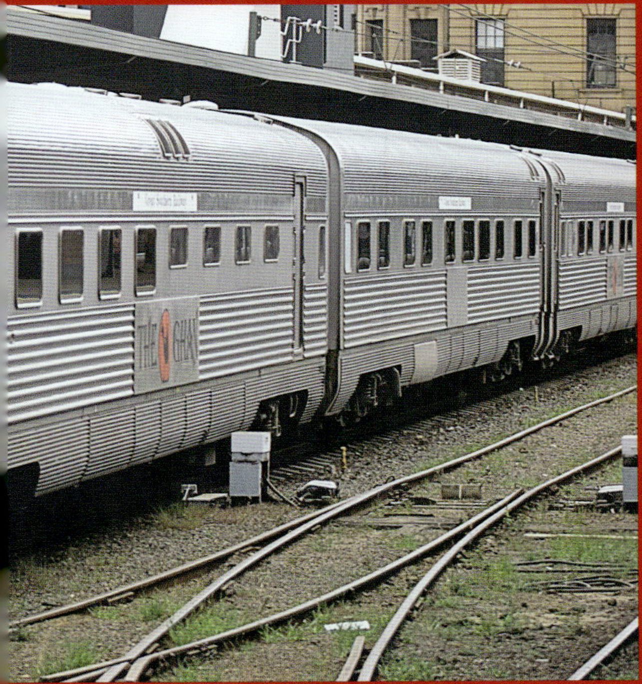

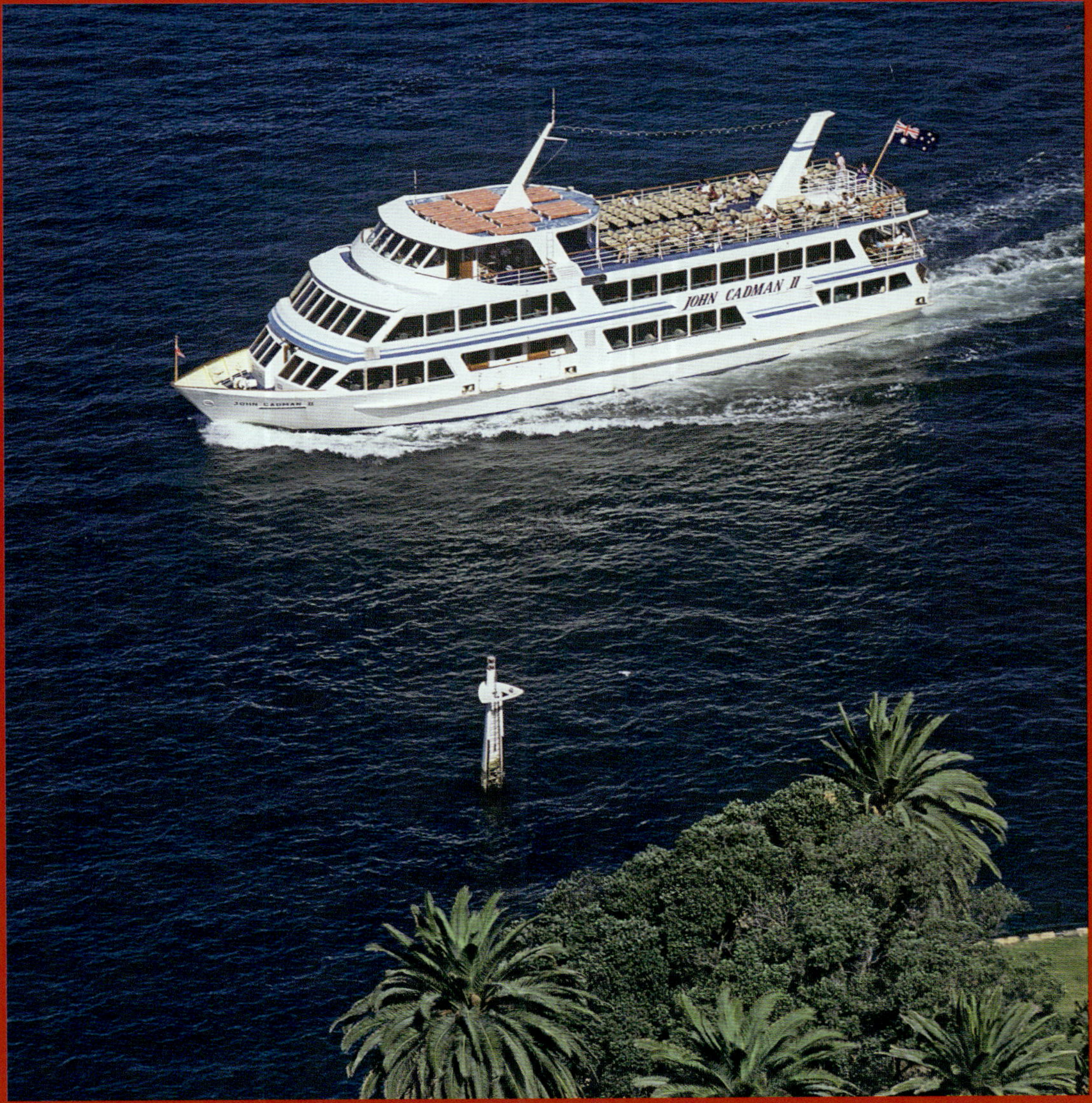

Ferry boats ply all the city waterways, none quite so frenetic as Circular Quay in Sydney, and offer a less costly way of viewing the city's waterfront sights than cruise ships and tours.
Next page: A spectacular fireworks display at Sydney Harbour Bridge.

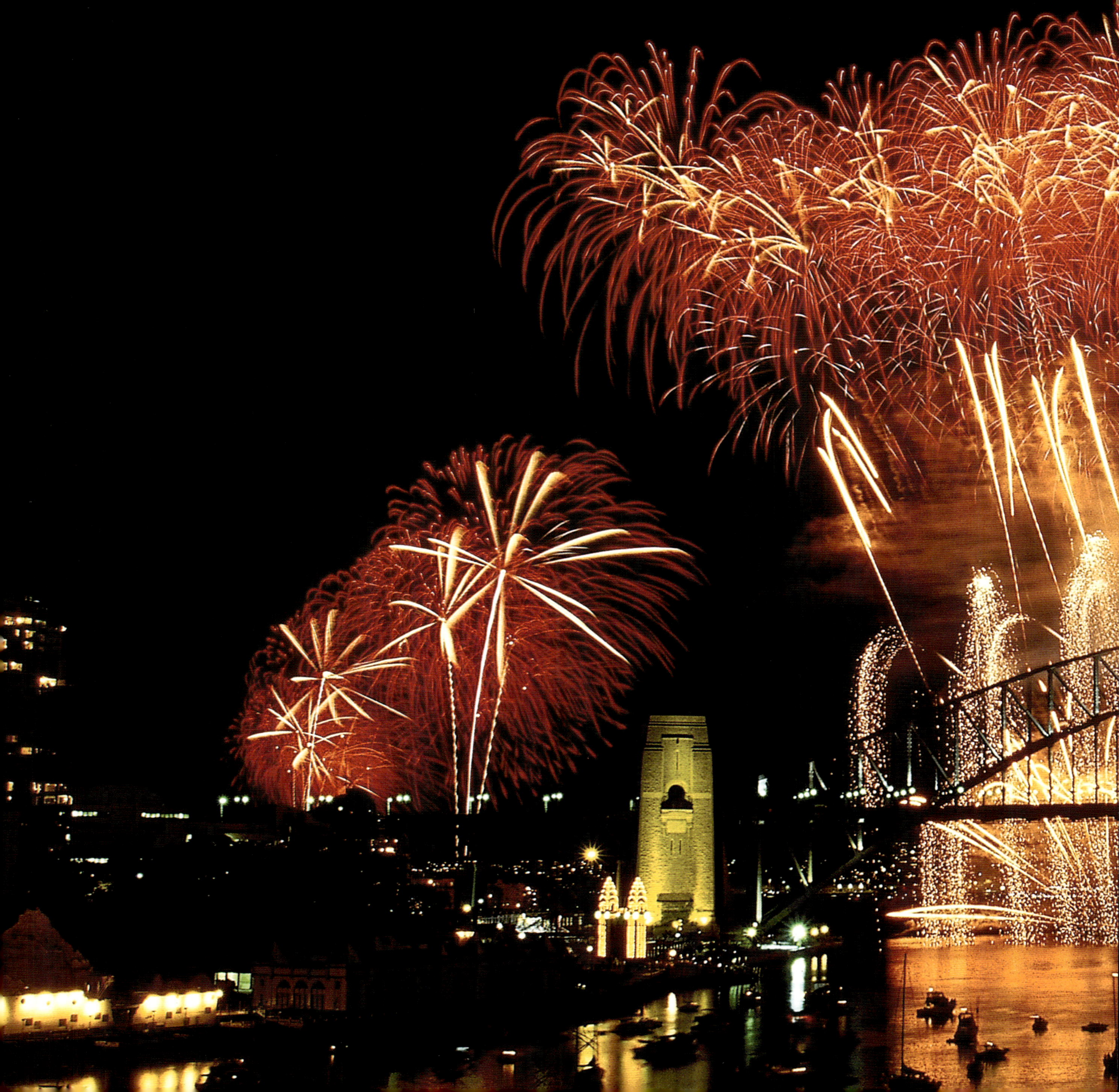

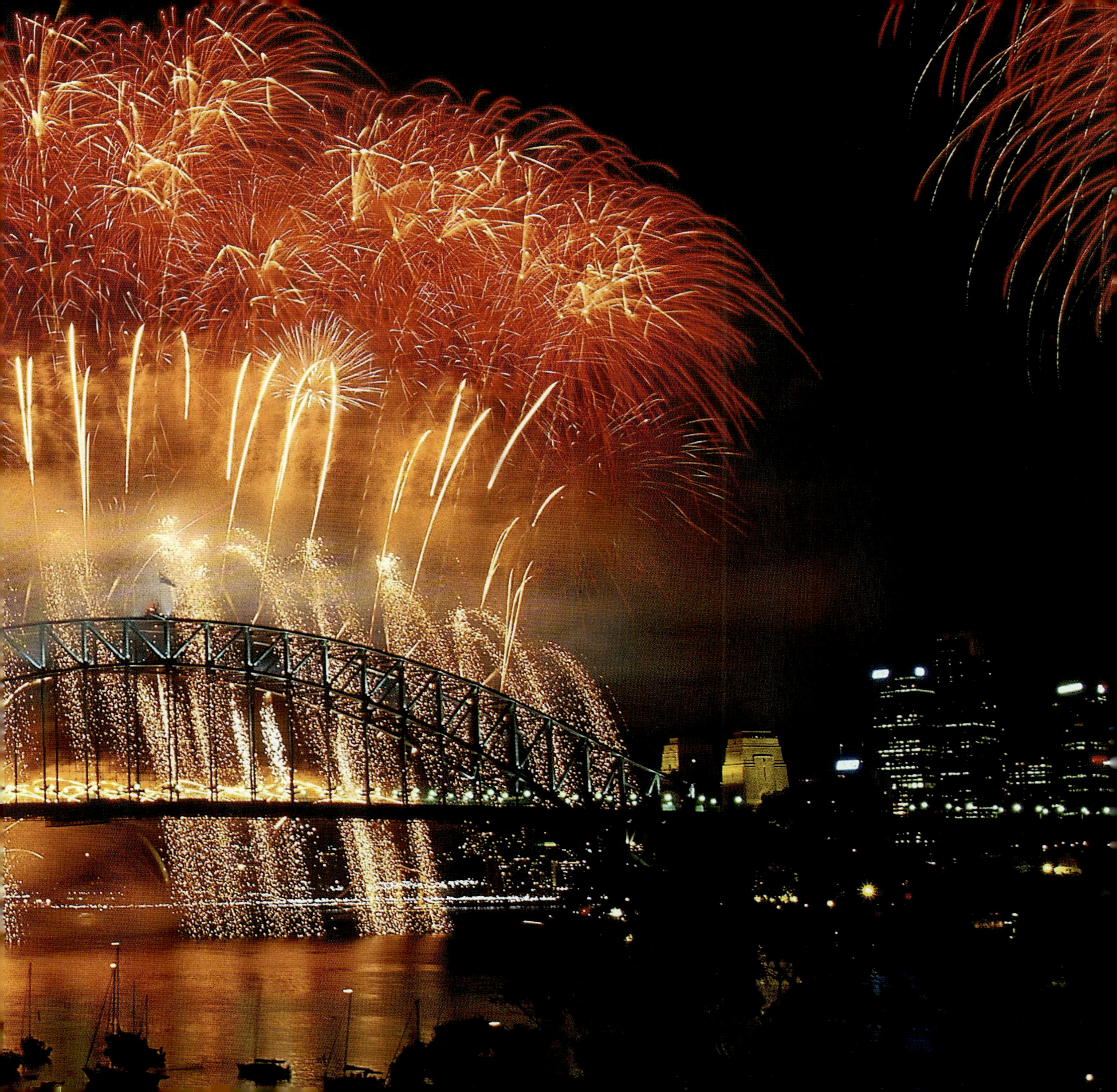

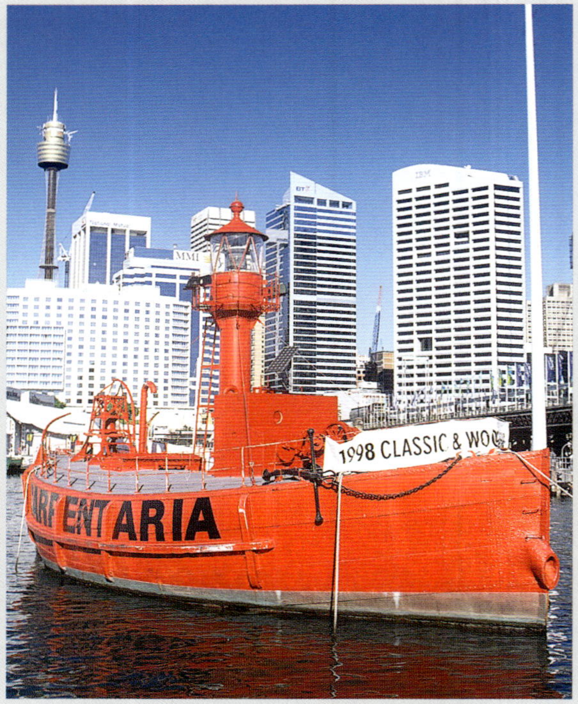
1998 CLASSIC &

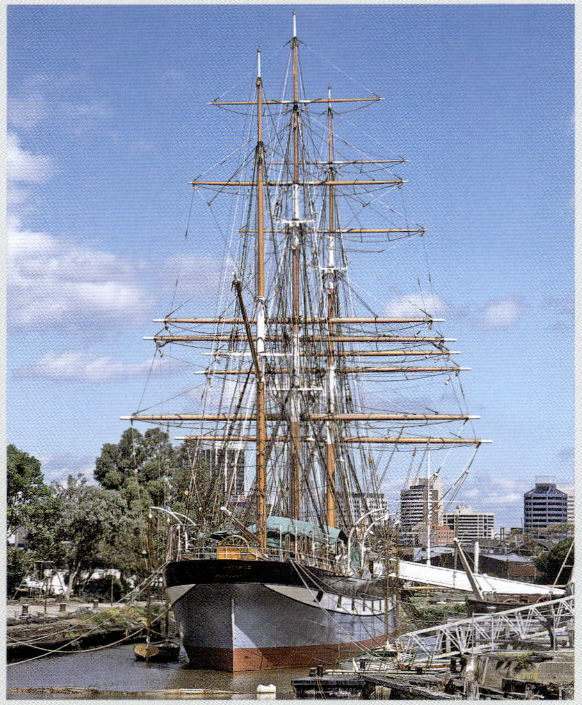

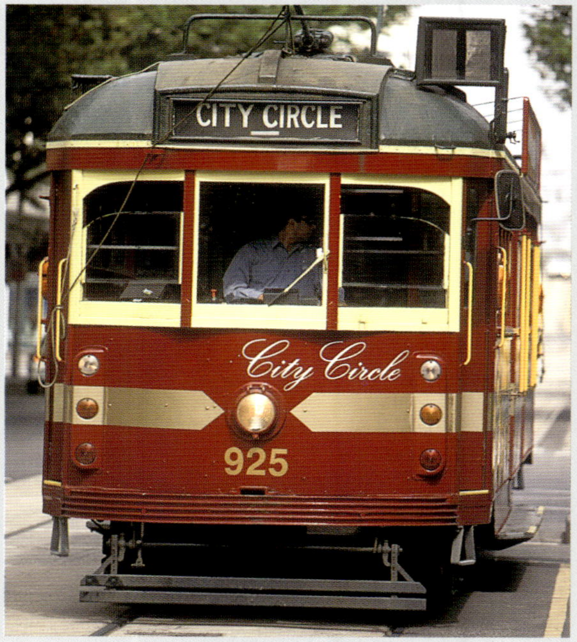
CITY CIRCLE
City Circle
925

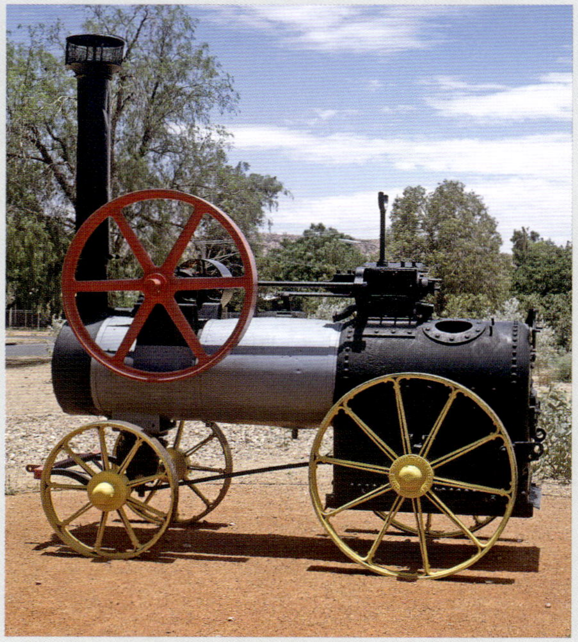

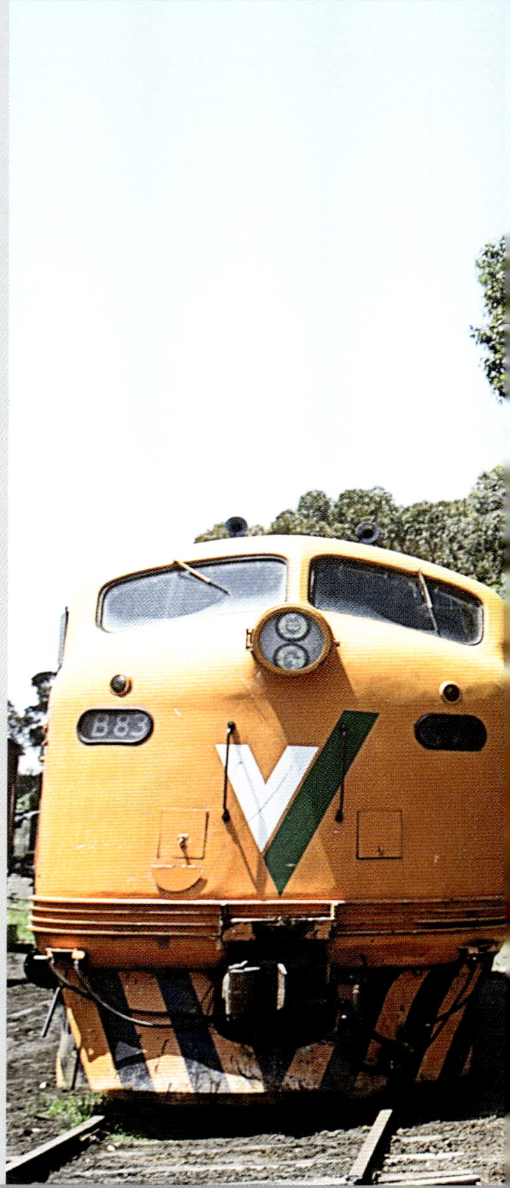
B83

BYGONE ERA

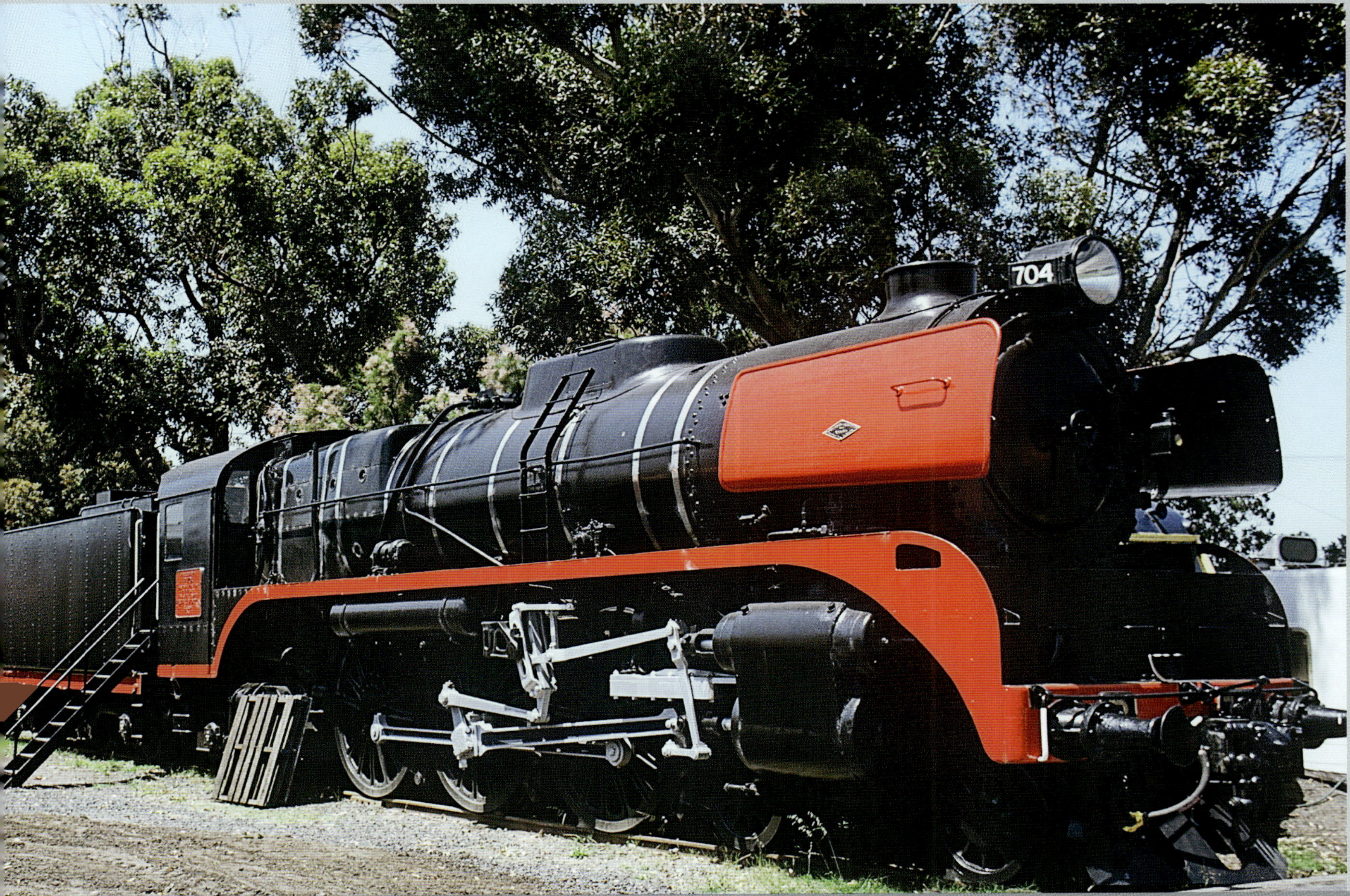

Modernization is all very well, but there is something lovingly nostalgic about the bright red lightship *Carpentaria* floating in Darling Harbour, Sydney, as part of the National Maritime Museum, and the magnificent rigging of the *Polly Woodside* tall ship tied up in Melbourne.

The City Circle tram in Melbourne is still operational and provides a free and easy way to get around the city center. Not so, alas, the old steam engine on display at the National Road Transport Hall of Fame in Alice Springs, or the old railway engines at the Melbourne Railway Museum.

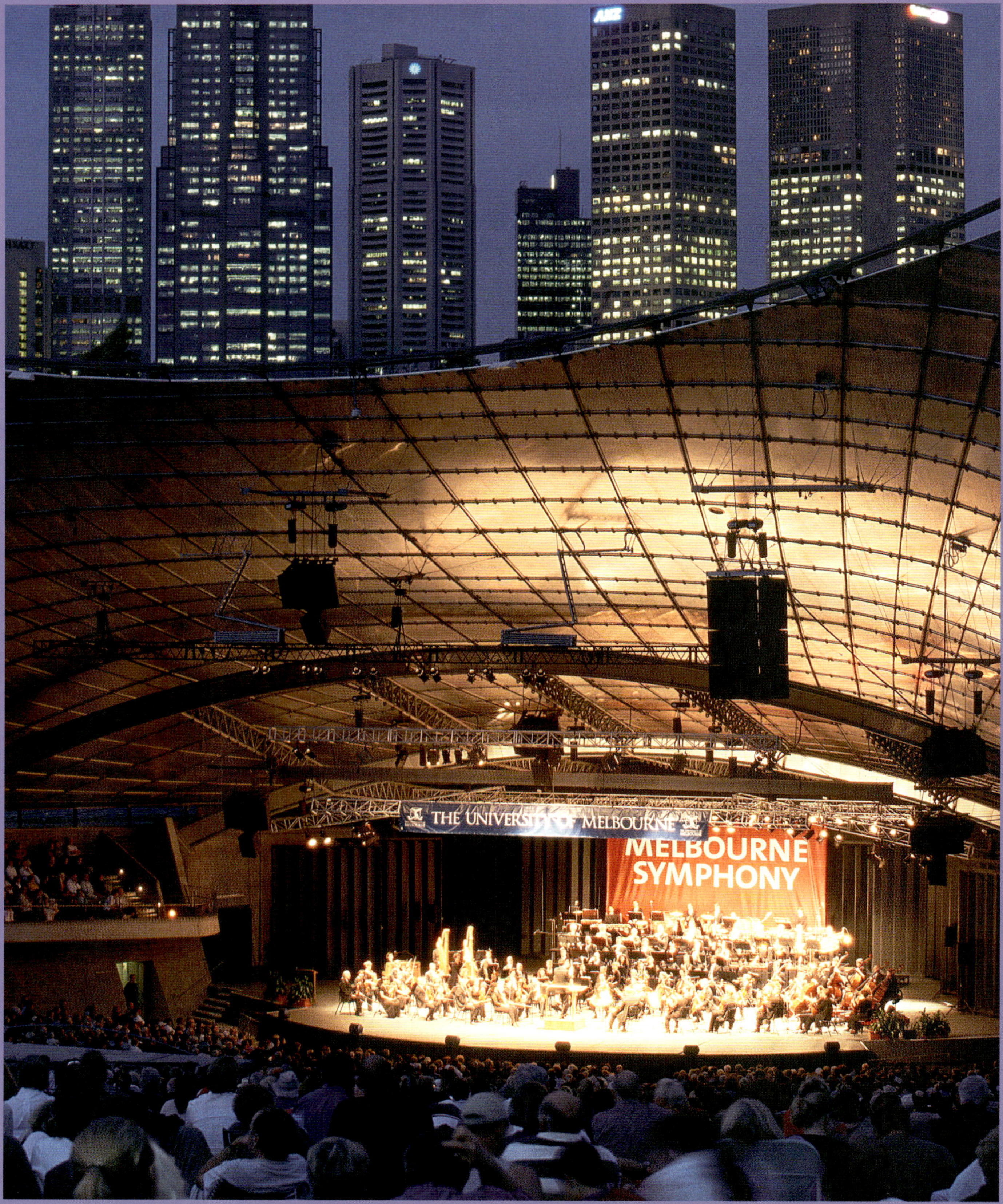
THE UNIVERSITY OF MELBOURNE
MELBOURNE
SYMPHONY

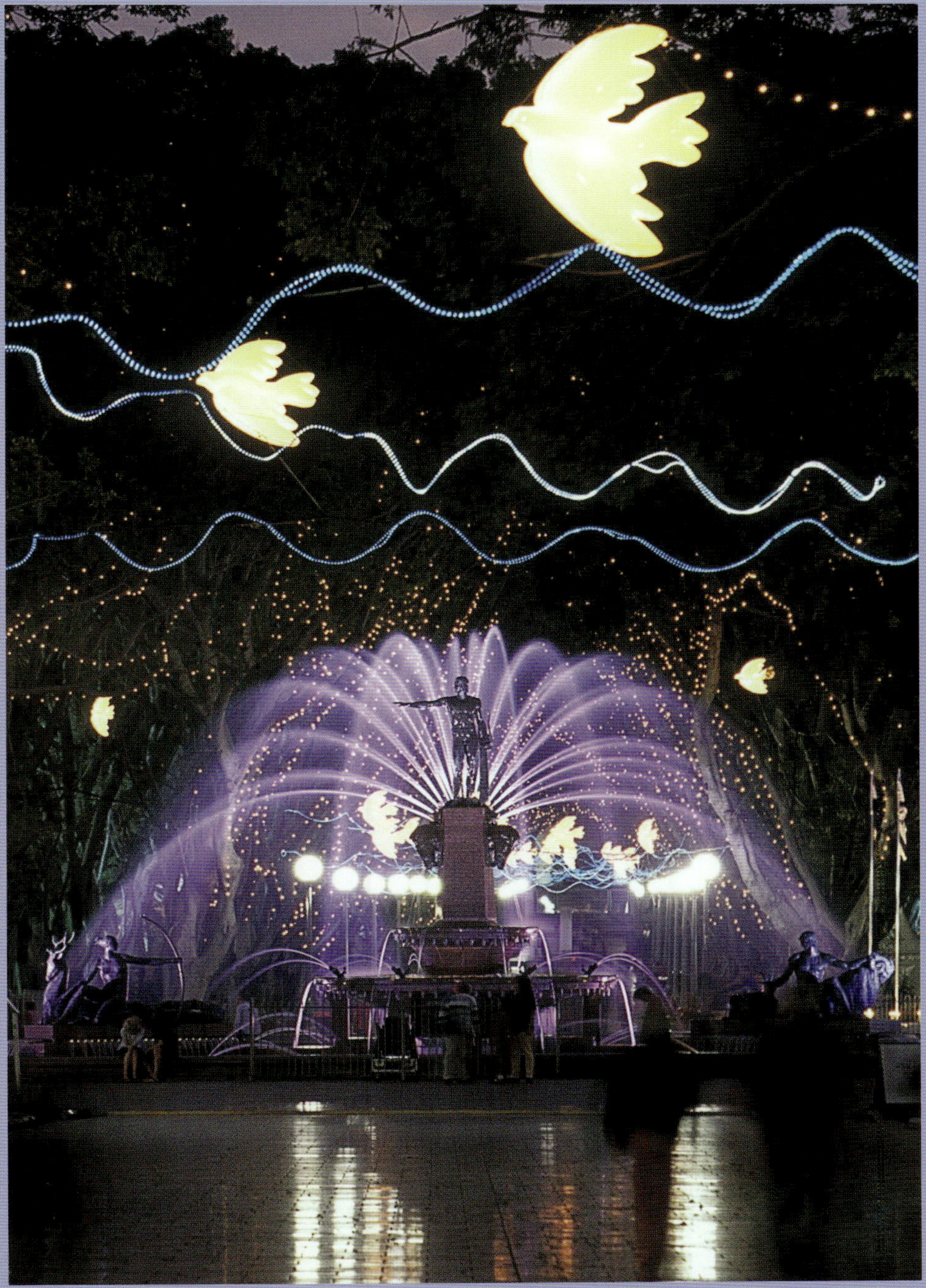

WORK HARD PLAY HARD

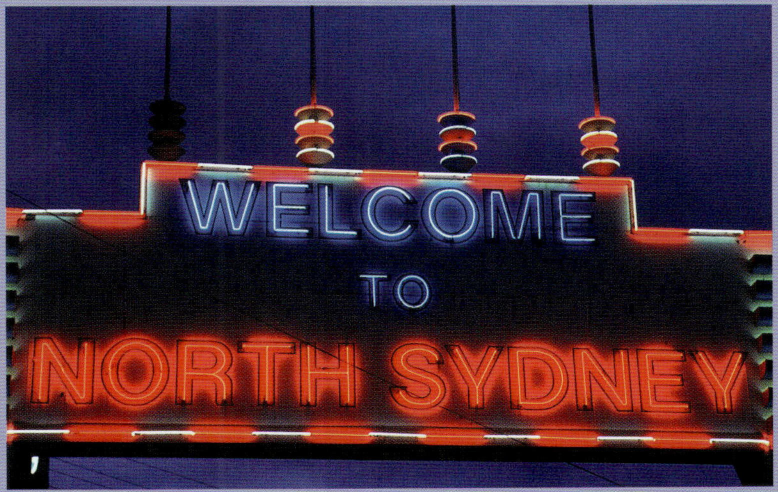

"Work hard, play hard" is a tiresome cliché, but it does serve to encapsulate the Australian approach to life. Society is fun-lovingly hedonistic, and balances the work ethic with enjoyment at all levels. Most of the cities have a fine symphony orchestra and outstanding auditoria in which they perform, but often many Aussies simply choose to go to a Festival of Lights, watch a firework display, or seize the chance to go swimming, surfing, sailing, or sunbathing.

FLOWER POWER

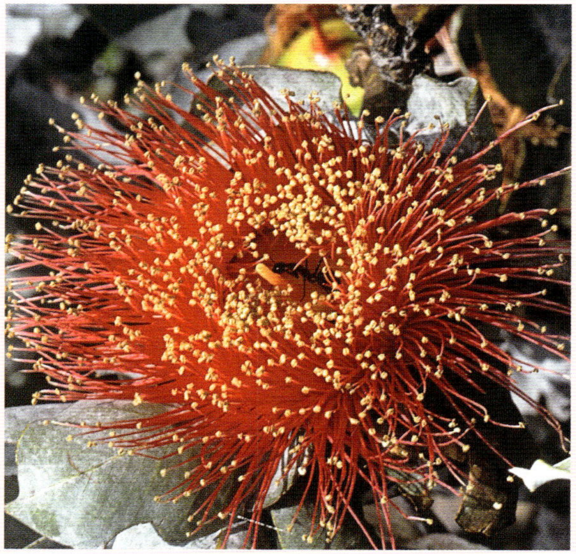

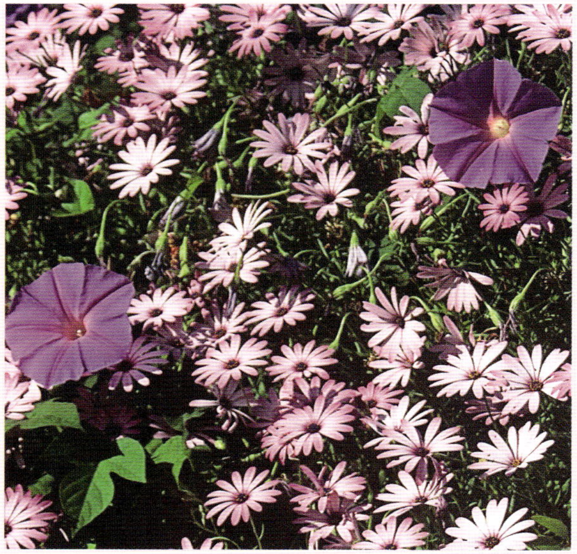

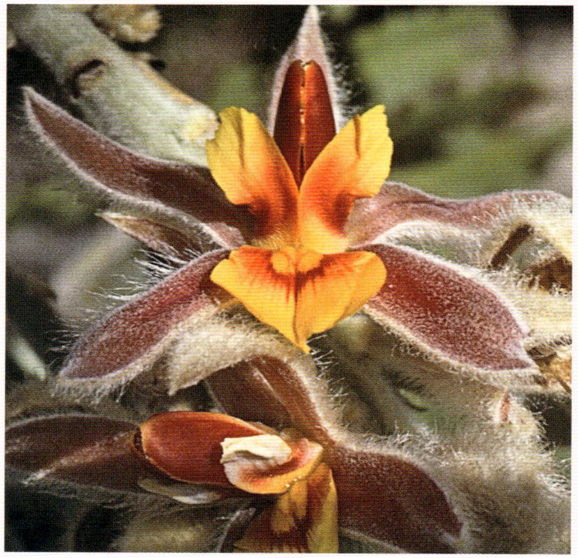

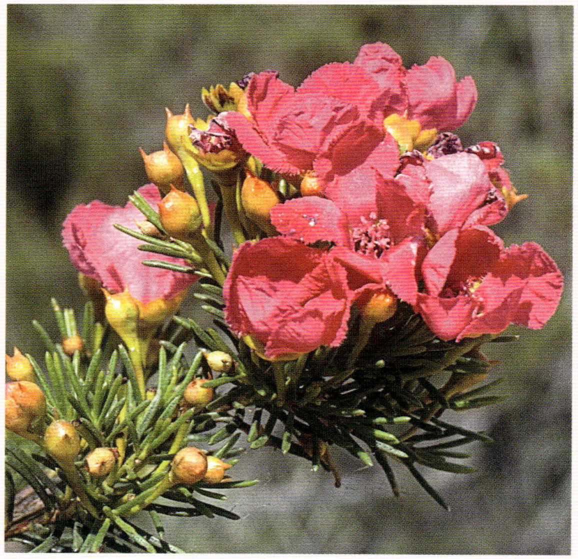

The Australian National Botanic Gardens modestly state that the total native species of flora in the country is in excess of 15,000, in addition to which there are another 2,000 naturalized species. Around 83 species are now presumed extinct—although a lonely stand of conifers, thought to have died out way before humans walked the earth, were rediscovered in Wollemi National Park in 1997, less than 65 miles (104km) from the center of Sydney. The diversity is bewildering, and many experts believe that hundreds of plants have yet to be discovered.

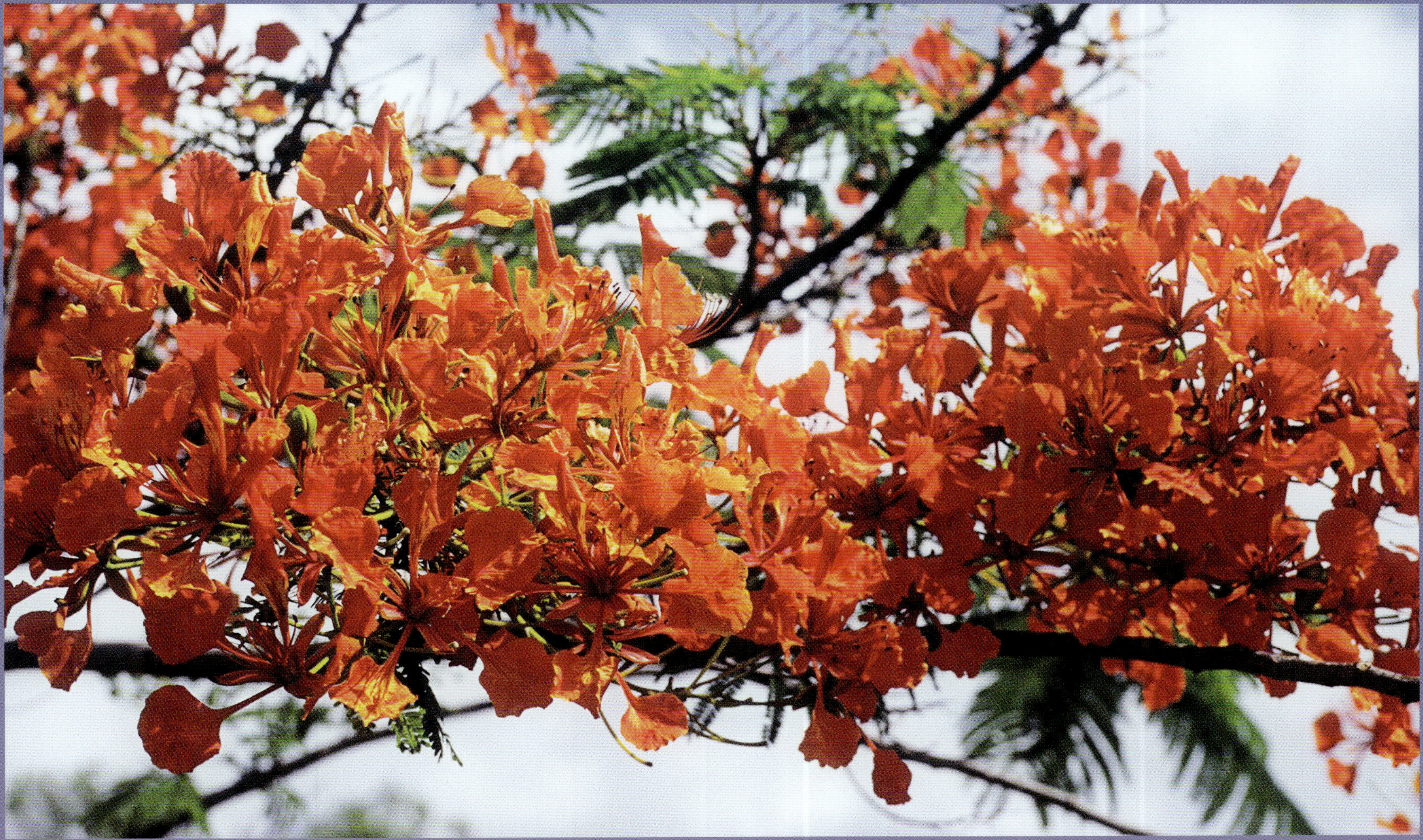

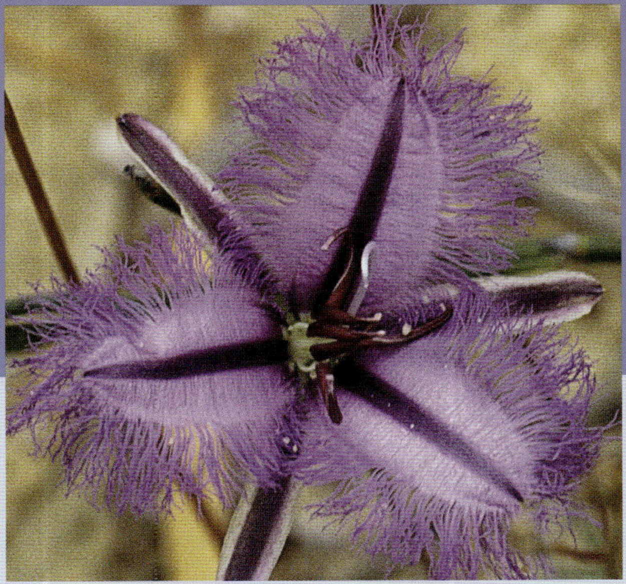

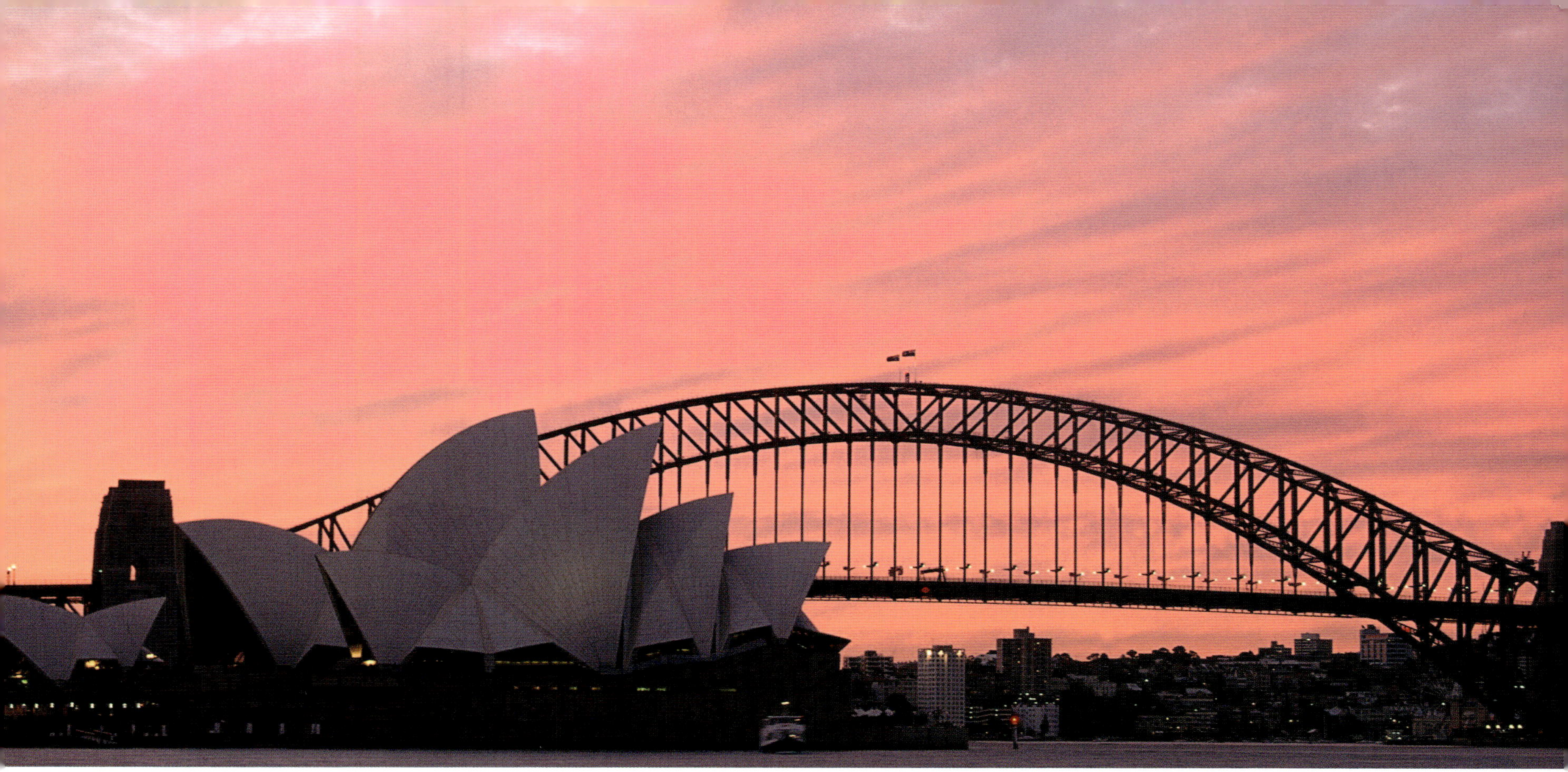

CREDITS

The Automobile Association wishes to thank the following organization for their assistance with the preparation of this book.

Australian Tourist Commission 55bc, 69r, 72bl, 75bl, 84b (**David Simmons**), 94, 95, 112br, 115r, 120/1, 124

The remaining photographs are held in the Automobile Association's own photo library (**AA World Travel Library**)and were taken by the following photographers:

Adrian Baker front cover bottom, back cover center left, 3cl, 5br, 19bl, 28bl, 28/9, 28br, 29cl, 29bc, 29br, 30tr, 34br, 36br, 37r, 42tl, 42bl, 42r, 43, 48br, 51tr, 52tr, 52bl, 55br, 57r, 64t, 64b, 65bl, 65br, 65tr, 70, 71r, 73bc, 73br, 74t, 74br, 76/7, 78tl, 78tr, 79tl, 83l, 85b, 86, 87l, 88l, 88r, 90, 91l, 91c, 91r, 100tl, 100tr, 100bl, 100c, 100br, 101bc, 107br, 113bl, 114c, 117, 122t, 122b, 123t, 123b, 128bl, 128br, 129bc, 130t, 131t, 132tl, 133cl, 138tc, 138bc, 138/9, 142tl, 142bl, 142br, 143b; **Andy Belcher** 6, 15, 17bl, 21bl, 28cl, 31, 35br, 50tr, 50br, 51bl, 52tl, 53l, 53r, 73bl, 75r, 78br, 84tr, 93bl, 97tl, 101tl, 103l, 106r, 124/5, 143t; **Bill Bachman** 4bc, 5bcl, 5bcr, 18bc, 21br, 22, 23t, 26/7, 35bl, 35bc, 40/1, 44l, 44cr, 45, 46/7, 47, 48t, 48bl, 49b, 51br, 54bc, 57l, 58t, 58c, 58b, 59, 66tl, 66c, 66br, 69l, 71tl, 82/3, 82, 83r, 84tl, 92bl, 92br, 93bc, 96, 97b, 98, 101br, 102tl, 102bl, 104/5, 107t, 107bl, 108, 112bc, 113bc, 116/7, 118/9, 125, 126tr, 128br, 138bl, 140; **Matthew Cawood** 74bl; **Steve Day** back cover right, 3r, 4br, 8/9, 11, 14, 22/3, 29tr, 39, 51c, 54br, 60, 62/3, 64, 66tr, 67tl, 67tr, 67c, 67br, 81, 92bc, 93br, 99, 101tr, 102r, 103r, 110l, 110r, 111, 113br, 114l, 126b, 127, 138tl, 142tr, 144; **Paul Kenward** front cover top, back cover center right, 3cr, 5bl, 18bl, 20, 21tl, 54bl, 55bl, 56l, 56r 57c, 61, 65tl, 67bl, 72br, 80tr, 115l, 120tc, 120bc, 126tl, 132br, 135, 141r; **Mike Langford** back cover left, 3l, 4bl, 18br, 19bc, 24l, 24r, 25tl, 25tr, 25b, 33r, 33bl, 38l, 44tr, 49t, 50tl, 50c, 71bl, 80l, 80br, 108/9, 128bc, 129bl, 132bl, 132c, 133cr, 133br, 134, 134/5, 136/7, 141l; **Christine Osborne** 68, 87r; **Simon Richmond** 10, 72bc, 75t, 79tr, 79br; **Lee Karen Stow** 12/3, 23b, 32, 34bc, 38r, 52br, 120bl, 133tl; **Steve Watkins** 16/7, 28tl, 30tl, 30b, 34bl, 36, 37l, 37c, 79bl, 89, 97tr, 106l, 112bl, 114r, 116, 120tl, 130b, 131b.